D0466105

The Question of Textuality

The Question of Textuality

Strategies of Reading in Contemporary American Criticism

EDITED BY

William V. Spanos
Paul A. Bové
and
Daniel O'Hara

INDIANA UNIVERSITY PRESS
Bloomington

Manufactured in the United States of America

CONTENTS

The Question of Textuality

imago homi nis
O AGIOS
MATT
heus

Introduction

Recurrence and Repetition: The *boundary 2* Symposium on the Problems of Reading in Contemporary American Criticism

> *A fact, a work is eloquent in a new way for every age and every new type of man. History always enunciates new truths. (974)*
>
> *The law of the conservation of energy demands eternal recurrence. (1063)*
>
> *"Timelessness" to be rejected. At any precise moment of a force, the absolute conditionality of a new distribution of all its forces is given: it cannot stand still. "Change" belongs to the essence, therefore also temporality: with this, however, the necessity of change has only been posited once more conceptually. (1064)*
>
> —Nietzsche, *The Will to Power*

> *As something communicated, that which has been put forward in the assertion is something that Others can "share". . . . But at the same time, what has been pointed out may become veiled again in this further retelling, although even the kind of knowing which arises in such hearsay . . . always has the entity itself in view and does not "give assent" to some "valid meaning" which has been passed around.*
>
> —Heidegger, *Being and Time*

> *Men make their own history, but they do not make it just as they please; they do not make it under circumstances chosen by themselves, but under circumstances*

directly encountered, given and transmitted from the past. The tradition of all the dead generations weighs like a nightmare on the brain of the living.

—Marx, *The Eighteenth Brumaire*

I

In the midst of the dialogue on *Hamlet* in *Ulysses*, Stephen Dedalus cunningly rings up the costs of Shakespeare's wonderful romance daughters. Marina, Perdita, and Miranda are all self-produced substitutes for Shakespeare's own dead daughter. Hamlet himself is a substitute for his dead son, Hamnet, just as Hamlet *père*, as Stephen even more cunningly shows, represents Shakespeare killed by Ann Hath-a-way. What Stephen knows here is what Freud and other post-romantics know about the compensatory character of art. And what Joyce accomplishes here in doubling the symbolic relationships of Shakespeare/Hamlet, Stephen/Hamlet, Shakespeare/Bloom, Stephen/Simon, Stephen/Joyce, and Bloom/Joyce is to help open the space of endless series of reflected signs which Derrida and Foucault, among others, have explored (and exploited) in defining the beginning conditions of post-structuralism.

II

Edward W. Said's "Abecedarium Culturae" has presented the purposes and implications of the central aspects of post-structuralist activity; the dissolution and dissociation of "man," "psyche," and "language" as inaugural centers against which traditional humanists such as M. H. Abrams, Wayne Booth, Nathan Scott, Denis Donaghue, and Gerald Graff have inveighed. Said has located the nexus of contemporary French thought in its power to displace dialectics with diacritics, to dissolve (central) "man" "as we know him," to recognize "man" as a "structure."[1] The sign, "man," no longer provides any ideological resistance to the corrosive multiplicity of the modern will to knowledge. Since it cannot any longer be "grasped," neither can it continue to privilege "comprehension."

For example, since Foucault is *both* a historical figure, i.e. an individual "author," and a "metaphor" or "sign," it is necessary to remember the theoretically enabling uses of this figure when confronting contemporary literary criticism's image of "Foucault":

> For if tradition and education train us to take man as the concrete universal, the pivot and center of awareness, then Foucault's prose, and concurrently his argument make us lose our grip on man. If we are inclined to think of man as an entity resisting the flux of experi-

> ence, then because of Foucault and what he says of linguistics, ethnology, and psychoanalysis, man is dissolved in the overaching waves, in the quanta, the striations of language itself, turning finally into little more than a constituted subject, a speaking pronoun, fixed indecisively in the eternal, ongoing rush of discourse. (B, p. 287)

Said's rendition of Foucault not only deftly deflects the traditionalist murmurings—now recuperating a plenary voice—that this post-structuralist criticism emerging from contemporary French thought is needlessly complex, obscure, non-referential—merely aesthetic self-indulgence[2]—but his trope also projects "Foucault" as a sign of man's bewilderment in the labyrinth of fractured self-reflections produced by and re-producing a series of suicidal disciplines. For to use both Foucault and Derrida's metaphor, writing and knowledge are "scenes" in the theater of "events," and "textuality" is the stage on which the scenes of the "human sciences" intermingle to create "man" as "the structure, the generality of relationships among those words and ideas that we call humanistic. . ." (B, p. 286).

Since it is true that man is a semiotic structure and since language and man are essentially rarefied refractions of images endlessly succeeding each other in textuality, one might say that "man" is perplexed, puzzled by the "tyrannical feedback system" of his knowledge, which hints that he and his actions might be only a set of reflecting and replicating signs drawn off into the infinitude of the parallax, "the eternal, ongoing rush of discourse." One might also say that, unlike its most traditional academic critics, contemporary French thought significantly does not ignore this system, but rather that it tries to find joy and knowledge in what it sees as a liberation from the ideology of "man" informing this parallax and also that it tries to overcome intellectually the dictatorship of the disciplines by locating itself subversively within the field of play generated by this feedback system. "Foucault," Said writes, "has been trying to overcome this tyranny by laying bare its workings. Most recently (in "The intellectuals and Power") he has ascribed that tyranny to its secrecy; just by naming, describing, classifying, where language and discourse pretend to 'unknowable' exigencies, the role of society and its class structure, for example, become evident" (B, p. 288).

We see in this rehearsal of "Foucault" that contemporary criticism delights in the displacement both of dialectics by diacritics and of totalized organic representations of history by disruptive comprehensive graphs of affiliated disciplines in the *epistémè*. Yet, more importantly, we also see that the contemporary critical dance has sought and found a thematics that it has christened "Foucault." For as Pierre Macherey has ironically suggested in calling him the Hegel of our generation, "Foucault" is all too inevitably, however unintentionally, being made to assume the role of the "founder of a new field of research" (B, p. 291), a kind of making which Hegel, Marx, and Nietzsche have demonstrated is fraught with the ambivalences of ancestor and hero worship. "Foucault's" activity dissolves the privileged ideological structures of humanism, and advanced contemporary criticism is "taking up" this activity into a set of figures compensating for this dissolution, supplementing "man's" semiotic being. That is, "Foucault" not only marks the secret hegemony of discourse, but its uncovering and overcoming (or sublating) as well.[3] For this "new" criticism, he figures not only the sublime beauty of the suicide of *homo sapiens* under its own microscopes, but the dead species' self-resuscitation in the hyperbolic extensions of its analytic methods to represent, reperceive, and reinscribe all "man's" works and histories as discursive "events." Following "Foucault," one might say that this process of contemporary criticism which we have described constitutes a Recurrence. And, while we know from many contemporary sources that important distinctions between origins and beginnings must be marked, we also know from Kierkegaard that the desire *to make, to will* new beginnings rather than *letting them occur* in the context of their occasion is a repeated self-enticement for the Western consciousness. Each willful repetition of this kind always accretes more positive knowledge, thereby echoing in the attempt to overcome the tyranny of disciplines, the very structures and effects of these tyrannical disciplines themselves. That is to say, each such beginning, each repetitive attempt at overcoming, is only an antithetical quest, a pursuit of one's own obsessive phantasmagoria, a reenactment of the whirling dance of death of the scholar embracing for the thousandth time the self-generated phantasm of his own method and intention. So that as Stephen Dedalus has it: "His own image to a man with that queer thing genius is the standard of all experience, material and moral."[4]

But "Foucault" tells us insistently that this Recurrence is an excess devoid of content. It must not be reduced to a place within a "particular discourse" or within individual scholarly phantasmagoria. For this Recurrence exists "outside" categories of being, becoming, and circularity; it is *un coup de dés*; in this, "Foucault's" adjacency to Derrida can be remarked: "It is at once the chance within the game and the game itself as chance. . . ."[5] Under the sign of Nietzsche this univocally recurring difference is first thought, first appears as thought. Can we ignore Nietzsche's "thought-event"? Must we not always pass through the Nietzschean critique of values? Daring to dance over and again within and across this Nietzschean limit marks the continuing novelty of "contemporary French thought." "Perhaps we should say that Nietzsche went as far as the thought of the Eternal Return; more precisely, he pointed to it as an intolerable thought. . . . But this intolerable nature must be considered because it exists only as an empty sign, a passageway to be crossed, the formless voice of the abyss whose approach is indissociably both happiness and disgust, disgust" (TP, p. 195).

Most of the papers presented in this Symposium do "dare" to think this empty sign. Since "Foucault's" rhetoric suggests that Recurrence exceeds the categorical restrictions of opposition within the same, even those essays which, when viewed conventionally, might seem to be in opposition to this Recurrence appear in fact to be scenes in the theater of this refracted thought. That is to say, more specifically, the difference between, for example, the ideology of humanism and its several post-structuralist critiques might blur within the pale light of the field of Recurrence. Could it be that difference masks Recurrence? Might it be that the dim echoes of earlier recurrences mark the limit of differences? Could it be that just as Bataille laughs at Hegel so, too, Recurrence laughs cunningly, silently, at those who "go beyond it," "correct it," or "reduce it"? [6] Is the conclusion that Recurrence draws all up into its space, defining the all in its emptiness? It is and opens up all space, the zero zone. Is it that which allows us to possess our own Difference: can one *will* a difference within the space of Recurrence? In our age, this is a space we have already designated "Foucault." Suspended in the pallid cast of shadows, our post-modern critical figures, in an activity that dimly revives disturbing earlier traces of it, play out dangerously the spider webs of their methods and desires, their intentions and passions, consciously, futilely, spinning their knowledge—mocking skeletal self-images—out of that "center" into the "formless voice of the abyss" the terrible mother as god:

> . . . Who, then, are they, seated here?
> Is the table a mirror in which they sit and look?
> Are they men eating reflections of themselves.[7]

The courage of this Foucauldian event—it is Donato who admits, speaking for all, that his project is failed—makes new thought possible, new mental events. One can think Poe with Riddel, the Orient with Said and Donato, and the Romantic poem with Brown and Arac. One can find present now in the critical events of this Symposium a new thought in which we hear the echoes of "Foucault" defining ours as the age of Deleuze:

> This thought does not lie in the future, promised by the most distant of new beginnings. It is present in Deleuze's texts—springing forth, dancing before us, in our midst; genital thought, intensive thought, affirmative thought, acategorical thought—each of these an unrecognizable face, a mask we have never seen before; differences we had no reason to expect, but which nevertheless lead to the return, as masks of their masks, of Plato, Duns Scotus, Spinoza, Leibniz, Kant, and all other philoso-

phers. This is philosophy not as thought, but as theater: a theater of mime with multiple, fugitive and instantaneous scenes in which blind gestures signal to each other. (TP, p. 196)

III

"As previously remarked, however, the ironic figure of speech cancels itself. It is like a riddle and its solution possessed simultaneously."

—Søren Kierkegaard, *The Concept of Irony*[8]

IV

boundary 2 initiated this Symposium in the Spring of 1978, hoping that a gathering of many of the leading theoreticians of our post-New Critical, post-humanistic critical scene would provide an especially fruitful opportunity for an exchange of ideas and for an assessment of where the American academy is now, more than a decade since the Johns Hopkins University Symposium on the "sciences of man" announced the presence of, indeed, "initiated," an entirely different set of rhetorics and procedures in American critical thinking. Perhaps the most obvious fact is also the most important. Whereas the gathering at Johns Hopkins involved many Europeans—Hyppolite, Barthes, Lacan, Derrida, and others—presenting their still somewhat alien ideas to a comparatively small number of other Europeans and initiated Americans,[9] the Binghamton meeting was essentially American with about four hundred in attendance—almost all of whom were familiar with and some of whom had worked with contemporary French thought and parallel models. Although not every one present gave assent to the basically structuralist and post-structuralist rhetorics in which much of the debate was carried out, nonetheless the success of post-structuralism in penetrating the academy's procedures and thinking marks precisely how effective the mechanisms for the distribution, consumption, and transformation of new ideas and new signs are in American critical circles. Perhaps symptomatic of this pervasiveness was the conspicuous absence from the debate of Harold Bloom's "home-made" brand of revisionism—a curious lacuna, to say the least.

This, however, is not to suggest a complete discursive uniformity reflected in the procedures and ideas of the participants. On the contrary, within the dominant post-structuralist rhetoric could be heard a number of other voices, testifying to the pluralism of the contemporary critical scene. Not only did Murray Krieger and Stanley Fish offer non-structuralist points of view on the needs of contemporary criticism, but Mark Poster and Michael Hays opened up the general socio-political theory of semiotics in their discussion of Baudrillard's critique of Foucault. And, perhaps most importantly, Edward Said, in a crucial gesture which marks him as in some ways paradigmatic, moved his own rhetoric and concerns beyond post-structuralism and, in his telling interrogation of de Man, introduced the Gramscian critique of cultural hegemony into a critical practice no longer tied to the merely refining academic textual analyses, a practice, that is, insisting on the "worldliness of the text." In an entirely different vein, Dennis Tedlock criticized Derrida's ascription of priority to writing over speech as the modality appropriate to post-metaphysical discourse through an analysis of the oral performance of the Quiche-Maya. And George Quasha and Charles Stein—graciously substituting for David Antin who had become ill in California—provided a dialogic exploration of the "open poetics" that informs much of the most interesting contemporary American poetry. Their performance of a Jackson MacLow "chant poem" stands so far outside the ordinary boundaries of interpretive activity that it cannot be reproduced here. A "script" of their contribution would be an immense misrepresentation, indeed, impossible. So the *absence* of their contribution—a sensuous, gestural event more physical and musical than verbal—from a *written* record of the Symposium's results is an appropriately eloquent testimony to the discordant otherness of their activity.

V

Although for the most part the Symposium speakers assumed that both American New Critical and Humanistic rhetorics are no longer viable alternatives for the critical intellectual in America, the papers of Jonathan Culler, Murray Krieger, and Stephen Crites and the discussions that followed them suggested that new alignments might be possible between, on the one hand, New Criticism and Humanism, and, on the other, structuralist poetics, post-structuralism, and phenomenology. There was, of course, a strong questioning of the privileged humanistic perspective throughout those papers—of Donato, Said, Riddel, Poster, Allison, and others—which continued the general post-structuralist critique of "man" and the Marxist effort to displace the "self" and the "author" from the humanistic center of a nexus of moral and causal codes. (To what extent this same critique was made of the "reader" within this network is not fully clear.) And, of course, there was also a rigorous reexamination and interrogation of "representation," of the "mimetic impulse," and, especially in Donato's presentation, of the possibility of the "recuperation" of the natural object.

In addition to these powerful critiques of some of the central ideals of humanism, Riddel and Brown demonstrably undermined the New Critical assumptions regarding the nature of organic form, while subtly subverting the legitimacy of the critical allegorization of a literary text. Yet, what must not be overlooked is the considerable number of participants in the audience who defended New Criticism and/or Humanism in what, in the present crisis of culture, can only be described as a sentimentally innocent and nostalgic way. Since it has not been possible to reproduce all of the audience's responses, a reader of this volume might mistakenly conclude that traditional critical points of view represented elsewhere by M. H. Abrams, Wayne Booth, Nathan Scott, Denis Donaghue, and Gerald Graff had no appeal at this conference.[10] On the contrary, so strong was this desire that at times the persuasive revisionist projects of Culler or Krieger were misperceived as appeals for simple reaffirmations of traditional academic procedures.

boundary 2 had anticipated that for many in the profession the challenge to traditional criticism had activated a "crisis." To adopt Heidegger's metaphor, when the instrument of analysis and representation upon which one had depended for so long in carrying out one's practice and in defining one's identity is challenged and fails, a crisis emerges explicitly in response to which one either tries to repair the broken tool or to find a new one. Stephen Dedalus's aphorism in *Ulysses* has it that a cracked glass is a perfect symbol of Irish art.[11] The same figure may represent the response of those who stare now unbelievingly at the shattered image of criticism hoping to find there the reflection which they feel was in place prior to the Postmodern critical moment. What one sees instead is *dispersal*: a broken, discontinuous, jagged series of fragments emptied of all illusory, mystifying traces of unity, revealed in all its particularity and unevenness—not the One, the Word, Identity, but the many, words, difference. The "one" who stares into the mirror is unmasked: there he finds the same figures of disruption, of failed recuperation, of the nostalgic desire to *create* or *project* or *re-present* or *re-collect* a unified *image* of critical activity—where none is to be found. We can connect nothing with nothing, one might say.

The death of meaning, of interpretation as the recovery of meaning, of the innocence of systems of representation, opened new space in which we can now see the diverse genealogies of contemporary criticism: Mark Poster's indebtedness to existentialism and Marxism as well as Baudrillard and semiotics; Said's adaptations of Gramsci and Foucault; Riddel's Derridean Heidegger; etc. Put more precisely and following Stephen Dedalus's metaphor, new images of the critic appeared in this Symposium, newer than even those we had already become partially familiar with in the decade in which French contemporary thought began to gain influence in America. Put most generally, however, the "Critic" in the papers presented at this conference appeared as a general intellectual, no longer restricting his or her procedures to textual analysis. Although the degree and nature of the movement beyond textual explication varies from, for example, Said's passionate insistence upon affiliating what one says about a literary text with history and power, to, for example, Allison's Derridean reading of the figure of "woman" in Nietzsche, there is no doubt that these papers show us that the critic can no longer be perceived as "legitimate" if he or she is merely an analyst of form, a discoverer of harmony and balanced tension, or a seeker after "objective" universal "human" ideals in art. Yet perhaps the anxiety a critic may feel in confronting *dispersal*, the eternal, ongoing rush of discourse, of *be-ing*, insecurely masks itself in a defensive concern for the mere play of institutional change within the profession. In any event, theory and theoretical praxis have replaced traditional Anglo-American "practical criticism" of the kind so long indebted to I. A. Richards and his New Critical progeny. But it does not yet seem fully clear if this new "theoretical practice" will mean anything more than the mere reduction of theory to methodology. The debate between Said and Donato centers precisely on the relative priority of "mathematics" and "physics," as Donato would put it. It is, however, clear that the Postmodern critic *must* now examine his or her procedures theoretically and always search in this insistent interrogation for new theoretical insights and modes of praxis in a powerful counter-tradition to the humanistic: Vico, Marx, Kierkegaard, Heidegger, Saussure, and their more contemporary heirs, Bataille, Gramsci, Althusser, Ricoeur, Lacan, Foucault, and Derrida.

The respondents often found that by retracing the speakers' relationships to the ideas and tropes of this counter-tradition they could supplement the original direction of the major presentation. This suggests not only the increasing genealogical awareness of the scholars in the academy—a willingness to examine the lived history of events—but how the critic is beginning to locate his activity between history and text, praxis and theory. This, we feel, is the space of *critical practice* most in need of and most rewarding to research and analysis. It allows above all for questions which have concrete historical implications. As Said suggests of Flaubert, for example, his novels are counter-representations of the Orient—powerless precisely because of their circumscription by imperialist accumulations empowered by the "science" of Orientalism.

However muted, if not unsaid, perhaps the essential contribution made by the Symposium is the extension of the post-structuralist critique of representation to the problematics of power, society, and competence as well as the recognition of the importance of the lived history of the tropes of the analytic systems of representation inscribed in the discourses and practices of the academy. Taken together these suggest the passionate interest of inter-ested individuals—willful, patient, careful—to extend the critical act to broader spheres of Western man's actions so as to understand them, judge them, learn from them, and, if possible, to correct them. They suggest "finally" an impulse, however constrained or contaminated by the Recurrence of discourse, to retrieve ("repeat") the idea and practice of criticism as the measure of "man's" centerless *occasion*.

VI

> *". . . do you want a name for this world? A solution for all its riddles? A light for you, too, you best-concealed,*

> *strongest, most intrepid, most midnightly men? —This world is the will to power—and nothing besides! And you yourselves are the will to power—and nothing besides! "*
>
> —Nietzsche, *The Will to Power*

William V. Spanos
Daniel O'Hara
Paul A. Bové

NOTES

1 *Beginnings* (New York: Basic Books, 1975), p. 286 (hereafter cited as *B*).

2 It might not, however, deflect the as-yet only partially articulated post-humanistic criticism that reads certain emphasis of the contemporary French insistence on the empty sign as a rehearsal of the neither/nor of American formalism, the privileged "irony" of New Criticism.

3 See Frank Lentricchia, *After the New Criticism* (Chicago: Univ. of Chicago Press, 1980).

4 James Joyce, *Ulysses* (New York: Random House, 1961), p. 195.

5 "Theatrum Philosophicum," trans. Donald F. Bouchard and Sherry Simon, in *Language, Counter-Memory, Practice*, ed. Donald F. Bouchard (Ithaca: Cornell Univ. Press, 1977), p. 194 (hereafter cited as *TP*).

6 See Jacques Derrida, "From Restricted to General Economy," *Writing and Difference*, trans. Alan Bass (Chicago Press, 1978), pp. 251-77.

7 Wallace Stevens, "Cuisine Bourgeoisie," *Collected Poems* (New York: Alfred A. Knopf, 1964), p. 228.

8 Søren Kierkegaard, *The Concept of Irony*, trans. Lee M. Capel (Bloomington: Indiana Univ. Press, 1968), p. 265.

9 See Richard Macksey and Eugenio Donato, eds., *The Structuralist Controversy: The Languages of Criticism and the Sciences of Man* (Baltimore: Johns Hopkins Univ. Press, 1970). It is worth noting that the sessions at Hopkins were held in 1966.

10 M. H. Abrams, "The Deconstructive Angel," *Critical Inquiry*, 3 (Spring, 1977), 425-38; Wayne Booth, "M. H. Abrams: Historian as Critic, Critic as Pluralist," *Critical Inquiry*, 2 (Spring, 1976), 411-45; Nathan A. Scott, Jr., "Gadamer's Truth and Method," rev. of *Truth and Method* by H. G. Gadamer, *boundary 2*, 5 (1977), 539 ff.; Denis Donaghue, "Deconstructing Deconstruction," *New York Review of Books*, Vol. 27, no. 10 (June 12, 1980), pp. 37-41; Gerald Graff, *Literature Against Itself* (Chicago: The Univ. of Chicago Press, 1979) and "Deconstruction as Dogma, or 'Come Back to the Raft Ag'in, Strother Honey! ' " *Georgia Review*, XXXIV (Summer, 1980), pp. 404-21.

11 James Joyce, *Ulysses*, p. 6.

Reflections on Recent American "Left" Literary Criticism

Edward W. Said

Never before in the history of American literary culture has there been such widespread and, on the whole, such serious, sometimes technical and frequently contentious discussion of issues in literary criticism. Certainly this symposium is one indication of richness of effort, if not always of result, and I doubt that any participant thinks that this contemporary battle of the books does not concern what he or she does as a teacher, critic, or scholar of literature. On the other hand there will not be automatic agreement on what the main or even the important issues are in the critical hurly-burly. It is probably true, for example, that even though many of the critical schools (among others, semiotics, hermeneutics, Marxism, and deconstruction) still continue to have their strict apostles, it is the case that the critical atmosphere is a mixed one, with everyone more or less in touch with, if not necessarily completely involved in, most of the reigning methods, schools, disciplines. Nevertheless it is almost certain that no one will underestimate the *sociological* as well as the intellectual importance of the large division separating adherents of New new criticism from those of the old, or traditional criticism. Not all critics are polarized by this often invidious division. But what is remarkable, I think, is that in debates between both sides there is a marked willingness to take positions simplifying and exaggerating not only one's opponent, but one's own team, so to speak. A deconstructionist speaking *sub specie aeternitatis* for vanguard criticism makes one feel that a challenge to Western thought itself is being portended when he analyzes some lines by Rousseau, Freud or Pater; conversely a critic who believes himself to be pronouncing in the name of sanity, decency and the family when he discusses the ideas of what humanism is all about, denigrates even his own work unintentionally by appearing to *simplify* the quite formidable codes of academic scholarship that make what he does intelligible.

Without thinking through all, or even a small number, of the aspects of this large opposition, we cannot properly hope to know in detail what really goes on in literary criticism and theory today, although, as I hope to show, we *can* speak accurately of certain patterns common both to criticism and to the history, society, and culture that produced it. One of my points will be that if the fierce polemics between say M. H. Abrams and J. Hillis Miller, or between Gerald Graff and the so-called Yale School, or between *boundary 2, Glyph,* and *Diacritics* and other little magazines seem to present very clear theoretical demarcations between old, or right-wing positions and new, left-wing positions, the divergence on both sides of the controversy between the rhetoric of theory and the actualities and results of practice is very nearly the same. This is of course always true in polemics: we argue in theory for what in practice we never do, and we do the same kind of thing with regard to what we oppose. Nonetheless, now we find that a new criticism adopting a position and a rhetoric of opposition to what is considered to be established or conservative academic scholarship consciously takes on the function of the left-wing in politics, and argues *as if* for the radicalization of thought, practice and perhaps even of society by means not so much of what it does and produces, but by means of what it says about itself and its opponents. True, there are important actual achievements to which it can point with pride, there are genuinely original, even revolutionary works of critical theory and interpretation, and these have in some cases been surrounded by a whole rhetorical armor of apology, attack, and extended programmatic elaboration: Harold Bloom's work and its repeated pro and con, come immediately to mind. But in the main Bloom's work and what it has produced in the way of anger and praise on theoretical grounds remains solidly within the tradition of academic criticism. The texts, authors and periods have stayed inside a recognizable and commonly agreed-upon canon, even if the words and phrases used to describe them vary considerably depending on whether you are for or against Bloom.

To such a thesis there is first the response that I, in my own turn, am being a reductionist, and second, that criticism after all is perforce restricted to the academy and banned—not only by virtue of its own politeness—from the street. Both objections to what I have so far been saying are justified in part: I can easily grant that, without at the same time giving up my point, which I shall have to make again in a different way. What I am trying to say (with an almost embarrassing generality) is that the oppositional manner of New new criticism conceals, or perhaps does not accurately represent, its ideas and practice, which, after all is said and done, further solidify and guarantee the social structure and the culture that produced them. This is not of itself a bad thing, except that the rhetoric delivering it says very much the opposite. Deconstruction, for example, is practiced as if Western culture was being dismantled; semiotic analysis argues that its work amounts to a scientific, and hence social revolution in the sciences of man; the examples can be multiplied, but I think what I am saying will be readily understood. There is opposition and oppositional debate without, in my opinion, real opposition. In this setting, even Marxism has often been accommodated to the exigencies of rhetoric (fierce ones) while surrendering its true radical prerogatives.

All of this is a very long way of explaining why in my title the word "Left" is enclosed in skeptical quotation marks. Perhaps also you will sense that I found the transition from the notion of the Left in politics to the Left in literary criticism a difficult one to make. Of course there *is* opposition between M. H. Abrams and Derrida or Miller, but can one say with assurance that what is at stake, which seems at most to be a question of whose super-structural visions are better, matches the apparent violence of the disagreement? Both new and old critics have been content for the most part to confine themselves, and to be confined, to the academic matter of literature, to the existing institutions for teaching and employing students of literature, to the often ridiculous and always self-flattering notion that their discussions and debates have a supremely important bearing upon crucial interests affecting humankind. In accepting these confinements the putative Left, no less than the Right, is very far from playing a left-wing role. Indeed I would go so far as to say that what distinguishes the present situation is, on the one hand, a greater isolation than ever before in recent American cultural history of the literary critic from the major intellectual, political, moral and ethical issues of the day with, on the other hand, a rhetoric, a pose, *a posture* (let us at last be candid) claiming not so much to represent as *to be* the affliction implied by true radical opposition to the *status quo.* A visitor from another world would surely be perplexed were he to overhear a so-called old critic calling a new critic "dangerous": what, this visitor would ask, is he a danger to? The State? The mind? Authority?

A quick glance at recent intellectual history reveals the story pretty well. No one would have any trouble finding a Left in American culture between the 20's and the 50's, as Daniel Aaron's book *Writers on the Left* will immediately testify. Certainly it is true that during those decades intellectual debate in this country was pre-eminently conducted in political language having a direct connection with actual politics; the careers of such men as Randolph Bourne and Joseph Freeman, for instance, are inextricable from the problems of war or non-intervention, class conflict, Stalinism and/or Trotskyism. If we feel that what they and writers like them wrote lacked the sophistication available to them in the criticism of their contemporaries—Eliot, Valéry, Richards and Empson—we also feel that their awareness of literature as literature (that is. literature as something more than ideological construct) was impressively strong. In the work of the best of them, say the Edmund Wilson of *To the Finland Station,* there is a very high order of intellect and scholarship, as well as considerable political sophistication and historical engagement, neither of which comes through as untreated propaganda or as what we have come to call vulgar Marxism. When, in this rather large and amorphous period that I designate simply as "recent cultural history" to distinguish it from the current moment, a major critic in the academy would seek to place himself responsibly in the world, we might get an essay such as F. O. Matthiessen's "The Responsibilities of the Critic," originally written in 1949. Matthiessen makes no pretense at being a Marxist, but he does make it very clear that the critic of literature must be concerned with the material with which Marxism deals along with "the works of art of our own time." The essay's controlling metaphor is a horticultural one: criticism can become "a kind of closed garden" unless the critic realizes "that the land beyond the garden's walls is more fertile, and that the responsibilities of the critic lie in making renewed contact with the soil." Not only does this mean that the critic is to acquaint himself with "the economic foundations underlying any cultural superstructure": it means

> that we in the universities cannot afford to turn our backs . . . upon the world. . . . The proper place for the thinker, as William James conceived it, was at the central point where a battle is being fought. It is impossible for us to take that metaphor with the lightness that he could. Everywhere we turn in these few fateful years since the first atom bomb dropped on Hiroshima we seem menaced by such vast forces that we may well feel that we advance at our peril. But even greater peril would threaten us if those whose prime responsibility as critics is to keep open the life-giving communications between art and society should waver in their obligations to provide ever fresh thought for our own society.[1]

There is an unmistakable implication in these remarks that the vast menacing forces of post-Hiroshima history can be kept at bay, and comprehended, by "fresh thought" which the critic provides. We might easily smile at Matthiessen's naiveté here, since today very few critics consider their work to be pitted directly against these, or any other brute historical forces. Moreover, as any reader of Paul de Man can readily tell you, the language of crisis is endemic to criticism, but, he would add warningly, unless language in such situations "turns back upon itself" there is more likely to be mystification and falseness than there would be either knowledge or real criticism. To Matthiessen, then, literature and criticism stand on and are nourished by the very same experiences out of which economics, material history and social conflict are generated. Such a proposition, in all its seemingly unproblematic ontological simplicity, is most unlikely to reappear today, when what de Man calls "the fallen world of our facticity" is considered to be matched ironically by a literature whose language, again according to de Man, "is the only form of language free from the fallacy of unmediated expression." And yet Matthiessen's achievement as a critic was a considerable one: books such as his *American Renaissance* reveal neither a deluded *schone Seele,* nor a crude sociologist of knowledge. The problem is to see how he spoke passionately and politically as he did of the critic's responsibilities and why, twenty odd years later, critics like de Man (whose present influence is really very estimable) direct their attention to the impossibility of political and social responsibility as Matthiessen, I think, envisioned them.

For de Man "philosophical knowledge can only come into being when it is turned back upon itself." This is another way of saying that anyone using language as a means for communicating knowledge is liable to fall into the trap of believing that his authority as possessor and communicator of knowledge, as well as his knowledge, are not bound by language, which in fact is only language and not immediate facticity. Literature on the other hand is basically about demystification, and according to de Man, "poetic language names this void [i.e., 'The presence of nothingness' supposedly denoted by the words of a literary composition whose essential task is to refer only to itself, and to be ironically aware of so doing] with ever-renewed understanding and, like Rousseau's longing, it never tires of naming it again." Such an insight allows de Man to assert that in its endless naming and re-naming of the void literature is most emphatically itself, never more strongly than when literature seems to be suppressed in order that mere knowledge might be allowed to appear. Thus:

> When modern critics think they are demystifying literature, they are in fact being demystified by it; but since this necessarily occurs in the form of a crisis, they are blind to what takes place within themselves. At the moment that they claim to do away with literature, literature is everywhere; what they call anthropology, linguistics, psychoanalysis is nothing but literature re-

appearing, like the Hydra's head, in the very spot where it had supposedly been suppressed. The human mind will go through amazing feats of distortion to avoid facing "the nothingness of human matters."[2]

Unlike Derrida, for whose work he was later to show considerable affinity, de Man is less interested in the force and the productivity of human distortion (what Derrida calls *impensé*) then he is in its continued, continuing and repeated performance, its insistence as insistence so to speak. This is why corrosive irony is really de Man's central problematic as a critic: he is always interested in showing that when critics and/or poets believe themselves to be stating something they are really revealing—critics unwittingly, poets wittingly—the impossible premises of stating anything at all, the so-called aporias of thought to which de Man believes all great literature always returns. These intellectual hobbles on the possibility of statement have not, however, inhibited de Man from stating and re-stating them on the numerous occasions when, more ably than most other critics, he analyzes a piece of literature. I would hesitate to call de Man a polemicist, but insofar as he exhorts critics to do something rather than something else, I would say that he tells them to avoid talking as if historical scholarship, for example, could ever get beyond and talk seriously about literature. Why? Because if great literature is already demystified, scholarship could really never tell us anything essential about it that, in a sense, the literature itself had not previously predicted: the most that can happen is that the critic is demystified, which amounts to saying that he acknowledges literature's prior demystification of itself.

I have no wish to use de Man as a representative of what is being done these days in literary criticism: his work is too important, and his talents too extraordinary for merely representative status. But I think that it is not unjustified to regard him as exemplifying an intellectual current opposing, in no very explicit way, what customarily stands for the norm in academic literary studies. The literary work for him stands in a position of almost unconditional superiority over historical facticity not by virtue of its power but in a sense by virtue of its admitted powerlessness; its originality resides in the premise that it has disarmed itself "from the start," as if by having said in advance that it had no illusions about itself and its fictions it directly acceded to the realm of acceptable literarity and form. These ideas of course express a major tendency in all symbolist art, a tendency valorized and made considerably interesting by every variety of twentieth century critical formalism: to paraphrase a famous remark by Mallarmé, underlying it is the notion that if the world exists at all it is to have ended up in (or as) a book, and once in a book then the world is left behind forever. Literature, in short, expresses only itself (this is a maximalist position; the minimalist view is that literature is "about" nothing): its world is a formal one, and its relationship to quotidian reality can only be understood, as de Man implies, by means either of negation or a radically ironic theory, as severe as it is consistent, whose workings depend on the equal and opposite propositions that if the world is not a book, neither is the book the world. These are perhaps not as unexceptionable as they may seem, especially if we remember the extent to which most criticism since Aristotle has admitted, in even its formalist branches, a certain amount of an often surreptitious and unadmitted mimetic bias.

But de Man's criticism garners some of its justified authority because de Man has been a pioneer, and indeed a perfect exemplification of European-style "metaphysical criticism" as some people like to call it. Here we rush headlong into the sociological as well as historical actuality that contemporary "left" or oppositional criticism in America is heavily influenced by European, especially French, criticism. One could give a number of reasons for the very dramatic change in language and tone that came over the American critical scene during the late 60's, and I do not intend here to spend much time doing so. But it is fair to say, I think, that among the effects of European criticism on our critical vocabulary and positions was a sense that the primacy of "English studies" in the literary field generally had come to an end. Most of the literary criticism dominating the academy, and indeed even the world of journalism, was based (in spirit if not always in fact) upon the achievements of British and American modernist writers, and also on a feeling that assumptions of national primacy—in all senses of that phrase—ought to dominate criticism. The believers in this idea include Arnold at the beginning, of course, later Leavis, Empson, Richards, and most of the Southern New Critics. I do not mean at all to say that these were provincial or local-minded men, but that for them everything outside the Anglo-Saxon world had to be bent around to Anglo-Saxon ends, so to speak. Even T. S. Eliot, much the most international-minded critic of the period until the early sixties, saw in European poets like Dante, Virgil and Goethe the vindication of such Anglo-Saxon values as monarchy, an unbroken non-revolutionary tradition, and the idea of a national religion. Thus the intellectual hegemony of Eliot, Leavis, Richards and the New Critics coincides not only with the work of masters like Joyce, Eliot himself, Stevens, Lawrence, but also with the serious and autonomous development of literary studies in the university, a development which in time became synonymous with "English" as a subject, as language, and as attitude.

At its very best "English" had Lionel Trilling, W. K. Wimsatt, Reuben Brower and a small handful of others as its prominent, deeply intelligent and humane, but very diverse, defenders. But it was challenged—well before the French efflorescence I believe—in two ways, one internal to it, the other external. Internally "English" produced only an implicit ideology, and no easily communicable methods: there are very complex reasons for this, and anyone attempting to describe the situation that prevailed would have to go into such matters as the revulsion from

Stalinism, the Cold War, the circumvention of theory, and the paradoxical unmediated, ahistorical association of values, commitment, and even ideas with "style." This is not the occasion to go into these matters since what I am most interested in is what, generally speaking, they produced intellectually: namely, a type of criticism based principally upon nothing very methodological, but upon endless refinement. In the sudden mood of competition and expansion that followed Sputnik, there were the various national security language programs funded by NDEA, and then there was English, which refined, without essentially adding to, our "strength" as a nation. The dissertation model was not the carefully researched historical monograph, but the sensitive essay: the English student became an adjunct to, and felt himself, I think, at a very far point away from what was important. The role of English was at best an *instrumental* one (this clearly was what Richard Ohmann and Louis Kampf were reacting to in the late 60's) although its best practitioners like Trilling, Abrams and Wimsatt were looked to as non-ideological reassurances that style, humanism and "values" really mattered. The net result of all this was an endemic flaccidity in English studies, for how far could one go in these circumstances along the road of mere refinement?

As an instance of how brilliant and resourceful literary refinement could become there was Northrop Frye, whose meteoric theoretical ascendancy over the whole field of English studies in the 50's and 60's can partly be accounted for by the climate of refinement (which he dignified and intensified in his *Anatomy*) and the historico-theoretical vacuum prevailing. As instances of how dull and enervating it all was, there was the huge agglomeration of various literary industries (Joyce, Conrad, Eliot, etc.) that had never even pretended to be a coherent part of the social and natural science march upon (or toward) knowledge. In a very unique and perhaps puzzling way then, literary modernity was associated first, not with the present, but with an immediate past which was endlessly validated and revalidated, second, with the production of a virtually unassimilable secondary elaboration of a body of writings universally accepted as "primary." The point to be made is that this body of secondary elaborations—like de Man's literary texts—was demystified from the start: it too pretended to no illusion about itself; it was secondary, harmless, and ideologically neutral, except within the internal confines of the more and more professionalized profession.

The second challenge was, as I said by way of contrast with what I have just been discussing, external. Here I have found it useful to employ the concept, seriously alluded to first by George Steiner I believe, of extraterritoriality. Again there are many things to be mentioned in this connection, and again I must be summary and selective. There was the greatly expanded paperback book market and with it the dramatic increase in the number of translations from foreign languages; there was the gradual impression upon "English" of such outside fields as psychoanalysis, sociology and anthropology; there was the decentering effect (under NDEA auspices by the way) of comparative literature, and with it the weighty prestige of genuinely extraterritorial critics like Auerbach, Curtius and Spitzer; and finally there was what now seems to have been a genuinely fortuitous intervention on our literary scene of ongoing European criticism, first through residents like de Man and Georges Poulet, then through more and more frequent visitors from abroad. It is important to mention at this juncture that Marxism became an intellectual presence to be reckoned with in this context of external challenge of importation from abroad: so far as I have been able to tell—and this is only a speculation—the kind of Marxism practiced or announced in university literary departments owes very little to the American radical movement that ended with the McCarthy period. The new Marxism came to this country partly as a result of the interest in French criticism and partly because of the general wave of anti-war agitation on the campuses. It did so in the form of sudden discovery and just-as-sudden application to literary problems. Its main weaknesses therefore were the comparative absence of a continuous Marxist theoretical tradition or culture to back it up, and its relative isolation from any concrete political struggle.

Between them, the internal and external challenges to English studies were decisive—but only in very limited ways: this is a crucial thing to understand, I think. During the great upheavals of the 60's the academic literary establishment, which had for years been accustomed to being a factory for turning out refined minds and essays, responded to the times with a demand at first for instant "relevance." In fact this meant only that the teaching and scholarship of literature should occasionally show us how the masterpieces were relevant to contemporary reality, that for example in reading Swift or Shakespeare we could "understand" man's inhumanity to man, or how evil apartheid was. I have little hesitation in saying that the much-vaunted MLA revolution brought only cosmetic changes of this sort, and these changes testified not to the will for change in various well-intentioned scholars, but rather to the depth and resiliency of an ideology of refinement which had effectively absorbed even this new, and potentially violent challenge. True, there was an extraordinary, not to say alarming tendency to overkill in the oppositional rhetoric of the late 60's and early 70's: the vocabulary became suddenly more "technical" and self-consciously "difficult," the Barthes-Piccard controversy was re-lived and even reproduced in many journals, congresses and departments, and it became *de rigeur*—indeed profitable for many of us—to aspire to the condition of "literary theorists," a position in departmental rosters virtually unthinkable a scant ten years ago. There was a peculiar (but, I am glad to say, a short-lived) search for "inter-disciplinary" projects, programs, "minds" and gimmicks, all of this accentuating the extent to which one could not (or perhaps ought not to) discuss a Donne poem without also referring to Jakobson, perhaps even to European Latinity, and at least to metaphor and metonymy. On the one hand therefore you had the appearance of a genuine new subculture of theoretical opposition to the old nationalist literary traditions institutionalized in the academy, and on the other, you had those old traditions fighting back with appeals to "humanism," "tact," "good sense," and the like. The question is whether in these instances Tweedledum and Tweedledee were really all that different from each other, and whether either had produced work that justified both the oppositional rhetoric of the one or the strong moral defensiveness of the other.

I am only concerned, however, with the "Left" side of the controversy, and in this connection my real beginning point is a pair of observations about what the Left has been, or perhaps still is, capable of producing. Consider first *that in American literary studies there has not in the past two decades been one work of major historical scholarship that can be called "revisionist":* I use this last adjective to indicate some parallel with what has gone on in American historical studies, in the work of Williams, Alperovitz, Kolko, and many others. I make the assumption that for there to be effective interpretation in what is, after all is said and done, a historical discipline, there must also be effective history, effective archival work, effective management in the actual material of history. Certainly the individual work of literature exists to a considerable extent by virtue of its formal structures, and it articulates itself by means of a formal energy, intention, capacity, or will: but it does not exist only by those, nor can it be said to be apprehended and understood only formally. And yet for the most part literary studies have been dominated, even in their Marxist variety, by an absence of the historical dimension, dominated indeed by the spirit of refinement I referred to a little while ago. Historical research on the Left has been neutralized by the notion that interpretation is based ultimately upon "method" or "rhetoric," as if either of those two defined the separate competency and dignity of the literary theorist. Moreover, the whole concern with oppositional knowledge (that is, a knowledge which exists essentially to challenge and change received ideas, entrenched institutions, dangerous values) has succumbed to the passivity of ahistorical refinement upon what is already-given, there, acceptable, and above all, already-defined. One looks everywhere and finds no alternative to the attitude that argues as to how, for instance, *Our Mutual Friend* can be understood better and better the more you see it in itself as more and more of a novel, which is, in this case, the more you study it, a finer and finer illustration of a very precisely reticulated theory of narrative fiction, whose conditions of readability and whose force depend on formal grammars, generative abstractions, and innate structures. There is a certain element of parody in my description, but a good deal of accuracy too.

The second observation is the other side of the coin, that literary studies on the Left, far from producing work to challenge or revise prevailing values, institutions and definitions, have in fact gone a very long way to confirming them. In many ways this is a more serious matter, and perhaps I had better speak about it in a bit more detail.

No society known to human history has ever existed which has not been governed by power and authority, and as Gramsci says repeatedly, every society can be consequently divided into interlocking classes of rulers and ruled. There is nothing static about these basic conceptions, since if we consider society to be a dynamic distribution of power and positions we will also be able to regard the categories of rulers and ruled as a highly complex and highly changeable pair of categories, in which many divisions and sub-divisions can be made. To use only Gramsci's terminology for the moment, we can divide society into emergent and traditional classes, into civil and political sectors, into subaltern and dominant, hegemonic and authoritative powers—and so on. Yet standing over and above all this activity is at least an idea, or set of ideas, and at most a group of agencies of authority, which gain their power from the State. The central reality of power and authority in Western history, at least since the period from the end of feudalism onwards, is the presence of the State and without wishing to argue this point at any great length here, I think that we would have to say that to understand not only power, but authority—which is I think a much more interesting and various idea than power—we must also understand the way in which authority, any authority, in modern society is derived (sometimes immediately, sometimes in highly mediated ways) from the power and presence of the State.

To a very great extent culture, cultural formations and intellectuals (artists, writers, critics, producers of culture like teachers, administrators, and the like) exist and are made possible by virtue of a very interesting network of relationships with the State's commanding, almost absolute power. About this set of relationships I must say immediately that all contemporary "Left" criticism, of the sort that I have been discussing, whether in France or in this country is stunningly silent. There are a few exceptions to this. Foucault is one, as is Ohmann; one would be hard put to name others whose criticism is directly concerned with the matter. Quite the contrary, nearly everyone producing literary or cultural studies makes no allowance in his work for the truth that all intellectual and/or cultural work occurs somewhere, at some time, on some very precisely mapped-out, and permissible terrain, which is ultimately contained if not actually regulated, by the State. If it is true that, according to an art-for-art's sake theory, the world of culture and aesthetic production subsists on its own, away from the encroachments of the State and authority, then we must still be prepared to show how that independence was gained, and more important, how it is maintained, or if it was ever maintained. In other words, the relationship between aesthetics and State authority prevails in the cases both of direct dependence or the much less likely one of complete independence.

The sense I now have of taking on far too huge an area of historical experience is intensified by the realization that cultural, theoretical, or critical discourse today provides me with no vocabulary, no conceptual or documentary language, much less a concrete body of specific analyses, to make myself clear. For the most part our critical ethos is formed by a pernicious analytic of blind demarcation by which, for example, imagination is separated from thought, culture from power, history from form, texts from everything which is "hors texte," and so forth. In addition we misuse and have been misused by the idea of what method is, and we have fallen into the trap of believing that method is sovereign and can be systematic without also acknowledging that method is always part of some larger ensemble of relationships headed and moved by authority and/or power. For if the body of objects we study—the corpus formed by works of literature—belongs to, gains coherence from, and in a sense emanates out of and reconfirms the concepts of nation, nationality and even of race, there is very little in contemporary critical discourse making these actualities possible as subjects of analysis or discussion. I do not by any means intend to advocate a kind of reductive critical language whose bottom-line rationale is the endlessly asseverated thesis that "it's all political," whatever in that context one means by *all* or *political.* Rather what I have in mind is the kind of analytic pluralism proposed by Gramsci for dealing with historical-cultural blocks, for seeing culture and art as belonging not to some free-floating ether nor to some rigidly governed domain of iron determinism, but to some large intellectual endeavor—what he calls systems and currents of thought—connected in numerous very complex ways to doing things, to accomplishing certain things, to force, to diffusing ideas, values, and world-pictures. If we agree with Gramsci that one cannot freely reduce religion, culture or art to unity and coherence, then we will go along with the following theses for humanistic research and study, remembering as we read Gramsci that for him philosophy and thought include art and culture:

> What must . . . be explained is how it happens that in all periods there co-exist many systems and currents of philosophical thought, how these currents are born, how they are diffused, and why in the process of diffusion they fracture along certain lines and in certain directions. The fact of this process goes to show how necessary it is to order in a systematic, coherent and critical fashion one's own intuitions of life and the world, and to determine exactly what is to be understood by the word "systematic," so that it is not taken in the pedantic and academic sense. But this elaboration must be, and can only be, performed in the context of the history of philosophy, for it is this history which

> shows how thought has been elaborated over the centuries and what a collective effort has gone into the present method of thought which has subsumed and absorbed all this past history, including all its follies and mistakes. Nor should those mistakes themselves be neglected, for, although made in the past and since corrected, one cannot be sure that they will not be reproduced in the present and once again require correcting.[3]

I have quoted the last sentence not because I agree with it, but because it expresses the didactic seriousness with which Gramsci believed all historical research should be conducted. But his main point of course is the (to me) very suggestive insight that thought is produced in order for actions to be accomplished, that it is diffused in order to be effective, persuasive, forceful, and that a great deal of thought elaborates on what is a relatively small number of principal, *directive* ideas. The concept of elaboration is crucial here, and has not been given enough attention by students of Gramsci. By elaboration Gramsci means two seemingly contradictory, but actually complementary things. First, to elaborate means to refine, to work out (*e-laborare*) some prior or more powerful idea, to perpetuate a scheme, a group of ideas, world view. Second, to elaborate means something more qualitatively positive, the proposition that culture itself, or thought, or art is a highly complex and quasi-autonomous extension of political reality and, given the extraordinary importance attached by Gramsci to intellectuals, culture and philosophy, it has a density, a complexity, and a historical-semantic value that is so strong as to make politics possible. Elaboration is the ensemble of patterns making it feasible for society to *maintain itself.* Far from denigrating elaboration to the status of ornament, Gramsci makes it the very reason for the strength of what he calls civil society which in the industrial West plays a role no less important than that of political society. Elaboration therefore is the central cultural activity, and whether or not one views it impoverishingly as little more than intellectual propaganda for ruling class interests, it *is* the material making a society a society. In other words elaboration is a great part of the social web of which George Eliot spoke in her late novels, but Gramsci's insight is to have recognized that subordination, fracturing, diffusing, reproducing as much as producing, creating, forcing, guiding are all necessary aspects of elaboration.

Thus thought, art and culture make up a large part of that upon which State authority depends, of that which the State governs. One could go as far as saying that culture—*elaboration*—is what gives the State something to govern, and yet as Gramsci is everywhere very careful to say, cultural activity (elaboration) is not uniform, is not mindlessly homogeneous. The real depth in the strength of the modern Western State since feudalism is the strength and depth of its culture, and culture's strength is its *variety,* its heterogeneous plurality. This view distinguishes Gramsci from every other important Marxist thinker of his period. In it he loses sight neither of the great central facts of power and how they flow through a whole network of agencies operating not by force but by rational consent, nor of the detail—diffuse, quotidian, unsystematic, thick—from which power inevitably draws its sustenance, on which power depends for its daily bread. Well before Foucault, Gramsci had grasped the idea that culture serves authority, and ultimately the national State, not because it represses and coerces, but because it is affirmative, positive, persuasive. Culture is productive, Gramsci says, and this—much more than the monopoly of coercion held by the State—is what makes a national Western society strong. Consequently, the intellectual is not really analogous to the police force nor is the artist merely a propagandist for wealthy factory owners. Culture is a separately capitalized endeavor, which is really to say that its relationship to authority and power is far from nonexistent: for one must be able to see culture as historical force possessing its own configurations, ones that intertwine with those in the socio-economic sphere, and then finally bear upon the State as a State. Thus elaboration's meaning is not only that it is *there,* furnishing the material out of which society makes itself a going enterprise, but that like everything else in what Vico called the world of nations, elaboration aspires to the condition of hegemony, with intellectuals playing the role of what Gramsci calls "experts in legitimation."

Because I value them, and consider them to be essential, I have pulled these ideas out of Gramsci to serve as a point of comparison with the historical and political ideas now propagated by oppositional, or avant-garde literary theory today. What I have been calling contemporary "Left" criticism is vitally concerned with various problems stemming out of authority: such problematics as that of the "return" to Marx, Freud, Saussure and others, the issue of influence and intertextuality, the questions of the *impensé* and the undecideable in deconstructive criticism, ideology as a factor in literary creation and dissemination. Yet nowhere in all this will one encounter a serious study of what authority is, either with reference to the way authority is carried historically and circumstantially from the State down into a society saturated with authority of one sort or another, or with reference to the actual workings of culture, the role of intellectuals, institutions, and establishments. Furthermore if the language of magazines like *Critical Inquiry, Glyph,* and *Diacritics* is brimming with sentiments of depth, radicality and insight there is never so much as a paragraph expended there on what in the way of ideas, values and engagement is being urged; nor, for that matter, will one ever stumble on a serious attempt made to characterize what historically (and not rhetorically) it is that we advanced critics are supposed to be opposing. One's impression is that the young critic has a well-developed political sense, yet close examination of this sense reveals a haphazard anecdotal content enriched neither by any knowledge whatever of what politics and political issues in our world are all about, nor by any awareness that politics is something more than liking or disliking some intellectual orthodoxy now holding sway over one department of French or another.

I do not think it is an exaggeration to say that oppositional Left criticism contributes absolutely nothing to intellectual debate in the culture at large today. Our bankruptcy on the suddenly glamorous question of human rights alone is enough to strip us of our title to humanism. Yet I do not by any means wish to downgrade the period of almost Renaissance brilliance through which technical criticism has passed in the last two decades. One can gratefully acknowledge that and at the same time add that it has been a period characterized by a willingness to accept the confinement and isolation of literature and literary studies *vis-à-vis* the world. It has also been a period during which very few of us have examined the reasons for this confinement, even while most of us have tacitly accepted, even celebrated, the State and its silent rule over culture—without so much, during the Vietnam and post-Vietnam period, as a polite murmur. My disappointment at this stems from an intellectual conviction that it is our technical skill as critics and intellectuals that the culture has wanted to neutralize, and if we have cooperated in this project perhaps unconsciously, it has been because that is where the money has been. In our rhetorical enthusiasm for buzz-words like scandal, rupture, transgression and discontinuity it has never occurred to us to be concerned with the relations of power at work in history and society, even as we have assumed that a text's textuality is a matter endlessly to be explored as something concerning other texts, vaguely denoted conspiracies, fraudulent genealogies entirely made up of books stripped of their history and force. The underlying assumption in all this is that texts are radically homogeneous, the converse of which is the extraordinarily Laputan idea that to a certain extent everything can be regarded as a text. The result as far as critical practice is concerned is that individualism of rhetoric in criticism and in the texts studied by the critic, are cultivated for their own sake, with the further result that writing is seen as deliberately aiming for alienation—the critic from other critics, from his readers, from the work he studies.

The compelling irony of this depressing isolation, given the way we (as part of the secular priesthood of what Bakunin called "the era of scientific intelligence") are viewed by our political masters is almost staggering. (In what follows I am indebted to Noam Chomsky's recent Huizinga Memorial lecture on the intellectuals and the state.) A recent Trilateral Commission publication, *The Crisis of Democracy,* surveys the post-60's era with some degree of concern over the masses' sense of their political demands and aspirations; this has produced a problem of what the authors (among them Samuel Huntington and Michel Crozier) call "governability" since it is clear that the population at large is no longer so docile as it once was. To this situation then the class of intellectuals contributes two things that derive directly from the two kinds of intellectuals contemporary democratic societies now produce. On the one hand are technocratic and policy-oriented, responsible intellectuals; on the other politically dangerous value-oriented "traditional" intellectuals. The second group is where, by any reasonable standard, we are supposed to be, for it is the members of this group that supposedly "devote themselves to the derogation of leadership, the challenging of authority, and the unmasking and delegitimation of established institutions." The irony is, however, that literary critics, by virtue of their studious indifference to the world they live in and to the values by which their work engages history, do not see themselves as a threat to anything, except possibly to each other. Certainly they are as governable as they have always been since state-worship became fashionable, and certainly their passive, though adulatory devotion to masterpieces, culture, texts and structures posited simply in their own "texts" as going, working, functioning yet finished enterprises poses no threat to authority or to values kept in circulation and "managed" by the technocratic managers.

But in more specific terms, *what is* the role of critical consciousness, of oppositional criticism? Since I only have a little time left to go into the matter, I shall have to confine myself to the study of the so-called modern period, which is what I know best. The relevant background in very schematic terms is as follows: as Raymond Williams has shown, words like *culture* and *society* acquire a concrete, explicit significance only as early as the period after the French Revolution. Before that, as I have tried to show in my own work, European culture as a whole identified positively as being different from non-European regions and cultures, which for the most part were given a negative value. Yet during the nineteenth century the idea of culture acquired an affirmatively nationalist cast, with the result that you have figures like Matthew Arnold making an active identification between culture and the State. It is the case, I believe, with cultural and aesthetic activity that the possibilities and the circumstances of its production get their force, their authority if you will, by virtue of a system of what I would call *affiliation:* that is an often implicit network of peculiarly cultural (as opposed to natural or biological or crudely ideological) associations between forms, statements, and other aesthetic elaborations on the one hand, and on the other, institutions, agencies, classes, and fairly amorphous social forces. Affiliation is a loose enough word both to suggest the kinds of cultural ensembles Gramsci discusses in the passage I quoted earlier, as well as to allow us to retain the essential concept of *hegemony* guiding cultural and broadly intellectual activity, or elaboration, as a whole.

I attach a great deal of importance to this notion of affiliation, and rather than trying to discuss it exhaustively let me try to suggest its general importance to contemporary critical activity. In the first place, as a general interpretive principle *affiliation* mitigates somewhat the facile theories of *homology* and *filiation* which, so far as humanists are concerned, have created the homogeneously utopian domain of texts connected serially, seamlessly, immediately only with other texts. By contrast affiliation is what enables a text to maintain itself as a text and this is covered by a range of circumstances: status of the author, historical moment, conditions of publication, diffusion and reception, values drawn upon, values and ideas assumed, a framework of consensually held tacit assumptions, presumed background, and so on and on. In the second place, to study affiliation is to study and to recreate the bonds between texts and the world, bonds which specialization and the institutions of literature have all but completely effaced. Every text is an act of will to some extent, but what has not been very much studied is the degree to which—and the specific cultural space by which—texts are made permissible. To recreate the affiliative network is therefore to make visible, to give materiality back to, the strands holding the text to the society, the author and the culture that produce it. In the third place, affiliation releases a text from its isolation, and imposes upon the scholar or critic the presentational problem of historically re-creating or re-constructing the possibilities out of which the text arose. Here is the place for intentional analysis, and for the effort to place a text in homological, dialogical or antithetical relationships with other texts, classes, institutions, etc.

None of this interest in affiliation—both as an analytico-theoretical principle of research or as socio-cultural process—is worth very much unless it is actively generated out of genuine historical research (and I mean that the critic is to feel himself making discoveries, making unknown things known—the model is perhaps a crude one), and it is ultimately fixed for its goals upon understanding, analyzing, contending with the distribution, deployment and management of power and authority within the culture. Let me put it this way: we are humanists because there is such a thing called humanism, legitimated by the culture, given a positive value by it. What we must be interested in directly is the historical process by which the central core of humanist ideology produced literary specialists such as ourselves, who have construed their domain as restricted to something called "literature" whose components (including "literarity") have been given epistemological, moral and ontological priority for the literary critic. In acting entirely within this domain then the literary critic effectively confirms the culture and the society enforcing upon him those restrictions; this confirmation acts therefore to strengthen the civil and political societies whose fabric is the culture itself. What is created as a result is what can reasonably be called a liberal consensus: the formal, restricted analysis of literary-aesthetical works validates the culture, the culture validates the humanist, the humanist is the critic, and the whole enterprise the State. Thus authority is maintained by virtue of the cultural process, and anything more than refining power is denied the refining critic. By the same token it has been the case that "literature" as a cultural agency has become more and more blind to its actual complicities with power. That is the situation we need to comprehend.

Consider now the issue formed during the nineteenth century by cultural discourse: one thinks immediately of people like Arnold, Mill, Newman, Carlyle, Ruskin. The very possibility of culture—I do not think that I simplify too much here—is based on the notion of refinement: Arnold's thesis that culture is the best that is thought or said gives this notion its most compact, but by no means its least powerful form. Culture is an instrument for identifying, selecting, valorizing, normalizing, affirming, certain "good" things, forms, practices, ideas over others, and in so doing it transmits, it diffuses, it partitions, it teaches, it presents, it propagates, it persuades, and above all, it creates and re-creates itself as a specialized apparatus for doing all those things. Most interestingly, I think, culture becomes the opportunity for a refracted verbal enterprise whose relationship to the State is always understated and, if you will permit the solecism, *understood.* The great realistic novel plays a major role in this enterprise, for it is the novel—as it becomes ever more "novel" in the work of James, Hardy, and Joyce—that organizes reality and knowledge in such a way as to make them susceptible to systematic verbal re-incarnation. The novel's realistic bodying-forth of a "world" is to provide representational or representative norms selected from among many possibilities: thus the novel acts to include, state, affirm, normalize, naturalize some things, values, and idea, but not others. Yet none of this can be *seen,* can be directly perceived, in the novel itself, and it has been the singular mission of most contemporary formalist critics today to make sure that the novel's remarkably precise articulation of its own selectivity appears simply as a fact of nature, and not of socio-cultural process. For to see the novel as cooperating with society in order to ban, reject, deform, and negatively capitalize, for example, what Gareth Steadman Jones has called outcast populations, is also to see how the great aesthetic achievements of the novel—in Dickens, Eliot, Hardy and others—result from a technique for representing objects, people, settings and values in affiliation with very specific historical and social norms of knowledge, behavior, and physical beauty.

In the widest perspective then the novel, and with it modern Occidental culture, is not only selective and affirmative, but centralizing and powerful. Apologists for the novel, among them nearly every novelist of note during the period, continue to assert the novel's accuracy, realism, etc., as well as the novelist's imagination, freedom of representation, etc.; the implication of this is that the culture's opportunities for expression are unlimited. What such ideas mask, *mystify,* is precisely the network binding writers to the State, and to a world-wide Occidental imperialism which, at the moment that they were writing, furnished them in the novelistic techniques of narration and description with implicit models of accumulation, discipline and normalization. What we must ask on the one hand is why so few "great" novelists deal directly with the major social and economic *outside* facts of their existence—colonialism and imperialism—and why too on the other hand critics of the novel have continued to honor this remarkable silence. With what, as elaboration, is the novel, and for that matter most modern cultural discourse, affiliated, whether negatively or positively, whether in the language of affirmation, or in the structure of accumulation, denial, repression, mediation that characterize major aesthetic form? How is the cultural edifice constructed in such a way as to limit the imagination in some ways, enlarge it in others? How is imagination connected with the dreams, the constructions, and ambitions of "official" knowledge, with executive knowledge, with administrative knowledge? What is the community of interests that for example produces Conrad and C. L. Temple's *The Native Races and Their Rulers?* To what degree has culture collaborated in the worst excesses of the State, from its imperial wars and colonial settlements, to its self-justifying institutions of antihuman repression, racial hatred, economic and behavioral manipulation?

Nothing in what I have been trying to say very rapidly here implies mediating or reducing the specific density of individual cultural artifacts to impersonal or anonymous forces supposedly responsible for producing them. The study of cultural affiliation necessitates an acute understanding of the specificity of objects, and even more important, of their intentional roles, neither of which can be given their proper due by reductionism or, for that matter by positivistic refinement. I would guess that Raymond Williams' term *cultural materialism* suits the methodological attitude I am trying to describe, although not necessarily all my views. In the main therefore I should like to see American literary criticism shedding its partly self-imposed and socially legislated isolation, at least with reference to history and to society. Given that the social sciences by and large have abdicated to the "technotronic" world of clinically specialized, streamlined knowledge, the void in responsible intellect, in informed reading—which is what we know how to do best—cannot be left that way by the literary intellectual. There is a whole world manipulated not only by so-called "reasons of state" but by every variety of ahistorical consumerism, whose ethnocentrism and mendacity promise the impoverishment and oppression of most of the globe. Unless someone is prepared to make clear and intellectually challenge the every-day realities of what it means and has meant to live in a society with interests, authority, density and power, we are heading for an era of depressing quietism. What is lacking in contemporary oppositional criticism is not only the kind of perspective found in Joseph Needham's civilizational approach to culture and society, but some sense of involvement in the affiliative processes that go on, whether we acknowledge them or not, all around us. I do not think that it is too much to ask intellectuals to attempt at very least to match their real situation with their real capacities, and at the same time, to recognize that historically they are as much the producers of history and the social dialectic, and of the possibilities of real knowledge and of real freedom, as any other members of society. But, as I have been saying over and over, these are matters to do with knowledge, not with refinement. I suspect that the most urgent question to be asked now is if we still have the luxury of choice between the two.

Columbia University

NOTES

1 F. O. Mathiesson, *The Responsiblities of the Critic: Essays and Reviews,* ed. John Rackliffe (New York: Oxford Univ. Press, 1952), p. 9.

2 Paul de Man, *Blindness and Insight: Essays in the Rhetoric of Contemporary Civilization* (New York: Oxford Univ. Press, 1971), pp. 17, 16, 18.

3 Antonio Gramsci, *The Prison Notebooks: Selections,* trans. and ed. Quintin Hoare and Geoffrey Nowell Smith (New York: International Publishers, 1971), p. 327.

The Politics of Literary Criticism

Evan Watkins

I think Professor Said's discussion has demonstrated a necessity to understand the relationships between criticism and other activities. And I don't want to suggest, in concentrating on the encounter between critic and poem, that there are a set of internal relations within the activity of criticism which must be described before one can talk about these connections to other things. Rather, my reason for emphasizing this particular relation, between critic and poem, has to do with the fact that it is too often conceived as having little to do with power or authority: because it is thought to rise above the problems of commitment, social awareness and so forth into a realm of pure description or pure scholarship; because it is understood as never quite getting to any real crisis of political awareness or never becoming any real political action; or perhaps most insidiously, as Said has shown, because one exaggerates the political relevance of methodological procedures at the expense of ignoring the actual interstices of a complex experience.

Perhaps the most obvious support for my contention inheres in the institutionalized opposition between artist and critic, to the extent that it has become one more division of labor. The critic amasses knowledge about an art he doesn't produce, and the artist, like some elegant and unpredictable animal driven by the instinct of inspiration, produces something he cannot talk about. I mention the opposition in this radical form because it was in effect canonized by Frye's *Anatomy of Criticism,* in the dictum that literature is dumb, only criticism can speak. Literature is something; criticism can know about something. More subtle, but just as important, is the division of the work of literature itself into a "surface structure"—defined, variously, as rhetorical, as intentional, as explicitly ethical, or as a sequence of "defense strategies"—and an underlying "deep structure," of myth, of language, of repression or whatever. For such a division of the literary work participates in the division of labor by apportioning literature into a surface which the author "intended," or of which he was at least aware, and an underlying pattern available only to the critic-analyst.

In this form, of course, the division seems to find powerful sanctions in the disciplines which can be brought to bear on the activity of literary criticism. A psychoanalyst, for example, does not expect patients to explain the basis of neuroses, any more than Lévi-Strauss expects the tribesmen to explain their structures of kinship or a linguist expects a native speaker of a language to have consciously available the system of phonetic differences which allows him to speak. Analogously, the critic should never expect to find the "real structure" of a poem made explicit by the author in the surface of the poem itself. Yet critics more often than not express a great deal of surprise when poets react with only tolerant amusement, and sometimes outright hatred, to such criticism. I remember a visiting poet at M.S.U., encouraged by my interest in new poetry, brought up short by a copy of Roland Barthes' *Critical Essays* on my desk. "You don't read that stuff, do you?" much as one might react to a narcotics agent at a rock concert.

However, his response seems to me altogether justified to the extent that any criticism which reserves knowledge of the "real structure" or "meaning" or "significance" of literature to the discoveries of the critical mind at work on it is ultimately totalitarian. No division is neutral, and certainly not divisions of labor. Thus for me the most immediately political consequences of much recent critical theory lies in its concern for the limitations of critical methods, not because they may be faulty instruments of insight, but because of how even at their best they can victimize both literary works and the critic writing about them. If, in fact, it is possible to recognize and describe a set of underlying structures which condition the production of meaning in literature, shouldn't this same recognition be extended to critical discourse as well? Isn't it necessary, politically as well as methodologically, to refuse any special privilege accorded to the position of critic?

In an interview in *Diacritics* a couple of years ago, Said cited R. P.

Blackmur as the most original genius of American criticism—a judgment with which I agree completely—and I want to return to an early Blackmur essay as a way of clarifying my point about this direction of recent criticism, and also as a means of suggesting my reservations about it. The essay is "A Critic's Job of Work," the point of it is precisely the victimization of criticism by its own best ideas, and the examples are as diverse as Santayana and Kenneth Burke, I. A. Richards and Granville Hicks. Just because of the extraordinary explanatory power of the methodologies developed by these critics, Blackmur argues that they too often end up by subjugating literature to their own constructions, making it merely a field to be explained, a sequence of texts dominated and tyrannized by the critical subject which observes them.

Recent theory, in its wholesale rejection of this "single field" model of human experience and its removal of the observing subject from the "center" of discourse, has of course radically extended and redefined Blackmur's reaction against the totalitarianism of critical analysis, as well as showing in convincing detail how criticism victimizes even itself at the point of greatest strength. Yet the fact remains that in the forty-three years since the essay was published, the paradoxical victimization Blackmur described has been built into the very terms of critical methods. Bloom's theory of misreading, like De Man's dialectic of blindness and insight, Girard's *méconnaissance,* and of course Derrida's deconstruction, all provide the means at hand to write, simultaneously, our critical essays twice, once as tragedy and once as farce.

One way to understand this critical doubling back on one's own procedures, and I have argued this way also, is as a kind of massive and baroque solipsism, with the real moment of blindness at the point when criticism should, and does not, contact actual poems. However, as Said has remarked before, it is not really the solipsism of self-defining methods which is dangerous, but their potential monotony. For where solipsism reduces oneself to the status of an inert object, monotony reduces others to the status of oneself, or to a system of discourse, which comes I think to the same thing. Thus rather than a *conclusion,* like Blackmur's, elicited from an awareness in the particular instance of how even the best critical method can tyrannize literature as its subject matter, a concern for the limitations of critical theory becomes instead a point of departure, one which reduces literary works to the same duplicity, the same inherent and problematic limits, as the method which appropriates them. Not surprisingly, a psychoanalytic criticism, for example, critically and intelligently attuned to how critics repress and deform their intentions, inevitably "discovers" in literary works a similar repression and a similar deformation.

Blackmur's corrective to these tendencies in criticism—which, like so many other tendencies, he discerned long before their institutional accomplishment—is at once simple and necessary: "Since criticism is not autonomous . . . it cannot avoid discovering within itself a purpose or purposes ulterior in the good sense."[1] Yet there seems to me two very different ways of understanding the first clause—"Since criticism is not autonomous"—which bear heavily on the possibility of a genuine "left" criticism in contemporary thought. The first recognizes as a given that "autonomy" is a fiction, a blind privilege accorded to absolute origins, and then proceeds in effect to insulate itself from the charge by claiming, precisely, an absolute origin in such recognition. So it is that blindness, that the *fact* of misreading, becomes less a discovery of specific limitations than itself a methodology calculated to recoup its loss of originality in the monotonous assertion that it is no better, and no worse, than what comes before and what comes after. Thus it is criticism which claims as its own unique and constitutive originality the capacity to determine that it has critical limitations in common with all discourse.

There is of course another way to understand Blackmur's stricture, and indeed, the progress of Blackmur's own thought is instructive, from "A Critic's Job of Work" to such splendidly iconoclastic essays as "Between the Numen and the Moha" and his four Library of Congress lectures ("Anni Mirabiles, 1921-1925: Reason in the Madness of Letters," collected in *A Primer of Ignorance*). The naiveté of "A Critic's Job of Work" inheres in Blackmur's belief that somehow literature itself is enough, that regardless of what critics say or don't say about it, the world it bodies into form has a life utterly its own. This is unfortunately a position that criticism has driven too many poets and artists to defend, and as an antidote to Frye's statement in *Anatomy,* even such naiveté has a salutary effect. But Blackmur can do better. The implicit premise throughout his posthumously published collection of essays, *A Primer of Ignorance,* realizes that criticism must bear the burden of responsibility for the continued life of literature in time. The truly frightening quality of literary works is not that they are monuments which intimidate approach, but rather that they have almost their whole history ahead of them. Said's book *Beginnings* is a reminder of what an important qualification inheres in that "almost." But for the moment I am more concerned with the implications of the other half of the proposition.

The responsibility Blackmur places on criticism implies an awareness that the literary work can be involved with other values, other beliefs, and perhaps what is most easily forgotten, other material conditions than one's own. Now "Otherness" as a category of insight and as a statement of displacement has certainly lost its terrors for us. And to the extent it has, the task of a "left" criticism remains one of re-introducing into this essentially idealistic category an understanding of its social and, to use a favorite word of Said's, its "worldly" import, where "Otherness" has little to do with the Symbolic, the vanished "trace" of Being, or even the reciprocal look of "The Other" on oneself described in *Being and Nothingness.* Indeed, "The Other" in these usages is nothing more than a way of disguising and *domesticating* the particular, contingent and disruptive intrusion of "an other" within every thought and action, including the activity of literary criticism. When theory makes poetics out of poems, this particular and contingent other activity is returned to the safety of one's own theory, reproduced in the image of our narrowly professional concerns. Poems become monotonous allegories of critical theory. Rather than the historical responsiblility to sustain a work of literature in time, one instead remains sealed within a timeless and ultimately metaphysical void. This is indeed the monotony Said has described in many different ways, where all that happens is that "one experiences the text making the critic work, and he in turn shows the text at work: the product of these interchanges is simply that they have taken place."[2]

Thus I would argue that the paradoxical result of a contemporary concern for "Otherness" is the return of criticism to the very model of experience whose break-up is announced again and again, that is, to the privilege accorded to the observing subject, the eye whose visionary light pores over the recesses of a layered field. For the attempt to maintain that there is a "field" without an observing subject is doomed from the beginning. The terms are always correlative. Even Derrida, whose work is intended to be ultimately disruptive of any such privilege, achieves his disruption only at the expense of conceiving yet another field: of anonymity, of script, of the written "I." Thus at the very point of expression, of the auto-affection of the speaking subject, Derrida discovers in Husserl the way in which such auto-affection is always already implicated in the anonymity of all discourse. Rather than disruptive of Husserl, rather than ulterior "in a good sense," I read Derrida's conclusion as a kind of comfort, a way of avoiding once more the constitutive shock of contact with another and different voice by the invocation of this field of anonymity, of Otherness as a total category.[3] When reduced to formula, as so often happens in writing which owes its terms to Derrida, Said's criticism remains exact: "the product of these interchanges is simply that they have taken place."

Said's statement can help explain as well the puzzling second half of my quotation from Blackmur, that once one recognizes that criticism is not autonomous, then one "cannot avoid discovering constantly within [it] a purpose or purposes ulterior in the good sense." For what has been written out of the situation Said describes is precisely an ulterior purpose in any sense. Once one knows that the best insight will be blind, the best understanding a misunderstanding, one's most personal statement implicated in anonymity, then one is free of any responsibility to determine an actual awareness of ulterior purpose, of all those concerns Said has spoken of tonight. There is only the monotonous and repeated assertion that of course such purpose is there, for someone else to discover later, where, as Barthes has it, one's critical metalanguage becomes but one more object—language for another or for oneself later on.

It is a truism of recent criticism that there is no pure speech. Yet the corollary seems to me less an emphasis on the institutional structures of language or the mediation of The Other than an awareness that what is already ulterior in any speaking is a silent and critical listening to what one says. No speaking precedes this silent listening; there is no residue of pure consciousness uncontaminated by the doubleness of speaking and hearing oneself speak. Such critical listening makes impossible a pure self-presence in consciousness. But neither can this impossibility be itself totalized as a field of anonymity. For listening as I conceive it is disruptive to the extent that it is always particular and contingent, ulterior insofar as it never quite lets the spoken words settle into the easily available patterns and codes of abstract linguistic behavior, and it is "in the good sense" because it makes necessary a continual movement beyond the static and central authority of intentional consciousness. Thus rather than a general and metaphysical freeplay of absence and presence at the noncenter of discourse, critical listening recognizes specific limitations which cannot be totalized.

Nevertheless, both Blackmur's work and Said's are reminders that criticism has responsibilities beyond an attentiveness to the nature of its own activity. To begin with, freedom from implication in the position of tyrannizing and privileged observer must become a freedom to engage the work of literature in terms which allow a kind of reciprocal creativity, and thus likewise the possibility that poems can talk back to critical theory. For the poem is also ulterior to the critical act, neither as The Other poised over against the observing critical mind, nor as merely another perspective which the critic must recognize and tolerate. The drama of speaking and listening I have described briefly as the means by which criticism comes into existence has its counterpart in the way a poem comes into existence. This means abandoning any abstract division of labor, and with it the idea that a poet is a kind of blindly inspired fool or the idea that he or she simply works out an intention as mediated by the generic conventions of language and learned response. Like criticism, a poem is a double movement of speaking and listening, a dialectic which the critic cannot afford to reduce to only another voice and which certainly cannot be generalized into a field of discourse.

The very best literature seems to me to complicate this situation still further. For what one realizes in Faulkner's *Absalom, Absalom!,* for example, is that Faulkner is not content to place Shreve McCannon within the texture of the novel as a single field shaped by Faulkner. Nor does he feel as a continual and disturbing "other perspective" the quite different conclusions about the Sutpens to which Shreve comes. Rather, and most finely in the long eighth section of the novel, he attends to Shreve's activity as it lofts out of a creative and silent meditation on Quentin's dilemma a sustained response that attempts to say something other than Faulkner's own sense of the Sutpen's history, just as Faulkner himself attempts to say something other than Shreve in his understanding of the Sutpens. Thus Faulkner's voice is doubly disrupted, by how he listens critically to himself, and by how he listens to how Shreve listens critically to himself. The greatness of Faulkner's genius is this humility, the willingness at once to commit himself to a response and yet to create in Shreve a capacity to create a radically different novel than Faulkner's own. And this difference is so important to Faulkner, not because he values a philosophical ideal of meaning as diacritical, but because, among other things, how one understands the institutions of racism and agrarian capitalism delineated in the story of the Sutpens is so very important in our own history.

Critics of *Absalom, Absalom!* should be capable of realizing in their work with the novel a doubleness as radical and as whole as what Faulkner achieves with Shreve. That is, they must first violate their own position as privileged observer by the critical and disruptive effort of silently listening to their own speech. And then they must go beyond even this, to attend to how Faulkner splits himself into two, three and even more vital centers of creative intelligence. Finally, they must commit themselves to a response to the novel which has as its very condition of existence the realization of that specific and contingent other complex of activity in Faulkner himself.

It is because of this intense and often painful drama of social interaction that I want to conceive of the critical act as political through and through and not only when it is put into relation with other and more obviously political behavior. Marx often speaks of a certain revolutionary impatience, a sense that one can feel at home in political activity only when it seems "big enough" or "important enough" to fulfill one's own sense of self-worth, or if it seems to have immediate connections to a massively concerted effort by countless individuals. What I would suggest about criticism as political activity is that the connections to others are forged at every point when one implicates criticism in the realization of a communal effort which thrives on the diversity of its members, and thus a communal effort that seems to me a very different thing than the corroboration of a scholarly community, the promulgation of culture, or the comfort of an anonymous field of discourse. This is not, of course, to imply that the practice of criticism is always and everywhere an appropriate political response to every situation. Nor, I think, is it to take refuge in a rationalization that if one does nothing else, at least literary criticism is obscurely important somehow in the "larger scheme" of things. For while, as Said has shown, it is necessary to think through the connections between one's activity as a critic and other activities, the reverse is also essential, that is, to realize even the most interior and private gestures of criticism as inaugurating a social and political world that is not, after all, so very different than what Said has suggested in his discussion of Gramsci.

Michigan State University

NOTES,

1 R. P Blackmur, "A Critic's Job of Work," in *Form and Value in Modern Poetry* (New York: Doubleday, 1957), pp. 347-48.

2 Edward Said, "Roads Taken and Not Taken in Contemporary Criticism," *Contemporary Literature,* 17 (1976), 334.

3 See my discussion of Derrida on Husserl in *The Critical Act: Criticism and Community* (New Haven: Yale Univ. Press, 1978), pp. 89-94

Historical Imagination and the Idioms of Criticism

For Edward Said

Eugenio Donato

We are gentlemen of Japan
On many a vase and jar
On many a screen and fan,
We figure in lively paint;
Our attitude's queer and quaint
You're wrong if you think it ain't. . . .

—W. S. Gilbert

The world has become sad because a puppet was once melancholy.

—Oscar Wilde

I signori . . . vivono di cose gia manipolate . . . non sono i latifondi e i diritti feudali a fare i nobili, ma le differenze.

—di Lampedusa

The nineteenth century's ironic realization that its self-awareness as well as apprehension of the natural and cultural environment were inextricably caught in the web of representation was all pervasive. The self could no longer be conceived of as a transparent unity acting as an originating intention upon a purely instrumental language or as the neutral locus of immediate perception. Nature stopped being a privileged origin capable of generating its own innocent spectacle or of serving as a repository for a "natural language." Finally, human institutions were no longer considered the incarnations of a divine plan or of laws transcendent by their origin or nature.

The self constituted by representation is both temporally and spatially self-divided. It was not necessary to wait for Freud to learn that the self is not continuous with its own past nor spatially adequate with its representations. The romantic problematic of memory, be it in poets such as Wordsworth and Coleridge, novelists such as Flaubert, or philosophers such as Hegel, always constitutes the self as the product of a representational system which does not allow for easy identities or continuities. Nature, caught in a perceptual and linguistic representational scheme, lost its privileged ontological status. More exactly, as De Man has convincingly shown, the romantic poets, aware of the exigencies of representation, through their representation of nature, allegorized the loss of a privileged "Natural Object." To this loss corresponded the view of society, illustrated by practically every novelist of the nineteenth century, as a system regulated by various representational mechanisms: money, desire, etc.

The objection can be made that this is a one sided view: after all, a Wordsworth or a Coleridge believed that through the privileged vision of imagination he could arrive at an original perception of nature, the "essence" of "things," and Hegel did construct, in spite of the negative temporal and spatial play of representation, a formidable dialectical machine to recuperate an essentially objective total history. But thus stated the objection fails to take into account priorities. If the romantics required elaborate and baroque philosophical mythologies to arrive at a privileged conception of the self or nature or society, it was because these entities had already lost their privileged status. The quest for immediacy and presence does not precede but follows irony. Recuperation is rooted in irony, not irony in recuperation.

I would like to generalize this point by suggesting that the critical attitudes throughout the nineteenth century to the present stem from the same romantic dilemma. Today, in fact, with the confrontation between the deconstructive critical idioms and recuperative criticism, we have reached the most acute form of this dilemma. Deconstructive criticism stems from the romantic problematic of representation and has systematically treated the text as ironic allegory of the analysis of representation. On the other hand, recuperative criticism has focused primarily on the *constructs* of a romantic mythology. The positions are not symmetrical for recuperative criticism has had to postulate as origin what is in fact a representationally derived, belated construct, namely the immediacy of an object or the authority of an intention.

When Nietzsche reiterated a leit-motif that runs throughout the nineteenth century by proclaiming the death of God, he emblematized the romantic problem of representation: God as origin, the ontologically privileged object or transcendental subject, is no more. The fact that he was once, but is no more, places him in an absolute past that cannot be recuperated as presence. After the death of God one is doomed, in Said's vocabulary, to repetitive representational beginnings rather than absolute origins. Nietzsche, however, writing precisely about the belief in absolute origins, was to add: "I fear we are not getting rid of God because we still believe in grammar."[1] Of the recuperative critics it could also be said that in not recognizing the representational nature of language they still believe in grammar and hence in a God dead at least since the beginning of the nineteenth century.

My purpose in this context, however, is not polemical. I would simply like to examine the way the romantic problematic of representation defined a specific domain, that of history, and, within that domain, examine the function of one specific metaphor, namely that of Japan.

Flaubert, in a number of striking statements, attributed the invention of history to the nineteenth century. Invention is, in fact, the wrong word since for Flaubert the century is characterized by its essentially historical nature. In a letter to Turgenev, for example, he writes: "One was a grammarian in the times of La Harpe now one is an historian, therein lies the whole difference" (*CS,* p. 414).[2] If we read the word "grammarian" in light of Nietzsche's statement, the eighteenth century presumably believed in language not as a representational system but as a medium that can maintain identities. On the other hand, to be a historian presumably excludes the belief in being a grammarian. The conviction that history constitutes the characteristic property of the nineteenth century is again stated by Flaubert in a letter to Edmond and Jules de Goncourt: "I like history with a passion. The dead please me more than the living! From whence comes this seduction of the past? Why have you made me fall in love with the mistresses of Louis XV? This love at any rate is something new in humanity. A sense of history was only born yesterday and that is perhaps the best that the XIX century has to offer" (*C,* p. 645).

If the dead are more seducing than the living, it is because the past as representation is more "real" than the present. The present has no possible privileged ontological status; the past, reduced to a series of representations, is the only possible "truth." Flaubert is extremely aware of this. In a letter to his niece Caroline, for example, he writes: "The Present is the least important of things, for it is very short, ungraspable. Truth is the Past and the Future" (*C,* p. 1620).

To Bouilhet he adds: "To establish something durable one needs a fixed base. The future torments us and the past holds us back. That is why the present escapes us."[3] The writer's present then is constituted by the past, more specifically, by the stored memories of the past. "The Past devours me, memories beseige me and overwhelm me and I don't hope for anything from the Future—nothing at all, that is my balance sheet" (*CS,* p. 792)!

It is the past, constituted as memory, that temporally and spatially divides the author from himself. From Trouville, Flaubert writes to Bouilhet:

> This trip to Trouville has made me go over the course of my intimate history. I have dreamt a great deal of this theater of my passions. . . . It is time to say goodbye to my youthful sadness. I do not hide the fact, however, that during the past three weeks they have returned like a flood. . . . At certain moments it would seem that the universe has immobilized itself, that everything has become statue and that we alone are living. How insolent nature is! What an impudent libertine face it has! We torture our minds trying to understand the abyss that separates us from it. But that which has even more the character of a farce is the abyss that separates us from ourselves. When I think that here, at this very place, in looking at this white wall decorated with green, I used to have palpitations and that I was then full of "Poetry," I am astounded, I am lost, I have vertigo, as if I discovered, suddenly, a fall of two thousand feet underneath me. (*C,* p. 420)

Let us postpone a consideration of Flaubert's strategy with respect to a nature which eludes his grasp and examine instead his attitude towards a past from which he is separated by an unbridgeable abyss. Not surprisingly Flaubert's present is the accumulation of his memories: "It is impossible for me to do anything whatever. I spend my time re-animating the past" (*C,* p. 1133). More importantly, however, living the present through past representations of memory leads the author to a nostalgia for a global historical past. This nostalgia will in turn constitute itself as a history in which the writer not only can, but does, live:

> Since I cannot see tomorrow, I would like to have seen yesterday. Why did I not live at least at the time of Louis XIV, with a big wig, well drawn stockings and in the society of Monsieur Descartes! Why did I not live at the time of Ronsard! Why did I not live at the time of Nero! How I would have talked with the Greek rheto-

> ricians! How I would have travelled on the big chariots on the roman ways and slept at night in inns with the priests of the Cybele vagabonding around! Especially why did I not live at the time of Pericles and dine with Aspasia crowned with violets and singing verses between white marble walls! All this is finished, this dream will never return. I have no doubt lived there in some past existence. I am sure of having been, under the Roman empire, the troupe director of some ambulant comedians, one of those funny characters who used to go to Sicily to buy women to make them into comedians and who were all at the same time professors, pimps and artists. Those scoundrels have beautiful mugs, In the comedies of Plautus, and in reading them it is as if memories return to me. Have you ever felt the historical shiver? (*C*, p. 341)

Through the historical representations of memory the individual can constitute himself as a subject of history. This capacity, or necessity, of the individual to identify himself with a mediated past history becomes the means through which a global history is made possible. If the whole of the nineteenth century is historical for Flaubert it is because the period is characterized by a global memory of past history, but is doomed by this very memory to repeat the past representationally. For example, for Flaubert the Commune is a repetition of the French Revolution which, in turn, only repeats the Middle Ages:

> As for the Commune, that is in its agony, it is the last manifestation of the middle ages. The last one? Let us hope so! . . . The Commune has rehabilitated assassins, like Jesus used to forgive thieves. And one nowadays robs the houses of the rich, because we have learnt to curse Lazarus, who was, not a bad rich, but simply a rich. "The Republic is above all discussion" is equivalent to the belief that "The Pope is infallible!" Always formulas! always Gods! (*C*, p. 1171)

In another letter to Georges Sand, Flaubert writes:

> We are splashing about in the after-birth (*arrière-faix*) of the Revolution which was an abort, something failed, a fiasco, "whatever one says." The reason being that it proceeded from the middle ages and from Christianity. The idea of equality (which constitutes the whole of modern democracy) is essentially a Christian idea which is opposed to the idea of justice. (*C*, p. 1207)

The constitution of history transforms it into a repetitive mechanism and renders the nineteenth century incapable of generating its own *original* history:

> Miserable though we are, we have, I believe, a great deal of taste because we are profoundly historical, we admit anything and place ourselves from the point of view of the thing to judge it. But do we have as much spontaneity (*innéite*) as we have comprehensitivity? Is a fierce originality compatible with so much largeness? (*B,* p. 645)

The nostalgia for the past becomes a nostalgia for the capacity of past historical periods to generate an original, grounded history.

History instead constitutes itself as an all pervasive textual encyclopedia:

> Ah! good tranquil periods, good wigged periods, you used to like standing squarely on your high heels and your canes. But our earth is trembling. Where should we take our resting point even admitting that we might have a lever? What we all lack is not style, nor that flexibility of the bow and of the fingers designated by the name of talent. We have a big orchestra, a rich palette, we know a great deal, perhaps more than people ever knew. No, what we lack is the intrinsic principle, the soul of the thing, the very idea of subject. We take notes, we travel, misery, misery. We become erudite, archeologists, historians, jokers (*gnaffes*) and men of taste. What does all that matter. . . ? From where to start and where to go? (*B,* pp. 627-28)

History thus encompasses atemporal dimensions which recuperate historically past societies and an aspatial dimension which anthropologically understands foreign societies. What is said temporally about the societies of the past corresponds spatially to the quest for the representational knowledge of societies different from our own. Nevertheless, history, constituting itself as historical or anthropological knowledge, precludes the possibility of a proper history or spatial identity for the nineteenth century. It must be emphasized again that the historical self constituted by the representations of a temporal past or spatial otherness is doomed to those representations and cannot identify with the object that stands behind them. Living with the representation of Rome does not make one a Roman any more than travelling in the Orient renders one an Oriental. To Louise Colet, who believed that through the representations of Rome one could identify with what a Roman was, Flaubert answers:

> Alas, no, I am not a man of antiquity, men of antiquity did not have diseases of the nerves like me, you also are neither Greek nor Roman you are beyond: romanticism has passed in between. Christianity, even if we wish to defend ourselves from it, has come to enlarge all this but also to spoil it, to put pain into it. (*B,* p. 300)

In short, Romanticism's paradoxical dilemma was that the realization of its historical modernity was but another form of belatedness.

I have quoted Flaubert extensively because his texts provide an elucidation and commentary on the Hegelian theme of the "End of History." For Hegel, the first, and necessarily the last, philosopher of a total and systematic history, the idiom of philosophy is constituted by the interiorized representational memory of history. History is finished. History ends precisely at the moment when it constitutes itself in philosophy, itself historical:

> As the thought-or-idea (*Gedanke*) of the World, philosophy appears in time only after the objective-reality completes-or-perfects its formative-education process (*Bildungsprozess*). When philosophy paints its grisaille, a concrete-form of like has [already] grown old; and it does not permit itself to be rejuvenated by [a] grisaille, only known-or-understood (*erkennen*):—the owl of Minerva begins its flight only at the coming of dusk.

This quote from Hegel's philosophy of right poetically reasserts what was already stated at the end of the *Phenomenology,* where Hegel, commenting on the nature of the knowledge that is to come at the end of history, writes:

> In its act-of-going-inside-of-itself, Spirit is submerged in the night of its Self-Consciousness. But its empirical-existence which had disappeared is preserved in this night. And this dialectically-overcome empirical-existence [that is, the existence which is already], past, but [which is] engendered-again from the Knowledge, is the new empirical-existence: [it is] a new [historical] World and a new concrete-form of Spirit. In the latter, Spirit must begin again in the immediacy of this form, and it must grow-and-ripen again starting with it; [it must do so, therefore] in just as naive a manner as if everything that precedes were lost for it and it had

> learned nothing from the experience of earlier [historical] Spirits. But *internalizing-Memory* (*Er-Innerung*) has preserved this existence, and [this Memory] is the *internal-or-private-entity, and in fact a sublimated* (*höhere*) form of substance. Therefore, if this Spirit, while seeming to start only with itself, begins its formative-education (*Bildung*) again from the start, at the same time it begins [it] at a higher (*höhern*) level.[4]

The contradiction is obvious: on the one hand, the past is "lost" and can be maintained only as representational memory (*Er-Innerung*), but on the other hand, the present can only be constituted by grounding it in these past interiorized representations. *Er-Innerung* is not, incidentally, memory proper for Hegel. Only after these primary representations have been recollected from the dark pit of memory can representation proper be said to exist. This secondary memory created by language is known as *Gedachtnis.*

I have purposely chosen to quote these two passages from Hegel which are examined by one of his greatest contemporary commentators, Alexandre Kojève, who has admirably summarized the problem:

> For Understanding or Knowledge of the Past is what, when it is integrated into the Present, transforms this Present into an *historical* Present. . . . (*RH,* p. 164)

> One can *understand* an historical World only because it is *historical*—that is, temporal and consequently finite or mortal. For one understands it truly—that is, conceptually or philosophically—only in "*Erinnerung*": it is the *memory* (*Erinnerung*) of a past real which is the *internalization* (*Er-innerung*) of this real—i.e. the passing of its "meaning" (or "essence") from the *external* Reality into the Concept which is *in* me, *inside* of the "Subject." And if the totality of History can be thus understood (in and by the *Phenomenology*) only at the end *of* History, a particular historical World can be understood only after its end or death in History. (*RH,* pp. 162-63)

In light of the preceding discussion it is not difficult to understand why an historical present can only come at the end of a history which it can only repeat. It is therefore puzzling to see Kojève hesitate in perplexity over the exact "placing" of the End of History. The End of History is not an historical "event" as much as it is a specific problem related to the representation of history. The "event" is not the end of history but the advent of a philosophy that constitutes the present historically rather than immediately, and therefore must postulate the end of history. This can be simply and unequivocably placed in the coming of Romanticism. Furthermore, it is also clear that we are still in the problematics inaugurated by that event—the problematics of belatedness. They do not permit any absolute breaks, and after Romanticism, the necessary series of new starts are each in fact only repetitive, belated beginnings.

It might be objected that I am over-privileging and historicizing the advent of Romanticism, but what I hope to have made clear is that the "event" of the advent of Romanticism is in fact a "non-event." As origin it gives itself the impossibility of origin—the inevitability of beginnings based on an origin which is only an abyss.

But let us return to Kojève and to his highly revealing discussion of the End of History. In spite of the lucidity of his own commentary, Kojève wrestles with the question of *when* to place the End of History and of what form it might take. In a note to the first edition of his *Introduction to the Reading of Hegel,* Kojève, after Hegel, places the End of History with the French revolution and sees the state of society in the past historical period as that of happy animality. He further argues that the Hegelian theme of the End of History is not inconsistent with Marx's view of history, except that Hegel has placed the End of History in the past and Marx in the future:

> The disappearance of Man at the end of History, therefore, is not a cosmic catastrophe: the natural World remains what it has been from all eternity. And therefore, it is not a biological catastrophe either: Man remains alive as animal in *harmony* with Nature or given Being. . . . In point of fact, the end of human Time or History—that is, the definitive annihilation of Man properly so-called or of the free and historical Individual—means quite simply the cessation of Action in the full sense of the term. Practically, this means: the disappearance of wars and bloody revolutions. And also the disappearance of *Philosophy;* for since Man himself no longer changes essentially, there is no longer any reason to change the (true) principles which are at the basis of his understanding of the World and of himself. But all the rest can be preserved indefinitely; art, love, play, etc., etc; in short, everything that makes Man *happy.* (*RH,* pp. 158-59)

Except for the grounding of the End of History as a specific historical event, such a reading remains consonant with a late romantic view of an historical period generated by the End of History as an eternal repetition of the same. The accomplishment of the End of History, however Kojève argued, was yet to come, placing the period between Hegel and the effective End of History in an historical no man's land.

In an important and lengthy note to the second edition, in fact, the only major change between the two editions, Kojève reveals that he has twice changed his mind. He initially believed that the end had already come. After arguing that the United States, Russia, and China are societies fundamentally identical in form and that they are nothing by the result of the consummation of the French revolution, Kojève singles out the United States as the most advanced form of a post-historical society and writes: "I was led to conclude from this that the 'American way of life' was the type of life specific to the post-historical period, the actual presence of the United States in the World prefiguring the 'eternal present' future of all of humanity" (*RH,* p. 161). I would not like to concern myself with this historical identification except to note that it is simply an extension of another romantic theme: the process of repetition applied to society will level it to a uniform state of undifferentiated mediocrity. Flaubert, for example, writes: "The world will become extremely stupid (bougrement bête). . . . For me it is almost certain that in the near or far future Society will be run like a school. The underlings will dictate the law. Everything will be in uniform" (*B,* p. 645). Nietzsche in the *Twilight of the Idols* more succinctly was to write: "The equalization of European man is today the great irreversible process."

But Kojève claims to have changed his mind a third time about the meaning of the End of History. It is this third interpretation that I find interesting from a theoretical standpoint. In spite of its length Kojève's comment deserves to be quoted in full:

> It was following a recent voyage to Japan (1959) that I had a radical change of opinion on this point. There I was able to observe a Society that is one of a kind, because it alone has for almost three centuries experienced life at the "end of History"—that is, in the absence of all civil or external war (following the liquidation of feudalism by the roturier Hideyoshi and the artificial isolation of the country conceived and realized by his noble successor Yiyeasu). Now, the existence of the Japanese nobles, who ceased to risk their lives (even in a duel) and yet did not for that begin to work, was anything but animal.
>
> "Post-historical" Japanese civilization undertook ways diametrically opposed to the "American way." No doubt, there were no longer in Japan any Religion, Morals, or Politics in the "European" or "historical" sense of these words. But Snobbery in its pure form created disciplines negating the "natural" or

"animal" given which in effectiveness far surpassed those that arose, in Japan or elsewhere, from "historical" Action—that is, from warlike and revolutionary Fights or from forced Work. To be sure, the peaks (equalled nowhere else) of specifically Japanese snobbery—the Noh Theater, the ceremony of tea, and the art of bouquets of flowers—were and still remain the exclusive prerogative of the nobles and the rich. But in spite of persistent economic and political inequalities, all Japanese without exception are currently in a position to live according to totally *formalized* values—that is, values completely empty of all "human" content in the historical sense. Thus, in the extreme, every Japanese is in principle capable of committing, from pure snobbery, a perfectly "gratuitous" *suicide* (the classical épée of the samurai can be replaced by an airplane or a torpedo), which has nothing to do with the *risk* of life in a Fight waged for the sake of "historical" values that have social or political content. This seems to allow one to believe that the recently begun interaction between Japan and the Western World will finally lead not to a rebarbarization of the Japanese but to a "Japanization" of the Westerners (including the Russians).

Now, since no animal can be a snob, every "Japanized" post-historical period would be specifically human. Hence there would be no "definitive annihilation of Man properly so-called," as long as there were animals of the species *Homo sapiens* that could serve as the "natural" support for what is human in men. But, as I said in the above Note, an "animal that is *in harmony* with Nature or given Being" is a *living* being that is in no way human. To remain human, Man must remain a "Subject *opposed* to the Object," even if "Action negating the given and Error" disappears. This means that, while henceforth speaking in an *adequate* fashion of everything that is given to him, post-historical Man must continue to *detach* "form" from "content," doing so no longer in order actively to transform the latter, but so that he may *oppose* himself as a pure "form" to himself and to others taken as "content" of any sort. (*RH,* pp. 161-62)

This passage is important in many respects. Kojève abandons, for any practical purpose, the futile effort to locate the End of History in a specific event. In spite of his vague references to Japanese history the argument is doubly spatial in nature. The reference to Japan is spatial inasmuch as Japan stands in a spatial, and not historical, relationship to European history, but, more importantly, all the Japanese practices noted are spatial practices in relation to Nature, and not to history, whose function is the de-naturalization of nature, the reduction of nature to cultural artifacts. This denial of nature through spatial practices is equivalent to an overvalorization of form with respect to content.

This discovery of Japan by Kojève should not be taken too literally, for it is only one episode in a series of texts which make of Japan an allegory for the problematics of form in general. However, before turning to some of these, I would like to briefly consider the problem of mnemonic representation with respect to nature in the nineteenth century and take Flaubert as an exemplary case.

In the letters of Flaubert quoted earlier, memory as representation induced two distinct forms of immediacy—one temporal, one spatial. In a temporal mode the mechanism of memory invested the present with a set of representations which prevented the present from grounding itself in any form of historical immediacy. Spatially the representations of memory will make it impossible to have a perceptual identity or linguistic adequacy with nature, that is, the "Natural Object" will be absent from representation. To repeat Flaubert: "How insolent nature is . . . one tortures one's mind trying to understand the abyss which separates us from it" (*C,* p. 420). The impossibility of finding perceptual or linguistic representations of Nature will lead perforce to a nihilistic critical epistemology. What is implicit and hopefully overcome in a Hegel or the early romantics will become explicit with a Nietzsche or a Flaubert who writes "Art is not reality" (*C,* p. 1818). If art can produce a representation of nature it is not by mimetic adequacy but as a pure representational construct. Artistic realism is in this sense the epitome of art. To quote Flaubert once again: "What a mechanical construct the natural is and how many ruses one needs to be true" (*C,* p. 380)! or "This mania of thinking that one has just discovered nature and that one is truer than one's predecessors exasperates me. The *Tempest* of Racine is as true as that of Michelet. There is no truth! There are only ways of seeing. Does photography give us resemblances: not any more than oil painting or even as much as oil painting" (*C,* p. 1942).

The function of art thus is not to arrive at any form of truth but to create illusions: "The first quality and the end of Art is *illusion*" (*C,* p. 426), and "I believe in the eternity of only one thing, and that one thing is *illusion,* which is veritably the truth. All the others are only relative" (*B,* p. 429).

This representational construct, which is and produces illusion, is for Flaubert nothing but Form itself.

> That is why I like Art. There, at least, everything is freedom in this world of fictions. There one does everything and finds every satisfaction. One is at the same time king and subject, active and passive, victim and priest. There are no limits; humanity is for one a puppet with bells that one rings with the tip of one's sentence . . . like the bowed soul deploys itself in the blue which stops only at the frontiers of Truth. Where Form is lacking the idea is absent. To look for one is to look for the other. They are as inseparable as substance is from color and that is why Art is truth itself. (*C,* p. 321)

Flaubert's famous statement of his wish to construct a "book on nothing" is nothing but the quest for pure form without content:

> That which seems to me beautiful, that which I would like to do, is a book on nothing, a book without exterior ties, that would stand by itself by the internal force of its style, like the earth which without being sustained is suspended in the air, a book that would almost not have a subject or at least where the subject would be invisible, if that were possible. (*C,* p. 303)

If representation is never adequate, perceptually or linguistically, to a natural object, a remark is here in order. Since Hegel, if not already with Condillac, it has been well known that perception is a tropological construct which always carries over a residue of the object. The question then is one either of recuperating the object by attempting to erase the effects of the tropological machine which engenders representations, or else of critically accentuating the tropological play of representation to minimize the effects of the residue and denouncing through a critical epistemology the illusions of any recuperative strategy.

It is quite evident that Flaubert for one is a critic accentuating the need to overemphasize form and minimize the residue carried by representation. Examining Kojève's arguments once again we can perhaps better understand why he needs to separate spatially form from content and valorize the latter by choosing Japan as an ideal post-historical society. The Japanese practices he quotes—the Noh theater, the tea ceremony and so forth—are cultural practices which denaturalize nature by a systematic use of highly elaborated representational forms. Flaubert does not mention Japan, but his attitude is not very different when standing in front of the Alps he yearns for the representational constructs that one would find in a Museum or a library: "I begin by declaring that the beauties of Nature bore me profoundly. . . . Decidedly the old man is not poetical, to all the glaciers of Switzerland he would prefer a library, a theater or a museum" (*CS,* p. 736).

The first systematic treatment I know of which relates the problem of form to nature and uses the example of Japan is the extraordinary dialogue of Oscar Wilde entitled "The Decay of Lying."[5] Wilde asserts from the outset the superiority of art over nature: "The more we study Art, the less we care for Nature. . . . As for the infinite variety of Nature, that is a pure myth. It is not to be found in Nature herself. It resides in the imagination, or fancy, or cultivated blindness of the man who looks at her" (*AC,* pp. 290-91). It is not then in the tropological residue of nature in perception that nature must be looked for, but in this secondary, artificial, formal representational construct which we call art. The realism of the naturalists is itself only an artifact that does not know itself qua artifact. Modern realism is constructed in the library:

> The ancient historian gave us delightful fiction in the form of fact; the modern novelist presents us with dull facts under the guise of fiction. The Blue-Book is rapidly becoming his ideal both for method and manner. He has his tedious *"document humain,"* his miserable little *"coin de la creation"* into which he peers with his microscope. He is to be found at the Librairie Nationale, or at the British Museum, shamelessly reading up his subject. (*AC,* p. 293)

Wilde, thus, distinguishes between two natures, both the consequence of the temporality generated in representation by its necessary mechanism of repetition: the nature "always, already" prior to representation, which leaves its residue there and which is hidden by representation, and another nature created by representation. What must be understood here is what we know only too well after Derrida—that representation cannot function without generating within itself the pseudo-presence of an "object." This "object," however, is secondary and derived with respect to the play of representation. The error—the error of recuperative criticism—is to identify this necessary but constructed object with an original "Natural Object," to place as cause what is an effect, as origin what is a product. Nietzsche had pointed out more than once that the error is a tropological one, that of chiasmatically reversing the temporality of representation and taking the "necessary after" for the "privileged before." To quote Wilde's priceless formula: "Where the cultured catch an effect, the uncultured catch cold" (*AC,* p. 312).

Pure form thus is a dream of a representation without an effect and Wilde names this dream Japan: "In fact the whole of Japan is a pure invention. There is no such country, there are no such people." The empirical Japan is not different from any other country:

> Do you really imagine that the Japanese people, as they are presented to us in art, have any existence? If you do, you have never understood Japanese art at all. . . . The actual people who live in Japan are not unlike the general run of English people; that is to say, they are extremely commonplace, and have nothing curious or extraordinary about them. (*AC,* p. 315)

Japan, as a metaphor for form, although without any ontological status, can be read in a representational scheme to restructure the perceptual effects of representation, to produce new perceptual effects, and to destabilize the illusion of a privileged nature:

> If you desire to see a Japanese effect, you will not behave like a tourist and go to Tokio. On the contrary you will stay at home, and steep yourself in the work of certain Japanese artists, and thus, when you have absorbed the spirit of their style, and caught their imaginative manner of vision, you will go some afternoon and sit in the Park or stroll down Piccadilly, and if you cannot see an absolutely Japanese effect there, you will not see it anywhere. (*AC,* pp. 315-16)

Roland Barthes on this point is interesting, but not illuminating. For Barthes, also, Japan is the dream of a pure form, the metaphor of a language without content, of a representation without effect:

> The dream: to know a foreign and strange tongue yet not to understand it: to perceive in it a difference without the possibility of having this difference recuperated by the superficial sociability of language, communication or vulgarity; to know, refracted positively in a new language, the impossibilities of ours; to undo our "real" by the effect of other decoupages other syntaxes; to discover unheard of positions of the subject in the enunciation, to displace its topology; in one word, to descend in the untranslatable, to feel its shock without softening it until the whole occident in us is shaken and we undo the rights of our paternal tongue, the one that comes to us from our fathers and that makes us in our turn fathers and proprietors of a culture that precisely history transforms into "nature."[6]

There is a problem, however, with Barthes' constant suggestion, in spite of his disclaimer that his Japan is imaginary, that, in fact, Japanese culture and its formalized rituals have succeeded in creating a pure form totally devoid of content and that, perhaps, if one went to Japan and looked at it with naive enough eyes one might be able to see such a pure form. What Barthes has forgotten are the exigencies of representation. If Japan can function as the metaphor for form towards western culture, it is because we can perceive in Japanese culture artifacts which denaturalize nature to a greater extent than our cultural forms do. The actual anthropological difference is one of degree and not of nature.

A far more interesting use of the metaphor of Japan is offered by a text of Heidegger's: "A Dialogue on Language between a Japanese and an Inquirer."[7] Inasmuch as the text implies an overview of an attitude towards language it involves the reader in a number of complexities which I shall disregard in this context to concentrate simply on the use of the Japanese interlocutor in Heidegger's strategy.

It might be useful at this point to remember that the opening lines of "The Saying of Anaximander" define "dialogue" as a necessary forum for the saying of an original saying which deals with truth and being, that is, for Heidegger, with language. The function of the dialogue, in the last analysis, to say appropriately the first saying, will necessarily bring forth a translation of that first saying. This should suffice in alerting us that neither the form of the dialogue nor the questions concerning translations of Japanese words are innocent.

The dialogue opens with a reference to an earlier dialogue that presumably took place between Heidegger and a certain Count Kuki. This earlier dialogue is not available to the reader but is now located at the start in the context of a funerary memorial. Count Kuki is dead; his remains are buried in the gardens of a temple in Kyoto. The Japanese interlocutor reminds his European counterpart that this funerary grove is a "place for reflection and deep meditation." In a sense, the dialogue is itself located in this funerary monument which commemorates an earlier dialogue concerning the relation of certain Japanese words and certain western words, a dialogue finally concerned with the ontological status of the artistic object in particular and with language in general.

We are told at the beginning that Count Kuki was concerned with giving a definition of the word *Iki.* The reader will in fact never be given a Japanese explanation of the word; the task would seem to be impossible. In the words of the western interlocutor: "We were discussing *Iki* and here it was I to whom the spirit of the Japanese language remained closed—as it is to this day" (*OWL,* p. 4). Nevertheless, the western interlocutor does seem to have an idea of what *Iki* means, but his definition, "A sensuous radiance through whose lively delight there breaks the radiance of something suprasensuous" (*OWL,* p. 14), remains within the realm of western esthetics, which is concerned with the distinction between the hidden and the apparent. To the western interlocutor's attempt to define *Iki* the Japanese speaker offers another word, *Iro Ku,* which seems to correspond

". . . exactly to what Western, that is to say, metaphysical doctrine says about art when it represents art aesthetically. The *aistheton,* what can be perceived by the senses, lets the *noeton,* the nonsensuous, shine through" (*OWL,* p. 14).

The possibility of translating Japanese words into western concepts is, however, quickly denounced by both interlocutors. If one can attempt the translation it is because there is in fact a process by which Japan has historically fallen under the spell of European metaphysics. In the words of the westerner there is a ". . . process which I would call the complete Europeanization of the earth and of man" (*OWL,* p. 15). The Japanese agrees, but with an important qualification: "The foreground world of Japan is altogether European or, if you will, American. The background world of Japan, on the other hand, or better, that world itself, is what you experience in the *Noh* play" (*OWL,* p. 17). Curiously, then, the "Japanness" of Japan is maintained, or rather, appears as different at the precise moment when Japan disappears in the sameness of western culture.

What is maintained is allegorized in a Noh play as a gesture which causes ". . . mighty things to appear out of a strange stillness" (*OWL,* p. 18). The possibility of the appearance depends upon an essential emptiness which is symbolized by the emptiness of the Noh stage: "The Japanese stage is empty. . . . To us, emptiness is the loftiest name for what you mean to say with the word 'Being'. . ." (*OWL,* pp. 18-19). Emptiness like pure form is *not;* yet without the emptiness no appearance would be possible.

What then is the function of Japan? To produce a number of words which are not words; to offer a number of linguistic entities which, although signifying an untranslatable void or emptiness, by their presence enable the understanding of the metaphysical representational scheme; to make it possible to apprehend the silence of silence through which speech becomes possible.

> I: Above all, silence about silence . . .
>
> . . . .
>
> I: Who could simply be silent of silence?
> J: That would be authentic saying . . .
> I: . . . and would remain the constant prologue to the authentic dialogue *of* language. (*OWL,* pp. 52-3)

If we were actively to forget the nostalgia for authenticity might we not recognize in the metaphor of Japan this silence about silence that which in a different critical idiom we have learnt to spell as differance with an *a?*

University of California, Irvine

NOTES

1 Friedrich Nietzsche, *Twilight of the Idols,* trans. R. J. Hollingdale (Harmondsworth: Penguin Books, 1968), p. 38.

2 Gustave Flaubert, *Correspondance* (Paris: Louis Conrad, 1927), hereafter cited as *C.* All quotes, unless otherwise noted, will be from this edition. The letters included in the four volumes of the *Supplement* will be cited as *CS.* My translation.

3 Gustave Flaubert, *Correspondance,* ed. J. Bruneau (Paris: Pleiade, 1973), p. 730, hereafter cited as *B.* My translation.

4 Both Hegel quotes are from Alexandre Kojève, *Introduction to the Reading of Hegel,* trans. H. Nichols, Jr., ed. A. Bloom (New York: Basic Books, 1969), p. 163, hereafter cited as *RH.*

5 Oscar Wilde, "The Decay of Lying," in *The Artist as Critic* (New York: Random House, 1969), hereafter cited as *AC.*

6 Roland Barthes, *L'Empire des Signes* (Geneva: Albert Skira, 1970), p. 13. My translation.

7 Martin Heidegger, "A Dialogue on Language," in *On the Way to Language,* trans. P. D. Hertz (New York: Harper and Row, 1971), hereafter cited as *OWL.*

Deconstruction: Beyond and Back
Response to Eugenio Donato, "Historical Imagination and the Idiom of Criticism"

Marie-Rose Logan

In the beginning of *The Sophist,* one of Plato's most speculative dialogues, Socrates, Theaetetus, Theodorus and the Eleatic Stranger decide to undertake the definition of the Sophist, the Statesman, and the Philosopher. They seek first to define the Sophist. Since the Eleatic Stranger is to lead the discussion, Socrates asks him whether he would prefer to present a long speech or to engage in a dialogue. To this question, the Stranger answers, "The method of dialogue, Socrates, is easier with an interlocutor who is tractable and gives no trouble: but, otherwise, I prefer the continuous speech done by one person."[1] Since the dialogical approach lies at the heart of the Socratic method, the answer is as rhetorical as the question. The comment of the Eleatic Stranger, however, reminds us that, in order to be able to develop a sustained argumentation, the speaker is to meet with an interlocutor who is at least willing to enter his frame of mind. Through a "response," the interlocutor presumably enters a similar intellectual contract.[2] Indeed, the Latin verb *respondere* means not only "to answer," "to respond," but also—like *spondere*—"to warrant," "to promise," "to bind." Yet, in the language of Roman eloquence, the term often acquired antagonistic overtones. When Cicero says, *respondeo orationi,* he means, "I refute your speech." On the other hand, the early Christians called *responsorium* a practice, borrowed from the synagogue, which consists in the singing of complimentary versicles.[3]

These prefatory remarks come to mind as I am about to respond to Eugenio Donato's "continuous speech" on "Historical Imagination and the Idiom of Criticism." Indeed, if I were to adopt the deconstructive critical idiom advocated by Donato, my response would probably turn out to be nothing more than a *responsorium,* an alternate chant. On the other hand, since I find myself in agreement with most of the issues Donato has brought up, I could hardly refute his speech. The position I will hence adopt will be that of a "tractable interlocutor" who would, nonetheless, like to press harder on some issues.

Let us consider first the issue of the idiom of criticism. The proliferation of a deconstructive terminology in such journals as *Glyph, Diacritics,* and the *Georgia Review* (under the editorship of John Irwin) leads us to the question whether the boundaries between "recuperative criticism" and "deconstructive critical idioms" are that clear. For, if such concepts as "deconstruction" and "differance" were to be used rhetorically, the thrust which presided over their emergence would be lost. Moreover, if deconstructive criticism were to become a paradigmatic and prescriptive mode of textual analysis, it would no longer be distinguishable from recuperative criticism.

In some respects, the critical exchanges which have been taking place recently under the banner of deconstruction are reminiscent of the intellectual exchanges which took place during the Renaissance. Let me explain this position, which might sound paradoxical given the fact that the humanists were intent on establishing a tradition which is today being challenged. Contemporary French thinkers have indeed accustomed us to think that "Man is occasionally *a* measure of things, but by no means is he *the* measure,"[4] whereas Erasmus, Budaeus, Colet, and More fostered the idea that Man is the sole object of man's study. Taking their cue from Cicero, they proclaimed that the concept, *humanitas,* embodied culture, dignity, and sociability. This *humanitas* was to be achieved through the practice of the *bonae litterae.* As M.-M. de la Garanderie has recently pointed out in *Christianisme et Lettres Profanes (1515-1535),* the expression *bonae litterae* was used as a generic term to designate an entire written tradition encompassing manuscripts and books already written and to be written.[5] Erasmus's contempt for the oral tradition and his reverence for the written one (*monumenta*) exemplify, in many ways, the humanistic ideal.[6] Yet, it is the very insistance on the *bonae litterae* which brought about the dilution of the concepts which Erasmus and his colleagues were trying to further. Their epistolary exchange, which reflects the wide range of their preoccupations, also denotes that arguing over the purity of their Latin expressions often took precedence over concern with the "political issues" of the time, notably the upheavals of the Reformation and the restructuring of the European powers. The *litterarum res publica* dealt, but at a distance (much as our critics do today), with the reality of the historical process. In a sense, too, their idiom, an *elegant* Latin (the epithet prevailed after Valla's *Elegantiae*) strengthened their fellowship as an intellectual elite; but, by the same token, it contributed to accentuate their divorce from the general culture of the period. In a letter to John Colet, Erasmus felt the need to write, "One quarrel springs from another, and with amazing arrogance we wrangle over trifles."[7] I do not think that we have yet come to the point of wrangling over trifles.

Derrida himself, however, reminds us that his philosophical strategy is not tied to, and thus reaches beyond the realm of, a specific terminology. In "Où commence et comment finit un corps enseignant," he attempts to clarify his own use of the term: "Deconstruction or, at least, what I have suggested by this term (which is as good as any other, but no better)—has thus always dealt with the apparatus and the function of teaching in general and with the apparatus and function of philosophy in particular and above all. Without limiting the specificity of what is at stake, I would say that we are but at a stage in the development of a systematic project."[8] Closely linked to the practice of teaching, the deconstructive strategy is thus conceived of by Derrida as an ongoing revisionary process. It is perhaps this aspect of deconstruction which should retain our attention within the framework of this conference. Indeed, by discussing the problems of reading in contemporary American criticism, we become aware of the ideological implications inherent in the models we use. Before turning my attention to the question of historical imagination which Donato has brought up in connection with the idiom of criticism, I would like to make a short digression. Although Continental criticism has played an important role in our discussion, we must not lose sight of the fact that—if you forgive the expression—Continental criticism is not the breakfast of every American critic. Stanley Fish, for instance, has debated the question of reading without referring to a single Continental critic. In fact, Fish's discourse unfolds strictly within the realm of Anglo-American principles ranging from Hume's notion of causality to Searle's speech act theory.

The French critic Michel Charles has recently published *Rhétorique de la lecture,* which echoes on Fish's description of reading as a trope of persuasion. A student of Genette and Todorov, Charles presents a reflection on reading which stems from a questioning of the so-called structuralist model of his predecessors. On Genette, he writes,

> . . . the figure is for Genette at once *technique* and *worldview.* This subtle interplay between silence and

critical discourse is thus not "simply formal." It is a matter of showing, revealing an aporia; it is, at once, necessary and impossible to talk about literature: necessary in so far as the literary object requires, in order to establish its status as such, reading and its "hyperbolic" form, criticism; impossible, in so far as each reading (hence each critique) modifies its object, if only because it names, gives meaning and always (more or less) "completes."[9]

Given the fact that the issue of reading has long been denied in American formalism and in French structuralism, the work of Fish and Charles might very well open new avenues or, at least, provide points of articulation for an encounter between the two models.

Let us now turn to the question of historical imagination. Donato has stressed that the nineteenth century "is characterized by its essentially historical nature." From there on, Donato relates Flaubert's historical constructs to the larger problematics of representation. This problematics enables Donato to proceed to a questioning which obliterates the received distinction between philosophical and literary discourse. For, if representational constructs are to be found in Flaubert, they are to be found in Heidegger and Kojève as well. In fact, the question of historical imagination relates not only to the philosophical and the literary discourses, but also to the historical discourse. In recent years, the status of historical discourse has been subject to investigations on both sides of the ocean. Let me take two examples: that of Hayden White and that of Michel de Certeau. Historians like J. H. Hexter or Peter Gay have attempted to examine the "craft" of the historian, but they have not proposed the kind of methodological revisions which White does.[10] In *Metahistory: The Historical Imagination in Nineteenth-Century Europe,* White explores the topic of historical imagination in authors ranging from Hegel and Michelet to Ranke, Tocqueville and Burckhardt. Yet, although he deals with philosophers and historians, and not with writers such as Flaubert, White applies, to the texts he considers, methodological criteria borrowed from Northrop Frye and from Kenneth Burke. Hence, he devises four modes of historical consciousness on the basis of the tropological strategy which informs each of them: metaphor, synecdoche, metonymy, and irony. A discourse originally devised to talk about literary texts is thus used to talk about other texts. Yet this gesture does not imply that White obliterates the received distinction between literary and historical discourses, since he never questions the status of the texts he exploits *qua* texts. His endeavor rather testifies to a long-lasting influence of formalistic modes of thought in American culture. In fact, White's book is written as a kind of defense of formalism against the pervading influence of contemporary European thinkers who "have cast serious doubts on the value of a specifically 'historical' consciousness, stressed the fictive character of historical reconstructions and challenged history's claim to a place among the sciences."[11] To be sure, in the 1960's, history vegetated in the shadow of the other social sciences—namely linguistics, anthropology, and psychoanalysis. At the moment, it seems, however, as though history is making a comeback on the French scene.

The publication of the three volumes of *Faire de l'histoire* in 1974 (one year after the publication of Hayden White's *Metahistory*) constitutes a turning point in the development of French historical practice. The three volumes include essays by Michel de Certeau, Andre Leroi-Gourhan, Emmanuel Le Roy-Ladurie, Pierre Vidal-Nacquet and others. These practitioners of history all appear in some way to have benefited from a confrontation of their discipline with linguistics, anthropology, and psychoanalysis. The most provocative among those essays is perhaps that of Michel de Certeau, "L'Operation historique," in which he questions the "concept of history." According to de Certeau, "history" designates "a practice (a discipline) and its result (a discourse) and their relationship."[12] The discourse of the historian is thus at once a discourse on history and a discourse on the historical discourse. As such it enjoys a status of its own:

> He [the practitioner of history] would indeed be an escapist, he would indulge in an ideological alibi if, in order to establish the status of his work, he were to have recourse to a philosophical *elsewhere,* to a *truth* elaborated and transmitted outside the channels through which, in history, any system of thought is linked to social economic, cultural loci.[13]

The thrust of de Certeau's gesture sends us beyond and back to what Derrida has called "deconstruction." For indeed, if the practitioner of history is not supposed to rely on philosophical premises, he is expected to adopt an attitude toward his discourse which is similar to that of the philosopher *vis-à-vis* the philosopher's own discourse. By the same token, the strategy of the historian, like that of the philosopher, is a strategy of watchfulness which enables him to operate on models borrowed from the other social sciences without losing track of the autonomy of his own discourse.

In this respect, the gesture of de Certeau is perhaps closer to that of Donato than to that of White. Yet, by its nature, it carries connotations which are not overtly present in Donato's discourse. Consequently, if American critics often reproach—and quite rightly do so—Continental critics for their strong bent towards theory, they might very well rethink, in the light of de Certeau's work, the warning of Schelling: "The fear of speculation, the ostensible rush from the theoretical to the practical, brings about the same shallowness in action that it does in knowledge. It is by studying a strictly theoretical philosophy that we become most directly acquainted with ideas, and only ideas provide action with energy and ethical significance."[14]

One very last remark: American poets do not perhaps exhibit the same fear of speculation as their fellow critics do. Can we not, indeed, perceive in the "idiom" of Wallace Stevens the Heideggerian "silence about silence" to which Donato alludes at the end of his paper:

> Yet the absence of the imagination had
> Itself to be imagined. The great pond,
> The plain sense of it, without reflections, leaves,
> Mud, water like dirty glass, expressing silence
>
> Of a sort, silence of a rat come out to see,
> The great pond and its waste of the lilies, all this
> Had to be imagined as an inevitable knowledge,
> Required, as a necessity requires.[15]

Columbia University

NOTES

1 Plato, *Sophist,* Loeb Edition (Cambridge, Mass.: Harvard Univ. Press, 1967), 217d, p. 269.

2 The role of the dialogue as a method of speculative investigation would deserve more attention than we can devote to it here. Let us note, however, that the response, although it bears similarities, also differs from the dialogue substantially: in the response, the two interlocutors are not given so great a chance to pursue the challenge of their encounter. I might also add that, in Western civilization, the dialogue has often contributed to fostering the synthetic (or syncretic) worldview. See, for example, Ibn Gabirol's *Fons Vitae* and Leone Ebreo's *Dialoghi d'Amore.* Today the interview (or "*entretien*") tends to fulfill a function similar to that of the dialogue. See, for instance, Jacques Derrida, *Positions* (Paris: Minuit, 1972).

3 Since the material for this chant was usually borrowed from Scripture, the practice tended to reinforce doctrinal principles. See J. A. Jungmann, *The Early Liturgy* (Notre Dame, Indiana: Univ. of Notre Dame Press, 1959), pp. 283 ff.

4 See Edward W. Said, *Beginnings: Intention and Method* (New York: Basic Books, 1975), p. 374.

5 Marie-Madeleine de la Garanderie, *Christianisme et Lettres Profanes (1515-1535)* (Paris: Champion, 1976), esp. pp. 36-38.

6 Although most humanists were interested in written works from a philological point of view, Erasmus and Bovillus discuss the relationship between speaking and writing in a more speculative manner. See M.-R. Logan, "Bovillus on

Language," *Acts of the Second Neo-Latin Studies Congress* (Munich: Fink, 1979).

7 Hans J. Hillerbrand, ed., *Erasmus and His Age: Selected Letters of Desiderius Erasmus* (New York: Harper, 1970), p. 31.

8 Jacques Derrida, "Où commence et comment finit un corps enseignant" in *Politiques de la philosophie* (Paris: Grasset, 1976), p. 65 (My translation).

9 Michel Charles, *Rhétorique de la lecture* (Paris: Le Seuil, 1977), p. 83.

10 J. H. Hexter's *Doing History* (Bloomington: Indiana University Press, 1971) and Peter Gay's *Style in History* (New York: Basic Books, 1974) represent esthetically oriented approaches to the historian's *"métier."*

11 Hayden White, *Metahistory: The Historical Imagination in Nineteenth-Century Europe* (Baltimore: Johns Hopkins, 1973), pp. 1-2.

12 Michel de Certeau, "L'Opération historique," in Jacques Le Goff and Pierre Nora, eds., *Faire de l'histoire* (Paris: Le Seuil, 1974), I, p. 34 (My translations).

13 Michel de Certeau, "L'Operation," p. 3.

14 W. J. von Schelling, *Werke,* ed. Manfred Schröter (Munich: Beck, 1958-59), III, p. 299.

15 Wallace Stevens, "The Plain Sense of Things," *Collected Poems* (New York: Knopf, 1954), p. 503.

Canticu graduum

Ad te levavi oculos meos
qui habitas in caelo
Ecce sicut oculi servorum
in manibus dominorum suorum
Et sicut oculi ancillae in manibus
dominae suae. Ita oculi nri ad dnm dm
nrm donec misereatur nobis
Miserere nobis dne miserere nobis
quia multum repleti sumus
contemptione
Et multum repleta est anima nra
obprobrium habundantibus
et dispectio superbis

Canticu graduum

Nisi quod dns erat in nobis
dicat nunc israhel
nisi quod dns erat in nobis
dum insurgerent homines in nos
forsitan vivos deglutissent nos

An Exchange on Deconstruction and History

Ed. Note: *Following Eugenio Donato's presentation, a brief debate occurred between Professors Said and Donato and others on the issues which both of their papers addressed. We present below a slightly edited version of their remarks.*

Edward Said: I'm sorry, I'm not sure that I can be as brief as you would like, because I have a number of things to say on what both of the speakers have said. I think these things are important for the general discussion of critical theory that we have been having here. Now, as you know, I have a great admiration for both of your work, and certainly I find absolutely nothing to disagree with on what you said about Flaubert and the whole question of the end of history as you discussed it, Eugenio. But let me preface what I have to say with one comment: that the notion of deconstruction is not a Derridean idea exclusively. That is to say—if you were to go before Derrida to Marx, for example, who in the *Eighteenth Brumaire* refers to the weapons of criticism, and before him, to Vico and so on, right back to Aristotle—there is an activity called criticism which exactly exists to use intellectual means to understand what it is texts are saying, what they are not saying, what they are doing. So, rather than repeat, you might say, the litany of virtues—and they are great—of the Derridean moment, I think it is important here to use the weapons of criticism to affiliate what you said with, in fact, history. Now, it would seem to me that to understand Flaubert in a real context, the larger context of his time, you'd have to say, first of all, that Flaubert is writing what he has to say about the present, his hatred of the present, his fear of the future, his nostalgia for the past and his sense of representation against something that was taking place, not only in France but in Europe generally, and that is exactly the *scientific power of representing the world*. Much of what you said, for example, Eugenio, about Flaubert should be read against Renan's *L'Avenir de la Science*, subtitled *Pensée du dix-huits cent quarante-huits*, published in 1890, in which he says that science is really the world, that the future of the world resides in science, because science can do certain things, among them philological things. Renan is not an original thinker by any means, but he represents the era of the spirit of things against which Flaubert as a novelist is reacting, that is to say, the *power* of science—philological science, natural science, social science—to deliver the world, to reconstruct the world—in the case specifically, since you were talking about it, of the Orient—regions of the world lost to Europe, lost even to the Orient which the scientists were delivering. The linguists did it—Sassez did it, Bopp did it, Schlegel did it, etc., etc. The list can go on indefinitely. But these people were able to go into the past and to represent the past in such a way that the past became actual in their writing, not only into the past but across great distances, into the Orient in particular. Flaubert's reaction, which you described brilliantly, and with which I have no quarrel whatever, was—and his novels are exactly a reaction to this—that the only thing left for the novelist to do is to criticize the representation, that is to say, by virtue of what you call deconstruction, and to show that the power of art is *precisely its powerlessness*, that it is *unable* to do what is going on at large in society.

That is to say, at the same time that Flaubert was writing about the loss and showing the nostalgia for the Orient in *Salâmmbo*, what he was talking about in *La Tentation de Saint Antoine*, the temptation of all knowledge which was now available to Europe, *was precisely being written out in the history of Europe*. Because you have, for instance, not only the invasion of the Orient by Napoleon at the beginning of the 19th century, but also the invasion by France exactly of Algiers in 1830. And during the entire 19th century you have a period during which European accession over the entire non-European world went to the extent of occupying 85% of the world. And it is against this vision of advancing recuperation precisely in the fundamental literal sense of the word, the recuperative march of science upon the rest of the world, that Flaubert finds himself working as a novelist, having nostalgia for the past, trying to create his own past in contradiction to what was taking place in his time. And this also applies to Hegel, because if you push further to affiliate *the rest of Hegel* to his assertion that there is only representation of the natural object, etc., it can be seen that for him it is finally within the *recuperative* and *totally representative power of the state to include everything which we have lost in nature*. That is to say, it is the structure of the state which is able to *deliver* the lost nature which has disappeared but which can be, in fact, reconstructed and restored, you might say, by the power of the modern state.

The point of all this is to note that the interest in Japan in Huysman, Claudel, Valéry, and others in the twentieth century has to be seen against this extraordinary background of *la découverte de l'Asie* as it was called, which meant, as you know, not just recuperation, but actual historical and political accumulation. It meant actual acquisition. And, therefore, as I see it, the novelistic project of Flaubert was, in fact, to institute a counter-acquisition or counter-accumulation by a narrative and descriptive technique of restoring *his* Orient as a kind of competing discourse to the other one. In so doing, he merely illustrated, as Lukács perfectly says about *Salâmmbo*, the singular powerlessness of the artist in *that* society. And that, I think, is the reading that in a sense completes what you're saying. I don't by any means think this contradicts what you're saying. But I *do* think that what is necessary here is to affiliate it with [history] and—the last point I wanted to make—one does not necessarily have to see this as a result of the *démarche Derridienne*. That is to say, this *kind* of criticism, "weapons of criticism," you might say, the Marxist critique, the Vichian critique, the Gramscian critique, or it could be the right-wing critique, etc., the great historistic projects of the nineteenth century, are all part of this. The last irony I would like to draw attention to is that the great deconstructive schema, which emerged out of Derrida—which is not noticed enough—is that Derrida, at the same time, through his method, is attempting in some way to recuperate all previous methods, too. I mean this is an important step that can be made. It is not just a free emanation in the spirit of science and so on, but the Derridean theory is precisely a theory to recapture all other theories and one has to see them in those power relations. You see, I think that is an important point to be made.

M.-R. Logan: Yes, but without going into Harold Bloom, I would say that that is the characteristic of any strong criticism, that, in a sense, you are a deconstructor, too.

Said: Marx was a deconstructor. . . .

M.-R. Logan: Fine, take Marxists, take deconstructors, call it whatever you want, you are the ones who have brought about that kind of awareness. So that is a parallel gesture; if it is not the same it is parallel.

Said: But I am trying to say that it cannot be done endlessly on the level of theory, or at least, of theory pretending only to be theory.

M.-R. Logan: I never said that. But I said we must not deny theory, we must not rush to practice. Which is exactly what you have been doing. Now, you know the whole question of the nineteenth century text and this use of the Oriental foreign countries is far more complex than we have expressed it here in one form or another. Because one could bring it about the way certain writers will use this fantasizing on the Orient as a weapon against their own society. And I'm thinking of Rimbaud, for instance, who as a young college student wrote poetry in Latin—again the distantiation of the language—right after Algeria had been conquered, right after the defeat of Abd el-Kader and said some day will come, some day they will overcome. Sometime the French will have to get out of Algeria. I mean, it is said almost as directly but in somewhat more poetic language. And he does the same thing with Africa: "moi, le nègre. . . ." and so forth.

Said: If I might first add an historical footnote. . . . This will amuse you, since I noticed that, as you were reading from Huysmans, Eugenio was nodding his head. Huysmans is an important figure for this discussion; for Huysmans was the Godfather of the greatest French Orientalist of the twentieth century, Louis Massignon. And Massignon's book, *La Passion de Husayn Ibn mansur Hallaj*, was dedicated to Huysman. At the same time, in other words, that Massignon admired, you might say, the decadence, the *fin de siècle*, the fatigue of a century coming to its end, he was working for the *Service de Renseignement*, the French Government. He was an agent, along with T. E. Lawrence, in the Hejäz, and his job was at the same time that he preserved his interest in the Orient as "decorative," etc., etc., he was acting in behalf of the French government as indeed was Flaubert when he went to the Orient. He was traveling around with French consular papers, making it possible for him to go through the Orient with the power of Europe. I think these things are important. . . . I'm sorry I took so long.

Donato: I will be perhaps as long in answering!

Said: I hope so.

Donato: I'll take my point of departure from something very marginal to what you [M.-R. Logan] said, in order to come to something that I think is at the heart of the problem, to the question of history. There is a point on which I disagree completely with Serres, and it has precisely to do with this problem of history, which we will leave until the question of "history" versus "real history" is taken up. In the nineteenth century, the classifications and the encyclopaedia do, indeed, become constituted by this accumulation of memory.

Said: And *"territory."*

Donato: But, I hope I made clear, the whole constructive recuperative movement that goes throughout the nineteenth century is accompanied by the deconstructive movement. However, if, for the moment, we remain within the deconstructive movement, that encyclopaedic project failed from the very beginning. It failed in its project in Novalis. Or if you take an encyclopaedic project like *Bouvard et Pécuchet*, it is a deconstructive and an epistemological critique of all the classifications which in fact represent an older science versus a new science. Then comes somebody like Michel Serres, who is a great historian of science—and a historian of science we have to cope with—who sees throughout the nineteenth century a certain number of breaks, but then, at a certain point, the scientific discourse becoming an absolutely overriding discourse with the only ontological grounding, a completely atemporal and non-historical discourse. There is a more interesting question which I could have gone through which connects, I believe, with what you were saying last night, that which—namely the quest for pure form—in fact, I was trying to describe. . . . Let us put the question in a broader way. Is there a way within representational history, not "real history," at least to create an historical space for science which it then erases in its own constitution? Is there a successful pure form? Indeed, in the nineteenth century we do see the birth of a successful pure form in the constitutions of mathematics *qua* totally independent syntax without any content. In that sense I would put it perhaps in shorthand notation. Before the *Cantos*, and so on, before the nineteenth century constituted this ideal form, there is no mathematics, there is only physics inasmuch as the reality of the mathematical object is always embedded in the real object. And, hence, mathematics becomes a mirage which literary critics use as an idea of pure form.

Said: You don't just find it in mathematics; you also find it in linguistics.

Donato: You find it in linguistics, you find it in music, and so on and so forth. So. . . . But, once a language like mathematics is constituted, or the same thing could be said with music, linguistics cannot be put on the same plane, because linguistics does not maintain that absolute synthetic form that mathematics maintains. Can you then say, we can just forget about mathematics? In a way your paper last night was saying, translating it into the problems that I'm focusing now, let us at some point forget doing mathematics and let's do physics. And, fine, let's by all means do physics, too.

Said: No, I agree.

Donato: But one cannot—let me elaborate this point a moment—one cannot give up the continuation of this fusion of mathematics and physics; one must allow mathematics to function in relationship to physics as that mirage of pure form with which it has to be integrated constantly. And yet their cleavage is always maintained and the two can never become adequate one to the other. So that brings me to another question about what you said. When you talk about "real history," I do not deny that there is a "real history" which is a totally different order from that which I was speaking of. The one thing I would deny is that after the beginning of the nineteenth century, after the analytics of representation are opened up, there is a way of talking of "real history" without talking about the problematics of representation of history. Treat them in any key you want, treat them in any ideology you want, treat them in any fashion you want, but those two things are not separable. In fact, this is, in part, the pregnant dilemma, the seminal dilemma that you are showing in your work on Orientalism. Because, indeed, the Orient is not the West, but the Orient gets constituted as an object within the Western representational scheme. But once it becomes constituted as an object, then the dialectic between the otherness of the Orient and the Orient as representation enter into a mechanism which you yourself show is inextricable, that we have to *read* and so on. But the dilemma then becomes if you try to do a radical critique of the enmeshing representation with the object, once the space of representation is open, where does it leave the object? In other words, the only alternative is to say there is a totally different thing there which has to be studied with totally different categories, independently from the constitution of this. But the thing is, in everything I'm saying, literary discourse does not have the privilege of mathematical discourse, and that's why it is doomed for me, once the space of representation is opened, to this constant repetitive mechanism which. . . . I really don't like this word deconstruction, although I use it, and wish I could have cast it in a different language from the language of deconstruction. What interests me at this point—and let me say what is behind all this in my own mind—is that in the last analysis, all of the systems that we have inherited from the nineteenth century are, whether they admit it or they don't admit it, caught within the analytics of representation. And all I'm saying is that, in this ironical moment, at least of the awareness inscribed in the analytics of representation, one is caught within the analytics of representation. What I want to say is that behind my project there is something. My project, failed as it may be, is, within no matter which representation scheme you want to choose, to do it from an ironic key, . . . But the question I want to raise is the problem of the "*Object*"—capital "O" in italics between quotes. This becomes extremely problematical and it still remains extremely problematical.

Said: I'm sorry, but may I respond? First of all, I agree with a lot of what you said, but I would not make the distinction between "History" and "real history." I don't know what that means. I never used that phrase. Exactly what I thought was particularly valuable and important in your paper was that it was done within, you might say, a historical dimension which I don't want to compare to something called a "real history." Quite the contrary, I want to open what you said, and because you gave it to me, I want to connect it with simply *more* history. That's what I mean. . . .

Donato: You used the word "real," that's what bothered me. . . .

Said: I don't mean to make an invidious distinction between "real history" and "deconstructive history" and so on. That's not the point. But the other thing about the object is a very important point. Now take this thing that I've been working on for a long time: I mean, it does seem, doesn't it, that all the descriptions of the Orient are, in fact, representations of the Orient? Then the question, which is a perfectly legitimate question to ask, if someone would ask it, is: "Well, O.K., if what you're saying is that the whole enormous tradition comprising sixty or seventy thousand books in a hundred years—never mind articles and so on—if this is all a structure of myths, or at least a structure, to use your word, of representation, which it is, then, *where is the 'real Orient'?* " And my point is precisely that there is no such thing as a "real Orient." Since the designations "Orient," "Occident," etc., all of these are themselves made. . . . And so the problematic status of the object remains or at least the nonexistence of the object remains. But, what is more important than that is that these representations which you talked about acquire the status of objects or representations *without* history, like mathematics. And this is, *I think*, true of linguistics, certainly in the models constructed in the first forty years of the nineteenth century by people like Humboldt and many others. These [representations] acquire precisely a kind of force which, although they seem to be abstract models, become, in fact, models for doing certain things. And what I'm talking about, what I'm interested in, is that these certain things acquire the status, for instance, of learning, the important status of knowledge. And at least in the limited case in which I have been interested, namely, the Orient, they become, in fact, the ways by which Europe administers and rules millions upon millions of people. Therefore, they are not simply representations which exist, you might say, in the discursive history that we write as scholars. They also become *facts* of a certain kind that have impinged upon events . . . I give the example of Macauley, who over and over again stood up in the House of Commons and said, "Well, here is the whole question of Indian education. There is now before the House the decision as to what we are going to allow these Indians to learn. Should we let them study in India, in the native languages, or are we going to let them do it all in England?" He then goes through a whole series of arguments proving abstractly, by a system exactly of representation, that represents English or European culture as *superior*. Well, this becomes then an administrative decision, because in 1835 the entire educational system of India was changed to an English system. So, here, as you might say, is a pure representation by Macauley, who had the force of power, standing in the House of Commons to, in fact, change the lives of people. I mean, I am interested in following these things out. So, I am not by any means saying that there are not representations, but that there are representations and representations. Some representations have power and some don't. The representations of Flaubert precisely are interesting because they don't have power and have to be read against the representations of power.

William Warner: I'd like to raise a question about Professor Donato's talk and ask you in some sense to relate it to Nietzsche's *The Uses and Abuses of History* as a way, perhaps, of re-engaging the debate between yourself and Professor Said. Because, it seems to me that Nietzsche annunciates a kind of admiration for the monumental historian, who is able to remake the past to generate the representations which effect or enable him to act in the present politically and locally, and then moves through the description of antiquarian history where we get a movement towards a kind of willfulness as knowledge, as interpretation. And I was wondering if it was possible for you to relate your analysis or your deconstruction of history to that sequence and then address the question: Is that a deconstruction of a historical moment of representation? Is that incompatible with a certain aspect of monumental history as, in other words, history acted, as well as politics in the present?

Donato: Well that would have been another question which I would like to discuss with Said following last night's paper. It's a very difficult question, and I think that, on the one hand, one can do an analysis of the problem, but the analysis of the problem will not bring one any closer to *praxis* of the problem. I think that mainly, indeed, within the nineteenth century, you have the coexistence of Macauley's historiography, which influences many millions of people in India, and then you have Nietzsche's historiography, which could be used against Macauley's, but which has no effect within the nineteenth century. So that between those two types of representation, by what critical strategy would one be able to produce a wedge? I have not thought the question out—and I am not ready to answer publicly—but I suspect that it would go through a problematic of values. And by going through a problematic of values, it would go also necessarily through the deconstructive moment of Nietzsche with relationship to values. Since you cannot avoid going through the Nietzschean moment, which suspends the kind of opposition that would permit you, within the context of values, to put stable oppositions, it would be impossible then, in fact, to be able to say, within this context, let's adhere to this representation because it permits an action outside. Actually, all representations, if one wishes them, would define a certain kind of action. There is no doubt about that. Now the question then becomes why one instead of the other. But one instead of the other goes through the Nietzschean problematic of values and the Nietzschean problematic of values undermines the whole problem in such a way that, in the last analysis, I think one is left with an act of Faith.

Stephen Crites: Yes, this is the question about the end of history and its Hegelian/Marxist context. I think there is an aspect of it, which Edward Said did not put forth in his lecture, that has some material bearing on the issue here. For Hegel, certainly, one of the things that happened with the notion of the end of history is precisely the collapsing of a certain kind of specialization of labor that is characteristic of the *historical* moment, a specialization, not only of work and means of subsistence but also of those special labors called philosophy, religion, aesthetics, politics. The subjects of his great lectures, all end by their collapse, or the overcoming of them as such, into something else that no longer represents the rigid kind of compartmentalization in which they have appeared historically. That bears on his notion of *Erinnerung*, which is not simply the representation of the past, but involves the taking in within the social substance of a people, the internalization of what had appeared to be merely representation, merely facts and events of the past, and this, understood as the outcome of history, it seems to me, is *mutatis mutandis*, involved in the Marxian notion of revolution—and revolution as the end of a particular kind of alienated history. What this means, I think, is partly that the sense, for instance, of the privileged position of the political over against the literary and philosophical theoretical substance of culture is not an adequate way of understanding the affiliations that exist in the different claims of authority that are recognized and represented. That is, there are types of authority—in this case, a certain sort of moral authority that is constituted precisely by the notion of the end or of this fullness or this abundance, understood as the end of history—that cannot simply be reduced, let us say, to aspects, hidden representations, of the authority of the state. What I'm saying as far as the question of affiliation is concerned, is that it is indeed more complicated and more fine grained than the notion that all authority derives in some sense from the state

Said: I agree. No, no, I didn't say that at all. Quite the contrary. My reason for soliciting Gramsci on this point was precisely to insist on the heterogeneity of the culture and the multiple, on some cases not only interlocking but contradictory, stands of authority which, nevertheless and in spite of this, are dominated by the structure of the state. Which is to say that the state is a kind of enormous, you might say, *spatial* configuration in which all kinds of authorities and activities, elaborations, etc., affiliate with each other, differently—at some moment one thing is more important than another and so on and so forth. It is by no means static and by no means rigidly hierarchical and dominated in the crude sort of deterministic way by the central administration. Of course, there are models for that. But that's not what I mean. Sorry.

Donato: Now, I basically don't disagree with that. The only footnote that I would add, though, to what you said, has to do with the encyclopaedic project of Hegel. Indeed, it is there and, indeed, he believes that it is successful. I think that one could do a close analysis to show that in some way the failure of that project is also already written in Hegel. But that is something that would have to be done.

Structuralism and Grammatology

Jonathan Culler

In organizing this conference the editors of *boundary 2* have asked us to consider the situation of contemporary American criticism, in which, as they say, various methods and rhetorics have been competing to replace the New Criticism. As one of the opening speakers, my job is to utter some debatable propositions so that they can be debated: I'm going to make tendentious remarks about the relationship between some of these competing modes of discourse. I chose my title because I had intended to concentrate on two competing discourses, which can be called roughly the structuralist and deconstructionist, and to look at a point of intersection, a moment of competition: Derrida's reading of Saussure in *De la grammatologie.* Though I shall do this briefly in order to discuss the relationship between structuralism and deconstruction, I respond to my place on the program by casting my net a bit wider and addressing the larger topic which the organizers call "The Question of Formalism: From Aesthetic Distance to Difference." In the competition among modes of discourse to replace the New Criticism, what has happened to formalism?

I think I can report that it is alive and well, doing very nicely.

Back in 1970 Geoffrey Hartman published a book entitled *Beyond Formalism*—hoping, perhaps, that everyone who was disenchanted with the New Criticism would buy it. But it turned out that what lay beyond formalism was more formalism. Indeed, as he argued in the title essay, the faults of those who have been called formalists "are due not to their formalism as such but rather to their not being formalistic enough." And he concluded that "to go beyond formalism is as yet too hard for us and may even be . . . against the nature of understanding."[1]

This is not a surprising conclusion. One might even say that to a sophisticated formalist, to one interested in the form of his own critical activity, it should be apparent in advance that beyond formalism lie only other formalisms (and perhaps one could also argue that before or in front of formalism there lies, already, formalism: "*toujours déjà.*") Now what is interesting about this situation is not the paradox itself—that beyond formalism there lies only more formalism (though for many of us this paradox may be a small erotic fillip)—but the fact that this paradoxical situation can be explained in two different ways. Let me briefly sketch these two accounts of why it might be impossible to go beyond formalism and then reflect on their implications.

The first account would say that formalism is the desire to explore the relations within a work or group of works, the desire to continue that exploration and to postpone for as long as possible the move which treats the work as means to some end. Since criticism inevitably makes that move and tells us what the work is an example of, what experience it produces or what truths it embodies—since criticism inevitably does this, this move does not lie beyond formalism, as an alternative to it, but is, on the contrary, a *telos* for formalist discourse. What lies beyond any given formalism are new ways of exploring an order of relations and of postponing the move which designates the closure of that order.

By this way of thinking, the New Criticism was not formalistic enough in that it restricted the relations it would consider to those between parts or features of a single work. Making the unity of the individual work its goal—what criticism had to demonstrate—it closed off the investigation of relations and interplay at a certain point to produce a thematic statement. While denouncing what he called the "Heresy of Paraphrase," Cleanth Brooks argued that the "characteristic unity of a poem lies in the unification of attitudes into a hierarchy subordinated to a total and governing attitude." The poet "comes to terms with experience;" the poem is a resolution of conflicts.[2] The formalism of the New Critics was designed to bring readers to the point at which a mimetic claim could be made for the poem: that it evoked a unification of experience: The poet's task, says Brooks, "is finally to unify experience. He must return to us the unity of experience itself as man knows it in his own experience."[3]

Now in the perspective of the first account of formalism one objects to the limitation imposed by the New Critics on the investigation of formal relations. Thus Hartman's attempt to go beyond Brooks's formalism involved, as he said, "a formalistic exercise in literary history."[4] The question of whether Wordsworth's Lucy poems return to us the unity of experience is postponed and they are read as critical revisions or transformations of 18th century lyrics. Nor is there any reason to stop here. One can have recourse to a wider intertextuality, attempting to relate the poem or poems to the institution of literature in general: its conventions, its most common structural models, its figurative modes. At this point, of course, one has a program which in one version has been called Russian Formalism and in another Structuralism, where a work can be submitted to extended formal analysis, studied in relation to the various properties of literary discourse which it exemplifies. The moment or point of totalization may be postponed for a very long time. Indeed, in works of poetics which explicitly seek to avoid interpretation, the strategy may be simply to label the work as an example of literary discourse. This is a very abstract totalization, but it still functions as a non-formal *telos* commanding the activity of formal analysis. That is to say, it imposes a closure by positing a content: the work can be seen as exploring, modifying, and thus commenting upon the systems of language and literature. There is always a content, even if it be only "I am a work of literature."[5] By this view which I have been sketching, the New Critics stopped too soon, ignoring vast orders of formal relationships, which structuralism, for example, set out to explore.

The second account of why one can not go beyond formalism would take a different tack, arguing that whenever criticism tries to identify a content conveyed by a form, it deludes itself and ends up reproducing a form. When one thinks one has isolated a content all one has in fact done is to translate one form or structure into another. One of the more familiar versions of this argument is deployed against Marxist critics and others committed to notions of representation: that what they appeal to as History, the solid content which a work represents, is as problematic a narrative construct as that from which they were appealing, and they have not moved out of the order of textuality at all. A more complex version of this argument would be that any attempt to escape formalism by asserting what a text really means is an allegorization which, in general, can be shown to have been deconstructed by the text itself, so that the move which asserts a determinate referentiality is not a move beyond formalism but a predictable move within the orbit of formalism.

I have left these two lines of argument very abstract because I am not at the moment trying to convince anyone of the truth or falsity of either. I am interested in the fact that there are two different ways of arguing that one can not go beyond formalism and in the different assumptions which mark these two lines of argument. The first made use of a notion of content (though a very relativistic one) as a kind of boundary which made formal analysis possible. The second, on the other hand, claimed that anything which was identified as content could be shown to be just more form. The first treated the distinction between form and content as a variable one but insisted on the importance of making it, whereas the second insisted that the variability of the distinction made it inappropriate and vitiated any conclusions based on it. As is doubtless apparent, one can identify these two modes of argument with structuralism and deconstruction respectively, and it is perhaps easier to show the appropriateness of these identifications if we change terms and instead of talking about form and content talk about *signifier* and *signified.*

Structuralism insists on the difference between signifier and signified: indeed, the radical difference and then arbitrary association of signifier and signified is the basis of its account of the sign. Deconstruction, on the other hand, demonstrates that any signified is itself a signifier and that the signifier is already a signified, so that signs cannot be authoritatively identified and isolated. However, by approaching the problem in terms of form and content rather than signifier and signified, one can see these movements as part of the larger "question of formalism" and one can explicate, in part, an apparently anomalous situation: structuralism and deconstruction seem in various ways opposed to one another; each of them is opposed to the New Criticism (whose faults are usually said to involve excessive formalism); nevertheless both can be identified with the impossibility of going beyond formalism.

Let me now consider more directly the relationship between these competing discourses by focusing on a situation of competition, Derrida's reading of Saussure in *De la grammatologie.*[6] The main lines of Derrida's argument are by now, I imagine, well-known: he reveals in Saussure a powerful logocentrism and phonocentrism on the one hand, and on the other the elements of a powerful critique of logocentrism and phonocentrism. On the one hand, Saussure is adamant in his condemnation of writing as derivative and corrupt—both inessential and dangerous. He privileges voice. Yet when he tries to explain the nature of language he is led to draw his illustrations from writing, and he asserts, unequivocally, that in the linguistic system there are only differences, without positive terms—a principle that sorts ill with the logocentric privileging of voice. It is, as I say, well known that Derrida's reading reveals these contradictory strains in the *Cours de linguistique générale,* which is the founding text for structural linguistics and structuralism. What is perhaps less well understood are the implications of Derrida's brilliant and scrupulous reading. Indeed, it is often taken as an attack on Saussure, just as John Searle has taken Derrida's reading of Austin as an attack on Austin.[7] We think of a deconstructive reading as an attack because we assume that self-contradiction (the self-deconstruction which a deconstructive reading reveals in a text) invalidates any intellectual enterprise. But one of the effects of deconstructive readings is to have shown us that the power and pertinence of a text is not inconsistent with the presence in it of a self-deconstructive movement. On the contrary, the power and pertinence of a text may depend to a considerable extent on the fact that it deconstructs the philosophy in which it is implicated.

In saying this, what am I saying about Saussure? First, I am saying, as Derrida shows, that the presence in Saussure of two motifs or lines of argument is not merely fortuitous: the result of accident or error. They are in a relationship of solidarity (albeit of solidarity that can lead to no synthesis), the solidarity of an aporia. It is important to understand why one line of thought implies the other.

In Saussure's argument, the further and the more rigorously he presses his investigation of the nature of linguistic units, the more he is led to deny that the linguistic signifier is in any way phonic, that sound itself, as material element, can belong to the linguistic system; he is led to the conclusion that in the linguistic system there are only differences with no positive terms.[8] It does not follow from this analysis, however, that Saussure's privileging of voice—his designation of writing as a representation of a representation which distorts that which it represents—is an unfortunate error which might have been avoided. The theory of the sign, which makes possible the Saussurian and post-Saussurian analysis of language, requires a privileging of voice. Why is this so? Because linguistic analysis (and by extension, semiological analysis, structural analysis) depends on the possibility of identifying signs—on the possibility of determining, for example, that *bet* is one sign and *pet* is another. The identification of signs cannot be carried out on the plane of the signifier alone, because the question is what portions of the signifying plane count as signifying units. To identify signs, then, one must be able to identify signifieds. A sequence is a signifier only if it is correlated with a concept of signified. We know *bet* and *pet* are different signifiers because each has associated with it a different signified. And if we ask how we know this, at what place or moment this association is given, the answer will ultimately refer to the moment of speech, the moment of utterance, when signifier and signified seem simultaneously present, unequivocally associated. When I speak, my words are not external, material objects which I first hear and then interpret. At the moment of utterance my words seem transparent signifiers which do not separate me from my thought; at the moment of speech consciousness seems present to itself; concepts present themselves directly, as signifieds which my words will express for others. Voice, as Derrida says, "is the unique experience of the signified producing itself spontaneously, from within the self, and nevertheless, as signified concept, in the element of ideality or universality."[9]

Since the possibility of grasping or identifying signifieds is necessary to the semiotic and structuralist project, it is no accident that structuralist theory should find itself implicated in phonocentrism and logocentrism. It is neither an accident nor, I want to insist, a mistake—an incorrect move. Let me quote another passage from the *Grammatology:*

> The privilege of the *phonè* does not depend on a choice that could have been avoided. It responds to a moment of economy (let us say of the 'life' of 'history' or of being-as-self-relationship'). The system of *'s'entendre-parler'* through the phonic substance—which presents itself as the non-exterior, non-mundane and therefore non-empirical or contingent signifier—has necessarily dominated the history of the world during an entire epoch, and has even produced the idea of the world, the idea of world-origin that arises from the difference between the worldly and the non-worldly, the outside and the inside, ideality and non-ideality, universal and non-universal, transcendental and empirical, etc.[10]

These are large claims. They may become more comprehensible if one notes that oppositions such as inside/outside, worldly/non-worldly, transcendental/empirical depend on a point of differentiation, a line of division where, for example, inside and outside meet: a point from which or with reference to which the difference between inside and outside can be conceived. The claim is that the moment of speech, where signifier and signified seem given together, where inner and outer are for a moment joined, serves as the point of reference in relation to which all these distinctions can be posited. The privileging of speech is thus the basis of our "logocentric" metaphysics.

Derrida does not argue that Saussure was mistaken in asserting the primacy of voice and founding linguistic analysis on the necessarily logocentric notion of the sign. On the contrary, Derrida's analyses of the ubiquity of logocentrism—even Georges Bataille can be shown ultimately to be a Kantian—show that analysis is necessarily logocentric, that even the most rigorous critiques of logocentrism cannot escape, since the concepts they must use are part of the system being deconstructed. There are, of course, various ways of resisting or playing with this system that one cannot escape, but it would be an error to suggest that Derrida and deconstruction had provided us with an alternative to structuralism and logocentrism. Grammatology, Derrida has said, is not a new discipline which could replace a logocentric semiology; "it is the name of a question."[11] Indeed, Derrida's discourse is a series of strategic manoeuvres and displacements in which he modifies his terms, producing a chain of related but non-identical operators—*differance, supplément, trace, hymen, espacement, greffe, parergon,* etc.—to prevent any of them from becoming concepts of a new science.

Derrida's reading of Saussure is an exploration of the self-deconstruction of linguistics and semiotics. Indeed, in the interview in *Positions* entitled "Sémiologie et grammatologie" he identifies his *double science* or double reading not with a mode of discourse which would lie outside or beyond semiology but with a special practice or attention with semiology: "One can say *a priori* that in every semiotic proposition or system of research metaphysical presuppositions will cohabit with critical motifs, by virtue of the fact that up to a certain point they inhabit the same language. Grammatology would doubtless be less another science, a new discipline charged with a new content or a new and delimited domain than the vigilant practice or exercise of this textual division ('la pratique vigilante de ce partage textuel')."[12]

In order to make apparent the implications for literary criticism of what I have been saying, I ought to explain the polemical thrust of my argument and identify the line of thought that I am rejecting. I think there are two positions which my account of the relationship between structuralism and deconstruction is implicitly criticizing. The first general position is one with which *boundary 2* often flirts. If I were to give it a name for ease of reference, I might call it "Ihab Hassan," or perhaps "The Post Position." This is a form of historical optimism which says—naively in my view—"we're post-structuralist, post-modernist, post-historical, post-logocentric; we're rid of all those old scientific and logocentric hang-ups, beyond it all." Proponents of "Ihab Hassan" believe, as Eugenio Donato recently put it, though he does not himself endorse this position, that for them "language sheds the burden of nostalgia and on the contrary accentuates its own playfulness, proclaiming unashamedly its incapacity to control its tropology."[13] Against "Ihab Hassan" one would cite Derrida himself, whose analyses are the best argument against the possibility of going beyond logocentrism. Attempts to escape may be extremely interesting or very boring; what is certain is that to believe one has escaped is naive.

The other position I am opposing is one I take more seriously. Since it's more diffuse and anonymous I will call it "George." "George" says that we need not take note of structuralism any more because it has been superseded by deconstruction, which has shown, among other things, that structuralists were wrong to think they could work out a science of literature. Deconstructionists use a lot of jargon, refer to too many philosophers, especially Germans, and go too far in their interpretations, but at least they see that their job is to interpret texts. "George" is, I suppose, a sort of native American know-nothing version of the position put forward by Hillis Miller in 1976 when he argued that critics influenced by continental criticism could be divided into the

> Socratic, theoretical, or canny critics, on the one hand, and Apollonian/Dionysian, tragic, or uncanny critics, on the other. Socratic critics are those who are lulled by the promise of a rational ordering of literary study on the basis of solid advances in scientific knowledge about language. . . . For the most part these critics share the

> Socratic penchant, what Nietzsche defined as "the unshakable faith that thought, using the thread of logic, can penetrate the deepest abysses of being, and that thought is capable not only of knowing but even of correcting it". . . . Opposed to these are the critics who might be called "uncanny". . . . These critics are not tragic or Dionysian in the sense that their work is wildly orgiastic or irrational. No critic could be more rigorously sane and rational, Apollonian, in his procedure, for example, than Paul de Man. . . . Nevertheless the thread of logic leads . . . into regions which are alogical, absurd. . . . Sooner or later there is the encounter with an "aporia" or impasse. . . . In fact, the moment when logic fails in their work is the moment of their deepest penetration into the actual nature of literary language, or of language as such.[14]

These are only the salient moments of an extended description of the two modes of criticism, but the point is clear: the canny and the uncanny critics both pursue a rigorously logical enquiry, but while the uncanny critics, who have no faith in logic, are rewarded with "deep penetration" into the nature of literary language, the canny, with their unshakable faith, are rebuffed. Miller's description makes the difference between structuralism and deconstruction primarily a matter of faith: of inwardness, of intention. Both follow logic but those who have no faith in logic are rewarded while those who have faith are punished for their confidence and, one presumes, pride—whose modern name, among literary scholars, is "science."

Leaving aside the question of faith, it is not hard to see that such an account re-enacts the favorite New Critical battle between poetry or humanism and science, and the history of this battle ought to make one suspicious of a critical move in which science once again plays the villain. One of the virtues of structuralism, after all, was to have called into question that opposition between scientific and humanistic discourse, both by analysing sciences as semiotic practices and by insisting that rigor and explicitness had their place in all forms of enquiry. Deconstruction has continued the questioning of the opposition between scientific discourse and other sorts of discourse and has shown that literary discourse can have the logical power and complexity that was previously thought the prerogative of philosophy and the sciences.

Miller sees structuralists as lulled by the promise of science into an unshakable faith that thought can penetrate the deepest abysses of being. It's hard to direct that accusation at Barthes and Genette, whom Miller mentions. The only description he offers of a critic deceived by thought is this: "a critic like Culler, with his brisk common sense and his reassuring notions of literary competence and the acquisition of conventions, his hope that all right-thinking people might agree on the meaning of a lyric or a novel, or at any rate share a 'universe of discourse' in which they could talk about it."[15] There is again the question of faith: the hope that right-thinking people will agree.

Since I'm accused of having an unshakable faith, let me prove Miller wrong by confessing that my faith has been shaken. Let me confess, more specifically, that my "faith in reason" has been shaken by Derrida's arguments. For those interested in faith this may settle the matter, but I would prefer to argue about critical practice rather than faith and intention, and here I can say with confidence that structuralism need not hope that right-thinking people will agree on the meaning of a novel, a lyric, or even on the meaning of a word. Structuralism can start from whatever effects it happens to observe: if it seems to be the case that readers disagree radically about the meaning of a lyric or a word, that is what requires explanation. Since no one has ever maintained that reading and interpretation were completely random processes, since on the contrary it is our experience that these are social activities which do involve a certain learning, then in principle there are facts to be explained: in particular, there are effects of communication to be accounted for. In describing codes, conventions, and logics, structuralism and semiotics attempt to identify the structures necessary to account for events.

This mode of explanation is a Saussurian legacy: confronted with speech events, the analyst describes a system to account for the events of *parole.* This is the primary mode of explanation in the human sciences and to it we owe much of our understanding. But as Saussure recognized, this mode of explanation leads ultimately to a paradox, for the system which is cited by way of explanation is not something given but is itself a result, a product of events. And when Saussure attempts to describe the relationship between historical events and the system, he specifies, on the one hand, that events do lead to modifications of the system but he must maintain, on the other hand, that "a diachronic fact is an event with its own rationale; the synchronic consequences which may follow from it are completely foreign to it."[16] We reach, in fact, an aporia in which Saussure must simultaneously assert and deny the causal connection between *langue* and *parole.* The logic of *langue* and *parole,* of synchronic and diachronic, of system and event, leads to the identification of a relationship which that logic cannot admit. We have here a version of the aporia of Derridian *différance: différance* is a difference always ready in place which makes meaning possible and an act or event of differing which produces the differences that it presupposes.[17]

It is another version of this aporia which Miller identifies as the insight of his first uncanny critic, Paul de Man: "The aporia between performative and constative language is merely a version of the aporia between trope and persuasion that both generates and paralyses rhetoric and thus gives it the appearance of a history."[18] Indeed, Miller recognizes that structuralism leads to the same aporias as deconstruction. Arguing that the crucial moment in the writings of the uncanny critics is the "encounter with an 'aporia,' " he writes, "In fact, the moment when logic fails in their work is the moment of their deepest penetration into the nature of literary language or of language as such. It is also the place where Socratic procedures will ultimately lead if they are carried far enough."[19]

If the point of arrival is the same in both cases, what is the difference between the canny and the uncanny critics? Miller puts it in terms of faith in reason, but it is also possible to argue, without raising such difficult questions as whether Roland Barthes has more faith in reason than Paul de Man, that structuralists do not seek the aporias as such or treat them as the primary insights. For structuralism, aporias are the result of methodological distinctions, as between *langue* and *parole,* synchronic and diachronic, performative and constative, literal and figurative, which are indispensable to an analytical program but which turn out to be undermined by the results of the program which they made possible. Structuralists are interested in what can be done with concepts that prove to be both necessary and problematic. Though Miller praises uncanny critics for insights into the nature of literary language (which is what *canny* critics are seeking), uncanny critics usually present their work as interpretations of individual texts, as a teasing out of its aporias. It is the canny critic—in this case Miller—who moves from interpretation to poetics by drawing the lessons about literary language and making the uncanny canny, transforming a "failure of logic" into an exemplary insight or a methodological concept. There is a relationship of interplay and solidarity here, between structuralist and deconstructionist discourse, which is more important for the present and the future of criticism than their alleged discontinuities.

Cornell University

NOTES

1 Geoffrey Hartman, *Beyond Formalism* (New Haven: Yale Univ. Press, 1970), p. 42.

2 Cleanth Brooks, *The Well-Wrought Urn* (New York: Harcourt, Brace, 1947), p. 207.

3 Brooks, *The Well-Wrought Urn,* p. 213.

4 Hartman, *Beyond Formalism,* p. 49.

5 The most obvious example of this move in structuralist writings is Lévi-Strauss's contention that myths ultimately signify the human mind which produces them.

6 *De la grammatologie* (Paris: Minuit, 1967), pp. 46-108. *Of Grammatology,* trans. Gayatri Spivak (Baltimore: Johns Hopkins, 1976), pp. 30-73.

7 See J. Derrida, "Signature, Event, Context" and John Searle "Reiterating the Differences: A Reply to Derrida," in *Glyph* I, (1977). Derrida's reply, "Limited Inc." is in *Glyph* II, (1977).

8 For detailed exposition of Saussure's argument, see my *Ferdinand de Saussure* (New York: Penguin, 1977), pp. 10-48.

9 Derrida, *Of Grammatology,* p. 20.

10 Derrida, *Of Grammatology,* pp. 7-8.

11 Derrida, *Positions* (Paris: Minuit, 1972), p. 22.

12 Derrida, *Positions,* pp. 49-50.

13 Eugenio Donato, "The Idioms of the *Text," Glyph* 2 (1977), p. 12.

14 J. Hillis Miller, "Stevens' Rock and Criticism as Cure, II," *The Georgia Review* 30 (Summer, 1976), 335-38.

15 Miller, "Stevens' Rock," p. 335.

16 Ferdinand de Saussure, *Cours de linguistique générale* (Paris: Payot, 1967), p. 121.

17 See Derrida, *"La Différance,"* in *Marges de la philosophie* (Paris: Minuit, 1972), pp. 3-29.

18 Miller, "Stevens' Rock," pp. 338-39.

19 Miller, "Stevens' Rock," p. 338.

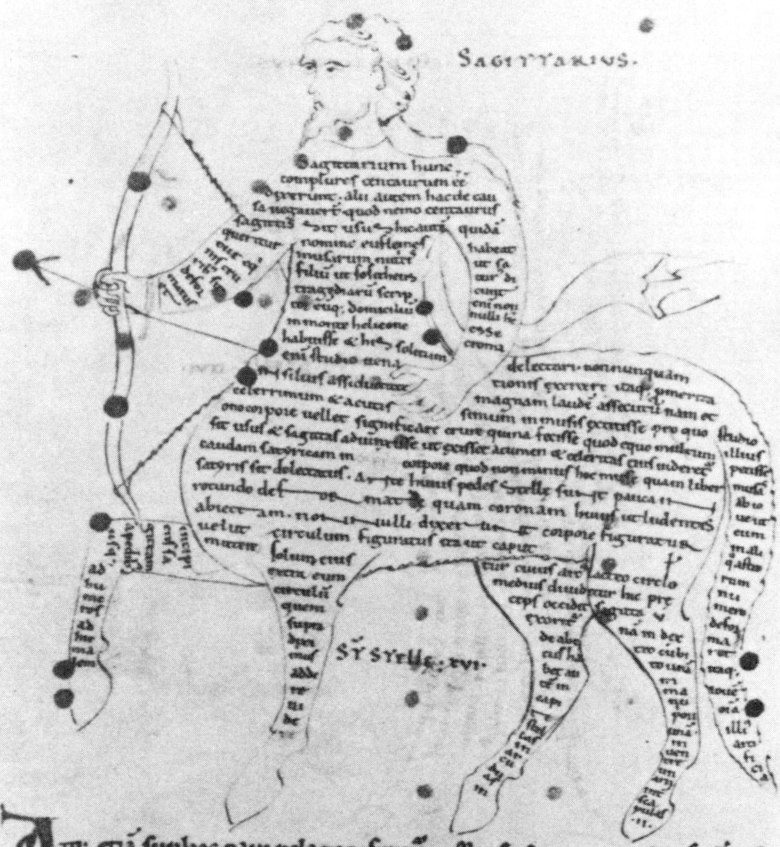

Atq; etiā sup hoc nauī pelagoq; ferat. Ostense sagittipotens soli cū susti
net orbē. Nā iā cū mini exiguo lux tēpore pstō ē. Hoc signū ueniens pote
rit pnoscere natiq. Iā ppe pcipitante licebit inserere nocti. Ut sese ostenderit
ostendat scorpi alte. Posteriore trahens flexū ui corporis arcū. Iā sup hē
cernes arcu caput ꝯminoris. Et magis erectū ad sūmū uersarier orbē.
Tum se se orion toto iā corpore condet. Extrema ppe nocte et cepheus con
detur alte. Lumborū tenus a pima depulsus ad umbras.

The Crossroads of Critical Consciousness: A Response to Jonathan Culler's "Structuralism and Grammatology"

Alwin Baum

Let me begin by acknowledging my general admiration for Professor Culler's exemplary contributions to a theory of structuralist poetics, a movement that, at the risk of privileging Gallic precedents, might best be considered *la nouvelle critique* in American literary criticism. I should preface my remarks with the further acknowledgment that I share in the pursuit of a structural poetics, or a semiotic theory generally. Thus, my response will appear more analytical than polemical, although I begin with a critique of certain paradoxical assumptions in Professor Culler's argument as a means to elaborate further the problematic arising from the premises and implications underlying the formalities of structuralism as well as the informalities of deconstruction.

In the midst of developing a persuasive rationale to illustrate that beyond formalism may lie only other formalisms, Professor Culler remarks, paradoxically, that even the most rigorously formal of critical analyses must yield inevitably to the teleology of asserting "what the work is an example of, what experience it produces or what truth it embodies."

At the same time, he suggests that formalist criticism has traditionally postponed as long as possible the "move to meaning," the discovery of the signified content articulated through the signifying text. These two remarks look forward to the problem of logocentrism raised in Derrida's reading of Saussure which Professor Culler invokes by way of illustrating that there is a certain aporia in any attempt to develop a coherent theory of signification; that, as Saussure discovered, finally one must "simultaneously assert and deny the causal connection between system and event." Another version of this paradox lies in Derrida's notion of *différance,* Professor Culler argues, wherein an act of differing (the imposition of meaning) must presuppose an extant system of differences (a signifying system) in which the act itself must necessarily be included.

It is another instance of a familiar phenomenological dilemma, and perhaps it is doomed equally to irresolution. Perhaps any notion of meaning in literary discourse must find itself mediated eventually in Derrida's infinite play of *différance.* However, this move toward indeterminacy could not itself escape the logocentric fallacy it is determined to deconstruct, at least if we accept Professor Culler's conclusion that in works of poetics designed to avoid interpretation (works which would include not only metafiction but Derridean deconstruction as well), "there is always a content, even if it is only 'I am a work of literature.' " Indeed, according to Professor Culler's line of argument, one would have to conclude that every discourse is ultimately metalinguistic, a reflection on its own system of differences.

While I am fully convinced of this ultimate aporia, I would argue, as Professor Culler does elsewhere, that it should be considered a theoretical paradox rather than a hermeneutic impasse—it should constitute a propaedeutic to semiotic analysis rather than a contradiction of its rationale. There is no reason why the structure (and the history) of literary discourse should not be considered in some way analogous to the structure of matter, an infinite series of embedded structures, where the search for an original content is as futile as the search for an irreducible particle. It is difficult not to imagine that buried somewhere inside the quark lies still another sub-atomic particle waiting to be discovered. And in the compulsive search for the elusive signified in the literary text, it is difficult to imagine that it would be anything other than a Carrollian "snark," standing at the threshold of semantic indeterminacy like a black hole in space. Yet the futility of the search for an ultimate content should not invalidate the discovery of patterns of significance in literary texts. Indeed, the primary contribution to literary theory of the formalist tradition, including structuralism and semiotics, has been to shift attention away from contextual analysis to signifying systems in the text, thus the enviable status of "bipolarity," "syntagm" and "paradigm," "deep-structure," and other concepts borrowed from linguistics to develop analytical models in literary theory. Yet these terms were developed initially to describe relatively finite phonemic, morphemic, and syntactic structures. It is obvious that the organizational complexity of language increases exponentially in accordance with the number of possible combinations beyond the morphological and the syntactic levels, the threshold of inversion where the signified usurps the space occupied by the signifer to become the center of a constellation of possible semantic codes. In fact, even Saussure felt compelled to abdicate the semiology of this constellation to the wider province of philosophy and social psychology.

In his argument to demonstrate the essential phonocentrism of Saussurean linguistics, Professor Culler remarks that "to identify signs . . . one must be able to identify signifieds. . . . We know *bet* and *pet* are different signifiers because each has associated with it a different signified." Yet there is an obviously significant difference between this phonological signified, which depends solely upon the bipolar acoustical opposition "voiced/unvoiced," and the complex signification that occurs at the level of textual organization where the recognition of similarity, of semantic association, comes into play. Yet, it is this level of semantic association which lends primary rationale to the semiotic project beyond linguistics. It is predicated upon the assumption that there is absolute organization not merely at the level of phonemic, morphemic, and syntactic laws (*langue*), but also at the level of *parole*—the act of speech constituting a text—the universe of the signified. But this project does not presuppose a "move to meaning," as Professor Culler suggests. Such a move would presume a teleological, or "transcendental" signified in contradiction to the fundamental axiom of Saussurean semiology, so influential in Derrida's deconstruction, that language is composed solely of differences without positive terms, that neither ideas nor sounds exist before the linguistic system.[1]

Professor Culler suggests a distinction between structuralism and deconstruction based upon the former's "move to meaning" and upon the latter's insistence that "anything which was identified as content could be shown to be just more form." Yet Derrida argues in the beginning of his *Grammatology* that traditionally, "the formal essence of the signified is presence" and that "it is not in itself a signifier, a trace."[2] The semiotic tradition, on the other hand, has been predicated upon the assumption that there is no content which is not structured in its turn as a signifier in another encodified relation. The familiar principle, fully acknowledged by Professor Culler in his *Structuralist Poetics* and elsewhere, is to show not what signs mean, but to illustrate the system of codes and rules governing their organization.

Much of this confusion about meaning seems to center on the difficulty of distinguishing, in any system of analysis, between an encodified relation of signifiers and a content, a signified. Indeed, the tradition of structural linguistics from Saussure to Greimas has served to accentuate the ancient, philosophical paradox of *identity* through its demonstration that any linguistic unit, like any material object, may be subdivided into constituent relations. The term *hawk* does not merely signify a species of bird. Obviously, it brings into play the paradigms of relative coloration, predatoriness, and migration, to name only a few taxonomic relations. Beyond these of course, no term exists independently of conventional associations and connotations—good/evil, aggressive/non-aggressive, free/confined, and so on in the case of the hawk. But the complexity accelerates when we take into account the essential fact that no term ever occurs in isolation; it is always textualized as part of the discursive system of the speaking subject, a speaker whose language is foreign to himself as subject, who speaks in a voice inherited from culture. Yet this textualization of the sign provides, paradoxically, much of the rationale for a semiotics as well, since it presupposes a finite system not only of rhetorical codes, but of conventional signified relations, however large and complex that system might be. Thus in a myth, the flight of a hawk may signify a period of the ritual calendar, a change of season, an abundance or a lack of game, and it is clear that all of these are interrelated. At the same time, it may signify a totemic classification (the migration of the "hawk" tribe, for example) or an economic exchange.

Now any of these encodifications may be considered a potential "meaning" of the sign, but that meaning is always virtual, and overdetermined, by virtue of its interdependence with all other signified relations within the text. And, by the same token, even if it were possible to isolate from this embedded structure of signified relations a "first level" order of signifiers, it would be clear that just as there is no absolute signified, *mutatis mutandis,* there can be no isolation of a signifier in a text. The minimal significant formula of a traditional narrative, for example, is not X, but X acting upon Y to effect change Z.

It is this diachronic axis of the text, at least the narrative text, which lends itself primarily to the supposition of a transcendental signified, a final meaning, since it carries within it the illusion of an origin and an end of action, conflict, and resolution. Yet even Vladimir Propp's formalist analysis of the folktale, which presumes to trace the laws governing an irreversible order of events at the level of the diachronic axis of narrative, must nevertheless draw upon a paradigmatic set of characters (hero, donor, magic agent, villain, etc.) and actions (departure, exile, fraud, struggle, marking, etc.) which presume at least some understanding of the cultural values and significance invested in the diachronic action of the text.[3] Conversely, Lévi-Strauss's analysis of the synchronic structure of myth, although drawn in disregard of narrative chronology, must inevitably assume at least a minimal diachronic movement—from lack to plenitude, for example—the movement characterized by Greimas as elemental to Propp's analysis.[4] Without that movement—given that it is polysemous, that the chain of signifiers is overdetermined—the notion of mediation would make no sense. There would be no grounds for assuming, as Lévi-Strauss does in an early essay, that the essential nature of myth is "to provide a logical model capable of overcoming a contradiction,"[5] an observation reminiscent of Cleanth Brooks's conclusion, cited by Professor Culler, that the poem invokes a unification of human experience through the resolution of conflicts.

The question is, what conflicts, and how are they encodified in a text? If we follow the rationale of the argument against the notion of a transcendental signifier as well as a transcendental signified, the question of the text arises even more enigmatically from the ashes of the alchemical fires of formalism and deconstructionism. Even the deconstructionists, Professor Culler remarks, see that "their job is to interpret texts." Yet the act of interpretation presupposes a symbolic displacement at the level of the signifying chain. It assumes that the *parole* of the text cannot be taken literally, that there is no literality, that the play of significations is subliminal. Nor are the structuralists any less insistent on this displacement of the signifier. Lévi-Strauss has remarked that the appearance of an evil grandmother in a myth need have nothing to do with grandmothers at all, much less with attitudes toward them on the part of the cultures which share the myth.[6] The relevance of the identity may lie only within the oppositional paradigms that it brings into play. And although it may be argued that we expect myths to be symbolic, the displacement of the signifier must be assumed to operate equally in a novel, or in any other textualized *parole.* With all due admiration for Freud's self-parody, a cigar may sometimes be a good smoke, but it may never be simply a cigar, either in dreams or in post-prandial reveries—it may be only a sign, a floating signifier waiting to discover its potential meaning in another chain of signification.

Yet this displacement, and the search for a latent content, or a "deep-structure," cannot presuppose an ultimate meaning any more than it can assume a literal one. If Lévi-Strauss discovers that the Oedipus myth finally brings into play the opposition of parthenogenesis versus bisexual reproduction, the conclusion does not imply that the myth may be reduced to this particular signification. The value of the analysis must lie primarily in the deconstruction of the text's semiotic relations at all levels, just as the interest of the opposition autochthony/bisexual reproduction lies in the role it plays in the entire system of cultural codes—communicational, legal, economic—where it becomes merely another signifier.

The deconstructionists may argue that this entropic character of the signifier presumes that any text may be considered best as an unlimited, "tropological" play of differences, but unlimited does not mean "unconstrained." Saussure has demonstrated clearly that there can be no *parole* which is not organized according to a rule-governed system of conventions, a *langue.* If he examines the signifier "out-of-play," as the center of a theoretically inexhaustible constellation of semantic paradigms, the interesting fact is that there are such paradigmatic terms and although the number of possible patterns is large, it is not "indeterminate."[7] In any case, Saussure's isolation of the signifier is heuristic; for the speaker of language, and for any reader or listener, the signifier is always "in-play," textualized in a motivated *parole.* It is clearly this motivation that validates the search for strategies of signification in any discourse—literary, schizophrenic, academic. And the text of speaking consciousness is always in-play as well, flowing in its uninterrupted stream like the phenomenal river of Heraclitus; thus, there can be no move to meaning on the part of the speaker whose text is never finished.

But there is a more compelling argument against the notion of teleological meaning, and against the accusation of logocentrism taken toward the structuralists, deriving from the difficulty of locating the synchronic banks of this same Heraclitean river. One may discover structured relations and patterns of signification in the text without presuming that it forms a closed system. Throughout the formalist tradition, the literary work is considered explicitly or implicity as the crossroads of cultural significations, an "intertextual construct" which can be read "only in relation to other texts" made possible by "the codes which animate the discursive space of a culture," as Professor Culler argues in another essay.[8] In the same place, he observes that the "death of the author" pronounced by Roland Barthes was immediately succeeded by the announcement of the birth of the reader considered as "the repository of the codes which account for the intelligibility of the text."

The codes animating the dialectic of the text, in the act of composition or reading, may only derive ultimately from the semiotic map of culture, a map which traces paths and intersections, but which is itself only the code of codes. It is ironic, but ultimately logical that the tradition of modern literary theory should presume to decipher that map even as it stands at the crossroads of this textual interplay of cultural consciousness. Lévi-Strauss prefaces his *Elementary Structures of Kinship* with E. B. Tylor's nearly century old observation that the tendency of modern inquiry is to assume that if law exists anywhere it exists everywhere.[9] It is the premise that has continued to dominate critical theory. One may argue that it constitutes a tautological aporia, since it presupposes a system of laws whose extent may never be realized, but it may be considered logocentric only if one were standing outside looking into a world that itself exists alone as a text. The flight of a hawk, the sound of Berkeley's tree falling in its invisible forest, a face—even when dead, as Merleau-Ponty suggests—all are condemned to express something, all become *signifiant* only when they are witnessed, when they are read as signs by a consciousness which engages each moment of its existence in the world as the trace of a floating signifier in its strategic interplay of *différance.*

SUNY – Buffalo

NOTES

1 Ferdinand de Saussure, *Course In General Linguistics,* trans. Wade Baskin (New York: The Philosophical Library, 1959) p. 120.

2 Jacques Derrida, *Of Grammatology,* trans. G. C. Spivak (Baltimore: The Johns Hopkins Univ. Press, 1976), p. 18.

3 Vladimir Propp, *Morphology of the Folktale,* 2nd ed. (Austin: Univ. of Texas Press, 1968).

4 A.-J. Greimas, *Sémantique Structurale* (Paris: Librairie Larousse, 1966), pp. 192-221.

5 Claude Lévi-Strauss, "The Structural Study of Myth," *Structural Anthropology* (New York: Basic Books, Inc., 1963).

6 Lévi-Strauss, "The Structural Study of Myth," p. 205.

7 Saussure, *Course,* p. 126.

8 Jonathan Culler, "In Pursuit of Signs," *Daedalus,* (Fall, 1977), 108.

9 Claude Lévi-Strauss, *The Elementary Structures of Kinship,* rev. ed., trans. J. H. Bell, J. R. von Sturmer, and R. Needham, ed. (Boston: Beacon Press, 1969).

Dixit dominus domino meo: sede a
dextris meis.
Donec ponam inimicos
tuos: scabellum pedum
tuorum.
Virgam virtutis tue e
mittet dns ex syon: do
minare in medio inimi
corum tuorum.
Tecum principium in die
virtutis tue: in splendo
ribus sanctorum ex utero ante
luciferum genui te.
Iuravit dns et non peni
tebit eum: tu es sacerdos
in eternum. secundum ordi
nem melchisedech.
Dominus a dextris tuis:
confregit in die ire sue reges.
Iudicabit in nationibus:
implebit ruinas: conquas
sabit capita in terra
multorum.
De torrente in via bibit:
propterea exaltabit caput.
Confitebor tibi dne
in toto corde meo:
in consilio iustorum
et congregatione.
Magna opera domini: ex
quisita in omnes volun
tates eius.
Confessio et magnificen
tia opus eius: et iusticia eius
manet in sclm sculi.
Memoriam fecit mirabi
lium suorum misericors et
miserator dns: escam
dedit timentibus se.
Memor erit in sclm testa
menti sui: virtutem op
erum suorum annuntia
bit populo suo.
Ut det illis hereditatem
gentium: opa manuum eius
veritas et iudicium.
Fidelia omnia mandata
eius confirmata in sclm
sclm: facta in veritate et equitate.
Redemptionem misit dns
populo suo: mandavit
in eternum testamentum suum.
Sanctum et terribile nomen eius:
initium sapiencie timor dni.

Poetic Presence and Illusion II: Formalist Theory and the Duplicity of Metaphor

Murray Krieger

I might well start by addressing the "crisis in formalism," except that it appears quaintly archaic today to speak of formalism as being in crisis, probably because formalism has now for some time been seen as a movement no longer vital, that is, as a movement for which no new usefulness could be found within a theoretical context which had outgrown it.[1] The death of formalism, assumed now for some time, has been followed by what most would feel to be the collapse of the many efforts to see it through any "crisis" invented in hopes of reviving it.

Yet let me be unfashionable enough to suggest that the assault on formalism (or at least on some versions of formalism) was launched on partly false grounds, so that the victory over it was announced over a misrepresented antagonist, an elusive enemy which had already slipped out of the grasp of the post-formalist terms that claimed to have vanquished it. We should thus examine the nature of the formalism which was under attack, the nature of the crisis caused by the attack, and the grounds of the attack, in order to discover the extent to which formalism may claim to have evaded its destruction, surviving in newer guises even as its demise was being taken for granted.

The impatience with formalism, which led to those counter-movements which supplanted it, rested upon a very narrow definition that, in effect, equated formalism with aestheticism as a doctrine which would cut the art object off from the world while treating only its craftsmanlike quality as an artifact. This narrow definition of formalism may have accounted for much of the doctrine of Russian formalism[2] as well as for the neo-Aristotelianism of the University of Chicago critics. The narrow definition would also account for some of the more mechanical practices of many of those parading under the banner of the New Criticism. But we would need a broader definition of formalism—one more concerned with the relations between the forms of art and the forms of personal or cultural vision—to account for some of the more daring philosophical possibilities that could be seen as extensions of the New Criticism. The formalism which most post-New Critical movements have destroyed is the narrow formalism, which isolated the work of art as a fixed ontological entity, an object, and went analytically to work upon it as upon Eliot's "patient etherised upon a table." Aside from the obvious unrealities involved in thus cutting off the art object from its creator, its audience, and its culture, this formalism—especially when translated into a literary criticism which deals with verbal sequences—seemed to require the assumption of an extremely naive epistemology, one which rests upon the mystification that posits the poem out there as a thing, and a self-sufficient thing at that, related to no others. Such a reification, made in the face of the sequential nature of language and experience, would have to neglect the treatment of poetry as a product of man and his discourse.

But a formalism more broadly defined escapes those restrictive charges which can be leveled against a theory which makes the poem into a static and isolated object. What I began by calling the crisis in formalism, then, I see as its need to redefine itself in this broad way, so that it can earn its right theoretically to open outward, as it frequently has opened at its best, and thus ride clear of the charges lodged against its more narrowly conceived shadow-theory. At its broadest, formalism must recognize (and has recognized) the several elements in the aesthetic transaction to which the word "form" may be applied. There is the imaginative form as it is seen, grasped, and (it is to be hoped) projected by the mind of the poet; there is the verbal form, at once diachronic and synchronic, that is seen, grasped, and projected in the course of the reader's experience; and there is the form that becomes one of the shapes which culture creates for its society to grasp its sense of itself. A shrewd formalism would try to account for and bring all these together. It would concern itself with that fixed spatial configuration of words on paper, but without ontologizing it into a static idol which would freeze into itself the humanly and empirically vibrant forms, whether phenomenological, psychological, or anthropological.

To the extent that formalisms have not worried about their epistemological mystifications and have indulged in uncritical objectification, they have not been shrewd. But as soon as we take into consideration that broader array of forms with which the formalist should concern himself, we come closer to that original sense of form bequeathed to us by its Kantian heritage, a sense of form which ties it at once to our vision of the world. This would make nonsense of those anti-formalist claims that denigrate the study of form by seeking to empty form out, excluding all worldly relations from it. If, on the contrary, we look at form as the primal agency of human functioning, we see in it the phenomenological categories for our coherent apprehension of the world's "given." It is what gives us the shapes of our world, the creation of the worldly stage and its objects within which we move, which we seek to manipulate though they often appear to manipulate us. Form in this sense is primal vision and, far from escaping reality for empty shows, it becomes the power that constitutes all the "reality" which we feel and know. A formalism deriving from such a fundamental notion of form—precisely the notion of form which philosophers have left with us for two centuries—must be phenomenological as well as anthropological from its very outset. If it is aboriginally aesthetic too, it is aesthetic in the sense of that word first given it by the philosophers who, deriving the term from *aesthesis,* meant by it no more than immediate sense perception. It is this immediacy of our perception of the objects which people our world, rather than the distanced observation of the techniques and patterned symmetries of art for their own sakes, upon which formalism, as a proper aesthetic, should concentrate. There would thus be in it neither vapidity nor unworldly dilettantism.

If we see the object within phenomenological terms, it is deontologized into an "intentional object" (though that should be enough for us); and this would permit the co-presence of all the kinds of forms I have been delineating—all under the aegis of illusions fostered by the particular intentionality which is functioning. In the spirit of Roman Ingarden, we can claim at once that the author as poet intended a form as his object, that the attending reader yet intends a form as his object, and that the moving verbal structure appears (though differently to each of them) to have intended its own form as an object and, as a formal object, appears to intend itself as an enclosed vision of the objects of a world, the world now having become its own world. The broad formalist hopes to find that these projected teleologies, though deriving from potentially conflicting perspectives, may be seen as converging. These several intentional objects draw their character from what our human and cultural (and aesthetic) habits of creating and perceiving forms expect them to become—nay, insist on their becoming—whether under the pressures of their being created or their being perceived. The poet does his work by using the habitual resources of language and the conventions of language considered as a medium for art both to encourage and to reinforce those perceptual habits. The reader tries to be responsive to the "objective form" as external stimulus with its own intentionalities, though his own habits, needs, and past commerce with the arts and their media (as well as his commerce with the world) lead to intentionalities of his own, whether or not he tries (vainly or not) to subject them to normative considerations.

Out of such intentional objects, discrete or overlapping, emerge the illusionary worlds of poet, reader, and the objects each intends to project or find. The illusion is what, as Gombrich has taught us, becomes our reality, what the world for now is seen as having become, either for the artist seeking to complete, in his medium, what seems to want to be completed that way, or for the reader seeking to confirm a pattern which he imposes in order to make the world he finds, or feels he should find in the object. And when the literary work works well, there is a congruence among these worlds, which encourages the satisfying mystification that it is *the* world of *the* object; and at an uncritical—an un-self-conscious—phenomenological level, it may even be so. Far from being static, spatially contained objects, however, these are worlds in motion, reflecting the diachronic character of verbal sequence and experiential flow.

These illusionary worlds, as our imaged realities, may also appear to be satisfying simulacra of "the world" outside, though that world has now been reduced not only to the bounds of our intentional perception but also to the capacities of language to enclose within itself what would seem to open it outward (except for those moments when it is viewed from within what we intend as an aesthetic act). Nor is the world any longer cognizable except by way of such illusionary reductions, or what Gombrich terms "substitutes,"[3] even if the substitutes are our only free-standing prototypes. The illusion is all; it is the seer's imaged reality, since there is no independently available reality against which the image can be seen as distorted or false, as a *de*lusion. Whatever hangover awareness we may skeptically retain of the fact that our aesthetic indulgence (in both the original and abridged sense of "aesthetic") is a "fiction," we yet permit the fictional to become the lens through which reality comes to us as reality. Thus we become provisionally persuaded of the presence of the poem as our present world, whatever the lingering suspicion we have about it as an intended presence only, as a mere substitute behind which is a real reality which would make it vanish as no more than a delusive appearance.

Within our qualified sense of its presence, then, the poem remains as a reduction of the world to the dimensions of humanly imposed form, a human metaphor that is supposed to "stand for" extra-human reality except that, by way of the illusion which is as much of reality as we intend, the metaphor is the formal expression of all that reality has become, has been compacted into. Since there is no universal archetype for it to reflect, it is a microcosm without a macrocosm behind it. That is, we cannot speak of a structured ontological totality out there (or macrocosm) since what lies behind our experiential "given" does not come to us bearing a form which would make it a cosmos until a human form is imposed upon it, at which time it becomes but another reduction, another metaphor, another microcosm. Using the old-fashioned meaning of "metonym" considered as a figure of speech, we could say that it functions metonymically—except that, as in the case of metaphor itself, we cannot firmly say or point to the larger term (or entity) behind the miniature image to which it has supposedly been reduced in order to serve our perceptual habits.

The poem, then, is a signifier which must carry its authenticity within itself since no external signified is accessible to us. But the nature of aesthetic intentionality, both for poet and for reader or audience within our culture, is such that close study of the signifier discloses its constantly enlarging capacity to be its own signified and to provide an ever-increasing sense of its semiological richness. Among the arts this is most spectacularly true of poetry, in which the nature of the medium is such that words can both exploit their meanings exhaustively and remake them utterly. But the presentational aspect of drama makes it perhaps the most spectacular of the genres of poetry in its power to make us aware of persons, happenings, and real consequences on the one hand, and of characters (or even mere actors), stage action, and curtained endings on the other. The poem's trick of being at once self-authenticating and self-abnegating enables it to proclaim an identity between itself as metaphor and its reality, a collapsing of the binary oppositions between signifier and signified, and yet enables it at the same time to undercut its pretensions by reasserting its distance from an excluded "real world." It is this acknowledged distance which seems to make the difference between signifier and signified impossible to bridge, since the signifier can find its formal nature only in the irreparable absence of the signified.

My last remarks depend upon an alliance between the terms "distance" and "difference" which is commonplace in the language of post-structuralist critical theory. I point this out to dwell for a moment on the fact that the title for our group in this Symposium, "From Aesthetic Distance to Difference," assumes some degree of opposition between the terms by suggesting that formalism has had to put up with history's demand that it move from one to the other. The notion of aesthetic distance or detachment has had a major place in that variety of formalist theory which developed in the wake of the formulations of Kant with their stress upon disinterestedness. The phrase itself can be traced back to the work of Edward Bullough and his influential pioneering essay on "psychical distance."[4] Clearly this doctrine refers exclusively to the relationship between the art object and its audience and, as a spatial metaphor, rests on the assumption of a fixed and insulated object whose separateness from its audience and their interests is the prerequisite for their aesthetic response to it. It is just a newer version of the classical view that insists, with epistemological naiveté, upon the objective status of that object out there which establishes itself by its distinctness from its viewers as subjects. The post-Kantian formalist asserts this view as the classical alternative to the nineteenth-century doctrine of empathy, a romantic view which calls for the overrunning of all bounds. It would obliterate all distance between subject and object and, instead, would require the subject to fuse with the object, to feel himself into it. Aesthetic distance seeks to reestablish the coolness needed for an aesthetic judgment of the object as a finite, made thing; it rejects as irresponsible enthusiasm the emotional subjectification of what it prefers to see as out there, apart from us.

With this disposition, aesthetic distance functions as an indispensable accompaniment to formalist critical theory, and it has contributed to the demise of formalism by its isolating of the object in space—even so temporal and fleeting an object as a poem. But if distance, as a spatializing metaphor, is a term we associate with formalism, it has also—though in a different sense—become associated with recent continental theorizing. For if formalist "distance" refers to space between audience and object, structuralist "distance" refers to space between signifier and signified, or between signifiers within a semiotic system. And this latter "distance" is essentially a synonym for the structuralist principle of "difference," representing the spatial gap, the hiatus, between differentiated elements. It has led post-structuralists to dwell upon the lack of presence in language, to the emptiness of the spaces marked by distance, now used as a spatial metaphor for the gap established by the structuralist principle of difference. This sense of the word would collapse the dichotomy between distance and difference which seems to exist within the formalist perspective (like that which provided the title for our group here).

Despite the implications of that title, however, one might argue that even the formalist devotion to aesthetic distance implies difference (instead of differing from difference) in that it indicates the extent of the difference between subject and object. But this should not suggest any closing of distance between formalist and structuralist perspectives, since the formalist object—however distanced and differentiated from all subjects—is at one with itself, achieving a present, undifferentiated identity (unlike the structuralist object). This internally unified fulfillment is observable to the formalist observer who, seeing the object as a distanced "other," responds to it disinterestedly as to a single, centered presence. He resists empathic involvement which would dissolve the distance and difference between his self and his object, for he would rather have a unity in the object which demands an exclusion of the self than, as in empathy, a unity of self-in-object (or object-in-self, for the two would be interchangeable). If this self-effacing formalist would freeze the object for analysis, the self-assertive alternative position loses it altogether in a romantic blur.

Of course, I must argue against the attempt to pit aesthetic distance against empathy in view of what I have said earlier about the capacity of a broader formalism to merge, within a phenomenological doctrine of intentionality, all the kinds of form which the narrow formalism would separate from one another with its naive epistemology. The narrow formalist performed this separation in order to eliminate what he saw as the form imposed by the author and the form imposed by the reader so that he might concentrate upon his metaphysical reification of the form of the "object itself" which was to be totally in control of the form "received" by the reader. Of course, this controlled stimulus provided the reader by the object is one that a critical epistemology beyond the narrow formalist's reveals has actually been projected by the reader's self. The circuitous route by which readers provide stimulating forms to which they then respond as if to a stimulating object—and the role that external stimulus, internally recast and cast outward again, properly plays—these become issues which only a phenomenology can resolve, though it must be resolution by overlap and merger rather than by exclusion. And the respective claims of detachment and self-involvement, of aesthetic distance and empathy, must be joined in ways the narrow formalist prevents himself from understanding. In the relation between the subject and object of experience one must account for identity as well as difference (that is, aesthetic distance), just as—earlier—I argued for identity as well as difference when, looking within the verbal artifact, I spoke of the relation between signifier and signified.

This is only to observe that the peculiar nature of the intentional object as aesthetic—whatever else it is—is surely duplicitous. This observation is confirmed wherever in it we look. Most obviously we find such duplicity in the peculiar status-in-being of fictional characters and actions, in the justifications we can make of them simultaneously as mimetic and as real. There is, perhaps, a more subtle doubleness within the single claim that they are illusionary, because when we take them seriously as illusion, we encompass both the mimetic and the real, the mimetic *as* real. As a dramatic performance unravels before us, this claim is both superficially and profoundly demonstrated in the paradoxical nature of the "stage reality" (to use an oxymoron which bears the paradox on its face). And the drama wants us to be alive to this doubleness, so that, with its use of its conventions, it is not loath to remind us of it, to have us look at it both ways—at the world of people and at the stage on which actors pose as the not-quite people we term characters: all the world's a stage and a stage is all the world. For whichever way we look, we look *as if* it was the world we were looking at. Thus illusion becomes self-conscious, thanks often to the devices of fictional self-reference. Even the most "realistic" of works use such conventions because, rather than trying to "take us in" (that is, to delude us), they prefer to show us how close they have come to doing so, how marvelously verisimilar their illusion is: one cannot appreciate the verisimilar without being aware that it is not the thing itself.[5] One might thus argue that no work is more illusionary than the most literally mimetic one.

Fictional characters and actions portrayed in narrative writing may not have quite so immediate a claim as drama does upon our illusionary capacities, but surely there is something equally duplicitous about their status-in-being. The illusionary reality of Tom Jones in Fielding's "history" of him is something Fielding is at great pains to leave us in no doubt about, and yet his make-believe status at every moment persuades us to yield to the as-if and follow his fortunes in a way appropriate to a true history, provided we retain an awareness of its mimetic basis. Thus poetry insists upon its ambiguous relation to reality-unreality in less literally mimetic modes of presentation than that of dramatic performance. A similar ambiguity is aroused by the confessional disclosures of the first-person persona in lyric poem or pseudo-autobiographical narrative, as we both indulge the responses to true autobiography or confession and, in mimetic awareness, withhold them for responses to the as-if-ness in the unfolding lines and pages.

Granted that the non-dramatic genres, existing only on paper or as voices which our eyes persuade us to hear, cannot afford us the blatant ambiguity of mimetic presence which the stage does; still our habits of reading and verbal imagination, and the intentionality fostered by them, create sufficient illusionary opportunities for duplicitous apprehension. Gombrich would quickly (too quickly, perhaps) grant that the visual arts, especially when representational, have an immediacy of illusionary possibilities which is denied to the non-dramatic verbal arts. (And even in the case of performed drama it is the other-than-verbal aspect, the spectacle of illusionary persons [or rather personae] acting, which is immediately illusionary, and not the words they speak [however these may imitate the act of speaking by real persons] .) There is the obvious fact that words are intelligible rather than sensible—arbitrary rather than natural signs, as aestheticians used to say—so that we must be aware that, in contrast to representational painting for example, there is no visible presence of any concept within them. Consequently, illusion in the purely verbal arts must come as a result of a strenuous, self-conscious effort, sturdily sustained by conventions which induce illusionary intentionalities among us if we attend to them.

Perhaps nothing in poetry is a more obvious illustration of this conventional effort than the age-old aural devices which focus attention upon the sensory character of words. Meter and rhyme, for example, call attention to the arbitrary element within the verbal medium which is capable of poetic manipulation without regard to meaning—a play among signifiers considered as absolutely empty of signifieds, in effect a play among the phonetic sequences themselves. Such exploitation of language as a sensory medium forces upon us an awareness of artifice, of conventionality, that allows us to return to the poem the illusionary character of which it seems to be deprived when we consider it strictly as intelligible discourse. For this concentration upon its sound (or rather its imagined sound, since we may be only reading silently) confers upon it the illusion of a physical presence, perhaps analogous to the sense of presence in the plastic arts or in dramatic performance. If this fixed sequence of words thus appears to take on body which makes it sensible as well as intelligible, then it may well be taken by us as a fully present entity, seen apart from the general system of language out of which it flows. Or so, at least, aesthetic intentionality, encouraged by the poet's manifestly self-conscious labors, permit us to say.

Further, this body of verbal presence can be seen as creating its own system of meanings with which it fills itself when we find arbitrary phonetic coincidences (like the pun, for example) being converted into substantive necessity. In the shrewdly extended pun, the accident of similar sound in differing words or meanings is forced to yield an identity of substance between them. We are to countenance their union because the two—though at variance with one another—have found a corporeal oneness growing out of the playful accident with which the pun was introduced. As I have demonstrated elsewhere, Shakespeare's sonnets are filled with brilliant examples of such verbal manipulation. What begins in the poem as an arbitrary system of sounds, arising out of an "aesthetic surface" which we normally expect to find in sensible media only but which convention has permitted us to find in verse, appears to develop into an utterly new system of meanings such as only this verbal system (with *its* compound of sound and meaning structures) can sustain as it creates it for our learned response. It is in this sense that I would argue for our viewing the poem as a *micro-langue,* a *parole* that has developed into its own language system by apparently setting up its own operational rules to govern how meanings are generated.[6] Though obviously the poem is but a *parole,* a speech act made in accordance with what the *langue,* as the general system of discourse, permits, it rises as a *parole* to become its own *langue* with its own set of licenses—within the intentionality of aesthetic experience and through the recognizable devices which encourage us to find a bodily presence in it.

Thus we have the illusion of its self-sufficient discontinuity with other discourse while our skeptical awareness of it as just another *parole,* continuous with the general system of discourse, remains to demystify that illusion. But we shall never read it in accordance with the intentionality we accord a poem unless we grant it this capacity to entrance us. This defense of a unique *parole* that creates its own *langue* is another form of my earlier plea for the reading that permitted signifiers to fill themselves with the signifieds they create. There is in poetry the need to overwhelm, under conditions of aesthetic intentionality, the binary oppositions (signifier-signified, *langue-parole*) constructed by modern semiologists to govern all language-functioning. But I ask that the exception for poetic discourse (along with the claim itself that there is anything like a poetic discourse) be entertained only *pour l'occasion* and under the prodding of what we habitually think we ought to find in poems, without our surrendering to its magic our stubborn common-sense view of language.

But even this provisional invocation of presence in poems, tied as it has been so far to their aural character, may seem to belie their character as writing and thus to ask for the sort of complaint lodged, for example, by Derrida against Saussure. The issue arises when we question whether we are considering the word as spoken (*parole*) or as written (*écriture*). The claim to verbal presence, a pious assumption in need of being demystified, is said to arise only because we think of the word as spoken and a spoken word implies a speaker, actively present and participating in a speech act. Thus a deconstructive critic can argue that the recognition of writing rather than speech as the major literary expression of our culture justifies his argument for verbal absence (by way of difference) over verbal presence (by way of identity). As *parole* requires the voice of a speaking presence, so *écriture* requires only the impersonal blank page filled with empty traces, arbitrary marks which lead away from themselves to testify to their unsubstantiality, to the field of utter absence in which they float. So the deconstructionist can use the transfer from *parole* to *écriture,* the removal of the word from the mouth to the page, as his argument to remove the myth of presence from discourse. My own use of the aural features of poetry, of the discovery and exploitation of the sensory features of the verbal medium, was meant to sponsor at least the illusion of presence, so that I must concern myself with what happens to my manipulation of the *langue-parole* opposition when it is systems and samples of *écriture* we have to deal with.

To begin with, there is at least as much of a basis for a claim to presence in writing as in speaking. The history of theory has produced at least as many mystifications in behalf of the one as of the other. We can easily reverse the argument summarized in my preceding paragraph to find writing as an inevitable stimulant for claims to presence, with speech as the antidote prescribed on behalf of absence. If we concentrate on the word itself rather than on its source, the products of the speaking voice seem anything but present: a sequence of fleeting sounds, gone in the air as they arrive, without even a momentary presence as they fly off on the wings of Zeno's paradox. Literature as voice and speech is a total surrender to the un-present domain of time. From this perspective it was the invention of the book, the cherished and highly ornamented thing of lines and pages and weight, which created a physical and spatial fix with which to catch the vanishing phonemes in order to make all of the literary work co-present, from beginning to end. It gave an enormous boost to a critic's formalist impulses and led him to ape critics of the spatial arts, the very arts used visually to enhance the written literary work and one's sense of its spatiality, its presence, with the attractive ornaments they provided. Hence the sacred Book and the interpretive industry provided by its sacralization.[7]

It is of course this industry applied to secular writings rendered equally sacred, which has come down even to the narrow formalists about whom I have worried in this essay. Indeed the tradition of mystification in this history of the Book and the theories of literary presence to which it gave rise has been a frequent subject for deconstructionist commentary. So, despite the fact that the speaker and his voice are absent in *écriture,* and despite the reduction of writing to marks on the page with their "differantial" motions, the written word provides a something-in-hand and a staying presence which gives "heft" to a temporal art. It encourages that reification of the literary object as object about which I earlier joined many others in complaining. Next to these claims to presence, one could argue, the implied presence of speaker and voice in *parole* is not very impressive, especially if our concern is with the word itself rather than its human source. For, whatever the sensuous presence of the spoken language, the dissipation of sound in air hardly encourages a secure feeling about it. Further, the speaker, however we may sense him when we hear his spoken word, is not *in* his word, cannot *become* his word, since only God *is* his created Word, converting that Word into substance, the onto-logical being of true presence. And His presence reveals itself to man only in writing, as the Word is transcribed into the sacred Book.

Let us agree, then, that the human need to reify our temporal encounters is reflected even more in our dealing with language in written form than it is in our dealing with language as spoken. Yet, beyond the mystifications created by this need, a sobering inspection of oral language sees (or rather hears) it fade away as it is spoken, and a sobering inspection of the written page sees the blankness of absent signifieds which the empty verbal signs finally cannot hide. Both the presence of the person in speech and the presence of the book in writing, however appealing in the human needs they satisfy, can be undone in a flash of anti-metaphysical skepti-cism which withholds belief in the God-in-the-voice or in the sacred, stay-ing authority of the Book. What I have said earlier about the poem as intentional *micro-langue,* however, bestows upon it the power, under the conditions of aesthetic illusion, to create a presence in the verbal sequence that does cut it off from the absences inherent in the nature of language generally. The signifier, which is seen as struggling against its nature to create the signified it contains, seems to have forced its god into itself and thus to have become fully substantiated. It is this fullness which creates the illusion of a self-sufficiency that justifies our treating the *parole* as its own *langue.*

I find this creative transformation to be impressed upon us as much by written as by aural effects, although my earlier argument for presence seemed to depend on phonetic coincidences arising out of the sensory properties of the verbal medium. Nor do we, in the act of reading, sort out what responses are owed to *parole* and what to *écriture.* The fact is that in reading poems (and I am discounting here the response to the oral performance of poems) our illusionary habits of response have taught us to *read* sounds. As much as it requires the illusion that its signified images are seen, the poem also requires the illusion that it is being heard as it carries forward—for those of us who know about it—its long-standing inherited aural character. Although puns, for example, often rest upon our aural recollection, they may also arise simply out of orthographic (and etymological) identities which never need go beyond the eye. Surely the reading of literature for the learned participant is a complex mélange of visual and quietly aural activities and sensory memories, making what is read a sample of *écriture* with significant intrusions from the realm of *parole.* And both the elements of writing which is read and the silent voice which is heard have their invisible and unheard universal structures behind them giving form to each, *langue* for the *parole* and *écriture* (as a general system) for the lines and pages before us. As I claimed earlier that in poems there were verbal manipulations which imposed an illusion of presence, thereby converting the *parole* into a *micro-langue,* so I would similarly see the piece of writing converted as we watched into a unique system of *écriture,* obedient to *ad hoc* rules created for the occasion. In both cases violence appears to be done to general systems with new rewards emerging out of such discursive subversion.

I am suggesting that one of the extraordinary impositions which poetry appears to work upon normal discursive systems is its creating the sense of being at once *parole* and *écriture,* borrowing from the character of each as it creates itself as a unique system. It is as if each of these aspects uses its opposition to the other to argue for its own presence, so that this double and paradoxical nature aids the creation of a complex micro-system out of what might seem to be the mutual blockage of a speaking system and a writing system which are each exclusive in their grounds for establishing presence and absence. The multiple devices in poems for turning verbal sequences in upon themselves vastly extend the powers of the medium to stir the feeling of presence when they can call upon the intertwined benefits of *parole* and *écriture* for mutual reinforcement. There comes to be the conviction of an always present speaker who is forcing language to become his-always-present-word, despite its tendency to be no more than fleeting sound; and the conviction arises in part because of the staying power provided by the play of written words, with their (apparently) fixed lines and stanzas permanently present before us on the page which takes its place in a book, a miniature analogue to the Book of Books, repository of the eternal creative Word. The mutual benefits of poem as speech and poem as writing help create the micro-system that evades the normal limitations of *paroles* and *écritures,* which fail equally to convince the wary reader of any presence in them.[8] Moved by these effects, one might thus define the poem as being (among other things) the interanimation of language both as speech and as writing, a single present micro-system out of the two impulses stimulated in the reader. The illusionary nature of his response is both double and ambiguous. As it has language turning upon itself in several ways, it exploits rather extraordinarily the special character of language as a medium at once visual and auditory, intelligible and sensible.

Our aesthetic intentionality that would see the poem as a mode of discourse in which the signifier has swallowed its signified and the *parole* its *langue*—as well as the poet's intentionality to create a verbal structure which can be so viewed—probably derives from human need as well as habit. The need to cultivate at least an illusionary sense of presence in language may well express our cultural nostalgia over the myths of presence which earlier ages could uncritically maintain but which growing skepticism has been draining away. Any attempted renewal of a claim to verbal presence would now have to be earned in the teeth of a wariness bred by the successes of two centuries of critical philosophy.

The history of our culture's sense of its language, with the gradual emptying of its signifiers, seems not unlike the layman's sense of the history of money as repositories of value and as a medium of exchange. Let us indulge the analogy for a moment. An obvious observation about the minting of coins in the modern developed nation is that there is an enormous difference between the value the coin signifies and the value of the metal it contains, indeed that the first, as an arbitrary signifier, is utterly irrelevant to the second. Let us assume, in this mythological history of money, that coin-making begins—long before the sanctions of the modern government—by creating objects of intrinsic value, say the solid gold piece. That is to say, coins contain materials of value: they *are* what they are worth. This would really be an extension of the bartering system, in which the intrinsically valuable coin serves as a general item of a certain quantifiable measure which can be exchanged for other more specific items one desires. But its value is *in* it: the value it signifies is limited to the value of the signified it contains.

Once governments begin to guarantee the exchange value of the coins they sponsor, then, to the extent that people have confidence in the government's capacity to make good that guarantee, a difference can develop—a larger and larger difference as governments and their stability grow—between what the coin intrinsically is and the value it signifies. From this point the phrase, "what it is worth," as directed toward the coin, becomes increasingly ambiguous. The coin is of course moving in the direction of becoming a purely semiological object which arbitrarily (though bindingly) signifies a value without having to contain it. The coin "has" value only in the most figurative sense, since there is no presence of value in it. The nation's monetary system, then, moves toward functioning like a language system. Still, however, the coin may nostalgically carry some small value in the metals within it. And in order to heighten the illusion of the now-absent intrinsic worth, it continues to be decorated, in some cases quite elaborately. The face of the sovereign may usually be reproduced on it as a symbol and a mnemonic warrant of its worth.

As inflationary pressures permit the coin to buy less and less, thus suffering a reduction in the value it signifies, the government must take care to reduce the value of the metal it still contains. The least valuable denomination of any currency, when it is a coin, always must avoid the embarrassment of containing more value than it signifies, as when a copper penny was discovered to have more than a penny's worth of copper in it. Here is too much signified for the signifier: the true presence of value is a danger to the entire semiological system and must be reduced at once. So the response to such inflationary pressure is to eliminate the lowest denominations, starting the monetary system further up the line, or to make even the lowest denominations an exclusively paper currency. Of course, paper currency would have been long since introduced for higher denominations as a silent acknowledgment that the monetary system had been reduced to a purely arbitrary status. (It is a constant irony that coins are usually reserved for the lowest denominations, while the higher denominations are paper currency, which can not have the slightest pretension toward intrinsic value. It is the frequency of exchange of lower denominations which argues for the use of metal—an argument which concedes utterly that the value of the tender itself is unrelated to the value it is to signify.) Nevertheless, it is the case that, even with the total elimination of intrinsic value, nostalgia coupled with national pride continues the practice of artful decoration and the use of the sovereign's face, even on the paper currency. And an advanced industrial nation can learn to make synthetic metals cheaply enough to retain coins in their lowest denominations in the interest of nostalgia and durability. But at this late stage there has been for some time little point in disguising the arbitrariness of the signifier and its utter dependence upon convention backed by the confidence of those who partake of it. However artful the decorations, there is no longer any illusion of value in the material product itself.

The history of book-making is enough like the history of coin-making for me to have used it as my example here—except that there was an obvious advantage in my being able to point to the agreed-upon degrees of value, whether in signifiers or signifieds, in monetary systems. But books also have an early career, which extends for a long time (and still is not altogether finished), during which their intrinsic value as a manufactured and ornamental product seems meant to serve as a material guarantee of the discourse within—a present, sensible accompaniment to the intelligible verbal code which was to have been the reason for the book's being there. More extremely, the book's existence as material art object may make its verbal contents irrelevant. But the original ornamented books—bibles and other religious works—wished to prove to frail humankind the divine presence within the book by marrying the sensible and the intelligible arts, an allegory of the marriage of flesh and spirit, which thereby guaranteed the appeal of the message by the richness of its embodiment. But, as with the actual gold we find as a material in some religious paintings, man's most precious goods—used symbolically—can physically create a present god even in the immaterialities of language. I hardly need remind anyone of the always growing deterioration of the material book, the increasingly naked display of the words themselves—for as little time as their pages and bindings will permit them to last. To the loss of the myth of presence *in* words has thus been added the loss of any pretence at an allegorical making of the material book itself as a presence.

Whether in coin-making or book-making, always there was the impulse to preserve the immediacy of sign systems as a potential form of magic by trying to get the god inside the signs. And invariably the movement in history has been to become more and more conscious of the absence of any god and the emptiness of discourse. Aesthetic intentionality, as I have been treating it, seems committed to creating an experience, and a stimulating object as its ground, which permits us again to feel the god within. That is, it wants to pack literary coins once again with gold, to feel in signifiers the signifieds that transform them from arbitrary to indispensable. If the rich materiality of the external book has for some time been denied to writing, the poet's task is to regain presence by turning the poem itself into an object—though an illusionary object.[9] Through an extraordinary manipulation of the words themselves, he seems to turn them into a newly filled system of signifiers which no longer drives us away from them in search of extra-verbal substance.

Still, the artificial nature of the poet's instrument and the fictional nature of his appeal clearly limit the magic of our experience to the realm of self-conscious illusion. But these become the terms which govern the way we want to see the poem and its world. The poem thus provides categories for our immediate aesthetic apprehension of our reality, if I may return to a theme with which I began. It helps constitute our aboriginal ways of perceiving and knowing, leading us to our primitive vision of a world of identities before our common sense reintroduces the logic of difference. The illusion is of fullness, and we take it seriously, though we are self-consciously aware of it as illusion and do not mystify ourselves by projecting it outward into an ontology. So we are in the untenable position of having at once to believe and to look skeptically at that belief; we have to subject ourselves to an illusion which we allow to become the phenomenological bounds of our consciousness, and yet we must summon the hardheaded critique which sees only an illusion, a figment.

I have been justifying a theory which talks out of both sides of its mouth in order to encompass identity and difference, as I earlier tried to find a broad intentionality which could speak about formal intentionalities that did not exclude one another. But my purpose is not simply to seek a friendly eclecticism that would embrace antagonistic positions or to make the more respectable claim to synthesis (and isn't synthesis what eclecticism often becomes when friendly hands take over the description from unfriendly ones?). Indeed, the relations between the opposed claims which I develop, as I seek to affirm both of them, are not meant to be mutually supportive; they are rather meant to be polar, though in a duplicitous way that permits polarity to become transformed to identity, but without being any less polar. By polarity I mean only the extreme form of difference, the logical consequences of the mutual exclusion between differential elements which turn them into binary oppositions. As mutually dependent as they are mutually exclusive, they undergo their will-o'-the-wisp transformations, leaving us unable to take our eye off either of them without losing the other.

As centrally poetic, metaphor furnishes the exemplary model for this complexity.[10] As we pursue each of the two poles of the poetic metaphor, we engage just the duplicity which I have been trying to describe. Our common-sense reading habits tell us to assume the distinctness between the two elements of the metaphor, one present and one absent, except that we also persuade ourselves to see only with metaphorical eyes and reduce all to presence.

What I suppose I am claiming is that our poetic habits (for both writing and reading poetry) encourage a paradoxical logic (or illogic) of metaphor. It requires us to entertain, in the operation of language and metaphor, or language *as* metaphor, the self-contradictions which allow us to view identity and polarity as I have suggested. In contrast to what discursive logic can recognize—the moment of opposition succeeded by the moment of compromise and reconciliation—in poetic metaphor the poles are to be seen as at once opposite, reversible, identical. These multiple views, mutually contradictory and yet simultaneously sustained, are permitted by the special character of fictional illusion, with its strangely duplicitous appearances and "realities." On the one hand, we perceive the tenor of the metaphor as collapsed wholly into the dimensions of the vehicle. That is, we see through the vehicle exclusively, reducing the world to it, finding it meaning-laden: we find it utterly identical with its meanings, or rather find its meanings in *it* as a fully embodied metaphor. All this we see though, on the other hand, we are also aware that the vehicle is *not* its meanings, is utterly separate from them, is *only* a metaphor for them, an empty verbal substitute. We remain conscious of the common-sense view of language, resigned to the unbridgable principle of difference on which it is based, and yet we permit the poem to seduce us into a magical view of language as creator and container, creator of what it contains, collapsing all (whatever its differential variety) into an identity within itself. Because we do not lose our consciousness that the language of the poem is still only language and thus differential (mere empty words with absent signifieds), we indulge the miraculous powers of the poem only as we remind ourselves that miracles cannot earn their name unless they cannot occur. Differences can be reduced to identity, via metaphor, only if concepts, as things (or their signifiers), lose their self-identity (which distinguishes them from all others) by becoming one another, over-running their bounds in defiance of the rules of property (and propriety). Metaphor becomes all-inclusive in the world it compacts within its identities and yet, in its consciousness of its artifice, it excludes itself, as mere illusion, from reality's flesh and blood. The illusionary basis of our commitment to the metaphorical fiction limits it to being an as-if commitment, complete in the magical verbal vision it provides, yet incomplete, even resistant, in that it allows us a skeptical retreat to the logic of difference.

I have elsewhere used a single quatrain from Pope's "The Rape of the Lock" as an extraordinarily spectacular example of this metaphorical duplicity — both by examining the language of the passage and, more broadly, by seeing in it a key to the master metaphor which is the constitutive principle of the poem.[11] I quote this passage and my commentary because I doubt that I can do as well in as little space to demonstrate this view of metaphor and of poem as metaphor.

> Pope forms his poem out of the tension between the sylph-protected, drawing-room evasions of time-ridden reality and the persistent biological promptings themselves. In several passages [he juxtaposes] the fragile China jar both to actual chastity and to his chaste and bloodless "toyshop" world. . . . But one of these passages takes this common metaphor of China and forces it at once to sustain the entire weight of both the delicate art world and the teeming continent itself.
>
> On shining Altars of *Japan* they raise
> The silver Lamp; the fiery Spirits blaze.
> From silver Spouts the grateful Liquors glide,
> While *China*'s Earth receives the smoking Tide.
> (3.107-10)
>
> Here is the utterly empty coffee ceremony rendered in a mock-heroic euphemism that seems unintentionally to bring in what this ceremonial world must exclude—the heaped, fleshly realities of birth and death. These are excluded as the decorative crockery from China excludes that peopled place itself: the refinement of the earthen rejects earth. We see "grateful Liquors," heated by "fiery Spirits," gliding from "silver Spouts"—a "smoking Tide" received by "China's Earth." Here is a ceramic charade of coitus, an artful imitation of history's brute

> facts that is also a metonymy that evades them. For it is an imitation that the poet's characters must take for all the reality there is, although the poet has shown us he knows better. . . .
>
> [I emphasize] the doubleness of the relationship between the aesthetic reduction and the resistant reality beyond: "China's Earth" . . . is the polished refinement of art—like that of the poem and of Belinda's toy-shop world. Though it is, in other words, the aesthetic reduction of China, the phrase itself carries in it the meaning of China's flesh, the endlessly peopled earth of that crowded land, but only to exclude it. As purified emblem, the earthenware is the metonym for the earth, a refined representative of it, and yet, of course, not at all like it: its artfulness excludes flesh, its precise manufacture excludes the numberless consequences of the chanciness of nature. Just so the other double meanings ("fiery Spirits," "smoking Tide") suppress what they suggest: the pouring of hot liquid from silver spouts in the coffee rites excludes—as its language, seeming to include, reminds us to associate it with—other "grateful Liquors" pouring from other spouts, filling China's earth as these fill another sort of China's earth. Much of this sort of doubleness—an exclusion whose language seems to spread its meanings to encompass what it, more narrowly, is seen as rejecting—occurs in other rites and games and mock battles throughout the poem, always reminding us what this purified world must neglect, as a prerequisite to its existence. The words seem bent on revealing the limitations of the world they describe, in their doubleness defining it by exclusion as well as inclusion. To return to the China example, we can say that, in reducing one kind of China's earth to another, the poem creates its emblematic metonymy (China for China, earth for earth) as its central metaphor (art for nature), while the fullness of its language denies the existential validity of the reduction. The metaphor, like the world of the poem, is brilliant, with a wrought surface ever admirable, but it is also reminding us constantly that, however satisfying its limited vision, it is not the world.

This example demonstrates that, within this uniquely sustained system, the very closing-in of the metaphor insists, through negative implication, on opening us (if not *it*) outward to embrace (while it rejects) the world.

What seems contradictory is made to hold together in this language.

The abstract relationship between the opposed elements in the poetic metaphor can be theoretically illustrated in a diagram I constructed some years ago to describe the opposed thematic extremities in post-Renaissance literature.[12] It demonstrated graphically this ambiguous give-and-take between the polarization and identification of these extremities. I now see that the applicability of the diagram is far broader than I realized, that it brought to definition certain more general tendencies which had been undercurrents in my theoretical work for many years. The diagram furnishes a model which moves beyond the thematic elements which inspired it, moves to the binary oppositions at the root of all aesthetic illusion. It accounts for their duplicitous character which forces their differential relations into identity without forgoing their polarity. As I have already suggested, these paradoxical workings of poetic metaphor—so contrary to the permissible logic of discourse—can be accounted for only by a system of relations between opposites which defies our normal sense of contradiction.

Let us imagine two diagrams: one, which I think poetic metaphor rejects, represents the conventional Hegelian conception of the tension between a pair of opposites followed by their reconciliation and synthesis, and then followed by the generation of further tension and further reconciliation. First there is a line of tension connecting the opposing pair, *A* and *Anti-A,* which are pulling apart from one another in polar repulsion, although they are also subject to pressure at either end to get them together. Under that pressure the line bows upward, becomes more and more bowed until it snaps, the two segments of the newly broken line now forming an inverted V. Repulsion has been converted to mutual reinforcement, with the high point of reconciliation the synthesis won at the apex. This is the *New A,* which once again generates its polar opposite, with which it becomes joined in a line of tension, and the synthetic process starts again, always moving from opposition to synthesis at higher and higher levels in a continually progressive sequence which like history is essentially linear.

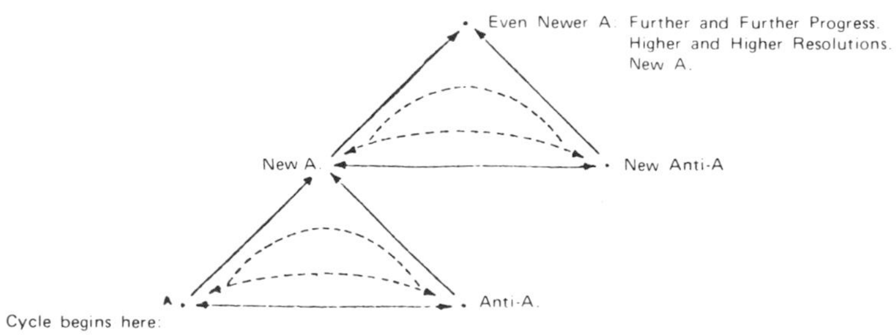

As description of language in poetry, this model seems to me delusive in its optimism and in the neatness of its movement from antithesis to union and back again. The firmness of its entities just does not seem responsive to the slippery behavior of the elements of poetic metaphor. Let me try an alternative diagram. The action of the opposing pair, *A* and *Anti-A,* starts the same way, with the tensional line of polar antagonism between them subjected to increasing pressure that bows it ever upward until it snaps, breaking into two segments which move upward toward union with each other. But this time I shall suggest that what appears to be their meeting point proves to be only a momentary illusion of their merging, a stage which they both move *through.* The directional arrows heading each segment go through the mid-point of meeting, continuing straight on their way to reasserting their polar relationships, though in reversed positions. Having started as polarities occupying opposed positions, they have come through an illusory moment of identification to occupy positions which are equally opposed, though now opposed also to their own earlier ones. Now the line of tensional opposition is regenerated between them and the cycle begins anew: at the end of the next stage, after moving through another momentary meeting point, they will each appear to be about where they started, only to begin the cycle once more and continue to move through the stages of opposition, identity, and reversal. Which pole, then, is which? How can we place any position for either of them in this movement which defies identity and difference alike and yet embraces both? Let me confess that, as I see them, the relations between the terms "identity" and "difference" themselves—at once opposed and touching and criss-crossing—are representative of the movements I am trying to describe.

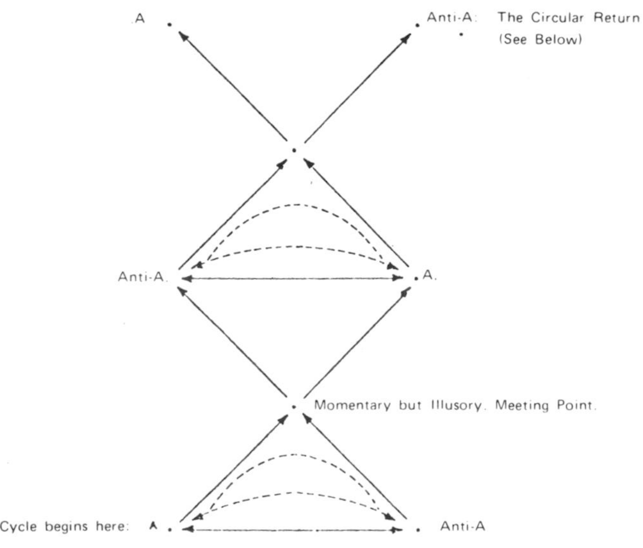

In contrast to the first diagram, this one is anything but progressive. The repeated pattern of reversal and return suggests instead a circularity. Perhaps we could simplify the demonstration and make it more accurate if we shifted the diagrammatic figure to a circle and put the opposed elements, *A* and *Anti-A,* at the poles, connecting them with the diameter that serves as the line of tension between them. Here too the fixity of position and opposition would be revealed as illusory only, once we became aware of the pointlessness of the circle: always turning, it has no isolable points around the indivisible circumference. Thus no single polarity can retain the pointedness needed to define itself and the diameter it creates. Each pair of poles constitutes only one of an infinite number of possible diameters, each with poles at its opposed ends. These polar extremities, as infinite, run into one another, thereby losing all possible definition, so that they all become ultimately identifiable. The certainty of eventual return for the poles is no greater than the certainty of their being inverted. Viewed from the perspective of metaphoric illogic, fixity and movement, along with identity and difference—and the very possibility of pointed definition and entityhood—all are illusions produced by the discursive necessities defined by the logic founded on the principle of

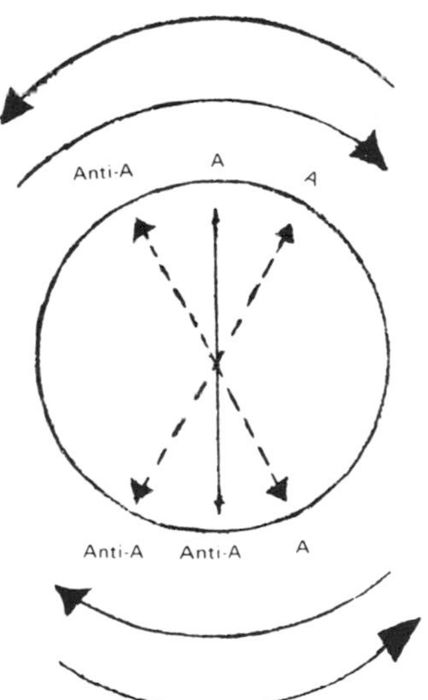

difference. But of course, from a logical perspective outside the grasp of the poetic moment, the paradoxical dissolutions prompted by metaphor are no more than ghostly visions, even if we find them expressive of the most immediate phenomenological responses of our consciousness.

As I now view the vain chartings of polar relationships in these diagrams, I see them as trying to account for all the binary oppositions which a language-oriented theory would have to treat, if—now—only as apparent oppositions: those between signifier and signified, vehicle and tenor, the metaphorical and the literal, poem and reality, word as substance and word as arbitrary marks on the page or a fleeting breath—and, behind all of these, identity and difference themselves. The illusionary doubleness, which I see within aesthetic intentionality as it characterizes the literary canon within our tradition, is built into our primitive sense of metaphor as we inherit it from earlier ages of literal belief in the magical power of words. Our belief is provisional and limited by the self-consciousness with which we address the nature of illusion.

We borrow our capacity to respond to such forms of metaphor—as the poet borrows those forms themselves—from the precedent of theological metaphors of presence. It is already the case in the Renaissance that poets take over and secularize Christian Neoplatonic paradoxes of divinity in humanity, spirit in materiality, unity in division (which is to say, identity in difference). It is the *form* of metaphor alone—with all its paradoxes—which is appropriated and our habit of metaphorical apprehension which is appealed to. The principle of transformation, of violations of verbal property, continues to be urged without any attendant substantive ontology or mystification. The demystification leaves standing the illusion created by the verbal structure, testifying to the need of our consciousness to *see* metaphorically and not just differentially. Even in a deconstructed form, then, the Neoplatonic habits of semiology persist, retaining a duplicity which limits itself to the realm of aesthetic illusion (in the original sense of that adjective). This claim turns out to be a defense of Matthew Arnold's old insistence that poetry does replace metaphysics once the latter has been demystified. In poetry as metaphor, the equations do provisionally hold, but only while they are seen as self-realized absurdities incapable of being held. Perhaps the most fascinating literary works in our tradition are those which recapitulate these teasing powers of metaphor and thereby become allegories of the metaphorical process itself.

Very late in *Tristram Shandy,* in the mock-romantic section (Volume IX) devoted to "The *Amours* of my Uncle Toby," the widow Wadman asks Uncle Toby a curious—but to her an almost desperate—question: "And whereabouts, dear Sir . . . did you receive this sad blow?" Given her secretly sensual concerns, she anxiously pursues the specific location of the wound received by Uncle Toby in battle in Flanders since she knows it to be in the area of the groin and worries about its possible effect on the marriage she hopes for. So, after all the delays invented through many pages and chapters and books by Sterne's ingenuity, she is ready at last for the answer. "And whereabouts, dear Sir . . . did you receive this sad blow?" Uncle Toby, remember, has promised, "You shall see the very place, Madam"—nay, more provocatively, "You shall lay your finger upon the place." And Uncle Toby is as good as his word, though at this final moment of disclosure he does not notice her "glance towards the waistband of my Uncle Toby's red plush breeches," since she expects him, as a start, to "lay his forefinger upon the place." After concluding his scale measurements, he takes her hand and lays her finger on the very place—the very place, that is, on his much treasured large map of the fortifications of the town and citadel of Namur, "the *identical* spot of ground where he was standing when the stone struck him." Sterne warned us much earlier, and repeats now, the claim that, after his lengthy study of the map, Uncle Toby "could at any time stick a pin" upon that "spot of ground." The widow's disappointment is more than matched by Uncle Toby's when he later learns the real object of her question and, shocked, breaks off his *Amours.*

Clearly, the issue between the not-quite-lovers is semiological and hermeneutic, revolving about words like "whereabouts" and "place." Whereabouts is the place where Uncle Toby received his wound? There are four "wheres" and "places" to which Uncle Toby may have been referring. Two of them would appear to be properly substantial signifieds, already ambiguous—one on the body of the man (in his groin) and one in the body of the battle (in the actual siege of the actual town of Namur in Flanders). But in Toby's mind a third "where" and "place," the point on the map, is a totally substantial signified, though of course as a map it will seem only an empty signifier to us. The final reality of the map is sufficient for Toby to take full comfort in it during those long weeks when he was first recovering from his wound. Yet of course Sterne is reminding us of the absurd confusion of signifier and signified when in two places[13] he has Toby refer to the point on the map as "the *identical* spot of ground" on which he received his wound. Further, Sterne reminds us of the absurd confusion of signifieds themselves, forcing us to remember the place on the body by insisting, in the same two passages, that Toby could stick a pin into it. But this is hardly the only time Sterne has offered us the geography of the body for the geography of physical space. For example, brother Bobby is earlier sent on a trip to the continent, we are told, because "the eldest son . . . should have free ingress, egress, and regress into foreign parts before marriage . . . for the sake of bettering his own private parts . . ."

To compound semiological confusions, there is yet a fourth kind of place to which much time is devoted in the novel, a place that falls somewhere between signifier and signified (between the large detailed map and the town itself) in that it has elements of each: the area on the bowling-green, "a rood and a half of ground," on which Toby and Corporal Trim constructed a miniature replica of a town in Flanders in order to follow the course of the war. Here indeed is a body of reality capable of giving Toby satisfaction even beyond that of his cherished map, though it does not—as we see in that final scene with Mrs. Wadman—detract from his sense of the substantive reality of the map too. But Sterne is capable of telling us that Toby took a ride on his horse out to Dunkirk without a suggestion that there is any other Dunkirk but the one reproduced on the bowling-green. The bowling-green reality, both signifier *and* signified, is dwelled upon at such length in the novel in order to reduce all semiology to absurdity. As a body of reality, it is even connected to the human body—that part of the body functioning in procreation—when Trim removes the weights which hold up the window to use them as "field pieces" on the bowling-green and the window falls, almost emasculating the young Tristram. ("You have cut off spout enow," Yorick says only half-metaphorically to Trim.) Here too the body of love may have to yield to the body of battle.

This reminder that the places of battle in the novel are inevitably yoked to the places in the genital area—the first working to the detriment of the second—returns us to the widow's question and Toby's response. We are surely to recall that earlier point in the novel when we were told, with Sterne's usual ambiguity, that "the wound in my Uncle Toby's groin, which he received at the siege of Namur, render[ed] him unfit for the service." Nor should we overlook the site of the battle which inflicted the wound, Namur, or ought we to spell it "N'amour," or even "no more"?[14] The very name "Namur," "place" of the love-denying wound, thus reinforces the prudishness Toby shares with his brother. But not with Corporal Trim, who, on the very page after Uncle Toby's version of "where" the "place" is, shows Mrs. Bridget (Mrs. Wadman's maid) that it was "here," having moved from the map to his body, putting her hand on the very place. But Corporal Trim much earlier rejected all language but the body's; and the story of his own wound and the therapeutic use of her hand upon it by the Beguine, which he recounted only shortly before as a preview of the final *amours* in the novel, indicates clearly enough the alternative reality to Toby's.

Where is the metaphor and where is reality in this discourse? Looking for reality, where can we find its "place" in this novel in which, as in the circle in my final diagram, nothing holds its "place"? Of the four kinds of wheres and places which Sterne provides in dealing with Toby's wound, we should remember that the one apparently literal signified—that town in Flanders, Namur itself (whose very nature is negative, if we are to believe the pun on its name)—is the only one which never appears in the novel. And of course, as far as Toby is concerned, neither does his own body exist, the "place" sought by Mrs. Wadman for which the point on the map represents "the identical spot of ground." The novel constantly turns away from such substantial signifieds as presumably real towns and real genitalia (only "presumably real" since the novel does no more than note their absence) to let us dwell among those newly substantiated signifiers—the maps and make-believe replicas which turn into linguistic realities for the hobby-horses which all the characters mount to ride off to their respective Dunkirks. Where conflicts between metaphor and reality are converted into conflicts among reified metaphors, language becomes the only enabling act: we recall Walter Shandy's auxiliaries (auxiliary verbs) marching off in order and presenting themselves to Toby, who converts him into *his* auxiliaries (soldiers) without really changing them at all. Again it is the language which is the reality, creating instantaneities of metaphor which collapse all the varied versions of reality into its own single identity of the word.

Tristram Shandy may thus be constructed around the fallacy of verbal reification—the conferring of a single substantial thinghood on empty polysemous words—as it is practiced by its several hobby-horse riders; but the novel is no mere game played among verbal ambiguities. It is rather a profound semiological instrument, tying visions of reality to a language which is potentially neutral, but is never neutral: it is only present, insisting on reducing all human realities to itself while acknowledging its own empty indifference to reality. Though what we are shown are the naive epistemological errors of Sterne's characters, these are compounded into the truth of the work's totality, which plays with us and asks us to have the patience to learn to play with it. We must take these reifications seriously as illusions which constitute an entire world for each of the characters. Thus Toby lives, on hobby-horseback, in mimesis of the one act in his life which has meaning, confounding ambiguous signifiers and signifieds in all-out sacrifice to the symbolic reality of his wound, the sole isolated fact.

But our sympathy for the seriousness of the illusions of the characters is cut short: we laugh at their illusory nature, assuming that we would know better. Sterne encourages our hold-out, anti-verbal skepticism by stimulating our sense of absurdity. We watch all the hobby horses, like Gombrich's "substitutes" for reality (foremost among which is, we remember, a hobby horse), while we are probably mounted up on our own. Tristram acknowledges as much when he shows us himself mounted up on his and riding, that is, writing this book. Or is he, as he suggests in Volume VII, *literally* riding as he flees through the continent, trying to escape that "arch-jockey of jockeys" who he feels is mounted up behind him and is in pursuit? But of course in this form death itself becomes just another metaphor, another hobby horse and hobby-horse rider. There are, then, no horses but hobby horses, though man is never anything but a jockey.

Sterne's many-leveled language, which would appear to be our only reality, is the one sure presence in a world where everything resists our touch and points us to a verbal map. Where signifieds and signifiers reverse and re-reverse their roles, what, besides the poet's language, is "here"? Where is the body of this reality before us and how does it relate to the body of words, if Sterne has persuaded us to grant his words body? How identical do the differences in the novel become for us who see the language create our awareness of them even as it collapses them into itself? What, then, is the book *about?* Where is its object of imitation? How can we touch the wound with which it has left us? We discover how difficult it is to answer precisely when, like Uncle Toby and the widow Wadman, we try to put our finger on the very place.

University of California, Irvine

NOTES

1 This is the second half of a two-part study. The first treats the subject from the perspective of Renaissance theory.

2 It is ironic that certain basic tenets of Russian formalism, which I treat here as too narrow a formalism to withstand the usual attacks against it, returned to become a bulwark of structuralism, which is one of the major anti-New Critical movements designed to supplant its formalistic insufficiencies.

3 I think especially of Ernst Gombrich, "Meditations on a Hobby Horse or the Roots of Artistic Form," *Meditations on a Hobby Horse and other Essays on the Theory of Art* (London: Phaidon, 1963), pp. 1-11. The most immediate argument for the claim that the "substitute" becomes the free-standing, indispensable "reality" (since the world is uncognizable outside it) may be at once grasped in the well-known Alain cartoon in *The New Yorker* with which Gombrich opens his *Art and Illusion* (London: Phaidon, 1960). In it, you will recall, the ancient Egyptian drawing class, rendered as conventionally drawn male figures seen only in Egyptian paintings, is trying to reproduce with mimetic precision the female model, a profiled figure which is the "woman" as represented in Egyptian paintings. There is, in other words, no pre-artistic or extra-artistic real world of either artists or models for us (or them) to perceive.

4 "Psychical Distance as a Factor in Art and an Aesthetic Principle," *British Journal of Psychology,* 5 (1912), 87-98.

5 I take these arguments up at greater length in *Theory of Criticism: A Tradition and its System* (Baltimore: Johns Hopkins, 1976), chapter 6 and the opening pages of chapter 7 (esp. pp. 182-83).

6 See my *Theory of Criticism,* pp. 188, 227-28 for a developed version of this argument.

7 For my own discussion of this history, see *Theory of Criticism,* pp. 146-48.

8 These are the failures which Derrida reminds us of. On the matter of speech vs. writing as it concerns the need to demystify any notion of presence, I find it unnecessary to choose between Saussure and Derrida. For in neither of them is there a theoretical concession to the illusion of language as a medium of art which can authenticate our response as a response to verbal presence. (I must at once acknowledge, however, the brilliance with which Derrida indulges this very capacity of language in his own writing.)

9 The climax of this movement occurs in the modernist's "ekphrastic" impulse (seen most clearly in poems from the Symbolists to Wallace Stevens) to get the object inside the poem via the concrete image which forces the poem to shape itself into its object of imitation.

10 I could speak of metaphor in the broad sense, in the way I spoke of it earlier as the reductive form, *multum in parvo,* through which we envision the intentional world of this poem. This is what I have in a number of other places referred to as a work's "master metaphor" (see especially *Theory of Criticism,* pp. 194-204). But this discussion may be the more easily followed if we think of metaphor also as the narrow rhetorical device, composed of tenor and vehicle and trying to lose the first in the second.

11 Krieger, *Theory of Criticism,* pp. 165-66, 196-97.

12 In *The Classic Vision: The Retreat from Extremity in Modern Literature* (Baltimore, Johns Hopkins, 1971), pp. 24-28.

13 I hasten to add, two "places" *in the text,* lest I be guilty of adding yet another level of ambiguity. The passages appear, almost verbatim, in Vol. 2, chap. 1 and Vol. 9, chap. 26.

14 To reinforce the pun with "N'amour" we should remember that it was Sterne himself who gives us the word, entitling Vol. 9 "The *Amours* of my Uncle Toby." I should like to thank my class in The School of Criticism and Theory during the summer of 1977, and Professor Stuart Peterfreund in particular, for the suggestions which enrich my discussion here.

T
FA
CTV̄
EST
IN TRICE
SIMO
anno· inquarto mense· inquinta m̄sis.
cum eēm inmedio captiuorum iuxta
fluuium chobar: apti sunt celi. &
uidi uisiones dei. Inquinta mensis

Parole Into *Ecriture:* A Response To Murray Krieger

George Stade

I am sorry to say that all I have for you this afternoon is a piece of *parole* rather than *écriture.* The reason is that I did not have time to write my response-to-be down. Well, that's not entirely true, for I intend to be entirely truthful. In fact, I have before me here some scribbled detritus of *écriture* to remind me of what I am going to say. No, that can't be true either. For how can you remind yourself of something that has not yet happened? My response is a long way from having responded. For it is an irrefragable law that it is not people who think, speak, write, or respond, but thought that thinks, speech that speaks, writing that writes, and responiality that responds. And who am I to refrag it?

These scribbled reminders, then, are in a double sense signifiers without signifieds. It is of the essence of reminders that they be present signifiers of past and absent signifieds, except that the past doesn't exist, except that the past of my response exists even less, except that the signified in this case lies in the future, which also doesn't exist. It's beginning to look as though what I have before me here is some kind of poem.

The truth is, reminders or not, I don't yet know what I am going to say, if we can pretend for a moment that it is I rather than speech who has not yet spoken, or has only spoken a little. These wretched pieces of *écriture,* it follows, signify nothing at all, nothing at all. That doesn't mean I intend to throw them away. I am not going to throw them away in spite of the fact that I can't see them without my glasses anyhow. I intend to go on looking down at them from time to time for dramatic effect. That effect would be lost if I were to pause from time to time only to look down at my empty hands, or rather the effect would be different. I gather, therefore, that there are degrees of nothingness.

Well, we seem to have gotten over that hurdle. For the time being anyhow. No, that can't be true, for it is the essence of hurdles that once you are over them, you are over them for good. You cannot uncross a hurdle. Once you have crossed a hurdle you can never again, never, never again be in the pristine condition of not having crossed it. All you can do is cross back over it again, going whence you came. Back onward we go.

In a moment I am going to read you a piece of *écriture.* I shall read you a piece of *écriture* from a book with Mr. Krieger's name on the cover. If you think I deduce from this fact that Mr. Krieger wrote the book, you have not understood me, you will never understand me, never, never understand me. This piece of *écriture* includes lines attributed to Pope, whatever that means. I mean *the* Pope, not the Pope, Alexander Pope rather than Paul Pope, although I can't see what difference (with an *e*) it makes, since whoever wrote the poem is just one more of the things absent from it.

Mr. Krieger said just now, though it seems ages ago, that we should read poetry under "the illusion of its self-sufficient discontinuity with other discourse." He says a poem is "a microcosm without a macrocosm behind it," "a unique *parole* that creates its own *langue.*" What I wonder is did Pope's *parole* become *écriture* once it was printed in Krieger's book? Should we no longer attribute it to Pope? Will that *parole* become *écriture* become *parole* again when I speak it? Should we then no longer attribute it to Krieger, but to me? Will that *parole* become *écriture* become *parole* become *écriture* again when it is printed in *boundary 2?* Should we then no longer attribute it to me, but to *boundary 2?* Is there a God after all? Let us hope not. Will it be a piece of *parole* or of *écriture* on the tape I hope someone is making of my response, for if no one is making a tape, my response will never again be a *parole,* never, never be a *parole* again. For a *parole* that has become *écriture* is like a hurdle that has been crossed. It has lost its innocence.

Here is the passage from Mr. Krieger's book, for although I bought the book, and paid for it through the nose, whatever that means, for some reason we go on saying it is Mr. Krieger's. Here it is. I should tell you that on the advice of Mr. Harold Bloom I mean to mis-read the poetry attributed to Mr. Pope. I intend, that is, to give it a strong reading.

All Nature is but Art, unknown to thee;
All Chance, Direction, which thou canst not see;
All Discord, Harmony not understood;
All partial Evil, universal Good:
And, spite of Pride, in erring Reason's spite,
One truth is clear, whatever is, is RIGHT.

Once nature has become art, every *is* is a *has*-to-be, every casual possibility a causal necessity.

With this conclusion to Epistle 1, Pope has brought us full circle with respect to where *An Essay on Criticism* began. It began with his justification of art through appealing to aesthetic principles—in effect, by treating it as a work of art ("All nature is but art, unknown to thee"). In short, he limits art by referring it to nature and limits nature by referring it to art; and he can do both because nature is from the start defined in accordance with the aesthetic principle of teleological order. Pope's tightly closed system collapses any distinction between art and nature, but collapses it on art's side—collapsing, that is, nature into art. Nature is the work of the Master Artist, with our mini-works, each of them a microcosmos, responding to the same rules, the same principles of order, of an indwelling and fully realized purposiveness.[1]

So far as I can see, Mr. Krieger has not read the poem under an illusion of its self-sufficient discontinuity with other discourse. He has read it, rather, as entirely continuous with a discourse of his own. He describes the poem as justifying some things, appealing to others, referring to still others, as defining things and collapsing distinctions. He draws out the poem's implications, attaches its signifiers to signifieds, measures it against a macrocosm of external meaning, and later on judges it, argues with it, finds it wanting, refutes it. This in spite of the fact that he has described a poem as a unique *langue,* an intentionality that intends only itself, a metonymy that is a metaphor of only itself, a signifier that signifies nothing but itself. What's going on here? Has Mr. Krieger gone crazy? No, he has not. In fact, he is sane to a fault, so far as theorists of literature go. The measure of his sanity is the difference (with an *e*) between his theory and his practice. In that respect he is like a hurdle that has been crossed or a *parole* that has become *écriture,* for the theorist who begins to practice thereby loses his innocence.

Especially for this occasion, I have rewritten the lines attributed to Pope so that they will better correspond with Mr. Krieger's theory:

Ah Sloopy, you're soapy, ah you're for me;
Ah Sis, un bumbah, land of oobla dee;
Ah waka, waka doo, doo waka dood;
Ah wonka, weevil, up to no good;
Go fry your hide, and your coiffure's a fright;
Something, something, whatever is, is RIGHT.

I think I can fairly claim that my poem is more discontinuous with other discourse than Pope's, which I never much liked anyway. To open the poem up again, I shall act upon a hint from Mr. Joseph Riddell. I am going to put a single parenthesis in the poem, just off-center, of course, smack between *waka* and *dood.*

According to Mr. Krieger's theory, a poem is at once illusory and real, mimetic and actual, metaphoric and literal, intelligible and sensible, self-authenticating and self-abnegating, at once *micro-langue* and *parole* and *écriture;* a there-not-there that combines absence with presence, identity with difference, projection with distance, aesthetic distance with structuralist distance. Well, that's one way of looking at it. No, that's not one way of looking at it, but many ways, heaped together. Mr. Krieger's terms, and his concepts, are jagged around the edges with shards of the contexts from which they have been excavated. They do not fit together, they do not jibe, they do not stimm, they are not esemplastic. They interrupt each other. His signifieds seep out through the spaces between his signifiers. What's left is a modification of Archibald MacLeish's old wheeze that "A poem should not mean / But be." Mr. Krieger's modification is to the effect that a poem should not mean, but seem to mean to be. It's an improvement, but not enough of one.

But the proper question for a pious Nietzschean such as myself to ask is not whether Mr. Krieger's way of looking at poems is the true way. The proper question is, why does he want to look at them that way, or ways? This question, in its Nietzschean form, presumes nothing about Mr. Krieger's biography. It is analogous to the Darwinian's question as to why fish have fins, which presumes nothing about the fish's biography, never mind his subjectivity. Fish have fins to swim with. They got them in response to the selective pressures of their environment. Mr. Krieger's way of looking at poems enables him to swim with the tide, which is something all sane men want to do. And so do sane women, for it is of the essence of sanity that when women are sane they are sane in the same way as men. Given an off-center universe, it does not follow, of course, that when men are sane they are sane in the same way as women. Mr. Krieger's theory evolved in response to the pressures of his critical environment, which is turbulent with currents of structuralist attack on formalism.

Mr. Krieger's theory has at least one more function, for like other symptoms of irresistable pressure, it is overdetermined. If, unlike Mr. Krieger, you were to put it into practice, it would serve as a defense. It would protect you from the dangerous solicitations of literature. It would excuse you from declaring yourself. To that extent, at least, it would make you into a new critic. Mr. Krieger's theory would rule out, for example, William Empson's reading of *Paradise Lost.* Empson read *Paradise Lost* as you would read Kafka, as a faithful representation of a repulsive and horrifying reality. Kafka can't be blamed for seeing the world as he did. He didn't like it either. But Milton, and his poem, endorsed a religion that consigns the vast majority of mankind to an eternity of the most exquisite tortures an ingenious divinity could devise. Empson saw this as a fault in Milton, and in *Paradise Lost,* not to mention Milton's God, and so do I. But Mr. Krieger's theory would hold that Empson and I were just riding our anti-Christian hobby horses. His theory holds, and I quote, that poetic language insists "on reducing all human realities to itself while acknowledging its own empty indifference to reality." I see this as a fault in Mr. Krieger's theory.

Would you say, then, that I disagree with Mr. Krieger? Not exactly. Do I agree with him? Not quite. What then do I do with him? I sympathize. I too would like, at least sometimes, to preserve the autonomy of literature, but not all literature. Not *Paradise Lost,* for example. If Milton were alive at this hour I would twist his nose for him.

I now have a confession to make. I've been playing a dirty trick on you. All the while I have been standing here responding, I've been spelling *écriture* with an "h" at the beginning. In French, I believe, that "h" would be silent. But as you have noticed, my French accent is an abomination. All the while I have been saying "*écriture*" to you, to myself I have been saying "he-creature." For to me, my absence or presence in what I am saying makes all the differance (with an *a*).

And now I have one more confession to make, for it is of the essence of confession that once you start, you can never stop. I've been lying to you. Every word I said is written down. That doesn't mean that my response was a piece of *écriture,* for while you were all out getting soused last night, I spent long hours memorizing it. I lied to you in order to make my response a fiction, a poem, as Mr. Krieger would say, for Mr. Krieger is given to the use of synecdoche. I lied because I wanted to remind you that fictive things wink as they will. Wink most when formalists wince.

Columbia University

NOTES

1 Murray Krieger, *Theory of Criticism, A Tradition and Its System* (Baltimore and London: Johns Hopkins, 1976) pp. 108-109.

Apres que moyse se feust ainsy parti des hommes et le pleur en fu failli et que les hebrieux eurent mise toute lesperance quilz avoient a luy en iosue. Josue commanda que le peuple feust appareillie a la bataille et envoya espieurs en iherico pour savoir leur voulente et leur vertu ad ce que ilz en eussent congnoissance. et il disposoit son ost aussi comme sil voulsist trespas

What Is Stylistics and Why Are They Saying Such Terrible Things About It?—Part II

Stanley E. Fish

I

I intend today to continue what Barbara Smith has recently characterized as my "saturation bombing" of stylistics.[1] As before, the focus of the discussion will be on the relationship between description and interpretation. In "What Is Stylistics, and Why Are They Saying Such Terrible Things About It?—Part I,"[2] I found that in the practice of stylisticians of whatever school that relationship was always arbitrary, less a matter of something demonstrated than of something assumed before the fact or imposed after it. Five years later, the situation has changed somewhat, but in terms of the claims traditionally made for and by stylistics, it is no more satisfactory, merely unsatisfactory in a different way. Charting that way will be the business of this paper, and I will begin by rehearsing my conclusions in advance:

1.) Stylistic analysis is of two kinds, but those who practice the art do not distinguish between them, even though the assumptions underlying them are contradictory.

2.) One kind of stylistics is incoherent, even on its own terms; the other *is* coherent on its own terms, but they are not terms which the stylisticians can comfortably acknowledge, because to acknowledge them would be to admit that the goal of stylistics—an objective account of form and meaning—is an impossible one.

The first point to be made, then, is that the proponents of stylistics literally don't know what they are doing, although, typically, they preface their analyses with programmatic statements that suggest a clear-eyed understanding of both purpose and method. Here are excerpts from the opening paragraphs of what Roger Fowler has dubbed the "new stylistics."[3]

> This paper starts from what might be called the Ohmann Hypothesis . . . "stylistic preferences reflect cognitive preferences."[4]

> It is a commonplace of literary criticism to observe that form and content in a poem are closely related. . . . Four poems by Wallace Stevens will be analyzed from a formal standpoint. Then an attempt will be made to show how the formal analysis is closely related to what the poem is about.[5]

> In the model of language production that is assumed for the purposes of this paper, a speaker or writer first constructs a lexical constellation which mimes a state of affairs.[6]

These paragraphs share a vocabulary, and in particular a set of related verbs: "reflect," "relate," "mime," and, in later appearances, "embody," "correlate with," and "express." Together they point to the central assertion of stylistics as it is forthrightly stated by Fowler: "It is possible to say the same thing in different words". It is an assumption that, as Fowler says, one *must* make given the two-stage procedure it authorizes. First, formal features patterns are discovered by the application of some descriptive apparatus, and then they are found to be expressive of or reflect or mime a meaning or a content which stands apart from them and which could have been expressed (or reflected or mimed by) some other pattern, or which could have been packaged in formal patterns that did not reflect it at all, but merely presented it. As Keyser observes, the "demonstration of a form-content correlation will be significant only if it is logically possible for the formal structure encountered in a poem to bear *no* relation to the poem's content" (*WS,* p. 597); that is, only if it is possible to point to a formal structure without already having invoked some interpretive principle.

It is here at the heart of stylistics that one feels the contradictory pull of two demands. Only if forms are separable from the meanings they encase and adorn can there be said to be a choice between them, and a question for stylistics to answer (what is the relationship between this form and that meaning?). But only if the relationship of the form to the meaning can be shown to be necessary (indeed inevitable) will its demonstration escape the charge of being arbitrary, of being capable of assertion in any number of directions.

Epstein's analysis of "Lycidas," line 167, is a small but instructive case in point. The line reads, "Sunk though he be beneath the watry floar," and it exhibits, he says, "a remarkable degree of objective mimesis through a combination of syntactic and phonological structures" (*SRA,* p. 54). The most important of these involves the "movements of the tongue and lower jaw," which by accomplishing "the stressed vowels of this line mime a motion from *mid central* to *high front* to *back.*" One wonders what Epstein means here by "mime"; as he typically uses it the verb indicates a relationship of distance, i.e., different *from,* but imitative *of;* but there is no distance between the movements of the tongue and jaw and the central, front and back positions which those movements successively occupy; those movements do not *mime* a motion, they perform it. The equivocation is of no consequence, except insofar as it is evidence of Epstein's desire to assert mimesis even in a case where he could have had the real thing. What *is* important, however, is what this motion (be it mimetic or performative) is itself said to mime: "The motion in turn mimes the relationship *low-high-low* expressed in the lexis—the body of Edward King on the sea floor (low) and the surface of the sea (high)." The high front vowels mime the notion "the watery floor far beneath which King has sunk." This is arbitrary in so many directions that one suspects it must be a parody. In the first place the two patterns—one phonological, the other lexical—are not parallel in a way that would allow the first to be mimetic of the second. The movement low-high-low occurs on a vertical plane, while the movement mid central-high front-back occurs on the horizontal or curvi-linear plane of the roof of the mouth (itself a metaphor which if taken seriously—and why not?—would at the very least complicate the problem of mimesis and give it a different shape than Epstein proposes.)

The only genuine parallel between the two patterns would seem to be the presence in each of three successive and alternating states or stages; but even this parallel will not bear examination, because Epstein's description of the "lexical constellation" (that is, of what the line is saying) is open to challenge. It is by no means obvious that the line expresses the relationship low-high-low; indeed it would make equal and better sense (and one in accord with Milton's practice elsewhere) to say that the movement described is from low (sunk) to lower (beneath) to lower still. In order to give the phrase "watry floar" the value of "high," Epstein has to treat it as a surface (a word he uses), but the effect of joining the two words (in what is almost an oxymoron) is to call attention to the way in which this particular floor does not have the properties of a surface (it is "watry"). The other or "low" pole in Epstein's pattern is provided by a genuine surface, the floor of the sea, but nowhere is it asserted that King rests there or anywhere else; indeed, for many the poignancy of the poem derives from that fact that the location of his body is unknown.

Of course this is a matter of interpretation, and I am not arguing for a particular reading of "Lycidas." My point is that Epstein's reading is no less an interpretation, and that rather than standing in an independent and confirming relationship to a structural pattern, it is produced by the exigencies of that pattern. Epstein asserts that the phonological structure is worth noticing only because of the "polar situation" it mimes; but in fact the dependency is the other way around: the line is read as it is because a structural pattern already discerned needs a meaning that it can be said to mime, and the critic is determined to provide one. (It could have been the other way around.) It is not that what Epstein does can not be done, but that it can not *not* be done because there are no constraints on the manufacture of the correlations his method uncovers. Is there a line whose articulation does not involve some back and forth movement of the tongue, and is there a sense which could not be brought into some relation (of expression, counterpoint, opposition, irony) with that movement? Even those verses which Epstein cites as instances of non-mimesis could be shown to be mimetic by someone sufficiently committed to the principle. All you need is a meaning and a formal pattern (any meaning and any formal pattern will do), and the pressure of the question "how do they relate?" and a relation will always be found.

II

It is certainly found by Keyser in his analysis of Stevens's "Anecdote of a Jar." He begins by declaring that "the immediate impression one receives upon reading this poem is that it is akin in some way to a painting" (*WS,* p. 586). This curious judgement is delivered as if it were a truth universally acknowledged, one that required neither defense nor explanation. Once delivered, however, it is abandoned as abruptly as it was introduced, and Keyser proceeds to a discussion of the poem's formal features. The most prominent of these, we are told, involves a succession of variations on the syllable *round:* "round," "surround," "around," "round" again, and "ground." Between the second and third stanzas *round* is replaced as an organizing principle by a series of *air* rhymes: "air," "everywhere," and "bare," and by the alliteration in the penultimate line of "bird" and "bush." An unexceptionable conclusion follows: "There is, then, a nonoverlapping succession of rhyming devices which appear in a serial fashion . . . beginning with variations on *round,* moving to end-rhyme, then to alliteration and terminating with identical rhyme between the first and last lines" (*WS,* p. 587). As always, the question is where does one go from here, and Keyser, who is nothing if not forthright, tells us: "If . . . there exists a relationship between form and meaning in this poem, it should be possible for us to find an interpretation congenial to the structure that we have already established, . . . the successive nonoverlapping series of rhyming devices" (*WS,* p. 588).

My point is that given this kind of determination it would be impossible *not* to find an interpretation that was congenial in the sense that it is available for correlation with the poem's structural properties. In less than a page and one half it is duly found, and then summarized: "A property of the jar is mentioned and the relationship of the property to the environment is specified. With respect to the property round, the jar made the wilderness surround the hill. With respect to the property tall and of a port in air, the jar dominated the wilderness. With respect to the property gray and bare, the jar contrasted its own barrenness to the implied life of the wilderness" (*WS,* p. 588). Basically, this is an expansion into a stilted language of the phrase "took dominion everywhere." It is followed by the promised relation of the poem's structural properties to its now discovered meaning. Keyser recalls that his formal analysis had uncovered a succession of variations on the syllable "round," which therefore dominates the first two stanzas of the poem just as the jar dominates the wilderness. Or in his inflated account: "The actual phonological shape of the property of the jar which, in English, takes the form of the word *round* imposes an order, just as the semantic property "round," which the jar possesses, imposes an order on the wilderness. Using the shape of the word *round* to impose an order on the poem parallels using the actual shape of the object to impose an order on the wilderness" (*WS,* p. 589). This relation, he continues, also "exists with respect to the second property, namely *tall and of a port in air.* Once again, the physical shape of a word used to describe the property, i.e. *air,* imposes a new rhyming order on the poem . . . and this parallels the imposition of a new perception on the wilderness by the semantic content of the phrases of which the word is part" (*WS,* p. 589).

The first thing to say about this is that Keyser cheats, even on his own terms, when he extends his argument from the syllable "round" to the syllable "air." Unlike "round," "air" does not describe that property of the jar which imposes an order on the wilderness. Only if the repeated sound were "all" (as in "tall") would the syllable function as he says it does, in an intimate relationship with the specified property. This, however, is an internal criticism of the procedure. The more serious criticism is that it is trivial because its shape is in no way constrained. Having decided that the poem is about the imposition of order, and having also decided that it would be desirable to find a formal pattern that mimes or parallels that imposition, it would be impossible not to succeed (just as it would be impossible not to find a theme which an already observed formal pattern might mime.) Some pattern or other—alliterative, assonantal, consonantal—will always be uncovered and designated as the dominating one, and in the unlikely absence of a suitable pattern, that absence could itself be interpreted as an ironic and deliberate (and therefore mimetic) non-mimesis which expressed or reflected the absence of a relationship between language and reality.

In other words, the exercise is an arbitrary one, ruled by the determination to *have* a relation rather than by a procedure which demonstrates it. The phonological shape of "round" imposes an order on the poem only if you have already decided that the poem is about order. That is, the pattern emerges under the pressure of an interpretation and does not exist as independent evidence of it. In the event of a different interpretation, the pattern would be seen differently and be evidence in another direction. One might decide, for example, that the poem was about the many ways of viewing a jar (as in the thirteen ways of looking at a blackbird); it would then be a series of puns: the jar is round; it is also a round; it is a superround (*super* is the Latin for "sur" and means over, above and on top of); and as the focus of attention it functions as a g-round. In the context of this reading, the pattern of sound would reflect difference and variation rather than similarity and order. Or alternately, one's reading might pay particular attention to the first person pronoun and regard the poem as the utterance of a limited persona, someone who is seeking the meaning of his experience, and fails to recognize it in the patterns of his own language: the repetition of "round," a syllable hidden in words which pay no particular attention to it, would then mime the psychological state of unawareness.

Of course it is not necessary that an interpretation be involved with the syllable "round" at all. Phonological patterns do not announce themselves naturally; they are picked out by an interested perception, and a perception otherwise interested will pick out another pattern. It is possible, for example, to read the poem as a meditation on nature in its benign and threatening forms. This distinction could then be seen in the migration of the syllable "ill" from "h*ill*" to "*wil*derness," back to "h*ill*" and then to "w*il*derness" again, and finally ending in the triumph of threatening nature when the sound is transformed into "w*il*d." My little phonological drama has the same status as Keyser's: his sounds dominate and order, mine migrate and oppose, but in both cases the pattern as perceived is the product of an interpretation and not independent confirmation of it. As I have said elsewhere, this is a game that is just too easy to play.

Keyser himself shows how easy it is when in a final paragraph he reinterprets his formal patterns as evidence for his impression that the poem is akin to a still-life painting: "The apparent framing of this poem between the repeated phrases *in Tennessee* which appear in the opening and the closing line of the poem provides a verbal counterpart of a frame to the still life in words" (*WS,* p. 589). Somehow Keyser doesn't see that his conviction that the poem is like a painting is what leads him first to see a repetition, then to characterize it as a frame, and pretends instead that the homology is between two independently existing systems. In the next paragraph he does it again (and he could have done it forever) when he succeeds (it is an assured success) in seeing in the phonological order an allegory of the poetic act. Here at least he has the right word, although it is applied in the wrong place. Whether or not the poem is an allegory, his performance surely is, in the discredited Ruskinian sense of reading a prefabricated meaning into patterns that have no necessary relationship to it whatsoever.

Allegory is also the mode of his analysis of "The Snowman." Here the formal description is of a syntax that has continually to be revised: while "the opening stanza constitutes what appears at first sight to be a complete sentence . . . the beginning of the next stanza indicates that an ellipsis has occurred and that the sentence which apparently terminated at the end of the first stanza is, in fact, the first member of a coordinate sentence" (*WS,* p. 590). The sequence repeats itself in the relationship between the second and third stanzas, when a "new ellipsis shows that once again we have been mistaken in our syntactic analysis, and we must now go back and reanalyze" (*WS,* p. 591). The pattern is varied somewhat in the last stanza, for "whereas the second stanza paralleled the first and the third paralleled the second, each time within a conjoined sentence, we now find that the last stanza parallels the first four, itself in a conjoined sentence." As a result, Keyser concludes, the poem consistently "demands that we analyze and then reanalyze yet again as we pass linearly and in time from one point to another in the structure" (*WS,* p. 595).

It is at this point that Keyser makes his characteristic move. Let us, he says, "look at the relationship between the formal device described above and the meaning of the poem." What he means, of course, is let us look for a meaning of the poem that can stand in an iconic relationship to the formal pattern we have discerned. That meaning is immediately found when Keyser decides, with some help from Stevens and Frank Kermode, that the poem is about the "need to perceive reality in a clear fashion" (*WS,* p. 596). In the course of the poem "we find that in the implied regimen needed to move toward a clear perception of reality, there is a constant change of perspective. Thus Stevens observes that to begin with, one must have a mind of winter, i.e. a particular state of mind in order to regard the frost. However, this state of mind is not in itself reliable for one must have had it for a long time in order to behold the junipers shagged with ice and not think of misery" (*WS,* p. 596). The conclusion can be seen coming from half a mile away, and in due time it arrives: "We saw that . . . the poem consists of a syntactic pattern whose main characteristic is that its structure at any one time seems clear but which, at the next moment, requires a complete reanalysis. . . . This designed need to change syntactic perspective cannot more closely parallel the sense of the poem which is to change one's outward perspective in order to more accurately understand reality" (*WS,* pp. 596-97).

In this wholly uninteresting reading the poem becomes a "how-to" manual, a developing set of directions for achieving a clear understanding of reality. Curiously, the reading would have been much more interesting if Keyser were more aware of what he is doing. He thinks that he is discerning an independent formal pattern and relating it to a content, but in fact he is eviscerating a pattern that is not, at least as he first comes upon it, formal. This is because his description is not, as he claims, of a syntax, but of a mind in the act of doing something; and it is therefore a description that follows upon a set of psychological assumptions about what people do when they read. What Keyser is assuming that they do is revise, and a complete description, one that was responsible to the principles that made it possible, would trace the career of that revising and not merely note it as preliminary to allegorizing it.

In other words, while in the analysis of "Anecdote of a Jar" there is no legitimate, that is constrained, direction in which one might go after pointing out the appearances of "round," here the direction in which one might go is built into the initial observation, but Keyser refuses to take it. This does not, however, prevent *us* from taking it, if only in order to see what kind of reading Keyser could have produced if he had seen what his own vocabulary so clearly implies: that the act of revising has as its object not merely a syntactic structure, but the structure of the reader's understanding. That is, each time we revise or reanalyze, what changes is not only our understanding of the syntax, but our understanding of what is required to regard the frost and the junipers; and the shape of that change is a complicating of what it means to "have a mind of winter." At first it seems to mean no more than that one's mind should be full of wintry thoughts or be unsympathetic in some undefined way; the phrase, in short, seems to be metaphorical. But then, with each realization that the syntax, and therefore the unit of sense, is not complete, comes the realization that the requirements for a clear and undistorting perception have grown tighter. They grow wire-tight in stanza three, where the newly specified requirement is "not to think / Of any misery in the sound of the wind." "Wintry thoughts," then, are precisely what must be avoided, and if we pause at the end of the line—"and not to think"—the injunction becomes even more sweeping; one must not have any thoughts at all: that is, one must efface oneself completely and become an observer so pure that he adds nothing to a reality which will be unmediated because he as a medium—as something obstructing—is no more. Only then, when he is nothing himself, will his self not be interposed between him and the nothing—the thing that is not an object of human thought—that is. But the reader who understands that this is what it means to have a mind of winter purchases that understanding at the price of being able to have one, since the act of understanding, of apprehending from a distance, is precisely what must be given up. What we finally discover is that what is required is a mind not active in the way it must be for the discovery to be made. The demand that the reader reanalyze does not parallel a program for the achieving of a pure perception; rather it is inseparable from the realization that such a perception is forever unavailable.

Now I am not claiming for this hypothetical reading that it is truer to the poem or to Stevens's intention than the reading Keyser actually performs; but that it is more likely to convince someone of its trueness because there is a clear line of argument from its uncovering of a formal structure to the stipulation of that structure's meanings. That is to say, given the assumptions already imbedded in the notion of revising, a reading which follows the career of that revising will have an immediate, persuasive force. There is no point in the reading where the analyst must stop in order to cast around for a meaning that can be related to his forms, because the description of those forms is at the same time a stipulation of their meanings. The assumption (it is Keyser's) that what a reader does is revise leads necessarily to an account of that revising, and that account is already involved with the determination and redetermination of sense. In short, in the second reading, the formal description is already an interpretation, and, in fact, the so-called formal elements come into view only because an interpretive assumption (about what readers do) is already in force. What Keyser does is detach his own formal patterns from the interpretive act which made them available, and then he proceeds to find for them an interpretation with which they have nothing, necessarily, to do. There is nothing inevitable about his analysis because at the crucial moment (when you would ask why *that*) the relationship between his form and his content is simply asserted. He would have achieved inevitability if he had only read out of his formal pattern the content it already, implicitly, had. And, indeed, this is what he does in the first of his analyses, although for reasons that should now be clear, he won't admit that he is doing it.

The poem is "The Death of a Soldier," and in it Keyser discerns three significant formal choices. Stevens has:

> 1. . . . selected verbs which can under no circumstances take agents.
>
> 2. He has selected the nonagentive use of verbs which can but need not take agents.
>
> 3. In the two instances where he has selected the agentive sense of a verb . . . he has displayed the verbs in a syntactic construction which requires that the agent be deleted from the surface of a poem. (*WS,* p. 582)

It is important to realize that these formalizations are different in kind from the others we have encountered, from the back and forth movement of the tongue, or the variation of a single syllable, or a syntax whose description becomes more and more complex. These patterns, at least as they are presented by Epstein and Keyser, are *purely* formal, and they acquire a semantic value only by being made icons of a meaning independent of them. Here the meaning is built into the formalization, and when the time comes all you have to do is read it out. Thus, when Keyser asks himself "whether there is a relationship between the suppression of . . . agency and the meaning of the poem?", the question is a rhetorical one because the suppression of agency *is* the meaning of the poem. I don't mean that it truly is, in some indisputable way, but that in the context of this formal description the specification of that meaning is inevitable, and this is enough to distinguish the analysis from those in which the specification of meaning is an act of prestidigitation. that is, Keyser can legitimately claim for this analysis what he claims for all the others (and if he doesn't claim it, it's hard to know what he *is* claiming): that the parallel between form and meaning could not be drawn in any other direction; and the claim can be made because it is *not* a parallel between form and meaning, but a spelling out of the meaning that has from the very beginning been the content of this formal category.

The curious thing is that Keyser feels obliged to assert the contrary and to deny the real coherence—a persuasive coherence—his analysis has. His conclusion makes that clear: "The manipulation of syntax and semantics to remove all vestiges of an agent . . . corresponds to the world of the poem in which there are no initiators" (*WS,* p. 583). The key word here is "corresponds," which is in the same line of work as correlates with, parallels, mimes, and reflects; it implies distance, but in this case there is none, because the notion of a world in which there are no initiators is derived directly (and not by way of correspondence) from a grammar without any visible agency. Keyser claims to have shown that "the form of his poem reflects its content" (*WS,* p. 584): but his formal description merely yields up the content it has always had. He refuses to see this because he is committed to keeping the two levels of his system separate; but in this example, at least, there is only one level; we can call it formal or we can call it semantic; what we can not do is maintain the fiction of a distinction.

III

That distinction, however, is essential to the stylistician's enterprise, since it is the availability of a purely formal component—of formal features that one can pick out independently of any interpretation of them—that allows him to claim objectivity for his analyses. We can now see clearly the choice that confronts the stylistician. Either he engages in an activity that is incoherent in its own terms because its assignment of significances is arbitrary; or he engages in a coherent activity whose terms do not allow him the claims he would like to make for it because the coherence is itself interpretive. In his analysis of Blake's "The Tyger" Epstein manages to engage in both activities at the same time. He first decides on the meaning of the poem: " 'Tyger' seems to record a moment of illumination, the moment when the nature of the fundamental energy of the universe became clear. There are, therefore, two aspects of this experience—memory of the sensation of mystic illumination, and awe before the object of perception" (*SRA,* p. 53). It is no surprise to find the assertion that "both of these aspects are reflected in syntactic structures . . . that communicate this moment with great power to the reader." Apparently, however, these syntactic structures are not available on the surface, since Epstein finds it necessary to create them.

His strategy illustrates something extremely important about this kind of analysis. When one interrogates a text with a grammar, one populates the text with the entities the grammar is able to recognize, that is, with entities that are a function of the grammar's categories; and if one of your categories is syntactic ambiguity, the question "is this text ambiguous?" will always be answered in the affirmative. Epstein puts that question to the lines "Tyger, Tyger, burning bright, / In the forests of the night." The first line, he discovers, can be read as either "The Tyger is burning," or "The Tyger is bright"; while the second line is ambiguous in several directions. The tyger could be burning or bright against the background of the forests of the night, or in the forests of the night, or within the forests of the night, and the phrase "forests of the night" could be predicating either thickness of the night or darkness of the forest. By the time he has finished, Epstein is able to speak of "this octuply ambiguous expression," and if we recall that each ambiguity exists in multiple relationships with the other seven, his mathematics are conservative. Now, having created this structure by means of a grammatical apparatus specifically designed to create it, Epstein declares that the information provided in the second, third, and fourth stanzas dissolves it by removing the ambiguities, so that when the first two lines reappear in the final stanza, they are "completely unambiguous," or in terms more appropriate to the art here being practiced: "Now you see it; now you don't."

I find this argument very strange. It asserts that in this last stanza contextual pressures are operating in such a way that the ambiguities noted in the first stanza don't arise; but those same or other pressures could just as easily have been operating in the first place. That is to say, one could have argued for historical or biographical or other contextual circumstances that would have removed the potential ambiguities of the lines before a reader ever came to them. What is Epstein's warrant for assuming that lines one and two of the poem are without context (not, in fact, a possible assumption), and are therefore available for an unconstrained quarrying for a grammatical apparatus? The question contains its own answer: the assumption of a-contextual circumstances is necessary if Epstein is to be free to "discover" a formal pattern that can stand in an iconic (mimetic) relationship to a sense already selected. In this case the process of fabricating such a pattern is so complicated that one tends to forget (as you may have forgotten) what the preselected sense is. In a triumphant conclusion, Epstein reminds us: "The movement from eight-fold syntactic ambiguity to single structure provides syntactic mimesis for the feeling of universal understanding with which the reader finishes the poem" (*SRA,* p. 67). The sleight of hand is transparent; the movement of the poem is entirely the creation of his analytic strategy; and that in turn is dictated by an interpretation which, rather than being mimed by a formal pattern, produces it. In short, the formal pattern is not there, in the independent sense claimed by the analysis, and even if it were, there would be no exclusive relationship between it and this particular interpretation. The movement from the complex to the simple could mime the change from a questioning of the divine mystery to its unthinking (that is, nonunderstanding) acceptance. Or it could mime an interpretation that Epstein specifically rejects: that the poem is spoken by a limited observer whose attempts to preconceive a reality too complex for him are finally given up. The point is that unless his interpretation is the only one that fits the "formal facts" (and remember that they are not really formal facts in the way he would have them be), the claim of mimesis is empty because there are no formal patterns or interpretations that could not be made into components of a mimetic relationship. In short, everything about this procedure is arbitrary; the interpretation is abritrary, the formal pattern is arbitrary; the link between them is arbitrary.

Epstein, however, is not yet done, and in the second half of his essay he produces an analysis as compelling in its own terms as this one is bizarre. The subject is still Blake's "Tyger," but the formalism is now speech act theory and the doctrine of illocutionary forces. Epstein distinguishes between yes/no questions, answerable by a simple assent or negation, and questions "to which the answer cannot be 'yes' or 'no' but which must be a phrase, a substitute for an interrogative pronominal, and whose syntactic class is strictly governed by the choice of interrogative pronominal," i.e. where, when, why, what (*SRA,* p. 70). The questions headed by some of these interrogatives are simple in form—"Where did you go?"—while others are more complex. An example would be "Whose hat is missing?", which assumes a situation previously ordered and understood. (There is a hat and no one has claimed it.) A given question may assume several prior levels of ordered understanding, and thus be a tertiary or even higher question. Such a question always implies that either the questioner or answerer "has already advanced beyond the point of confronting an unordered situation." Epstein finds that in lines like "What immortal hand or eye, / Could frame thy fearful symmetry," Blake proposes secondary and tertiary questions which are not preceded by the appropriate primary question. The result is "to rob the questions of the power to elicit information of which the questioner is ignorant." They are "not really questions at all, but disguised exclamations." The situation of the reader is thus uneasy; he listens to the form of questions, but is aware at some level that they are disguised exclamations, and therefore questions that he cannot even begin to answer. In stanza five, however, the questions are in "perfect canonical form"—"Did he smile his work to see?"—and they come as a great relief because "the construction of an answer can at least begin for them. Thus the 'true' questions in stanza five act to release tension previously created by the asking of questions subtly false in form" (*SRA,* p. 73).

Now one can quarrel with this, but the quarrel would be with the account of the different kinds of questions and their effects on readers, but given that account, Epstein's conclusions follow. If there is any magic in the sequence, it is at the beginning, where the formal apparatus is introduced. Two points should be made about that apparatus: 1. It isn't formal in the strictest sense since it contains information about responses and takes into account not only the situation of utterance, but the situations prior to utterance. 2. It is not a finished thing, but is in the process of being constructed. Epstein is forthright about this, noting that he is depending to some extent on rules not yet formulated and labelling his approach, quite properly as "tentative." These two points will allow us to make a third by way of a question. What would happen if Epstein were to come up with a new formulation of the rules governing questions? One is tempted to answer that the description of the poem would change, but when the categories in dispute are as basic as the structure of questions or the properties of verbs, there is literally nothing to describe. That is, if descriptive categories are themselves interpretive (because they are open to challenge) they are constitutive of their object rather than being faithful (or unfaithful) to it; and when one system of formal rules gives way to another, the result is not a new description of the same poem, but a new poem. Epstein's analysis of the questions in "The Tyger" is not persuasive because it matches up to the poem, but because it produces the poem: one interpretive structure—a theoretical account of interrogatives—leads inevitably to another—the poem he proceeds to "describe." There is certainly a coherence to the procedure, but it is a coherence that begins and ends in interpretation, without ever touching base with a fact or a pattern that is *independently* specifiable.

Another way of putting this is to say that in the more coherent (and therefore more persuasive) of these analyses, the construction of the grammar and the construction of the poem are going on at the same time. Indeed, they are the same activities. This is especially clear in Donald Freeman's analysis of Keats's "To Autumn."[7] Freeman's exposition is subtle and complex, but basically it is an argument about the verbs "load," "bless," "bend," "fill," "swell" and "plump" as they appear in the following lines:

> Conspiring with him how to load and bless
> With fruit the vines that round the thatch-eves run;
> To bend with apples the moss'd cottage-trees,
> And fill all fruit with ripeness to the core;
> To swell the gourd, and plump the hazel shells,
> With a sweet kernel. . . .

Freeman notes that in the surface structure all of these verbs are transitive, and are to some extent causative, while in their underlying forms "plump" and "swell" are intransitive, and "fill" has at least one intransitive reading. It is possible, he continues, to argue that "load," "bless," and "bend" also have underlying intransitive readings. One need only add the suffix "en" to them to see that they denote states in the process of coming about. "*Just as the thickened . . .* underlies *John thickened the sauce,* so does *the hazel shells plump[en]* underlie *to plump the hazel shells,*" and similarly with "bend*en,*" "load*en,*" and "bless*en*" (*TA,* p. 6). Freeman concludes that by embedding these basically inchoative verbs in a surface structure marked "transitive," Keats achieves an effect basic to the meaning of the poem. The underlying subjects of natural and apparently independent states—the trees which bend, the shells which plump—are made into the objects of Autumn's all-powerful agency. Rather than the fruit filling with ripeness (where "ripeness" is the answer to the question, "in what manner does the fruit fill?"), the fruit is filled by Autumn, who uses ripeness in the accomplishing of her work. Normally, "with fruit," "with apples," "with ripeness," and "with a sweet kernel" would not be instrumentals, but in this construction they become the means by which Autumn loads, blesses, bends, fills, swells, and plumps. Each of these instrumental phrases, rather than being the result of a verb's action (the vine is loaded—with what?—with fruit), becomes the object of Autumn's action (Autumn loads the vines and she loads the vines with fruit.) The overriding agency of Autumn, by making everything her object, makes everything her instrument, even the sun. She conspires with him in the sense of using him; she conspires, and the instrument of her conspiring is him, and the complement of his instrumentality is all the subsidiary instrumental actions: loading, blessing, bending, etc. Thus as instrument, the sun "becomes a part of the objects upon which it is employed (the fruit, the apples, the ripeness, the sweet kernel) just as they in turn become . . . a part of the objects upon which they are employed as instruments (the vines, the trees, the fruit, the hazel shells.)" "On this reading," Freeman concludes, "the sun can be seen . . . as a meta-instrument for Autumn, the ultimate agent of all the natural forces in the poem" (*TA,* p. 10).

I find this all elegant and persuasive, but it is also interpretive from the very first word to the last. Like Keyser, Freeman believes otherwise. He sees his reading of "To Autumn" as a demonstration of "syntactic mimesis, imitation by the poem's syntactic structure of its subject matter" (*TA,* p. 12); but this is to give himself less credit than he is due. The syntactic structure and the poem's subject matter are not brought together in the analysis; they are created by the analysis as the building of the one produces an account of the other. Freeman admits as much in a footnote where he attempts to argue that the pattern he discerns represents options chosen by Keats from alternatives in the deep structure. But the enterprise, as he himself says, founders, because linguists disagree about what is in the deep structure, and therefore about what would be alternative derived structures. Nevertheless, he remains convinced that the inchoative-causative pattern in "To Autumn" reflects a preference, although, as he says, a preference over what is a question he cannot answer. The answer is obvious. The preference of one grammar over the other is not the author's, but the critic's, and what it reflects in his reading of the poem, a reading which is the very content of his formal categories. The point has been made by J. P. Thorne, who acknowledges that his grammatical analysis of a poem follows rather than precedes his understanding of it, and therefore cannot stand in a relationship of confirmation to that understanding: "The whole point of constructing a grammar [for a poem] . . . is that it provides a way of stating clearly the interpretation that one finds."[8] Just so. Freeman's specifying of the inchoative-causative pattern is not an act preliminary to interpretation; it is itself an interpretive act, and the specifying of the poem's "subject" matter is nothing more than a transposition of that act into a more discursive and less technical vocabulary. In short, when Freeman chooses one grammar rather than another he is choosing one meaning rather than another and is therefore choosing one poem rather than another. Eugene Kintgen has remarked that given the number of competing grammars and the disputes concerning their basic categories, "two stylistic analyses of the same text written at different times may . . . associate different phenomena, and make apparently different claims about the text."[9] I would go even further; the two grammars would be making different texts.

With that statement I come to the end of my argument and can return to its beginning and to my conclusions. There are two varieties of stylistics and neither of them will support the stylisticians' strongest claims. The one falls apart in the middle because there is no legitimate way (and every illegitimate way) to relate its formal and semantic components; in the other the formal and semantic components are so perfectly related that the distinction between them is lost: its stages are interpretive from the first to the last. The stylisticians often perform these two kinds of analysis without seeing the difference between them, because they remain committed to a form/meaning distinction even when they have in their practice abandoned it. That is, they begin by assuming that a form can express many meanings and that a meaning can be clothed in many forms, and it is an assumption that they persist in even when demonstrating how much semantic content—how much meaning—their formal categories have. In short, they refuse to acknowledge their dilemma. Either they can continue in an activity that is wholly illegitimate, or engage in an activity which, while legitimate, is not, in the sense they desire, formal. They can still claim rigor and precision, but it will be rigor in the unfolding of an interpretation, and precision in the stating of that interpretation.

Some of you will have noted that this same dilemma is writ larger in the history of transformational grammar. On the one hand there are those who have argued for an independently motivated syntax to which a semantic component must then be added in some *ad hoc* or artificial way; and on the other, those whose syntactic categories are already so laden with semantic content that the distinction between them finally disappears. The lesson to be drawn from the plight of stylistics is a hard one, especially for those who still dream of a criticism, or even of a linguistics, that begins with free-standing and independent formal facts, and builds up from those facts to the larger world of discourse: the dream, in short, of an analysis that moves in a principled way from the objective description of a text to its interpretation. What I have been saying is that every description is always and already an interpretation, and that therefore the first act of any criticism, and especially of a linguistically based criticism, is to constitute the text.

Finally, I should point out that the argument of this paper differs considerably from that of its predecessor. In "What Is Stylistics and Why Are They Saying Such Terrible Things About It?—Part I", the focus is on the arbitrary relationship between the specification of formal patterns and their subsequent interpretation. Here my thesis is that formal patterns are themselves the products of interpretation and that therefore there is no such thing as a formal pattern, at least in the sense necessary for the practice of stylistics: that is, no pattern that one can observe before interpretation is hazarded, and which therefore can be used to prefer one interpretation to another. The conclusion, however, is not that there are no formal patterns, but that there are always formal patterns; it is just that the formal patterns there always are will always be the product of a prior interpretive act, and therefore will be available for discerning only so long as that act is in force. Or, to end with an aphorism: there always is a formal pattern, but it isn't always the same one.

Johns Hopkins University

NOTES

1 See "Surfacing from the Deep," in *On the Margin of Discourse: The Relation of Literature to Language* (Chicago: Univ. of Chicago Press, 1978), pp. 157-201.

2 In *Approaches To Aesthetics,* ed. S. Chatman (New York: Columbia Univ. Press, 1973), pp. 109-52.

3 See "The New Stylistics," in *Style and Structure in Literature: Essays in the New Stylistics,* ed. Roger Fowler (Ithaca, N.Y.: Cornell Univ. Press, 1975), pp. 1-18; p. 8.

4 Donald Freeman, "The Strategy of Fusion: Dylan Thomas' Syntax," in *Style and Structure in Literature,* p. 19.

5 Samuel Jay Keyser, "Wallace Stevens: Form and Meaning in Four Poems," *College English,* 37, (1976), 578 (hereafter cited as *WS*).

6 E. L. Epstein, "The Self-Reflexive Artifact," in *Style and Structure in Literature,* p. 40 (hereafter cited as *SRA*).

7 "Keats's 'To Autumn': Poetry as Process and Pattern," *Language and Style,* XI, No. 1 (1978), pp. 3-17 (hereafter cited as *TA*).

8 "Generative Grammar and Stylistic Analysis," in *New Horizons in Linguistics,* ed. John Lyons (Harmondsworth, England: Penguin, 1970), pp. 194-95.

9 "Is Transformation Stylistics Useful?" *College English,* 35, (1974), 823.

sed post pressura studia: in domo domini profecimus laboramus. Illi interpretati sunt ante adventum Christi, et quod nesciebant dubiis protulere sententiis; nos post passionem et resurrectionem eius non tam prophetiam quam historiam scribimus. Aliter enim audita, aliter visa narrantur; quod melius intelligimus, melius et proferimus. Audi igitur, emule; obtrectator, ausculta. Non damno, non reprehendo lxx, sed confidenter cunctis illis apostolos prefero. Per istorum os mihi Christus sonat, quos ante prophetas inter spiritalia carismata positos lego, in quibus ultimum pene gradum interpretes tenent. Quid livore torqueris? Quid imperitorum animos contra me concitas? Sicubi in translatione tibi videor errare, interroga Hebreos, diversarum urbium magistros consule. Quod illi habent de Christo, tui codices non habent. Aliud est si contra se postea ab apostolis usurpata testimonia probaverunt, et emendatiora sunt exemplaria Latina quam Greca, et Greca quam Hebrea. Verum hec contra invidos. Nunc te deprecor, Desideri karissime, ut quia me tantum opus subire fecisti et a Genesi exordium capere, orationibus iuves quo possim eodem spiritu quo scripti sunt libri in Latinum eos transferre sermonem. Incipit liber Genesis.

In principio creavit deus celum et terram. Terra autem erat inanis et vacua, et tenebre erant super faciem abyssi, et spiritus domini ferebatur super aquas. Dixitque deus: Fiat lux. Et facta est lux. Et vidit deus lucem quod esset bona, et divisit lucem a tenebris. Appellavitque lucem diem et tenebras noctem. Factumque est vespere et mane dies unus. Dixit quoque deus: Fiat firmamentum in medio aquarum, et dividat aquas ab aquis. Et fecit deus firmamentum, divisitque aquas que erant sub firmamento ab hiis que erant super firmamentum. Et factum est ita. Vocavitque deus firmamentum celum. Et factum est vespere et mane dies secundus. Dixit vero deus: Congregentur aque que sub celo sunt in locum unum, et appareat arida. Factumque est ita. Et vocavit deus aridam terram, congregationesque aquarum appellavit maria. Et vidit deus quod esset bonum, et ait: Germinet terra herbam virentem et facientem semen, et lignum pomiferum faciens fructum iuxta genus suum, cuius semen in semet ipso sit super terram. Et factum est ita. Et protulit terra herbam virentem et facientem semen iuxta genus suum, lignumque faciens fructum et habens unumquodque sementem secundum speciem suam. Et vidit deus quod esset bonum. Factumque est vespere et mane dies tercius. Dixit autem deus: Fiant luminaria in firmamento celi, et dividant diem ac noctem, et sint in signa et tempora et dies et annos, ut luceant in firmamento celi et illuminent terram. Et factum est ita. Fecitque deus duo magna luminaria: luminare maius ut preesset diei, et luminare minus ut preesset nocti, et stellas. Et posuit eas in firmamento celi ut lucerent super terram, et preessent diei ac nocti, et dividerent lucem ac tenebras. Et vidit deus quod esset bonum. Et factum est vespere et mane dies quartus. Dixit etiam deus: Producant aque reptile anime viventis et volatile super terram sub firmamento celi. Creavitque deus cete grandia et omnem animam viventem atque motabilem, quam produxerant aque in species suas, et omne volatile secundum genus suum. Et vidit deus quod esset bonum, benedixitque eis dicens: Crescite et multiplicamini et replete aquas maris, avesque multiplicentur super terram. Et factum est vespere et mane dies quintus. Dixit quoque deus: Producat terra animam viventem in genere suo, iumenta et reptilia et bestias terre secundum species suas. Factumque est ita. Et fecit deus bestias terre secundum species suas, et iumenta et omne reptile terre in genere suo. Et vidit deus quod esset bonum, et ait: Faciamus hominem ad imaginem et

Critical Persuasion: In Response To Stanley Fish

Joseph F. Graham

I have mixed feelings, now that I find myself in the position of having to respond to Stanley Fish. Were I at all clever, or at least clever enough to hope to hide my embarrassment, I would find something to say about the host and the parasite, comparing myself to a parasitic host. But I would soon get lost in the dialectics of such a subtle relation.

I also have mixed thoughts about this response, for I can imagine several different ways of responding to this stimulus. Stanley Fish is indeed stimulating; he is a great stimulus—one of the best stimulants in academe. And we have all felt his effect on our mental organs. He does stimulate, in all the senses of that curiously jaded word: arouse, activate, excite, urge, provoke, instigate, goad, spur, prod, prick, inflame, fire. . . . See *animate,* or so says the dictionary. And he may not be cheap, but he is legal—though some students have been warned about getting too high on Fish.

One response—and this was my first—could be framed in answer to the following question: Who is Stanley Fish, and why does he have such terrible things to say about stylistics? The answer would then be constructive, instructive. A second response—though perhaps the first reaction of a stylistician—could be characterized by a slightly different question: Just who is this Stanley Fish after all, and why does *he* have to say such terrible things about *us?* The answer then would be more aggressive. Personality may seem to make all the difference, the difference between a positive and a negative response, and I suppose that many feel and some even think that Fish either turns you *on* or turns you *off.* He leaves few indifferent. There is a cult of personality in contemporary criticism, and his is one of the most striking. It has the force to strike discord: if you are not with us, you are against us.

It may be possible to feel both of these responses, without being tepid or just timid. I would hope to understand them both, without suggesting any middle ground, any moderately safe position in-between, for I think that such extremes are not as distant as they may appear. They are related in some way, in an almost logical way, that I will try to elaborate. My argument will run roughly as follows: If the positive response is valid, and what we can say for Fish is true, then the negative response is also valid, and what we can say against him is also true. This may sound like a contradiction, and it would be, were the antecedent and the consequent of the same logical type. There is an important difference between the two which makes their correlation all the more interesting.

A positive response to Fish might inspire us to argue for the therapeutic value of his work in literary criticism. This is no poison, but a cure for our critical malady, for that kind of positivism which remains a threat to the very life of criticism, its full health and humanity. Such an argument might then suggest that Fish has helped to do for criticism the type of job once required in analytic philosophy, to combat that same disease of the mind suffering under its own constraints. We could then turn back to Wittgenstein or perhaps to Quine for original examples of vigilance against that simplified epistemology which would divide all knowledge, by making terms either observational or theoretical, statements either synthetic or analytic, and further separating psychological contexts of discovery from logical contexts of justification. But the word has been out for some time now that the positivist idea of science is mistaken for both history and theory, so that you can find much of the same criticism in any number of books and articles, in Hanson, Feyerabend, Toulmin, Kuhn, Lakatos, Agassi, and many more. There is no immaculate perception, no neutral language of description, no strict logic of induction, and no simple progress from ignorance and superstition to science and enlightenment. These dogmas of empiricism have been attacked on all sides, with devastating results. Science now appears more arbitrary but in many ways less forbidding because more speculative and even more intuitive, since the emphasis has shifted from the rigors of a closed system to the risks of open research.

It may seem strange that such a clear message should have to be repeated with any insistence for the benefit of those working in stylistics, especially since the very same message has figured so prominently in linguistics, in the transformational linguistics which serves as a model and provides the method for the most recent work in stylistics. From the very beginning, Chomsky has been adamantly and even militantly opposed to the kind of mindless empiricism—alias, behaviorism—so congenial to most structural linguists. He has denounced their naive belief in the possibility of some mechanical discovery procedure which would somehow produce a significant theory when fed raw data—whatever that may be—arguing that neither the linguist nor the child could possibly learn a language, each in their different but analogous ways, according to the strictly empirical method of induction, since grammar, whether explicit and scientific or implicit and psychological, is necessarily under-determined by the evidence of ordinary speech. Without some initial hypothesis to restrict the class of possible languages or the class of possible grammars, nothing could ever be learned. The same type of argument had already been made by Saussure in terms of the irreducible specificity of language structures and the consequential autonomy of linguistic science, but it was so much more forceful in generative terms, because the study of syntactic structures revealed a degree of complexity requiring for their representation a line of derivation which had to be psychologically real rather than just formally adequate as was the case for the syntagmatic and paradigmatic principles of Saussure. His idea of structure was compatible with a data-processing model favored by the Americans, whereas transformations were not; they could only be mental operations, procedures required for and yet easily demonstrated by the regular interpretation and production of sentences in natural language.

It could just be that the message was lost in the passage from language to literature, or it may be that the lesson has to be learned again for the study of literature, since the difference between the two will not allow any direct or literal transfer of procedures from the one to the other. What counts in language does not necessarily count in literature or not necessarily in the same way. And for that reason grammar cannot be applied to literature with the expectation of infallibly significant results. At times it would seem as if Fish were saying little more, and such mild words of caution could only be taken well, as well meant. And if this were the case, or if it were only the case, his voice would be one of many warning about the dangers of linguistic imperialism in the study of literature. Grammar is not enough to interpret literature, despite whatever Jakobson might have said in more sanguine days, for it has to be interpreted anew for literature, not just for literature in general, but also for each and every literary text in particular. The purpose of such grammar to correlate form and meaning in a systematic fashion can be shared by linguistics and stylistics at least in principle, but that correlation has to be double rather than single, and perhaps even n-tuple in some cases where the relation between text and grammar is especially oblique.

Having hedged my last statement with an "at least in principle," I may turn to face the full brunt of the attack on stylistics, for Fish seems to be opposed to the very principle of there being any such correlation between form and meaning for literature and even for language.[1] He finds in that very principle both the initial assumption and the fatal presumption of all stylistics. In a passage from "What is Stylistics . . . Part I," which echoes Hubert Dreyfus against the program of artificial intelligence, Fish writes the following:

> the more reasonable inference would be that the difficulty lies not with the present state of the art but with the art itself; and this is precisely what I shall finally argue, that the establishment of a syntax-personality or of any other paradigm is an impossible goal, which, because it is also an assumption, invalidates the procedures of the stylisticians before they begin, dooming them to successes that are meaningless because they were so easy.[2]

Even if we have to accept the curious logic of this passage on faith—I can think of at least one massive and quite significantly related counter-example—the point being made seems fairly clear. Stylistics is impossible in principle, if we understand by stylistics what most stylisticians hope and would have us believe, namely that it is possible if not as yet feasible to correlate form and meaning in some regular, systematic, and ultimately mechanical fashion. And thus the argument which Fish proposes would be crucial indeed, for he presents himself as the Gödel of stylistics whose limitative theorem will put an end to something like Hilbert's folly—that was my counter-example now turned analogy. Roughly and briefly, there can be no algorithm for stylistics and, by extension, none for any mode of interpretation adequate to literature.

I would take this analogy to the theory of formal systems quite seriously, though not quite literally, but seriously enough to suggest that it informs the entire issue which I take to be the nature of critical argument, the issue of whether it be some kind of proof or some kind of persuasion. For reasons of strategy, my guest and host cannot fully acknowledge the analogy which has to be handled with care, for he can hardly admit wishing to provide a proof against proof, nor can he even press it too hard without losing its force. Here the art is suggestion. And thus Fish can easily destroy the analogy, which would be mine literally, by simply denying it, even though meant to represent his rhetoric not to repeat it, since that very attempt seems to be the most serious mistake. One I cannot help but seem to commit and worse to defend, however perversely, unless it were even more perverse of me to just seem or just act so.

If Fish does not or cannot provide a proof against the possibility of any proof for the interpretation of literary texts, he tries to persuade us that such a project is impossible. And at the heart of this persuasion is the conviction that such proof is artificial rather than natural, and dangerously perhaps treacherously inhumane. He also uses the word "perverse". Fish is a humanist arguing as if in defense of an endangered species. There is a sense of crisis in some of what he writes, a sense of mortal conflict between two cultures, a crucial struggle of men against machines, with stylistics serving as a fifth column—harboring those who act traitorously and subversively out of secret sympathy for the enemy: a digital computer. This may sound too melodramatic to be true, but a reading of Part I is quite revealing. The sweet syrup of existential phenomenology flows free in many a line, like the following:

> It would be a mistake to underestimate the desire to which it [a dream book] appeals: the desire for an instant and automatic interpretive procedure based on an inventory of fixed relationships between observable data and meanings, meanings which do not vary with context and which can be read out independently of the analyst or the observer who need only perform the operations specified by the "key". It is a desire as new as information theory and as old as the impulse to escape from the flux and variability of the human situation to the security and stability of a timeless formalism. (*PI,* p. 110)

There is hardly any of this emotional appeal in Part II, and I introduce it here only because it is important to recognize the necessity of such a grand style, for his persuasion must touch our own sense of humanity, our proud sense of difference. It is an appeal to heart and minds, which also plays on our fears, our threatened sense of that difference, our visceral response rallying in support of our wounded pride. We cannot fight the machine, that indifferent enemy, but we can turn against those of our own kind who have sold out to the opposition. Collaborators like Keyser, Freeman, and Epstein have to be rooted out, they will be our downfall, our decadence.

Before I get carried away with my own rhetoric, and thus fall prey to incoherence by trying to persuade against persuasion, an abrupt return to the problem of proof, as it appears in the piece that you have just heard. There is an argument with a definite logic, an argument which analyzes and criticizes the false logic of stylistics, and which then proposes a different logic to explain the relations between form and meaning, between description and interpretation, between literature and criticism.

The initial and essential charge against the stylisticians is simply, though devastating in its simplicity, that they do not know what they are doing. And further that if they did know, they could no longer do it. The theory and the practice of stylistic analysis are thereby inconsistent, though necessarily inconsistent. It could not be otherwise and is therefore incorrigible. It cannot be salvaged, saved, or redeemed, for it is "doomed"—a word that recurs—though doomed to success, but this kind of easy, inevitable success is obviously the worst kind of failure.

It would be difficult but no doubt rewarding to analyze the terms of this charge in detail, for it contains its own incoherence, which is a type of ambivalence playing back and forth on the values of knowledge and action, discovery and demonstration, when in fact those very differences are at stake in the argument. There is a most subtle manipulation of logical and practical principles (e.g., contradiction and incoherence) to elicit the sense that these two are one—it certainly cannot be proved logically, nor just shown practically. The art of demonstration is deft, almost deceitful. And we might be tempted to turn Fish against himself to say that he does not know what *he* is doing. But he, of course, never claims to know in that sense—but then what sense is that—in the sense that knowing is the representation of doing, its spectacle and spectator. To know is to do it and that is all there is to it!

The relation between description and interpretation is said to be arbitrary in every case; it is never demonstrated but always assumed (before the fact) or imposed (after the fact). The stylisticians present their case for the correlation between form and meaning in terms of an inductive argument: if that is the form then this is the meaning. And thus the observation (the discovery) and description (presentation) precede interpretation. Whether in fact any of the stylisticians actually proceed in this manner, in this order, can hardly be known; we do not have the experiment but only the results. This point, or rather the point of this difference has to be ignored or just neglected by Fish. He has to assume or at least pretend that the two are the same, for his own idea of knowledge as practical experience cannot tolerate such a split; he keeps insisting upon the need to close the gap between observation and interpretation, as if he were unable to imagine, except as some form of perversion, the desire to separate the two. And so it is that the stylisticians are accused of incoherence, for the order of discovery is really deductive rather than inductive: theory precedes fact, interpretation precedes observation or description, just as meaning precedes and determines form. But this recognition leads to a second charge of arbitrariness, because it then said that the interpretation *produces* the description, the theory *produces* the facts.

If we turn to the logic of form and meaning, the same pattern emerges. The relation appears to be conditional in either case. Induction: if this is the form, then that is the meaning. Deduction: if that is the meaning, then this is the form. But in both cases the relation is arbitrary because there are no constraints imposed. The form of the argument comes from the propositional logic, where the material truth of individual propositions, both the antecedent and the consequent, has to be known independently. Of course the propositional logic is known to be recursive (i.e. decidable). There is an algorithm, because truth-functions are mechanical. But an argument remains arbitrary without any substantial correlation among the propositions beyond their truth value. What is required to prove such a correlation is first a biconditional: this is the meaning if and only if that is the form, or this the form if and only if that is the meaning. And that biconditional has to be valid, for only such a form in the predicate logic could possibly represent an equivalence of predicates and thus an identity of subjects—analogous to the monism presented in Part I, "thus there is only style, or if you prefer, there is only meaning" (*PI,* p. 150, n. 39). But the predicate logic, even of the first order, is notoriously non-recursive (i.e. not decidable); for it there can be no algorithm.

And thus it seems as if there were no hope to establish a regular relation between form and meaning, as if all relations were arbitrary, being relations rather than functions, in the mathematical sense of function: a restricted relation of many to one or one to one. And if indeed the correlation is subject to synonymy (several forms and one meaning) and to ambiguity (one form and several meanings) of such high degree—but just how high is too high—then it seems, as so many of the counter examples and counter readings proposed by Fish are supposed to prove, that "the search for a paradigm of formal significances is a futile one" (*PI,* p. 120).

But all is not lost, for we not only can but actually do correlate form and meaning all the time, almost all the time that is, for some of us have tried but failed in an attempt to fix this fluid operation as a rigid connection, for we succeed only when we follow our inclination—doing what comes naturally—to read coherently and consequently, that is, consecutively from expectation to confirmation and new expectation. The model is hermeneutic, a phenomenology of reading which is true or perhaps valid, precisely because it refuses to claim truth, for such truth implies another model of reading which is false, that of the stylisticians who would separate form and meaning, in order to prove something true or false. They prove anything and everything, consequently nothing.

I have neither the time nor the desire to rehearse the objections that have long been raised against phenomenology and recently repeated in France. Fish surely knows them, and he clearly shows respect for the consistency of structuralism in a note to Part I:

> the structuralists dislodge man from his priviledged position as the originator of meanings, and locate meaning instead in the self-sufficient operation of a timeless formalism. The difference is that they do

> consciously what the stylisticians do inadvertently; they deliberately raise the implied antihumanism of other formalist methodologies to a principle. (*PI*, p. 139, n. 30)

Rather I am anxious to insist that Fish does well to insist upon the special value of his own particular method or manner. It is certainly more effective in most cases than that of the formalists (e.g., the stylisticians) or even the structuralists, and it is more effective for the very simple and very good reason that it is psychologically real, or at least more realistic psychologically than its competition, and finally realistic enough to recognize the need for some competition, some real opposition. This type of polemic has great appeal, because it appeals to our own sense of ourselves, our best sense of ourselves, or our sense of our best selves. It is flattering, for it suggests that we can do it after all—with a little help from our friend. And yet it is also threatening, or at least chastising, for it requires that we mend our ways and make amends by renouncing our false friends, the rigid formalists. There is drama in the demonstration, a good story with a few laughs and a few chills. Here is real human interest—what more could anyone want, especially in a classroom?

Another aspect of this realism is the appeal to our foreknowledge. His manner mobilizes what others would explain, and thus like a traditional grammar need only evoke or inspire. The formalist or broadly scientific pursuit of knowledge assumes a false idea of learning for the very purpose of explaining that learning. It proceeds as if we do not know what we know precisely in order to learn what we know, but then and thus to learn it as if from scratch. This is not only difficult but also unnatural, and the analogy to the computer is suggestive to that extent. We are not machines, but if we imagine ourselves as machines we might learn how and why we are not. This program will never be popular; it seems so perverse. It is much easier to soothe our fears that we may be just machines after all by refusing even to pretend. And it is safer not to play at being both actor and spectator at the risk of losing identity through strange fascination with impossible roles.

Actually I hold no brief for the stylisticians, and I am certainly not prepared to defend their readings against Fish, when his are almost always more interesting and much more convincing. His friendly persuasion works on all of us. And some may simply wish to conclude by saying, in echo of his own words about the structuralists, (*PI*, p. 139, n. 30) that one may disagree with the assumptions impelling his enterprise, but one cannot accuse him of being unaware of those assumptions, and thereby granting that because he is fully consistent, unlike the others, you have to accept or to reject his position on the basis of those fundamental assumptions. It would thus seem as if we finally were faced with an irreducible and inevitable choice: either Fish or his foes. And we then would simply have to decide, unless that forced option were in and of itself an assumption both hidden and false, and we could rather decide against any simple decision, on the grounds that such an option is neither exclusive nor exhaustive. The case to be made is that in his attempt to force the issue about the possibility of proof in literary criticism, Fish has actually adopted an algorithm of his own, a different type of algorithm, a higher but no better type which operates the same way at a different level. His is a second-order, meta-critical algorithm providing a decision procedure for criticism rather than literature. And this is what gives that cloying effect to his story and style—good against evil in a modern morality play. Some of us are more demanding, though few perverse enough to require an argument for mortality and rigidity against vitality and flexibility.

The realism fails at this point of reflection, as the argument lapses, almost collapses, into the belief, which is more like faith, that proof in criticism has to be either mechanical or rhetorical, and further that such a difference must be easy to grasp however difficult to accept. The mistake is to confuse contrary and contradictory by refusing to distinguish *all* and *some,* which belong to the predicate logic. Once the range of proof has been reduced to axiomatics, it becomes absurd to believe that anyone could expect to devise such a method of proof for an empirical subject, since it is then enough to know just the meaning of algorithm to recognize the absurdity, no less than the impossibility. Both the methodology and the psychology are thus implausible when taken literally, but they are still implausible when taken otherwise, for what could be more literal than an algorithm? To allow a difference of degree in proof is to abandon the model of a rigorously deductive system and to settle for the most probable, though such a concession can hardly come as a defeat or even as a surprise, except perhaps to those with great expectations. Fish must have known and felt some of that temptation which he would now spurn. Most of us can give up algorithms, without any loss, without any qualms, but we do need proof, some kind of proof to be sure. This residual demand for proof seems to confound and confuse those like Fish who show a preference for all or nothing. And yet it is just plain silly to require that proof be axiomatic—in the strictest sense, algorithmic—or not be proof at all, for there could then be no proof in any empirical science. That kind of proof is rigorous indeed, but in this context simply ridiculous. Not even elementary arithmetic can be proved in that way.

There is often a point in Socratic dialogue where the exchange fails, because one of the parties just refuses to go on, either opting out or flouting the logic of consequence. Socrates is then helpless; his appeal to reason has been rejected. And Fish seems to imagine himself in such a predicament, as he seems to expect and even to accept such an irreducible opposition from the stylisticians. They will never change but still pursue their impossible goal, to know what cannot be known, or not known in that form of knowledge, but known and even familiar to those who are willing, being wise enough, to realize that such desire for the impossible is the only real obstacle to our having the possible. And in these terms opposition becomes incomprehensible, completely arbitrary and yet somehow necessary. But it has to appear perverse, willfully and infinitely negative, only because all differences are reduced to oppositions, when and where to understand is normally to agree. There is good reason to disagree at this very point and to argue against Fish by resisting his attempt to restrict our choice. To do this we have to break out of the double bind which would keep us from commenting on his message without having to contradict it. The force of his argument is to force us to decide on his terms, either for or against, but agreement under such conditions could only be weak or false.

By way of conclusion, I would simply suggest that most of us are probably convinced that the logic of interpretation for literature is too complex to be decided mechanically. And we are quite happy that Fish should provide evidence to support that conviction, evidence of the type found in phenomenology, even though we may not be completely satisfied. It is not from ingratitude nor from perversity that we require more than evidence, that we ask for a theory. Fish might then reply, in echo of the later Wittgenstein: But there simply cannot be any such theory, and if you could only understand *that,* you would be satisfied with the evidence. Many were not satisfied with the original response, and some were even infuriated by what they took to be an insidious anti-intellectualism, a dogmatic defeatism, which was really skepticism. However unreasonable it may seem, there are those who will not be satisfied with less than proof that interpretations cannot be proved in some way, which would at least require a better definition of terms. Though well-disposed to Fish, they are not content with his persuasion, for they continue to insist that evidence is not theory, any more than meter reading is physics, any more than text reading is poetics. This is simply and finally to insist upon the difference between describing our performance and explaining our competence for the interpretation of literature, because that very difference is essential to maintain, even if we were eventually to prove that Fish was right after all. And he could well be right in his critical persuasion, though without any crucial reason to make that difference.

SUNY-Binghamton

NOTES

1 Fish has an idea of language consistent with his idea of literature. In a piece to appear in *Critical Inquiry,* he mounts an attack on the very principle of meaning usually attributed to Frege and generally assumed in linguistics.

2 "What Is Stylistics and Why Are They Saying Such Terrible Things About It? (Part I)," in *Approaches to Aesthetics,* ed. S. Chatman (New York, Columbia Univ. Press, 1973), pp. 109-52. (Hereafter referred to as *PI.*)

e
a
b
c

Decentering the Image: The "Project" of "American" Poetics?

Joseph N. Riddel

> Our debt to tradition through
> reading and conversation is so
> massive, our protest or private
> additions so rare and insignificant . . .
> that, in a large sense, one would
> say there is no pure originality.
> All minds quote. Old and new
> make the warp and woof of
> every moment. There is no thread
> that is not a twist of these
> two strands.
>
> —Ralph Waldo Emerson

> Everything we do must be a repetition
> of the past with a difference.
>
> —William Carlos Williams

> The whole of great art is a struggle for communication. . . . And this communication is not a levelling, it is not an elimination of differences. It is a recognition of differences. . . .
>
> —Ezra Pound

I

I begin by putting the question in quotation marks. "American literature" is an oxymoron — a notion of the belated original, of the immaculate opening of an old closure. "American literature" has always been inscribed in such a questioning parenthesis, because its dream of "making it new," of realizing itself originally, begins with the contradiction inherent in the notion of original or creative "literature," or an original secondariness. What is called the modern, and "American literature" has always been "modern"—that is, inscribed as both an end and a beginning between two notions of history—is always an "event" that is logically anterior yet historically posterior to that literature we call traditional or classical. "American literature" has always played in the paradoxical margins of the "new." One has only to remark the double sense of "tradition" that obsesses our modernist experimenters, the makers of the modern Image, to understand the contradiction Paul de Man finds in the privileged notion of the "modern." To "make it new" means in one sense (e.g., T. S. Eliot's) to supplement the tradition, to add something to an already completed whole; but it also means to repeat the moment of some pure origin that has been obscured by history's lengthened shadow, and hence to re-write the whole. "American literature," we might say, is a search which repeatedly suspends the dream of literature, the dream of totalization, of poetic closure. In this, of course, it simply makes explicit, by repetition, the subversive element in all literature, the "double sense" contained in every "sense of an ending." Once achieved, The Great American Novel would be the end of "American literature"; that is why we have so many of them, and why it is always "to be written."

William Carlos Williams's long poem *Paterson* puts the question of the "American" crisis most directly: how can a new beginning be original? "How to begin to find a shape—to begin to begin again, / turning the inside out: to find one phrase that will / lie married beside another for delight?" In its context this question leads directly to a quotation, a statement once made by the British poet George Barker: *"American poetry is a very easy subject to discuss for the simple reason that it does not exist."* It is always situated in a borrowed language, and in a tradition that, as Emerson saw, would not close. To "exist," an American poetry would have to write that closure, and repeat an opening that had already always begun. In Emerson's sense, the poet of the present must be the genius: "Next to the originator of a good sentence is the first quoter of it . . . there are great ways of borrowing. Genius borrows nobly." Williams and his poem compose one figure, one more repetition, in a line of so-called American Adamic poets, running, let us say for historical convenience, from Emerson's call for a purely American idiom to Olson's announcement of the forward thrust of "Projective Verse." This is a somewhat arbitrary line, not a "history" at all, but a metaphor for all the new beginnings that dot the "development" of an "American poetry" which does not yet exist.

Indeed, we might explore one sequence of those repetitions, where the historical possibility of an unbroken, continuous development does seem present, as the measure of the "project." I am referring to what literary history calls the "Imagist movement," obviously an international rather than an American revolution, but a movement nevertheless closely tied to Emerson. For Imagism led successively to movements with counter-names—Vorticism, Objectivism, even Objectism—and to in-mixtures with continental movements like Dada, Surrealism, and Cubism. From Emerson to Olson, there is not a straight line but a movement of appropriations, of decenterings, of repetitions that manage to keep the possibility of an "American" poetry open. That possibility is perhaps most vividly inscribed in the wonderful figure by which Olson defines the American: "We are the last 'first' people."[1]

"I take SPACE," Olson writes in *Call Me Ishmael,* "to be the central fact to man born in America, from Folsom cave to now" (*CMI,* p. 11). Space, he says, is "prime," is of the beginning; it is an origin which "history" necessarily erases and cannot recall, except in its utopian fiction of perfection. But for Olson, space is neither absence nor plenitude. It is original homelessness, or restlessness (Hegelian?), of the self which awakes to itself as already bound in the other, in geo-graphy. Space is what was violated in the "Original Act . . . the First Murder." For Melville, as Olson puts it, Shame takes precedence "to any Eden." Shame is "of Prime." In the beginning was the act, and in the knowledge of that act the "concord of Space . . . was curdled" (*CMI,* p. 83). Yet, the Olson/Melville myth is not a teleological myth of *felix culpa*, of an original Unity violated and a redemption tentatively promised. Shame already preceded Eden. What was shattered with the First Murder was the "concord" of Space, original difference. In the "Original Act," space was displaced as history, the hierarchical and authoritarian history of the West, logocentrism. Man arrogated to himself centrality or priority, of which Emerson's central man is a last, late repetition.

For Olson, man's original state was always already Shame, the condition of need. Man is a secondary condition, prefigured as the wanderer who has always repeated the primordial "First Murder," itself a figural event inscribed in the moment of all writing. As Olson says, the "tale of the Great Tower [of Babel] is as ultimate a legend as the Flood, Eden, Adam" (*CMI,* p. 96). In the beginning was random distribution, space as difference. Man is an "outrider," a wanderer, in space; his first knowledge is of himself as other. His first need is for community, communication; for the (original) writer is the "figure of outward" or "figure of forward." Man is forever deprived of his sources, is never central. So that man's belated appropriation of the center, which Olson identifies with humanism, lies in the very origins of metaphysics and radiates through the literature of the West, particularly in its preoccupation with "narrative."

For Olson, Melville's crisis, realized both thematically and psychologically in his radical and obsessive questioning of narrative, repeats the structure of "mythic consciousness": he "agonized over paternity" and "demanded to know the father" (*CMI,* p. 82), leading him to a displacement of the "father" that makes problematic his whole canon. His mythopoeic imagination lured him toward an origin that was originally violated. The author/writer is originally a foundling. And Olson sees Melville's late capitulation to Christianity as coincidental with his refusal to write, his abandonment of a narrative that was directed against the history of narrative. Melville reembraced the "white guilt" and a "promise of a future life" (*CMI,* pp. 92, 100), but this false return to a symbolic father stifled the "myth power" and with it the guilt implicated in writing, since writing *is* murder, the "First Murder," the displacement of the father and the projection of "space." This "First Murder," then, is not an event from which everything following derives, but the sign of an originally impure origin. It is, in Olson's figures, irreducibly a scene of writing, a beginning without origin.

Call Me Ishmael is the first of Olson's manifestoes of a new writing that would repeat, yet be different from, a first writing, considering that the very notion of a first writing can only be represented in writing. His essay "Projective Verse" is a second. In the history of modern poetry, he once speculated, the year 1950 would align with the year 1910, to bracket Modernism. The advent of "Projective Verse" would complete and supplement the experiments of Imagism, and begin again the invention of poetry. Olson's "project," like Melville's, goes back to come forward, repeating and displacing the Image, repeating the succession of openings and closings that mark the spatial history of cultures, of cities, and thus of writing. Hence Olson's interest in a non-phonetic writing, in what preceded logocentrism. Hence his reading of Melville's double career: of writing as a murder of the father, and the guilt that led to silence, Melville's late capitulation to the "promise of a future life" or a return to the father.

Melville goes back, as Olson says, behind the great Hellenic elevation of the logos in order to know "the great deed and misdeed of primitive time" (*CMI,* p. 85). He is a "Beginner—and interested in beginnings. Melville had a way of reading back through time until he got history pushed back so far he turned time into space" (*CMI,* p. 14). For Olson, this origin is/was multiple, a chaos, and not an origin at all. To go back is not to seize the origin, to recuperate some paradisal space, but to begin again the "deed and misdeed" signified by writing. Olson's new beginning rejects (figuratively) everything that lay between Homer's writing and Melville's.[2] That is, it rejects (or at least puts in question) representation, humanism, and history. What Olson comes to call projective (and also con-jectural, in the sense of throwing together) writing would re-inscribe a spatial doubleness into the linearity or narrativity of Western literature, thus re-marking the problematics of representation which Olson feels has been silently suppressed with the appropriations of Homer (and mythic consciousness) by the humanist literatures of the "tradition." Homer and Melville, then, bracket the epoch of humanism; they are both inside and outside the "history" their art opens and closes. Olson's Melville, as he suggests in his *Mayan Letters,* repeats Homer's deconstruction of Mediterreanean myth with his own deconstruction of the Pacific myth. Melville writes an end to humanism, to the Emersonian dream of the "central man," just as Homer writes an end to the myth of wandering (writing) and makes possible, if not inevitable, the era of the hero, of return and redemption (the closed circle of representation).

It must be the project of a post-modern poetry, says Olson, to repeat the "figure of outward," to go back behind Homer in order to come forward beyond Melville and Romanticism, and thus to open up once more the possibility of generative repetition. To be post-historical, however, is an impossible possibility. Original writing repeats the violent moment that marks the rupture between pre-history and history, i.e., the space or scene of writing itself, and reveals the artifice of those historical categories. Olson/Melville wants to "go back" to (to repeat) the founding of prehistorical cities, where the invention of writing marks the selection that is "culture," an origin that is never pure and simple. To "go back" to these places is to repeat and reappropriate their act of first writing, an archeological adventure that is also archeo-clastic, since the writer does not reappropriate the old signs (as in grave robbing) so much as he repeats the violence of opening a site. He therefore goes for the center, as into a pyramid (*CMI,* p. 99), not to retrieve a meaning lost or buried in past forms, but to effect a new writing, a pro-jecting and con- jecturing of old signs that is the "beginning" of writing. Olson gives us the figure of the poet, in Gilles Deleuze's phrase, as Egyptologist, who descends into the crypts in order to read the secret language of hieroglyphs.[3] The "archeologist of morning" (it is the metaphorical title posthumously given to Olson's collected shorter poems) dismantles the myth of origins, only to construct another, a fiction of impure origins. He produces, in Deleuze's terms, a "literary machine," an "anti- logos." Olson reads out of Melville's writing, his worrying over the father/center, the whole history of Imagism and the need for a "Projective Verse" as the next radical decentering of "modernism."

Olson, of course, is re-writing a particular chapter of "American" literature, or better, displacing that chapter from its position as the conclusion, the final repetition, in the history of Western literature, to the position of yet another "beginning." He needs to displace the origins of an "American" literature from Emersonian logocentrism to an even more original notion of beginning, and this involves him in nothing less than re-writing or doubling the concepts of "beginning" and "re-presentation," that is, erasing them.[4] Olson's appeal to Melville's "mythopoeic" imagination may appear to compromise his entire project, particularly if one traces the notion of mythopoeisis to its Jungian formulations, as Olson seems elsewhere to do. But in Olson the mythopoeic is never inscribed in the power of some arche-type, some universal center, that governs the continuity between origin and image. On the contrary, the site of the mythopoeic is a place of violence, of the great "deed and mis-deed" which underscores the need for creative discontinuity. Olson re-writes, as it were, the genealogical fable of Western literature.[5]

Olson's privileged text is *Moby Dick,* a protean work for anyone ready to extend Olson's arguments to a commentary on the "scene of writing."[6] Had he extended his inquiry to *Pierre,* however, he might have viewed Olson's worrying over the "father," and the genealogical/representational metaphor and the question of original writing, indeed of the possibility of "American" literature, as even more radical and problematical than *Call Me Ishmael* admits. I will restrict my commentary here to one brief part of that novel, which has been the subject of a most brilliant essay by Edgar Dryden, precisely on this same problem; of the entanglement of the metaphors of genealogy and representation in an American novelist's efforts to articulate his tainted originality.[7] There is a chapter in *Pierre* entitled "Young America in Literature" where Melville deals satirically with the prevailing notion that a young country might begin again, in all innocence, to produce an art, at once nationalistic and universal, out of something as spontaneous as "poetic nature." The youthful Pierre had written a number of things, juvenilia, marked by the "pervading symmetry of his general style," but he has not composed a "mature" work nor anything like a "book." When he finally decides to become a writer in seriousness, he finds a pair of editors who have recently switched professions, from tailoring to publishing, and who arrange for him to produce his first book, in the "Library form," as they put it. What they project for Pierre is a canon, but cut to the whole cloth, made on the "Sample of a coat."

If the satire is directed at anything other than Emerson and his original quoting or appropriations of Carlyle, it is surely a reminder that writing has always been implicated in a series of conventions and complications which preclude the thinking of its primal origin in the "poetic nature." Pierre discovers the project of his Collected Works to involve the "Library Form: an Illustrated Edition" and a whole series of productive constraints and economic demands that make the notion of author fairly anonymous. Pierre finds himself embroiled in an economy of production where there is always a remainder; he is an author, literally, without a distinct "signature."

The theme is entangled with Pierre's obsessive questioning of his identity and, as Dryden shows, is complicated throughout by the question of his name. (Whether, indeed, he takes his proper name from a living or dead rock, from the sacred origin of the Bible and its living ground or a dead nature.) Publishers repeatedly ask him for a "biography" which he cannot deliver, reminding us, perhaps, that Emerson had always claimed that history is "biography"—the "lengthened shadow of a man," in Eliot's acid phrase. Writing, Pierre discovers, implicates him in the worldly economy of textuality. The author becomes a "sort of publisher"; "the age of authors [is] passing," Pierre declares. Young America usurps the innocent's dream of originality, of radical innocence, and implicates its authors in a chain of fraternal production, a capitalist enterprise of textual production that abolishes the romantic dream of the "author" and subordinates his originality to the collective designs of the "tailor." From this appropriation of his innocence Pierre draws a bitter lesson: "Youth must wholly quit, then, the quarry, for awhile, and not only go forth, and get tools to use in the quarry, but must go and thoroughly study architecture." He must give up Nature and study craft, but when he turns to method, to architecture, he must learn another ironic lesson, that architecture reveals the artifice of the construction of origins. Once again, Pierre finds the self to be defined by an artificially constructed house. His identity, as author, is not naturally derived, nor is it singular: "Never was a child born of one parent."

Still later, when Pierre attempts his first "mature" or "comprehensive work," he must come to terms with this democratic economy of production, in which there is not one but many authors of every text. Only now he must contemplate "originality" in terms of his implication in both a paternal and fraternal nexus of production: "most grand productions of the best human intellects ever are built round a circle, as atolls (i.e. the primitive coral islets which, raising themselves in the depths of profoundest seas, rise funnel-like to the surface . . .)"; a "book," then, composed out of "reading," of heterogenous materials acquired by a "random but lynx-eyed mind, in the course of . . . multifarious, incidental, bibliographic encounterings." Pierre "would climb Parnassus with a pile of folios on his back"; he would layer his book out of the compilations of other books, so that no master book might command his production, or be represented in it as master, since "all existing great works must be federated in the fancy." Federal production not only abolishes the notion of author but disturbs the logocentric notion of an orderly movement between origin and image. As several commentators on this remarkable chapter of the novel have observed, none more convincingly than Dryden, any idea of the natural origin of art is suspended.

At the end of a series of reflections, which began in the figure of the "book" as an "atoll," or the sedimentation of skeletal forms into the shape of a mountain, the narrator elaborates yet another figure of the book, this time as the exterior of the "soul" of man, cast in the architectural shape of the pyramid, itself a composition of hetereogeneous elements, a tomb that is produced to house the body of the King, the "mummy [which] lies buried in cloth on cloth." The explorer or reader of the pyramid or book seeks its center, moving through and re-moving layer upon layer, seeking the "unlayered substance." But a stratified reading does not uncover the unstratified. The "central room," and I will not repeat the whole of this famous passage, is empty, "no body is there!" Neither the King nor the author. The pyramid, which Melville elsewhere notes is made on the model of natural mountains, represents instead the "atoll." Neither nature nor its representation is anything more than a representation; neither house their origin. Neither atoll nor pyramid is natural. The "book," then, is not a representation of nature, but a text, the texture of a representation, of nature as always already an architecture, a technic, a text, a construct. And it is interesting that in the one paragraph separating these opposing yet complementary metaphors of the "book" (as circle upon circle, as atoll) and the "sarcophagus," Melville poses the figure of the traveler in Switzerland who can never see, let alone achieve, the peak of his Alps. The traveler comes "at last to gain his Mont Blanc" only by paying a severe price, a "tithe" he cannot calculate. The mountain top (itself a figure of remote, inaccessible origins, and hence unimageable, as Eugenio Donato has revealed in a recent essay[9]) is as absent as the King in the pyramid. And "far over the invisible Atlantic, the Rocky Mountains and the Andes are yet unbeheld." It is just this natural origin that is never beheld, except in a belated image that can never represent it fully but can only stand for its absence, like a textual construct.

So American literature begins, not by inventing or recuperating an authentic origin, but by repeating in radical innocence the double vision of Romanticism, a Romanticism obscured, as Paul de Man has shown, in those idealized readings of its recuperation of nature, of immediacy.[10] In Wallace Stevens's figure, the poem has always already taken the place of a mountain. The problematic that de Man and Donato find in the Romantic Image—that the image not only signifies the murder of the "natural object" but makes unthinkable any natural origin—lies at the very heart of the question of "beginnings" which "American literature" poses to itself: that it can never, in the language of *Pierre,* take an "overtopping view of these Alps," but must build a machine to bridge the abyss its questioning repeatedly opens up.

II

I turn now to one of those curious paradoxes of literary history: to a text which may be said to tie together a movement of "American poetics" from Emerson through Pound to Charles Olson. It is also a text inscribed in the discontinuity of that movement: a text composed only as lecture notes by its author, but revised and published in a collection of essays by the poet (Ezra Pound) who made the most effective use of it and whose own poetry turns upon the double sense of what it elaborates. The text is Ernest Fenollosa's (non-)essay "The Chinese Written Character as a Medium for Poetry."[11] Its centrality to the modernist experiment is all the more illuminating because of what Hugh Kenner has called its "history of interesting mistakes."[12]

In *The Pound Era,* Kenner submits the essay to extensive examination, but he focuses on two crucial aspects of its argument: (1) Fenollosa's discovery in the Chinese written character of a vital relation between language and reality, or between culture and nature; and (2) Fenollosa's curiously limited understanding of Chinese writing, particularly his assumption that Chinese writing is non-phonetic. Fenollosa had gone to Japan to teach philosophy; a student of Hegel and Emerson but not a linguist, he remained there many years seeking the reunion of two cultures. His interpretation of Chinese writing is refracted through Transcendentalism: "A true noun," he writes, "does not exist in nature," nor does a "true verb." Language, like nature, is therefore only apparently marked by the grammar of the logos, by dualism. Nature is not made up of things (nouns) and motions (verbs), but of things which move and a motion which is only that of moving things. Similarly, Chinese language is not constituted by "parts" of speech with discrete functions. Fenollosa opposes to this the abstract structure of Western grammar, which legislates the priority of subject to object and heightens the arbitrary relation between signs and facts, or abstractions and concretions. (The terminology, of course, is riddled with problems, since facts and concretions here would be, in effect, signifieds.)

Thus Fenollosa both identifies what modern linguistics has recognized as the irreducible doubleness of the sign (accentuated by the mark of a written language and repressed in spoken language) and interprets Chinese writing as a primordial script that preceded the dualisms of the West as they are manifest in phonetic writing. To put it in terms which would perplex a contemporary philosopher of language, Fenollosa gives nonphonetic writing the status of primordiality and associates phonetic writing with secondariness and abstraction. The neo-Hegelian rewrites not only Aristotle, but Hegel. The Chinese written character reminds Fenollosa of what Emerson had always claimed nature to be: vital and thus verbal. All words were originally charged with transitive power. Western nominalization, its elevation of the subject, was for Fenollosa a rupture of language from its natural origins. Most interestingly, in Fenollosa's writing of a history of language's westering and fall, its loss of primordial (and natural) power, his interpretation locates itself in the full authority of Transcendental idealism, for which Nature is both God and grammar.

"Things," Fenollosa writes, "are only the terminal points, or rather the meeting points of actions." Nouns are both formal and transitive; all language is verbal, thus temporalizing, though it temporalizes in the sense of unfolding or explicating. Form and power are one in nature, as Emerson had argued. Fenollosa remarks that our tendency to isolate either the motion or the location (verb or noun) reveals the limit of conceptuality already built into Western grammatology. But he conceives of an original language which transcended that limit, not in its adequation with nature but in its own graphic naturalness. Ideogrammic writing, he claims, is neither purely pictorial nor purely abstract, neither a representation nor an arbitary substitution, but the very law of nature itself. Like a hieroglyph—and unlike others, he does not distinguish between ideographic and hieroglypic writing—it is not an "arbitrary symbol," not a sign that displaces what it signifies, but a "vivid shorthand picture of the operations of Nature," a synecdoche. The Western degradation of writing beneath speech does not trouble Fenollosa. In its Orient, language was at once speech and writing, the power and the law folded in one. As "vivid shorthand," at once visual and nonrepresentational, this writing is "close" to, yet not identical with, nature. It is the truth of nature, then, its idea as action. Here he gives a certain, unique twist to Hegel. Language is the becoming of nature, nature as becoming. But the grammar of nature—which as we will see has no grammar—excludes the negative. In Chinese writing, strangely, Fenollosa finds the ever-presence of becoming, a writing which bears on its face the entire history of presence.

The double sense of his theory shows up in Kenner's analysis of Fenollosa's "misinterpretation": the view that all Chinese writing is nonphonetic. According to Kenner, that is a common mistake of Western scholars who tend to study only a limited number of radicals. And Kenner offers a corrective, while praising Fenollosa's discovery of the ground "truth" that relates natural language and nature: the continuity of "process." Fenollosa "needed to suppose," Kenner writes, "that all ideograms followed one principle so that by gazing into them as into living monads he could expand, miraculously concentrated, the Emersonian organicism he had brought to Tokyo from Cambridge."[13]

(Parenthetically, I should note here that Kenner never questions the adequacy of the organic metaphor, nor its Emersonian authority. A deconstruction of Emerson's theory of language might reveal, indeed, that nature is always thought on the model of language rather than the reverse. If we heed the wisdom of Harold Bloom's view, that "Deconstructing Emerson is . . . impossible, since no discourse ever has been so overtly aware of its own status as rhetoricity,"[14] then we have to conclude that nature arises, indeed originates, only in a text. But for Bloom, rhetoric remains primarily speech, located or oriented in the trope of will, in the power of a "psyche" or a subject, which though irreducibly a trope, originates by and in its form. Kenner, on the other hand, never feels the need to question either the metaphor of natural origin or the problematical notion of an Image through which is translated, with exactness and clarity, the otherwise unseen laws of nature, an Image simultaneously representational and presentational. If Emerson cannot be deconstructed, however, it is nonetheless possible to show that nowhere in his writing can Nature, or God, or Unity, appear outside a linguistic chain. One brief example: in the early essay *Nature,* the chapter on "Language" appears as the third stage of a circular or dialectical movement, translating nature as commodity into Idealism, a circuit that Spirit must traverse to fulfill itself, yet a circuit that is itself Spirit. And, the stage of language repeats and completes the entire circuit: "1. Words are signs of natural facts"; "2. Particular natural facts are symbols of particular spiritual facts"; "3. Nature is the symbol of spirit." There is no distinction between signs and symbols. There is a continuity between origin and difference, one and many, idea and representation: "A Fact is the end or last issue of spirit." In Derrida's terms, Emerson's siting of language, and Kenner's use of it to explain the Fenollosa/Pound derivation of ideographic precision, is "pneumatological" and not grammatological:[15] "material facts" must preserve an "exact relation to their first origin," the "substantial thoughts of the Creator." No deconstruction of Emerson is necessary to reveal that any importation of the Emersonian circle to the Orient is a doubled dream of recuperation by supplementation. If Fenollosa needed to recover the power lost when the West forfeited Eastern graphism, his reparation of the circle necessitates the importation of idealism, of language as spirit and breath, of the soul back into the abstract body, as Leibniz saw it, of the Chinese written character, a restoration of the organic roots to the body of the radical. Like Hegel, Fenollosa celebrates the triumph of the very Western language that has divided up Eastern nature, a nature whose totality, we have seen, is only thinkable as an organic and logocentric circle.)

As a "shorthand" picture, Fenollosa's radical would at first appear to be a privileged representation. Yet he (and Pound) insist on calling it "presentational" and productive. It is, therefore, an interpretation, productive of equations, of laws that govern culture's relation to nature. Indeed, it signifies the orderly transformation from nature to culture. As a "shorthand" system, language is a figuration of force which produces and maintains a field of differences. Or like a transistor in an electrical circuit, it signifies the order of a discontinuous repetition. Pound, in a footnote to the essay, and again in his Vorticist book, *Gaudier-Brzeska,* calls both Image and Ideogram the "language of exploration" or "interpretative metaphor" and employs the metaphors of electrical circuits and cinemato*graphic* projection to exemplify the new organicism. Writing, then, occupies a space of origin (of complex rather than simple origin) which maintains differences by producing or multiplying them. This nature (this grammar) will not close. Its unity is not simple, is never a non-difference.

Fenollosa's nature is a grid or graph that inscribes only "objective lines of relations." and "relations are more real and more important than the things which they relate." The forces of nature function as resistances; they are unequivocal; they branch rather than reunite, producing a kind of doubling or disseminating effect that refuses any return to univocity. And Fenollosa employs a metaphor which will become familiar in modern poetry—the concept of potentiality held within the seed of an acorn. The seed, however, is a figure for culture, for cultivation, for the "city." Thus Fenollosa blindly collapses culture and nature into one organic figure: the city is a body, like the ideographic sign, of spirit. Systems of nerves, he argues, grow like a culture, like roadways connecting towns, ports, and so on. Every system is literally a radical, and thus rooted in what Fenollosa calls an "identity of structure." "Had the world not been full of homologies, sympathies, and identities," he says, "thought would have been starved and language chained to the obvious." "Thought" precedes language, which expresses or exteriorizes that true origin, natural law. But the circularity of Fenollosa's argument undoes itself. Rather than uncovering the unity of ancient roots, it reveals a branching of the origin. If as Fenollosa argues, "Nature has no grammar," then nature cannot be thought in terms of unity. We recall Nietzsche's identification of God and grammar in *Twilight of the Idols:* "I fear we are not getting rid of God because we still believe in grammar."

Fenollosa employs still another problematic metaphor of the "history" of language: that it develops through "quasi-geological strata," of metaphor upon metaphor, a geo-arche-ology. Nature is a kind of palimpsest. Moreover, nature is, as he says, a myth, the spatial interpretation (*aletheia*) of the invisible, the movement from invisible to visible. Thus, language explicates. But Fenollosa must preserve this appearance of nature from its death. A geological unlayering, an archeological excavation, would reveal, he argues, that the text of nature is grounded in a primordial life that sustains a continuity between original language and its historical repetitions. Thus the Chinese radicals, the "visible hieroglyphics," bear on their faces their whole "etymological history" while Western languages (characterized by the discontinuous representations of phonetic writing) have imposed upon our poets the need to "feel painfully back along the thread of our etymologies and piece together our diction."

On this point, the essay becomes aberrant. Ideograms are concrete, and thus natural symbols, yet abstract like Hegel's hieroglyphs, in that they are a "shorthand" of a nature which is a law. They are graphs, a shorthand, of nature's "clues." Thus Nature is a system, a structure; the "relation" of its "clues," the presence of "homologies" and "identities," affords man a "bridge" between the visible (or empirical) and the invisible (truth or logos). The ideogram and, by extension, an ideogrammic poetry, would be a "bridge" between visible and invisible, but only because the poem, or art, is a graph (interpretation) of nature's visible model. Language cannot properly have its origin in either the visible or invisible, in either nature or spirit. The ideogram as bridge has no foundation, but is itself the ground. It is therefore *radical* in two senses, of a root that will not return to its root, an originary force that is not, as such, original.

The modern reader of Hegel—that is to say, of Derrida's readings of Hegel—cannot help remarking that Fenollosa's privileging of the "visible hieroglyphics" of Chinese writing against the secondary and arbitrary signs of phonetic writing, and hence his privileging of the poetry over philosophy, is something more than a simple misreading of Hegel—Hegel Emersonized, as it were. In a sense one might even say that this version of Emerson anticipates Heidegger, both in its treatment of poetry as the language of unconcealment and in its disruption of the thinking of a metaphysics it seems everywhere to confirm. Derrida himself suggests that it was modern literature, before even the analytics of philosophy or science, which began the systematic dislocation or decentering of the "founding categories" of metaphysics, the representational order speech/writing. As Kenner points out, Fenollosa seems to ignore the fact that phonetic writing was never absolutely excluded from ideographic writing (though in the essay he does acknowledge some phonetic radicals). But as Derrida shows, the rebus-like effect of Oriental writing breaks or constellates the sign into an irreducible double which can never allow the unity of sound and mark. Thus a language "structurally dominated by the ideogram" gives "testimony of a powerful movement of civilization developing outside of all logocentrism," since this language can never presume to encounter "reality."[16] Fenollosa, however, celebrates the "graphic symbol" because it is not representational, but a "force." Yet he continues to think historically: Chinese language retains its primordial power, the power of direct, innocent observation, while Western language has grown "pale," losing contact with its natural origin, so that a recuperation of Chinese graphism will close a circle and complete a history. His fable of the origin of language as writing rather than speech employs the figure of its being primordially "verbal" rather than "nominal": "The sentence form was forced upon primitive man by nature." Strangely enough, this syntax is the order of causation. Yet, causation is figured as a discontinuity, the sentence not as complete thought but as the *"transference of power":* "The type of sentence in nature is a flash of lightening," a unit of redistributed force. The syntactical force of nature is open ended. Nothing returns to a subject. Process branches into a discontinuous play of forces.

At this point, what seems like an incoherent argument for the natural origin of language produces the possibility (or necessity) of a double reading: Kenner's or Derrida's. On the one hand, all the elements of organicism or logocentrism are there: in the notion of language as a "metaphoric advance," and poetry, particularly the "graphic symbol," as a "centre" throwing "about it a nimbus of meanings." Thus, the "graphic symbol" is presentational and interpretative at the same time, making the continuity between culture and nature, the origin of culture in nature. Kenner reads Pound's faith in the classical precisions of graphic language as an efficient archeology, a recuperation of primordial language or proper naming. Derrida, on the other hand, cites Pound and Fenollosa, in *De la Grammatologie,* because of their "irreducibly graphic poetics [which] was with that of Mallarmé, the first break in the most entrenched Western tradition." Like Nietzsche, he adds, they "at first destroyed and caused to vacillate the transcendental authority and dominant category of the *epistémè:* being."[17] If the "graphic symbol" is Fenollosa's "centre," then it is a non-centered non-centering center, always already multiple. And nature is not an agent, but already a play of forces, a constellated and constellating field.

Fenollosa's concluding example of the triumph of ideographic precision is the graph for the English sentence "The sun rises in the east." He explains it as follows: "The [ideograph of the] sun, shining, on one side, on the other the sign of the east, which is the sun entangled in the branches of a tree. And in the middle sign, the verb rise, we have further homology; the sun is above the horizon, but beyond the single upright line is the growing trunk-line of the tree sign" Derrida must have been illuminated by the very precision of this placement of Western metaphor, the "sun" as origin entangled in the branches of a tree, eclipsed in its origin, distributed across the branchings of a text which is its origin, the site of its appearance. Fenollosa would hardly have understood this unnatural and perverse reading.

III

What we call today the Imagist movement—and even Vorticism—is not a method deriving from Fenollosa's text, any more than it is the method of a single experimenter.[18] In fact, whether it can be called a method at all is questionable; and so far as it is the name for a historical group or movement, it bespeaks the heterogeneity of literary history. Nevertheless, Fenollosa's text was seminal for Pound, as it was not for other Imagists, but one cannot speak of its "influence" on his theory, and certainly not on his theory of the Image. Still, one can read Pound's Imagist theory through a text which, after all, was first published as an appendix to a collection of Pound's essays, edited with a few explanatory notes, in a manner that must have concealed its own accidental origin. For the essay itself is a Poundian reconstruction, out of Fenollosa's notes, and the accidents of its own "organic" form await the explanation of a textual editor. In his notes to the text, Pound transcribed Fenollosa's speculations into his own. He chose to emphasize their mutual discovery of "interpretative metaphor" in contrast to "ornamental metaphor," either metaphor as "analogy" or as symbolism—that is, interpretation which translates, carries over, displaces, transcribes; a metaphorics that disturbs the theory of metaphor. Pound's theory of the Image is not simply a postulate of form or style, but a theory of generative and dislocating force—in a sense, a theory of translation, or better, transcription. The Image, by which he means the poem as a condensation (Fenollosa's "shorthand" cypher), defines stylistic precision as an "objectification" which overthrows the *aporia* between two senses of figural language (or rhetoric), between trope as visual representation and trope as displacement, between form and force. In Pound's definitions, the Image (i.e., the whole Poem) is always a "node" or "cluster" of figures, a constellation of radical differences, and a transformative machine which represents a movement across these points of difference. The radical, the Image, is a "field"—in short, originarily a text.

The Image, Pound writes, may be defined as an "intellectual and emotional complex in an instant of time." And Pound confesses that he takes the word "complex" from a London psychiatrist and follower of Freud, Bernard Hart. As a "complex" the Image would suggest something like a Gestalt, according to Herbert Schneidau,[19] and would therefore constitute a kind of mapping (and thus a figural displacement) of its object. But the Image has no object as such. It displaces time (linearity and succession) into a figural space (a "moment of time"), producing a formal mirage (a *sens*). The unconscious has no time, nor any object. It is displaced as time, as consciousness, and thus as a movement of images. Time, therefore, does not represent, but is presented as the explicit (and explicatory) movement of language, its presencing/absencing. Time is a play of figure. The poem as Image, then, can only translate by constellating this play of images. Pound's psychological metaphor for the Image as "complex" anticipates the deconstruction of Freud's Unconscious as a term for presence or for non-difference, and the dreamwork as a *mise en scène* of writing. The "complex" is an Image of differences known only in the play of translations. The "complex" is translation and interpretation of symptoms, signs, and not of "experience." The Image is a layering of images, or other texts.

The well-publicized tenets of Imagism speak of the Poem as a "direct treatment of the 'thing,' whether subjective or objective," in a way that throws interpreters off the track, since it suggests a return to immediacy as objectivity. But "thing" is already in quotation marks, like Nietzsche's "Thing-in-itself," or already a figure of some "object," and what is "direct" in this definition is the "treatment," of signs or symptoms. The Image is curative, then, only in the sense of interpreting, of bringing to consciousness (as form, visibility) and throwing off. The force of writing disseminates by radical displacement, by condensation, staging, transcribing. Thus the tenet arguing for strict economy—to use no descriptive, ornamental, or unnecessary word—and the tenet rejecting metronomic repetition (set verse rhythm) for variations governed by the play of the "musical phrase," suspend both the notions of immediacy and mediation, and suggest a poetics that precedes the thinking of the play of presence and absence. Pound's Image recapitulates, by reproducing the primordial event of a writing without origin, of a writing at the origin.

Pound's own example of the characteristic Image poem speaks of superpositions, the gliding of one image over the other. But superpositioning, while suggesting a pure spatiality, must include the temporalizing play, the succession of images which repeat one another in their difference, repeat by weaving together or inscribing that which cannot be reduced to a singularity. That is why Kenner can interpret the little "Metro" poem as a repetition and condensation of Persephone's eternal return, literally of opening or blooming: "The apparition of these faces in the crowd; / Petals on a wet, black bough." "In a poem of this sort," Pound wrote, "one is trying to record the precise instant when a thing outward and objective transforms itself, or darts into a thing inward and subjective."[20] The "instant" is movement itself, caught in a complex of superimposed differences, of crossing lines of force. Superpositioning cannot escape successivity, the act of the second image displacing the first even as it carries forward the memory of that sign displaced, negated, repeated, and effaced. There is no perception here, certainly not of nature; the natural image originates in a mythic text.

In Pound's "Metro," the textural contrast of fallen petals on a background that once sustained them carries forward an "apparition," that is, a previous image or a trace that effaces itself. An image of falling or dying nature, which includes a living blooming nature, recapitulates an image of remembered presence or of presencing that includes its own death. The play of images is patternless outside of the textual field, the interpretation. That is, the textural weave, the projection of an "experience," is a remembered "perception" superscripted upon a mythic text of repetition. Pound discovered his modern Image of Persephone/Kore in an appropriate place: the Metro or Underground is a place of transversal, crossing, the translation of appearance/disappearance. The Image is a scene of writing, a figuration of its own condensation. One has only to recall Pound's own anecdote (in *Gaudier-Brzeska*) of the experience which triggered the poem (it was not really an experience in the "Metro" but a reflection of the significance of formalizing or rendering that already remembered moment). The poem went through several versions, or textual condensations, until the final Image becomes a map of the process of displacement and reinscription. If the poem re-tells the myth of Kore, or of *aletheia,* it renders it as a violence of writing. While the poem may be an Image of spring, of unconcealment, of blooming, it also is an Image of the "apparition," of the appearance of the sign/Image itself, the appearance of which, like Kore's face, inscribes its own death. For if the poem has anything at all in common with the Kore archetype—and I am by no means convinced that Kenner's insight is anything more than an arbitrary critical analogy—it is because Pound's text, like the "original" myth, is a graph of "memory," of remembering, and not a representation of nature's becoming.

More than two decades after his radical polemics on behalf of Imagism had produced its stylistic revolution, Pound recognized the problem of earlier Imagist definition to lie in the mimetic prejudice associated with the term "image," and he sought to reemphasize the temporality (the praxis) which Vorticist theory had featured: "The defect of earlier imagist propaganda was not in misstatement but in incomplete statement. The diluters took the handiest and easiest meaning, and thought only of the STATIONARY image. If you can't think of imagism or phanopoeia as including the moving image, you will have to make a really needless division of fixed image and praxis or action."[21] Pound's use of *phanopoeia* refers to a lexicon developed much earlier, which also includes the terms *melopoeia* and *logopoeia.*[22] These three terms, which correspond to the three tenets of Imagism, suggest the movement or play of images (*phanopoeia*), of sounds (*melopoeia*), and of meanings or ideas (*logopoeia*). The common property of each of these elements is movement or "play." In *phanopoeia,* the images are "thrown," not intended. The visual is reinscribed as a play of differences (that is, in writing) which decenters any imagistic representation. More significantly, Pound gives *phanopoeia,* the throwness or play of images over one another, a privilege over *melopoeia* and *logopoeia.* Like Fenollosa, therefore, he gives priority to the image as hieroglyphic writing, and thus to the graphic play opened up in the non-origin that is language.

On the other hand, although Pound repeats Fenollosa in attributing to nature the genesis of this play, he does not assume that nature governs the system of language it presumably sets in play. Like Nietzsche, he views nature as a field of irreducible energies, of conflicting forces. The poetic imagination, as in Nietzsche, is seminal—and Pound, at least in one place, follows Nietzsche in suggesting that the brain consists of seminal fluid from which images spurt like "ejaculations."[23] Like seeds these images lead a life independent of the source (the brain) which begets them. Divorced from the naturalism of the description, which Pound only halfway embraces since he is commenting on Remy de Gourmont's *Natural Philosophy of Love,* the metaphor subscribes to an origin that is already diacritical, like the two hemispheres of the brain. The origin was irreducibly a play of seminal differences. Thus graphic or image play is the primary language of this productive dynamic, but the images are not natural—they are neither exteriorizations of an interiority, nor representations. They *present* only their own play of energies. The "image," then, "is not an idea. It is a radiant node or cluster," a "Vortex," a form that resists any collapsing of differences into unity.

This freedom from the commanding origin, this play of originating forces, informs the modern long poem. The praxis of the moving image puts in question the idea of the unified or autotelic text, or the thinking of poetic closure. It also resists the possibility of a text commanded by any one of its elements: a controlling theme, a privileged point of view, authorial intentionality, image cluster, or central symbol. The possibility of the long poem opened up by the decentering of Imagism was, in fact, contrary to any New Critical holism that was derived from it. For example, Kenneth Burke (who is hardly a subscriber to such holisms) has employed the metaphor "qualitative progression" to account for the continuity between elements that were quantitatively or logically irreconciliable, suggesting that the long poem developed by a kind of inner dialectic in which similar residual qualities overcame heterogeneous quantities to move the poem toward totalization and closure.[24] Another Burkean term, "perspective by incongruity," offers a similar psychological and dialectical explanation of the linked analogies between otherwise incoherent or heterogeneous elements. The struggle to domesticate or acculturate *The Waste Land,* to make it "readable" and thus to shore "fragments" against our psychic ruins, becomes a model to interpret all those long poems, like *The Bridge* and *The Cantos.* The model of metaphysical conceit or Symbolist synaesthetics is called up to justify incongruity and fragmentariness as an inaugural movement that signifies the ultimate yoking and reconciliation of opposites, the poem's triumphant closure upon itself, its becoming an object, synecdoche of the universal One.

In an essay contemporary with *The Waste Land,* Eliot advocated what he called the "mythical method" as the way by which the modern writer, faced with the chaos of modern history, might find a "model" of order for his work to imitate, to repeat as a structural ground.[25] Lacking a coherent system of belief or a credible idea of order, the modern writer, he suggested, must either appropriate one from a past writing, as Joyce did in *Ulysses,* or fabricate his own system, as Yeats had in *A Vision.* In either case, the appropriated or fabricated system would serve as an a priori source of images, a privileged point of reference. This timeless fiction (i.e., a circle totalizing its images, themes, etc.) not only lends authority to the signs or images appropriated from it, but signifies the general form of mastery or totalization. Thus allusion, quotation, reference, and the like, reenact the gathering or regathering of the many into the one. The essay is a restatement of Eliot's idea, in "Tradition and the Individual Talent," of the "ideal order" of "existing monuments" which composes the "timeless" tradition—the "presence" of history repeatedly manifest in the body of artistic forms. The "mythical method," and its primary strategies—reference, citation, allusion, and quotation—confirm art as "timeless" repetition of the same, repetition as incorporation. That which governs this repetition is a logos, a logocenter or *spiritus mundi,* that appropriates language and speaks, in the poem, simultaneously of its presence as an absence. In Eliot's most striking metaphor, the "tradition" or "existing order" of art is always complete, and each new work alters it "if ever so slightly," therefore supplementing its completeness. The same must be claimed for every poem. Its incorporation, literally, of the fragments and archives of a previous art, incorporates the absence of the origin. All texts supplement that which supplements them, displacing that origin which commands their ultimate effacement.

This thinking of "reference" or allusion functions within a certain nostalgia for the center, and within a movement of an absent presence (language) that defers the return to center. "Past" signs inscribed within a system of "present" signs mark the time of a history: Eliot's "turning world" that repeats the "still-point." There is no master text but a library of simultaneous texts, the tradition; even the Bible is only another catalogue of the distanced Word. One might argue that allusions or references within individual poems function in the same fashion as do new poems in the "existing totality" of the "tradition." But whereas Eliot saw this, within the metaphysical view of history and textuality, as the unity of a becoming and thus a repetition of the Same, Pound's Imagist-Vorticist theory opens up the question of textuality by putting in quotation marks the authority of Being. What his poetics makes necessary is the "repeat of history," but a repetition as in a fugue rather than a quartet, a repetition that does not close or return absolutely upon itself.[26] Where allusion might suggest a past and privileged point of reference, Pound's repetition inscribes without reducing the fragment, the sign of the present-past. Hence that past is already textual, or pre-textual. Pound's Vortex literally winds itself upon a previous text, reinscribing it. But by inscribing the past text into the present text, Pound underscores the architechtonics of the repetition, the construction of one house upon another. The past text is never the present text. And the present text, insofar as it alludes to a past text, is never fully present. The time of the poem is the time of its play, its translation, the time produced in its signature of its own operation. Presence is a formal construction, and a mirage, always already an Image.

In one of those unorthodox examples which characterize the *ABC of Reading,* Pound compares modernist poetic method to that of the contemporary "bookkeeper" who employs a "loose-leaf system."[27] This system separates "archives" from "facts that are in use," and allows the bookkeeper to retrieve either past or present facts and to "use" them in a relation not dictated by chronology or nostalgia. The example characterizes Pound's sense of the modern Image. The facts of a poem are not references, except as they refer to another text. And every fact in use (present fact) may have an intertextual relation to an "archive" (the signs of the past), but only in a spatial relation. "A loose-leaf system," which is more modern than a palimpsest, redistributes the chronological reference but does not violate the force or play of alterity. It does, however, suspend the privilege of the "archive." Detail can be retrieved or left out of play, but no detail commands the system totally.

The "loose-leaf" system makes possible a new interpretation of "use," of usage, and therefore reinscribes within the possibility of poetry an anti-usury. A privileged pre-text does not rule the system; nor are "archives" relegated to a place of sacred significance, of archeological fragments from which one can remount the stream of history or memory. What is meaningful is the play of signs, not their reference to a lost or concealed meaning. The present facts repeat the "archives," but with a difference. This kind of system resists the wearing out (effacement) of facts that allows Pound to associate linguistic imprecision with economic inscribes and produces endlessly, makes it a writing device that repeats original creation, that is, original coinage. The Image moves because it resists equivalences. When Pound borrowed the archeological figure of the *paideuma* from Leo Frobenius for the "complex of in-rooted ideas" that governed the structure of every culture, he named a center or origin that was radically complex, and inseparable from the "play" (the *paidia*) that Plato saw as the danger of language.

At this point, however, it is time for a textual leap. What Vorticism opens or doubles (the question of textuality as representational or productive), Pound amplifies in *The Cantos.* On the other hand, the degree to which Pound participated in a radical re-opening of the idea of literature is repeated and, indeed, pro-jected in the work of Charles Olson. It is there that we began, in Olson's decentering, in his return to Melville to follow Melville's wandering/writing. To return to Olson, then, is to return to the disruptive "project" of a "post-Modernism" which has only the privilege of a certain repetition already inaugurated in the "beginning of writing."

IV

Olson's poetry, like his criticism, inscribes itself from its beginning in a field of old texts, the "limits" enclosing every individual subject. "Limits / are what any of us / are inside of . . ." (*MP,* p. 17). The limited self is only a force in a field of forces, and not a commanding subject of history, the hero. Its "limits" are its language, the field of language in which every subject arises, a field it can never command. The self has no proper beginning. It produces no history or teleology: "there is no 'history.' (I still keep going back to, the notion, this is (we are) merely, the *second time* (that's as much history as I'll permit in, which ain't history at all . . ." (*SW,* p. 113). (This history, like Olson's parentheses, will not close.)

To go back to come forward, as Olson said of Melville, is to seize the beginning as already begun. The poet is "merely, the *second time."* His originality is already a repetition, a temporalization that disrupts the notion of a "first" time by marking its figural nature. The poet who is the *first* to look *again* at the "start of human motion" (*MP,* p. 15) repeats the Original Act, the First Murder, in the sense that he fractures the dream of some original, recuperable purpose. Olson's poetics begins as a determined attack on logocentrism, and thus on the Modernist poetry, like Eliot's, that presumes to totalize the great (Western) tradition. In his "Letter to Elaine Feinstein," which has become an official postscript to the essay on "Projective Verse," Olson writes of his own archeological researches into the earliest languages as a decentering of the Image: "I am talking from a new 'double axis': the replacement of the Classical-representational by the *primitive-abstract. . . .* I mean of course not at all primitive in that stupid use of it as opposed to civilized. One means it now as 'primary' " (*SW,* p. 28). Thus the image as representation, as "referential to reality," is seen as the nostalgic invention of "history." Olson's leap backward into prehistory destroys the teleological fiction which had displaced the localism of preclassical culture. The ancient "Image, therefore, is vector," centered on a " 'content' (multiplicity: originally, and repetitively, chaos)—Tiamat: wot the Hindo-Europeans knocked out by giving the Old Man (Juice himself) all the lightning" (*SW,* p. 29). The "primary," the first, is force—already multiple and temporalizing. Like Olson's punctuation, the Image disseminates rather than closes.

"We have lived long in a generalizing time," he writes in "Human Universe," and that means since "450 B.C." (*SW,* p. 53). Our language is inescapably metaphysical and obscures the history of language's invention in a myth of origins—the fall. "Unselectedness," says Olson, "is man's original condition" and culture emerges by selection, by "act." Man is a force who signifies himself as a mark, as writing. Man begins as the already begun. There is no inaugural selecting act, no Adamic naming, but only babble (Babel) and the beginning as selection.

For Olson's poet, the first act is to displace the fiction of origins, to reintroduce "intention" as Desire: "the old Kosmos—or order imposed on Chaos in the creative beginning from it by Spirit of Desire, and by all three of mud, and then from mud the World Egg—becomes a condition, even if with a more precise vocabulary, of each one of us . . ." (*SVH,* p. 51). In this *Special View of History,* chance and accident precede and displace the fiction of original unity, generating "history" as a space of play. Life genetically occurs as "autoclytic multiplication": "Life is the chance success of a play of creative accidents. It is the principle of randomness seen in its essential application; not in any serial order imposed at random on either change or accident . . . but in the factual observation of how creation does occur: by the success of its own accident." (*SVH,* p. 48). "Ontogeny creates phylogeny" (*SVH,* p. 49). In the beginning was a chaos, a freeplay, the cultural space or graph Joyce called "chaosmos." "Selection," as in the act of writing, has no privileged beginning. To recall Williams, there are no ideas before things and no "things" without "relation." Selection begins in seeing the local difference, in "factual observation," or looking. Looking is not perception, however, not the constitutive act of a subject. Nor is it empirical ordering. Looking is situated at the place where selection begins, in the first accidental marking of difference and relation, a grammar governed by neither subject nor arche, an an-archy, a multi-centered field:

> There are not hierarchies, no infinite,
> no such many as mass, there are only
> eyes in all heads,
> to be looked out of
>
> (*MP,* p. 29)

Language, however, is already informed with hierarchies. The language of poetry appeals to the unity of the Word and thus to the commanding presence of the "old Man (Juice himself)" who possesses all the "lightning." To recuperate the cultural origin in "selection" is to seize a beginning already begun, to recover the play of writing. Selection is not *aletheia,* but a productive interpretation, an act of appropriation. Thus when Olson calls this recuperation a return to "speech" and "breath," it is not the speech of logocentrism, but language marked by an irreducible doubleness, hieroglyph or ideogram: "Logos, or discourse, for example, has, in that time [since 450 B.C.], so worked its abstractions into our concept and use of language that language's other function, speech, seems so in need of restoration that several of us go back to hieroglyphs or to ideograms to right the balance. (The distinction here is between language as the act of the instant and language as the act of thought about the instant.)" (*SW,* pp.53-54). There is an inaugural disruption here: of the priority of Being to language. "Selection" does not originate in a "subject," but in the accidental encounter. At this point Olson identifies speech with performance, with the "act" that shatters representation.

Despite the evidence which tempts one to locate Olson's poetics in the oral tradition—his preoccupation with "breath," for example—it is graphic selection that precedes logos. The return to speech as act or performance, like the return to "glyph" writing, is an attack on "manuscript" and set verse (the text as representation of thought or expression of self) and therefore upon phonetic writing. Speech, as we will see, becomes for Olson the energy of quantified differences, which has a doubling, a projective and con-jectural effect. It is the act which gives the poem "solidity" by breaking up the prescribed grammars, decentering the narrative "line" into the spatial field of "elements," thereby restoring to the textual space the "play of their separate energies" (*SW,* p. 21).

The irreducible element of verse is "breath," Olson claims, and not the metered foot. Breath is the mark of temporalization, of a broken and breaking movement, of "spacing." It therefore sets off and marks the productive force of the "smallest particle" of verse, the syllable. The "syllable" is irreducible difference, signifying both the temporal and spatial play of language. It projects, resisting any center or centering tendency. And this allows Olson to make a distinction which for many critics has seemed contradictory. The return to the elements of breath and syllable has been encouraged, he argues, by the typewriter, by a writing instrument which has made possible "space precisions" and therefore the necessary marking and projecting of syllabic difference. The machine, as Olson argues, produces the graph for a reading; it produces a text that in its turn can never govern a reading. Olson's graphic (machine) text is not only a play of elements; it pro-jects multiple readings or voicings that play off its play. Thus Olson, whose poetics derives at least indirectly from oral formulaic scholars like Milman Parry and Alfred Lord, and from classical scholars like Eric Havelock who have followed Parry and Lord, links himself to an oral poetics by the very instrument which puts that "tradition" in quotation marks. Olson's poetics, that is to say, opens the idea of the text to performance. Every performance transcribes and projects a difference; it tropes the trope, as in de Man's sense of the *aporia* that opens up the play and hence marks the lack of mastery between conative (philosophical or nominative) language and performative (literary or rhetorical) language.

The contribution of the machine, "space precisions," may be seen to take on a significance beyond the practical spacing or scripting for reading performance. Spacing is inseparable from the elementary quantification or temporalization of verse. And as Derrida indicates, a notion of spacing is fundamental to any thinking about writing.[28] Can Olson's literal emphasis on spacing be elided with Derrida's? Spacing for Derrida is an irruptive function of writing, of marks or grammatic indications which signify the displacement of the sign by a following sign; the *blanc* and the *hymen* (which may stand for the doubleness of all graphic or punctual marks) are syntactical indicators which give place to signs and thus mark their incompleteness, their doubleness. Spacing for Derrida, therefore, becomes a sign (or non-sign) of the impossibility of any sign's holding a fixed significance. Spacing suspends the semantic depth of the sign. It disrupts the place of the sign even as it inscribes the representational mirage. Spacing is projective and productive or disseminating. We may confidently assume that Olson's concern for spacing goes beyond technique; for his project demands nothing less than a clearing away of the illusion of the closed text, and particularly of the Western, Mediterranean, classical notion of representation.

Derrida's thinking of writing as spacing/dissemination, as a "productive, positive, generative force,"[29] can help us understand what has become, especially for Olson's detractors, a nearly nonsensical formula for "projective" verse. If the "syllable" is the simplest element of verse, that element includes its double: it "is only the first child of the incest of verse (always, that Egyptian thing, it produces twins!)" (*SW,* p. 18). Its twin is not simply a repetition of the same, but a radical doubling—the syllable's twin is the "line." A syllable commands only its displacement, projecting temporally both word and line, producing the unfolding breath unit: two children, two irreducible units, the twins of difference. Here, then, is Olson's formula for the pro-ject: "the HEAD, by way of the EAR, to the SYLLABLE/the HEART, by way of the BREATH, to the LINE" (*SW,* p. 19). The syllable is uttered in a *place* of irreducible difference and thus signifies a presence that is not present to itself. The syllable contains its own double, the temporal movement of the "line." The line, in its turn, is a unit marked by the inevitable next "breath," it signifies its own disruptive, discontinuous play, like a path cut through space, like a geograph.

The syllable is of the "head," then, because it is the elementary constituent of a semantics, or a semantic mirage. It is also of the "ear" because it demands alterity, or temporalization. It is the elemental unit which must be combined to make the word. The word, therefore, is never singular or nominative, never out of play. And the line is of the "heart" (not the sentimental organ of a unified interiority, but the temporal beat) because like all "life" it moves, advances, repeats, or is disseminated through a play of differences. Or as Olson redefines his concept in an interesting combination of metaphors: the "head . . . ear . . . syllable" makes possible the "PLAY of a mind"; the "heart . . . breath . . . line" provides the "threshing floor for the dance" (*SW,* p. 19). Play is *différance;* the dance is its decentered repetitions. The two are inseparable and irreducible. Unlike the logocentric "line," Olson's poetic line refuses any closure of its circulation.

Its play projects an ever-expanding unit, a "FIELD," the poem itself. This field cannot be "centered," that is, commanded by a single intentionality or privileged object. It is, rather, a space of relations, of forces always already begun: "each of these elements of a poem can be allowed to have the play of their separate energies and can be allowed, once the poem is well composed, to keep . . . their proper confusions" (*SW,* p. 21). This play dissolves the referential function of the sign and reinscribes it within a new system of relations, projecting new fields, not recuperating old ones.

Dance and process are other Olson metaphors for this movement. He relates them to a methodology of "limits," to a poetry set against the logocentric dream of totalization (and thus totalitarianism). In seeking a new methodology, he says, it has been necessary to deconstruct the old methods, to "turn the totalitarian" (*LO,* p. 106). The new methodology will be based on the model of the city, not the modern city but the early cities of Sumerian and Mayan culture, those ancient places of man's gathering which have survived history in the traces of their indelible invention, writing or hieroglyphs, that is, their invention of history as writing. From 3378 B.C. until about 1200 B.C., he conjectures, "civilization had ONE CENTER, Sumer, in all directions"; thus, Olson concludes, "a city was a coherence which, for the first time since the ice [age], gave man the chance to join knowledge to culture" (*HU,* p. 19). Coherence, however, is not a closed system. In contrast, the historical civilizations which followed in Greece and Rome tried to totalize this coherence by locating the center in an idea of man, in humanism. They were marked by logocentrism and by the rise of the "hero"; Man displaced the community of men (or discourse) as center. In *Letters for Origin,* Olson relates his search for a new methodology to a deconstruction of the epoch of the hero:

To cohere means to stick together! To hold fast, as parts of the same mass!

And coherence is defined as connection or *congruity* arising from some common *principle* or idea

Now if I slug in juxtaposition and composition by field, METHODOLOGY as a word of more import than technique—as a word also as proper to the change of procedure demanded of us in the face of TOTALITY—may be more of the cluster of force i take it it is.

But let's go back to root: to *methodos,* and look!

with a way,

with a via, with a path (weg, that which died, and does not die, which it is any man's Job—and more so now, when the old way is dead, long live the methodology

in other words, the science of the path—what could be more exactly what we are involved in—it is not the path, but it is the way the path is discovered! (*LO,* p. 106)

The classical principle of totalization, of ideational centering, has displaced the coherence of the open or multicentered field in Olson's special (a spatial) reading of history. Method as projection or quest has given way to ethnocentrism and thus authoritarianism. *Methodos* disrupts representation, the law that makes us follow the path, and returns us to that act of cutting the path. To reappropriate the elementary twins of verse, syllable and line, recapitulates the reappropriation of Sumer. Coherence is a work of construction, not an imitation of Truth. Like Pound, Olson appeals to the archeological metaphor, but the archeologist does not presume to recuperate presence. Rather, in his re-search of method, he seeks that cutting edge, the "way" to cut a path and not some path to follow. He seeks the disruptive, productive tool of writing.

For some of Olson's acolytes, his theory advocates a present reappropriation of the past, an authentic return to an authentic "time," to the prehistorical purity of an oral tradition. But Olson is not nostalgic. The past, whether an ideal prehistorical culture or an authoritative past text, is neither the object of his desire nor a point of privileged reference. The remote cultures summon him because they are like a mysterious writing; he would decipher their method, not their meaning. Olson's effort, then, is to recapitulate the process of a "first writing" as the generation of coherence, as a desire for and thrust toward the Center. In this regard, the Center is the place of the dance and of the play of the mind, a scene of writing, as it were. The ancient city exemplifies man's selection; it is a labyrinth that was purely and simply made, not a representation of an idea, a city of God. To go back means to open up again that "play of creative accidents" which precedes all totalitarian cultures. In Olson's view the modern poet thinks he has written the closure of history and therefore of poetry. What stands between the "post-modern poet" and the figural act of first writing is the history of accumulated texts. To cut through these texts demands a repetition of original research, whether this means going to an archeological site to study a culture whose language has not been deciphered (like the Mayan's) or following the method (the way) of the new scientific analysts, the archeologists or geographers, linguists, and revisionary historians.[30]

An Olson poem may graph or map an old document or old text in the same way an archeologist might open up a site. Its purpose is not to sanctify old texts or uncover their origin, but to decipher the crux that led to their writing. Old texts incorporate the doubleness of history. To use a favorite Olson metaphor, history is a Moebius strip, a single surface that always returns upon itself; it is not the exterior of some interior presence, not simply the expression of God or the "unity of a becoming." History is a single surface of successive events, like successive perceptions, that return into themselves, cross through each other, repeat themselves, but always with a difference. Each repetition is an asymptote. Olson therefore calls this a method of "Document" as opposed to the method of "Narration"; for in the latter, the narrator as personal interpreter dominates the movement of the text and governs its closure. The poem as "document" throws together (thus con-jectures) old texts, mapping them, so as to "re-enact" their making (*HU,* p. 127).[31]

Present poems do not absorb old texts, but take movement, a kind of spacing, from them. Documents decenter the lyrical voice, the centering or narrative subject. But the poet's performance (method) also decenters the documents. Affiliation maps and demythologizes the fiction of narrative or filiative order. In the juxtaposition of documents, the author does not determine the field, since there is a multiple of authors. "Curiosity," says Olson, drew man's attention to the things around him, including the detail of other human objects. This motivated his measurings, his cosmic interpretations (*SW,* p. 58). This interpretive act inscribes or maps the "Spirit of Desire." Like the Dresden codex, Stonehenge, and the ruins of Angkor Vat, the poem will be a projective machine, not some nostalgic sign of a past, or past-present. The poem—that is, the post-modern poem which aspires to be original, a first poem, in that it must repeat what is seen by the "first human eyes . . . / at the start of human motion (just last week / 300,000,000 years ago" (*MP,* p. 15)—must be a "glyph," a mark in nature, a mark signifying the intercourse of man and nature, the place of man, his placement toward nature, the meeting point of an irreducible difference. Thus the poem is not recuperative but productive. Yet, it is a threshold, like the "skin" where man and nature interact, the place of the dance or play of a difference, of opposites which can never be dissolved into one. Olson, then, can argue, like Vico and Rousseau, that original language was figural, poetic. Yet it is instrumental. If the "instrumentation of selection" is always located on this "threshold" (*SW,* p. 60), it precedes the self as subject, just as it precedes nature as object, or any originary Being. The "skin" is a "cutting edge," not a thing or a place at all, but the field of language marked in every "glyph." No history can begin from this non-origin, this "skin" which is neither an inside nor an outside. No single "way" can be retrieved from its cutting. In the beginning was *methodos,* the cutting edge, the threshold. To recuperate method, however—to go back to go forward, to recover the thrownness, in both Heidegger's and Olson's sense—is to overcome at last "American" belatedness, or to put its nostalgia in the parentheses of a "literary history." The "project" of an "American" poetics, if one can condense a history that does not exist, has been to invent a machine of its own origins—to invent or reinvent "language," an "Image," where the fiction of Being can be entertained, not as that which has been lost and can be recuperated, but as that which has been invented as a pure fiction so that it can be destroyed, or deconstructed, in the "beginning again." The "project" of "American" poetry has always been an-archic rather than archeo-logical, or as one would say, archeo-clastic, a myth of origins that puts the myth of origins in question, that puts itself in question. It is a poetry of uprootedness, of radical innocence, of the radical origin, the radical as origin—the "decentered" "Image."[32]

UCLA

NOTES

1 Charles Olson, *Call Me Ishmael* (New York: Reynal and Hitchcock, 1947), p. 14. I will hereafter use the following abbreviations for works by Olson: *CMI—Call Me Ishmael; HU—Human Universe and Other Essays,* ed. Donald Allen (New York: New Directions, 1967); *LO—Letters for Origin: 1950-1955,* ed. Albert Glover (London: Cape Goliard/Grossman, 1969); *MP—The Maximus Poems* (New York: Jargon/Corinth, 1960); *SVH—The Special View of History,* ed. Ann Charters (Berkeley: Oyez, 1970); *SW—Selected Writings of Charles Olson,* ed. Robert Creeley (New York: New Directions, 1966).

2 One should doubly emphasize here that Olson doesn't exclude all writers who fall within the period of Western literature, since Shakespeare is his model of the "mythic" and universal imagination never containable in this "history." *Call Me Ishmael* is a pioneering, speculative study of Melville's appropriation of Shakespeare.

3 Gilles Deleuze, *Proust and Signs,* trans. Richard Howard (New York: Braziller, 1972), pp. 91, 167. The book was first published in France in 1964, revised and supplemented in 1970.

4 The reference here is to Jacques Derrida's destruction of Husserl's presentational phenomenology: "somehow everything 'begins' by 're- presentation',"

which "means that there is no 'beginning' and that the 're-presentation' we are talking about is not the modification of a 're' that has *befallen* a primordial presentation." See Derrida, *Speech and Phenomena,* trans. David Allison (Evanston, Ill.: Northwestern Univ. Press, 1973), p. 45n. This is a translation of Derrida's *La Voix et le phènoméne* (1967).

5 In his "Nietzsche, Genealogy, History," in *Language, Counter-Memory, Practice,* trans. Donald Bouchard and Sherry Simon (Ithaca, New York: Cornell Univ. Press, 1977), pp. 139-64, Michel Foucault distinguishes between a nostalgia for origins and the concerns of genealogy: "The genealogist [of morals] needs history to dispel the chimeras of origin . . ." (p. 144). The Nietzschean genealogist is concerned with the gaps, the lapses, the intensities, the agitations—in short, the discontinuities and not some thread that links history with an ideal, simple origin. Thus Foucault reads the Nietzschean genealogy as an indifference to the "father." Melville, even as Olson reads him, worries over the questions of identifying the father/origin and of deriving an identity from him. The author, then, always lives in the uncertainty marked by genealogy.

6 See, for example, Rodolphe Gasché, "The Scene of Writing: A Deferred Outset," *Glyph I* (Baltimore: Johns Hopkins Univ. Press, 1977), pp. 150-71.

7 Edgar Dryden, "The Entangled Text: Melville's *Pierre* and the Problem of Reading," *boundary 2,* 7 (Spring 1979), 145-73.

8 This and subsequent quotations from *Pierre* are from the Northwestern/Newberry edition, ed. H. Hayford, H. Parker, and G. T. Tanselle (Evanston and Chicago, 1971).

9 Eugenio Donato, "The Ruins of Memory: Archeological Fragments and Textual Artifacts," *MLN,* 93 (1978), 575-96.

10 See Paul de Man's early, more phenomenologically oriented essay "Intentional Structure of the Romantic Image," in *Romanticism and Consciousness,* ed. Harold Bloom (New York: Norton, 1970). The essay first appeared in 1960.

11 First published in Pound, *Instigations* (New York: Boni and Liveright, 1920), pp. 357-87.

12 Hugh Kenner, *The Pound Era* (Berkeley: Univ. of California Press, 1971), pp. 192-231, esp. p.230.

13 Kenner, *The Pound Era,* p. 230.

14 Harold Bloom, *Wallace Stevens: The Poems of Our Climate* (Ithaca, New York: Cornell Univ. Press, 1977), p. 12.

15 Jacques Derrida, *Of Grammatology,* trans. Gayatri Spivak (Baltimore: Johns Hopkins Univ. Press, 1976), p. 17.

16 Derrida, *Of Grammatology,* p. 90; also, p. 91.

17 Derrida, *Of Grammatology,* p. 92.

18 Some of the following section was treated, in a slightly different way, in my

essay "Pound and the Decentered Image," *The Georgia Review,* 29 (1975), 565-91.

19 Herbert Schneidau, *Ezra Pound: The Image and the Real* (Baton Rouge, La.: LSU Press, 1969), pp. 99-100.

20 Ezra Pound, *Gaudier-Brzeska* (1916; rpt. New York: New Directions, 1970), p. 89.

21 Ezra Pound, *ABC of Reading* (New York: New Directions, n.d.), p. 52.

22 See Ezra Pound, *Literary Essays* (New York: New Directions, 1954), pp. 25-26. The terms are repeated elsewhere, esp. in *ABC of Reading.*

23 Ezra Pound, Postscript to Remy de Gourmont, *The Natural Philosophy of Love,* trans. Ezra Pound (New York: Liveright, 1922), pp. 295-96.

24 Kenneth Burke, *Counter-Statement* (Chicago: Univ. of Chicago Press, 1957), pp. 124-25.

25 T. S. Eliot, " 'Ulysses,' Order and Myth," *The Dial* (November 1923); rpt. Mark Schorer, et al., eds., *Criticism: The Foundations of Modern Literary Judgment* (New York: Harcourt, Brace, 1948), pp. 269-70.

26 See *The Letters of Ezra Pound, 1907-1941,* ed. D. D. Paige (New York: Harcourt, Brace, 1950), p. 210.

27 Pound, *ABC of Reading,* p. 38.

28 See Jacques Derrida, "La double séance," in *La Dissémination* (Paris: Seuil, 1972), pp. 198-317; also, *Of Grammatology,* p. 203 and *passim.*

29 In Jacques Derrida, "Positions," *Diacritics,* 3 (Spring 1973), 41n.: "As *dissémination,* as *différance,* it includes a genetic dimension, it is not simply the interval, the space constituted between two . . . but spacing . . . the operation or in any case movement of separation. This movement is inseparable from temporization—temporalization . . . —and from the *différance,* the conflicts of force which are at work."

30 Among Olson's models of objective scholarship, one should mention certainly the geographer Carl O. Sauer; the linguist Edward Sapir; the mathematician Georg Riemann; Werner Heisenberg, for his radical modification of relativity; the anthropologist Leo Frobenius, whom Pound found so central to the modern; the Greek scholar Eric Havelock; and several archeologists who had uncovered and decoded the sites of Sumer. These are scholars who have advanced the search and effected a "change of paradigm" (to use Thomas Kuhn's phrase) in their discipline, without presuming to have arrived at or recuperated the Truth. Theirs is the method of "Document."

31 See Derrida, *Of Grammatology,* pp. 107-8: "one should meditate upon all of the following: writing as the possibility of the road and of difference, the history of writing and the history of the road, of the rupture, of the *via rupta,* of the path that is broken, beaten, *fracta,* of the space of reversibility and of repetition traced by the opening, the divergence from, and the violent spacing, of nature, of the natural, savage, salvage, forest . . . ; it is difficult to imagine

that access to the possibility of a road-map is not at the same time access to writing."

32 This essay will appear, under the present title, in *Textual Strategies,* ed. Josue Harari (Ithaca: Cornell University Press, 1979). For this reason, the title has been changed from the Symposium title.

Writer as Reader: An American Story

Edgar A. Dryden

> The development of the normal transitive sentence rests upon the fact that one action in nature promotes another; thus the agent and the object are secretly verbs. For example, our sentence, "Reading promotes writing," would be expressed in Chinese by three full verbs. Such a form is the equivalent of three expanded clauses and can be drawn out into adjectival, participial, infinitive, relative or conditional members. One of many possible examples is, "If one reads it teaches him how to write." Another is, "One who reads becomes one who writes." But in the first condensed form a Chinese would write, "Read promote write."
>
> —Ernest Fenollosa

Following the hint of Fenollosa's suggestive example, I want to begin with the observation that Professor Riddel's admirable essay in inscribing parentheses, in placing quotation marks, in declaring and asserting situates itself as a scriptive performance rather than a reading as such. Like the postmodernist project that it maps, it implies that one who reads becomes one who writes. Reading in this context is no passive and parasitical activity, the pale complement of the original and glamorous act of creation itself. On the contrary, it is productive and active, associated with the practical researches of Egyptologists and archeologists who open up sites and descend into crypts in order to decipher and repeat the mystery of an original act of writing. The method of repetition, moreover, is that of the document rather than that of the narrative, for it is one that throws together, maps, and reenacts. The poets who dot the line Professor Riddel traces read in order to find a starter for their own activity, recognizing as Emerson does that " 'He who would bring home the wealth of the Indies, must carry out the wealth of the Indies.' There is creative reading as well as creative writing."[1] This reading/writing problematic, as Professor Riddel brilliantly shows, informs the tradition of American literature shaping not only the project of American poetry but that of the novel as well. With the novel, however, there are special problems that derive in part from its dependence on story and narration and the related idea of a naive and enchanted reader. I want briefly to introduce a few of those problems here in the form of a supplement (in the sense of adding to an already completed whole) to Professor Riddel's paper.

Hawthorne and Melville put the problem most directly, for in their cases reading does not always promote writing. Hawthorne, of course, recognizes that writers are readers too, the act of creation one of unweaving and reweaving the texts of others. His tales are "twice-told" not only in the sense of being "musty and mouse-nibbled leaves of old periodicals, transformed by the magic arts of . . . friendly publishers into a new book,"[2] but also in the sense of being interpretations of events, objects, and stories from the past. His starting point as a writer is most often an "Old Time Legend," some object or scrap of gossip from the past pregnant with an undisclosed meaning which he sets out to uncover for his reader. The most explicit treatment of this theme, of course, is found in Hawthorne's discussion of the source of *The Scarlet Letter.* The story, he tells us, derives from his reading of a faded Scarlet A, which presented itself as "most worthy of interpretation," and "several foolscap sheets, containing many particulars respecting the life and conversation of one Hester Prynne."[3] In both cases Hawthorne's reading is the last of a series of interpretations. As Charles Feidelson notes in his seminal discussion of this episode, everyone in the novel reenacts the scene in which Hawthorne attempts to read the meaning of the letter,[4] and the letter is interpreted in a variety of ways by Hester and her contemporaries as well as by Hawthorne and the reader. Hester herself, moreover, is the "text of the discourse[s]" (*CE,* p. 85), not only of puritan clergymen but also of the "aged persons, alive in the time of Mr. Surveyor Pue . . . from whose oral testimony he had made up the narrative," and his narrative, in turn, forms the basis of *The Scarlet Letter.* Hawthorne seeks to uncover the "dark meaning" (*CE,* p. 31) in the faded A as well as the "traces of Mr. Pue's mental part, and the internal operation of his head" (*CE,* p. 30) contained in the "half a dozen sheets of foolscap" (*CE,* p. 33). And, as Hawthorne is Pue's commentator, so the reader is his, seeking in Hawthorne's text the illusive meaning of the mysterious A as well as the features of its current interpreter. No matter how interpretations proliferate, however, something will always remain hidden, for the wonderful A "gives evidence of a now forgotten art, not to be rediscovered even by the process of picking out the threads" (*CE,* p. 31).

It is that "forgotten art" which haunts Hawthorne's career as a writer. For him the processes of weaving and unweaving which constitute the acts of writing and reading are not productive enough to justify either activity. His career ends with the realization that because these activities are dependent on "old delightful ideas of the past, the associations of ancestry, the loveliness of an age-old home—the old poetry and romance that haunt [the] ancient villages and estates of England," to engage in them is to "give up the chance of acting upon the unmoulded future of America."[5] Even a demystified view of story is unacceptable to the modern American who is building a new world, for story remains tied to the past and to a myth of origin in the form of the seductive idea of our ancestral home. Such seductions are rejected explicitly by Hawthorne in the uncompleted romances as they are implicitly in *The Marble Faun.* To be a writer is to remain in exile in the Old World; Hawthorne, at the last, returns to the New.

For Melville, even more than for Hawthorne, the writer is at first a reader. His creative powers depend on the scope of his reading, "spontaneous creative thought" being a process whereby "all existing great works are federated in the fancy; and so regarded as a miscellaneous and Pantheistic whole."[6] The text of *Moby-Dick,* for example, is woven more from the threads of the texts which fill Ishmael's library than it is from the lines and ropes of the whaling world. Indeed, Ishmael's relation to that world is that of a reader to a text, and he tries to organize and arrange it as he has previously done his library by establishing a bibliographical system. Moreover, reading is not an easy or a passive activity. In "Hawthorne and His Moses" Melville distinguishes between that reader who sees Shakespeare as a "mere man of Richard-the-Third humps and Macbeth daggers," who responds to the "popularizing noise and show of broad farce, and blood-besmeared tragedy," and the more discriminating reader who is "content with the still, rich utterances of a great intellectual in repose."[7] In the place of "blind, unbridled" (*HM,* p. 542) reading, Melville proposes a deep, careful one which is capable of discerning those truths which the writer "craftily says" or "insinuates" (*HM,* p. 541) in his texts. As Ishmael demonstrates when he tells the Town Ho's Story by "interweaving in its proper place the darker thread [the secret part of the tale] with the story as publicly narrated on the ship,"[8] story-telling is the process of conveying a dark truth that will only be available to the reader whose response is in the form of a deep and probing examination.

Melville soon finds, however, that both writer and reader are themselves woven into the fabric of story. *Pierre* and *The Confidence Man* are records of his discovery of the extent to which writer and reader are entangled in the web of fictions which surround them. In *Pierre* he attempts to distinguish between the "countless tribes of common novels" which "laboriously spin veils of mystery only to complacently clear them up at last" and those "profounder emanations of the human mind" that never "unravel their own intricacies, and have no proper endings" (*P,* p. 141); but he then goes on to demonstrate the way in which the "infinite entanglements of all social things, which forbid that one thread should fly the general fabric, on some lines of duty, without tearing itself and tearing others" (*P,* p. 191), make it impossible either for a writer to produce an original text or for a reader to respond to it in any but a mystified way. "Like knavish cards, the leaves of all great books [are] covertly packed," and any new author but packs "one set the more" (*P,* p. 339). As *The Confidence Man* makes clear, all stories are at least twice told and are designed, primarily, to divert and charm. Here the writer is portrayed as the Confidence Man, a contradictorily derivative but original character who has no fixed identity, and readers—both naive and suspicious—are represented by his many victims. Writing is a sham and reading the activity of fools.

The unpublished fragments of Hawthorne's last years and Melville's long period of silence following the publication of *The Confidence Man* are in one sense reactions to the discovery of the extent to which man is the prisoner of the already known and written. Both writers are overwhelmed by the exhaustion of possibilities and dismayed by the realization that their relation to their readers is based on deception and bad faith. However, in their willingness to investigate fully the limitations of story rather than to displace story by focusing on its historical or moral dimensions, they suggest the possibility of a fiction which emphasizes story and reading in the face of exhausted possibilities. Writing of such a literature of exhaustion, John Barth insists that the "used-upness of certain forms or exhaustion of certain possibilities" is "by no means necessarily a cause for despair." The important thing is to be "aware of what one's predecessors were up to." With that knowledge, it is possible to rediscover "validly the artifices of language and literature—such far-out notions as grammar, punctuation . . . even characterization. Even plot!"[9]

Barth's starting point as a novelist is an undisguised fascination with the "element of story—just sheer extraordinary marvelous story," that is to say, "yarns—elaborate lies." "Scheherazade's my avantgardiste," he says after commenting that the "nouveau roman isn't . . . my cup of tea."[10] Nevertheless, Barth is as aware as any student of *la nouvelle critique* of the problematic nature of such categories as consciousness, selfhood, origin, and end. A sense of the fictive status of these categories lies behind his impulse to "imagine alternatives to the world," to "re-invent philosophy and the rest—make up your own whole history of the world."[11] His books, as he says, are "novels which imitate the form of the Novel by an author who imitates the role of Author," and no one is more aware of the subversive effects of imitation than he is:

> If this sort of thing sounds unpleasantly decadent, nevertheless it's about where the genre begins, with *Quixote* imitating *Amadis of Gaul,* Cervantes pretending to be the Cid Hamete Benengeli (and Alonso Quijano pretending to be Don Quixote), or Fielding parodying Richardson. "History repeats itself as farce"—meaning, of course, in the form or mode of farce, not that history is farcical. . . . The first attempts . . . to imitate actions more or less directly, and its conventional devices—cause and effect, linear anecdote characterization, authorial selection, arrangement, and interpretation—can be and have long since been objected to as obsolete notions, or metaphors for obsolete notions: Robbe-Grillet's essays *For a New Novel* come to mind. There are replies to these objections, not to the point here, but one can see that in any case they're obviated by imitations of novels which attempt to represent not life directly but a representation of life. In fact such works are no more removed from life than Richardson's or Goethe's epistolary novels are: both imitate "real" documents, and the subject of both, ultimately, is life, not documents. A novel is as much a piece of the real world as a letter, and the letters in *The Sorrows of Young Werther* are, after all, fictitious.[12]

The effect of an imitation is to repeat the source in parody and thereby to reveal its fictive nature. This process, as Barth suggests, is built into the art of story-telling and may be one reason why that art has always been regarded suspiciously. The words "once upon a time" can at once comfort and unsettle, for they both come from the past and break from it. For Barth and his characters this contradictory quality is the aspect of story which most fascinates. Consider, for example, the enthusiasm of Harvey Russecks in *The Sot-Weed Factor:*

> "No pleasure pleasure me as doth a well-spun tale, be't sad or merry, shallow or deep! If the subject's privy business, or unpleasant, who cares a fib? The road to

heaven's beset with thistles, and methinks there's many a cow-pat on't as well. And what matter if your folk are drawn from life? Tis not likely I'll ha'met 'em, or know 'em from your telling if e'er I should! Call 'em what names ye will: in a tale they're less than themselves, and more. Besides which, if ye have the art to make 'em live—'sheart!—thou'rt nowise liable for what the rascals do, no more than God Almighty for the lot of us. As for length, fie on't!" He raised his horny finger. "A bad tale's long though it want but a single eyeblink for the telling, and a good tale short though it takes from St. Swithin's to Michaelmas to have done with't. Ha! And the plot is tangled, d'ye say? Is't more knotful or bewildered than the skein of life itself, that a good tale tangles the better to unsnarl? Nay, out with your story, now, and yours as well, sir, and shame on the both o' ye thou'rt not commenced already! Spin and tangle till the Dog-star sets i' the Bay—nor fear I'll count ye idle gossips: a tale well wrought is the gossip o' the gods, that see the heart and hidden o' life on earth; the seamless web o' the world; the Warp and Woof . . . I'Christ, I do love a story, sirs! Tell away!"[13]

Like Barth himself, who in writing *The Sot-Weed Factor* set out to "make up a plot fancier than *Tom Jones,*"[14] Harvey delights in the spinning and tangling of tale-telling. At issue here is not truth or meaning but an uninhibited joy in the performance of the virtuoso who "with the aid of *very special gifts*" and with the knowledge that all possibilities are exhausted manages to speak "eloquently to our still human hearts and conditions."[15] Harvey is, we recall, a character in a novel which imitates the eighteenth-century Novel, the creation of an author who imitates Fielding and other Authors, and the metaphors which he uses to express his enthusiasm suggest the problematic relationship between source and copy. The fact that Harvey simultaneously and contradictorily attributes pagan, Christian, and realistic sources to story suggests a systematic putting into question of previous values that leads to a vision of the human world as a web of words.

The naive reading which has been associated with the novel from its beginning may not be innocent at all since the form itself can be seen as socially and ontologically subversive. The special delight novel readers experience when they give themselves to the magic of story may not represent a passive, unquestioning acceptance of the codes and conventions of their society. The very act of turning away from what is, to feign belief in what is not, violates the natural attitude and ultimately puts it into question. So it is that the story which so delights Harvey Russecks reveals "an itch for all we lose as proper citizens—something in us pines for chaos, for the black and lawless pit" (*SW,* p. 628). For Barth a good story is at once evidence that "human works can be magnificent" (*SW,* p. 356) and a revelation of that "black cosmos whence we sprung and through which we fall" (*SW,* p. 364), a perception which manages to dignify both the naive and enlightened attitudes and to illustrate nicely Professor Riddel's suggestion that American Literature is a fiction that exposes the idea of a privileged world.

SUNY-Buffalo

NOTES

1 Emerson, "The American Scholar," in *The Complete Essays and Other Writings,* college ed. (New York: Modern Library, n.d.), p. 51.

2 Hawthorne, *Complete Works* (Cambridge: Riverside Press, 1883), III, 389.

3 Hawthorne, *The Centenary Edition of the Works,* eds. William Charvat, Roy Harvey Pearce, and Claude Simpson (Columbus: Ohio State Univ. Press, 1962-), I, 32 (hereafter cited as *CE*).

4 Feidelson, *Symbolism and American Literature* (Chicago: Univ. of Chicago Press, 1953), p. 10.

5 Hawthorne, *Complete Works,* XI, 505.

6 Melville, *Pierre; or, The Ambiguities,* eds. Harrison Hayford, Hershel Parker, and G. Thomas Tanselle (Evanston: Northwestern Univ. Press, 1971), p. 284 (hereafter cited as *P*).

7 "Hawthorne and His Mosses," in *Moby-Dick,* eds. Harrison Hayford and Hershel Parker (New York: W. W. Norton, 1967), p. 542 (hereafter cited as *HM*).

8 Melville, *Moby-Dick,* p. 208.

9 Barth, "The Literature of Exhaustion," *The Atlantic* (August 1967), pp. 29, 31.

10 "John Barth: An Interview," *Wisconsin Studies in Contemporary Literature,* 6 (1965), 5-6.

11 Barth, "Interview," p. 8.

12 Barth, "Literature of Exhaustion," p. 33.

13 Barth, *The Sot-Weed Factor* (New York: Grosset & Dunlap, 1964), p. 625 (hereafter cited as *SW*).

14 Barth, "Interview," p. 7.

15 Barth, "Literature of Exhaustion," p. 30.

vre point lauoir · leu en quel
conque leu.

Cy apres sensuit lystoire
circes qui fut une tresreno

Destruction/Deconstruction in the Text of Nietzsche

David B. Allison

The paper I'd like to present—"*Destruction/Deconstruction* in the Text of Nietzsche"—is composed of two parts, two quite different parts. The first and shorter part deals with the issue of a deconstructive style *within* the text of Nietzsche, and the second is concerned with such an operation as performed *upon* Nietzsche's text—i.e., by someone else and from without. The second part, then, concerns a stylistic fold or doubling-up of interpretation: the example or model I have chosen for this is a text with which most of you are no doubt familiar, Derrida's recent work on Nietzsche, entitled *Spurs: Nietzsche's Styles.*[1] For the earlier account of an immanent deconstruction, I have turned to the analyses of Paul de Man.

To what extent is my presentation phenomenological? Perhaps only etymologically—to the extent in which one can "lay out" or "say" something about the phenomenon of a text. This certainly seems to be the sense that both Derrida and Heidegger accord the term. Indeed, Heidegger himself remarks in one of his last works,

> The age of phenomenological philosophy seems to be over. It is already taken as something past which is only

> recorded historically along with other schools of philosophy. But in what is most its own, phenomenology is not a school . . . its . . . essential character does not consist in being *actual* as a philosophical school. Higher than actuality stands possibility.[2]

Now, it was precisely with this in mind that Heidegger began what he called the *Destruktion* of Western thought, namely, a laying-out of the possibilities already implicit in Greek thought, possibilities that have *not* developed into, and thus, have not constituted the history of metaphysics as such.

Heidegger conceived this project, he tells us, during the period in which he served as Husserl's assistant. By 1922 the problematic issue of *alētheia* had already provoked him to question the adequacy of phenomenological method: how could a phenomenon be fully presented, much less grasped by consciousness, if its very appearing was *grounded* in concealment? Indeed, if concealment itself was found to be enigmatic, was itself concealed? It was the set of possibilities opened up by this concept of truth as *alētheia* that guided Heidegger's project of *Destruktion* from its initial formulation in *Being and Time* until the final texts of *On Time and Being* and *The End of Philosophy,* where Heidegger renounced the very concept of *ground* as being perhaps the most conventional of all metaphysical categories. And it is only at this point, Heidegger claimed, that thinking could be freed from the history of metaphysics, thence to enter into and give rise to its own possibilities.

We should note that Derrida follows a similar itinerary: what Derrida addressed, however, was not the history of metaphysics as such, nor the thought of the presocratics, but rather their axiomatic condensation in the work of Husserl. If Heidegger, by a process of "remembrance" and "retrieve," finally questioned tradition through the *Destruktion* of (its) *ground,* and by the thought of *Ereignis* and poetic thinking, so does Derrida perform this in his analysis of Husserl's *Origin of Geometry* and the *Logical Investigations* by deconstructing the concepts of *archē, telos,* sign, and phenomenological intuition. And, perhaps more positively, by instituting the thought of *differance,* alterity, and, for want of a better word, indeterminacy or undecidibility. Moreover, he does this *as* Heidegger did—by deconstructing the metaphysics of "presence."

So much by way of a nominal introduction. How does this lead us to the issue of deconstruction in and upon the text of Nietzsche?

I

If the recent literature is at all indicative, it seems practically impossible for a contemporary reader of Nietzsche not to encounter Nietzsche's texts except by way of Heidegger and Derrida.[3] Let me simply advance this as a claim. But if you accept this claim, something becomes strikingly obvious about previous Nietzsche criticism: with few exceptions, the earlier analyses resulted in a *systematized* Nietzsche—one that had positive and well-defined ethical, epistemological, and ontological theses; theses, moreover, which were codified, consistent, and hierarchical, rigorously argued for, and to all appearances conclusive. The range of these interpretations, needless to say, was vast. At one time or another, Nietzsche was variously held by his early critics to be anything from a neo-positivist to a transcendental esthete. One concern however, was held in common by most of these "philosophical" interpreters: to make *sense* of Nietzsche, one had to modify if not sacrifice what they considered to be the stylistic *excess* of his writing. Much as in contemporary Plato criticism, one at best pays lip-service to the style or dramatic construction of the dialogues—in order better to find a system of logical argumentation and demonstration, which, we are invariably told, is in any case invalid and wrong-headed.

But if the conventional systematic reading of Nietzsche chose to *dispense* with the complex issues of his style, a more recent school has ventured the other extreme—and has become lost in an exclusive, if not rhapsodic concern with style alone. The outcome of this kind of tortured reflection is the claim that Nietzsche had *no* doctrines, no position that might not easily be replaced by any other.

Both the systematic and rhapsodic readings perform their own kind of violence, then, and both reduce Nietzsche's text to a series of theses or non-theses.

Perhaps as a response to the rhapsodic reading, a newer orientation has emerged, one which explicitly calls itself a "deconstructionist" reading. The foremost representative of this movement in the United States is no doubt Paul de Man. And it is largely to him that we owe a renewed and vigorous reading of Nietzsche. While he acknowledges his own indebtedness to Derrida and to what I would call the rhapsodic school (e.g., Bernard Pautrat, Sarah Kofman, Georges Bataille, Phillipe Lacoue-Labarthe, and Jean-Michel Rey), his work is distinctly his own. What is perhaps most important in de Man's reading of Nietzsche is that he anchors the Derridean project of deconstruction firmly within the stylistic mechanics of the text itself (rather than, for instance, subjecting the text in a supervenient way to these techniques). The outcome of this method is the attempt to establish the nature of textual authority and the permissible range or extent of its semantic assertions. Thus, in two extremely important and well-known articles, "Genesis and Genealogy in Nietzsche's *The Birth of Tragedy*" and "Nietzsche's Theory of Rhetoric," he makes the claim that deconstruction is an immanent operation—performed in and by the text on at least two levels, the explicitly narrative and the metalinguistic levels.[4]

These two levels operate in such a way that (for Nietzsche, at least) the narrative teaching is undermined by the rhetorical dynamics of the text—both on the level of the narrative itself and by the ground of its own genesis. When de Man discusses *The Birth of Tragedy* in his earlier article, he shows that the truthful narrative (which can knowingly distinguish the reliability of what it represents) is orchestrated *against* the narrative of an unmediated representation of will. Thus, he argues, Nietzsche's

> narrative falls into two parts, or what amounts to the same thing, it acquires two incompatible narrators. The narrator who argues against the subjectivity of the lyric and against representational realism destroys the credibility of the other narrator, for whom Dionysian insight is the tragic perception of original truth. (*GG,* p. 51)

What would follow from this opposition of truth and non-truth, of Apollonian and Dionysian, of illusion and non-illusion? To decide these issues, de Man continues, the text "has to run the risk of having to decree the loss of its own claim to truth." Indeed, this would seem to be the claim he has to defend. It is at this point that de Man turns from the discourse and narrative to its genetic foundation:

> Have we merely been saying that *The Birth of Tragedy* is self-contradictory and that it hides its contradictions by means of "bad" rhetoric? By no means; first of all, the "deconstruction" of the Dionysian authority finds its arguments within the text itself, which can then no longer be called simply blind or mystified. Moreover, the deconstruction does not occur between statements, as in a logical refutation or in a dialectic, but happens instead between, on the one hand, metalinguistic statements about the rhetorical nature of language and, on the other hand, a rhetorical praxis that puts these statements into question. The outcome of this interplay is not mere negation. *The Birth of Tragedy* does more than just retract its own assertions about the genetic structure of literary history. It leaves a residue of meaning. . . . (*GG,* p. 52)

This residue of meaning presents itself in such a way that it can be translated into what he calls "a secondary statement . . . about the limitations of textual authority." What *is* this residue of meaning? It is surely not systematic, for, as he says, it "remains beyond the reach of the text's own logic and compels the reader to enter into an endless process of deconstruction."

What the reader finds, then, in this *residue,* are formulations "in which every word is ambivalent and enigmatic." Why is this? Because their *source* in the "will has been discredited *as* a self," it can no longer give an account *of* itself *as* a self. Thus the pretended fullness of the Dionysian language appears as the "absence of meaning and the play of [an] endless tension of a non-identity, a pattern of dissonance that contaminates the very source of the will, the will as source" (*GG,* p. 52).

The problem here is that the Dionysian narrator is *only* a metaphorical representation of the natural will, as is the language he speaks and the music he plays. Thus, there can be no natural claim to his authority in language or music. What in the text of *The Birth of Tragedy* can be made as a statement about nature, that is, as a truth claim about the essence or nature of things, cannot survive this original translation *into* metaphor. The genetic model of discourse is founded squarely on the metaphorical transfer which inaugurates the Dionysian and Apollonian narrative in the first place. De Man concludes that such a model is not unique to *The Birth of Tragedy.* Rather, this dependence on the discontinuous ground of metaphoric and aphoristic formulations "turns out to be a recurrent structural principle of Nietzsche's from the start." Ultimately, metaphor loses its authority to make any claim. As de Man argues,

> if genetic models are only one instance of rhetorical mystification among others, and if the relationship between the figural and proper meaning of a metaphor is conceived, as in this text, in genetic terms, then metaphor becomes a blind metonymy and the entire set of values that figures so prominently in *The Birth of Tragedy*—a melocentric theory of language, the pan-tragic consciousness of the self and the genetic vision of history—are made to appear hollow when they are exposed to the clarity of a new ironic light. (*GG,* p. 53)

It seems, then, that very little of the vaunted "semantic residue" surfaces at all within Nietzsche's text, save for our own awareness that we are condemned to a continual series of cancellations, precisely on the level of meaningful statements. At the genetic level, we are already subject to the ironic characterization *of* the tragic statement—which irony leaves a "hollow" where the significant values in question were to have arisen.

The metalinguistic reflection on rhetoric is even more pointed in de Man's later article, "Nietzsche's Theory of Rhetoric"—where he convincingly shows that "the linguistic paradigm *par excellence*" is the trope, the figure of speech (especially metaphor, metonymy, and synecdoche). Indeed, Nietzsche himself claimed, in his lectures on rhetoric dating from 1872-73, that " 'No such thing as an unrhetorical, 'natural' language exists that could be used as a point of reference; language is itself the result of purely rhetorical tricks and devices" (*TR,* p. 35).

Such a conception of language clearly forbids the possibility of a literal truth. Thus de Man insists that we are further and further driven "into the complications of rhetorical delusion." In the end, any proposition or part of a proposition results in what he calls "an exchange of properties that allows for their mutual persistence at the expense of their literal truth." And this is an irremediable situation from which we cannot extricate ourselves. The deconstructive character of the Nietzschean text consists ultimately in a rhetorical process of endless reversals and substitutions. In de Man's words, "one more 'turn' or trope added to a series of earlier reversals will not stop the turn towards error." From the very outset, therefore, philosophical reflection would be bound to the literary and rhetorical "deceit" it traditionally labors to discredit (*TR,* pp. 40-43).

What then, one might ask, staves off the Nietzschean text from total self-destruction, from total cancellation, from being a "hollow"—devoid of any significance at all? De Man is sorely pressed to answer this; he concludes in an odd way that

> The wisdom of the text is self-destructive . . . . , but this self-destruction is infinitely displaced in a series of successive rhetorical reversals which, by the endless repetition of the same figure, keep it suspended between truth and the death of this truth. A threat of immediate destruction, stating itself as a figure of speech, thus becomes the permanent repetition of this threat. . . . It follows that the entire system of valorization at work . . . can be reversed at will. . . . This exchange of attributes involving the categories of truth and appearance deprives the two poles of their authority. (*TR*, pp. 43, 45)

All of which is to say: the text of Nietzsche is at once true and false, neither true nor false, successively true and false.

Curiously enough, de Man has gone both too far and not far enough: it seems as if the text deconstructs itself right out of existence, but all the while *only* on the supposition of a precedent ground, which is variously introduced and invoked by de Man as will, presence, truth, error, illusion, nature, self, self-consciousness, or art. The proposed deconstruction, then, only survives to the extent it does by virtue of implicitly postulating a non-figurative ground of truth and being—even if the discourse *itself* can neither attain to nor express this transcendent ground.

Elsewhere, I have shown how it was the purpose of the Nietzschean discourse to bring this ontotheological ground into question, precisely by *employing* a metaphorical conception of language that would be framed, by analogy, to the *metamorphic* nature of Will to Power.[5] The articulation of each would be understood according to its diacritical or differential character. The advantage of this view would be to preserve the possibility of a meaningful and coherent thematic, without basing it on the simple referential character of a proper, non-figurative language. To be fair, de Man himself tends towards this direction in the later essay.

At the end of his paper on "Nietzsche's Theory of Rhetoric," de Man announces that his reading should best be seen as a preparation for examining the text of *Thus Spake Zarathustra.* Surely, this would be *the* work to examine. But what would be the result? Another "hollow"? Another voyage into the metaphorical subversion of every thematic or "philosophical" teaching? Another series of narrative feints, mutually cancelling one another? Indeed, *Zarathustra* is often considered to be just that: a standing contradiction between the exuberant affirmation of the first three books and the sobering denial, the nay-saying of the final book, written some two years later.

But Nietzsche himself is consistently clear about the seriousness of this text and its overall positive character. Three and one-half years after its completion, in *Ecce Homo*, he continues to call *Zarathustra* his greatest inspiration, the one that stands above and apart from all others. During the period of *Zarathustra*'s composition, he writes to von Gersdorff: "Don't be put off by the mythic style of the book: my entire philosophy is behind these homey and unusual words, and I have never been more serious."[6] Nietzsche thus seems to be fully aware of the stylistic and rhetorical resources of *Zarathustra;* yet far from resulting in a *cancellation* of the narrative or in an *evacuation* of its teachings, these stylistic resources intensify and unify both the narrative and the teaching. It is in this sense that he can say, in *Ecce Homo,*

> Let anyone add up the spirit and good nature of all great souls: all of them together would not be capable of producing even one of Zarathustra's discourses. . . . The most powerful capacity for metaphors that has existed so far is poor and mere child's play compared with this return of language to the nature of imagery. . . . In every word he contradicts, this most Yes-saying of all spirits; in him all opposites are blended into a new unity.[7]

Perhaps *Zarathustra* is exemplary in that Nietzsche concentrates his contradictory, metaphorical expression in so *many* images throughout the text: wheel, sun, snake, ring, journey, homelessness, wave, sea, cave, mountain, arrow, animal, child, etc. But what is most important about this concentration is that each image, however fractured, points to a unity or unifying process, one that finds its highest instance in Zarathustra's own teaching. The unity, bred *from* the most extreme opposites, after all, *is* the very definition of the Overman: the Overman is the meaning of the earth. He who can will the prospect of an Eternal Recurrence of *all* things will redeem the earth. And what is this Eternal Recurrence but the most complete expression of the Will to Power?

In all this, there is no master sense, no non-figural meaning, none of what de Man terms a "zero degree of figurality" (*GG,* p. 52), nor is there a discrete or transcendent *ground*—above or beneath. Indeed, Overman, Eternal Return, and Will to Power are *themselves metaphors* in each of Nietzsche's published works. When they were provisionally analyzed as non-figural concepts by Nietzsche, he saw fit *not* to publish these analyses. The deconstructive operations within Nietzsche's text do, as de Man suggests, take us back to the metalinguistic genesis of the narrative train. But this is *not* an analytical or deconstructive *terminus ad quem,* as de Man seems to think, nor does it result in the *cancellation* of significant statements at the level of the explicit narrative teaching. On the contrary, deconstruction should do precisely the opposite: it should, if at all possible, fill in the suspected hollow with all the resources that *lend* significant value to any one statement. In the case of the Nietzschean text, this in fact occurs: the metaphorical circulation of signs constitutes this value, just as the metamorphic circulation of force constitutes the sum of relations as Will to Power, and defines this very "moment itself" as one configuration, one set, in its eternal process of transformation.

II

The kind of deconstruction practiced by Derrida is far more of an operation *upon* the text. In his *Spurs: Nietzsche's Styles,* Derrida performs—and "performs" is perhaps too weak a word—what he calls an "affirmative" and "contemporary" kind of deconstruction. There, he radically extends what in his earlier work he called a "decentering" of the text. By following out his own programme of a "*supplementary* form of interpretation," which would consist in pursuing the "genetic indetermination" or the "seminal adventure of the trace," Derrida affirms what Nietzsche had long ago claimed: that the text finally disappears beneath its interpretation.[8] But for both Nietzsche and Derrida, this is the normal state of affairs. Since there is no "immaculate perception" there can be no simple return "to the texts themselves," to some immaculate or original edition.

If de Man's immanent deconstruction had emptied the text and shown it to be a hollow vessel, for Derrida the text now becomes a positive receptacle, not only furrowed out by an ever-changing and ampliative series of codes, but also traversed by what Heidegger referred to as *paths* of thought which often lead nowhere: *Holzwege, Feldwege.* Such paths often terminate abruptly; or, they can generate their own axes of development and continuity from within. Derrida suggests just such an entrance into the text of Nietzsche. He begins his account with what he calls an *erratic exergue.* Interestingly enough, this brief and erratic exergue explains nothing. But inasmuch as one can talk about the *kind* of deconstructive operation that Derrida performs upon a text, it is arguably the most pointed and instructive example in the entire course of his work.

The text of *Spurs* begins with an exergue—then, i.e., with a *space* which is *below* the inscription, or, outside the printed message of a coin. Let me quote this:

> From this, Nietzsche's letter [to Malwida von Meysenbug, November 7, 1872], I shall snip out the bits and pieces of an erratic exergue.
> *". . . At last my little bundle is ready for you, and at last you hear from me again, after it must have seemed I had sunk into a dead silence. . . . [We] could have celebrated a reunion like that of the Council of Basel, which I recall with warm memories. . . . For the third week in November, and for eight days, a glorious visit has been announced—here in Basel! The 'visit in itself,' Wagner and wife. They are on the grand tour, intending to touch on every main theater in Germany, on this occasion including the famous Basel "DENTIST," to whom I own a debt of thanks. . . . You see, my* Birth of Tragedy *has made me the most offensive philologist of the present day, to defend whom could be a true marvel of courage, for everyone is of a mind to condemn me."*

Then the text begins:

> The title for this lecture was to have been *the question of style.*
> However—it is woman who will be my subject. (*S,* p. 31)

Several questions are immediately suggested here, in the space of this brief exergue. Derrida calls it an "erratic" exergue—that is, one that *wanders.* The term "erratic" comes from Heidegger (*die Irre*), and Derrida often invokes it. It suggests wandering away from the truth, into error. It is a term for the necessary deviance that accompanies any reflection about truth or Being: if one seeks to open up or to follow a *path* of thought, one must perforce be attentive to the edge, the outside margin of that path, which defines the path and sustains its very directionality. The term is also reminiscent of Nietzsche's own description of himself and his kind: "we nomads, we wanderers."

In this *snippet of* a letter, Nietzsche mentions six things: (1) A wrapped package—an envelope or gift—whose contents are *not* mentioned. (2) That he has been *silent* of late—he has *not* written Malwida von Meysenbug for some time. (3) He would *like* to reconvene a meeting, a reunion, in Basel—in the near future. (4) Wagner will shortly arrive in Basel. (5) The visit will include the attendance of a famous Basel "dentist"—the term "dentist" is in double quotes. He is one to whom

Nietzsche owes a debt of thanks, of gratitude. (6) Finally, he speaks of the poor reception given to his *Birth of Tragedy,* and the defensive posture he must assume. Six things, then: a package, his silence, a meeting, Wagner's arrival, an unmentioned yet apparently important dentist, and his defensiveness. Let us say that Derrida's *snippet*—which is a cutting *up,* or *out,* of a letter by Nietzsche—let us say that this snippet conveys a sense of mystery or enigma; perhaps of presentiment and expectation. Some things have happened—and these are unclear. Other events are yet to happen—and these are also unclear. All of which is to say that the events of the letter, that which takes place, the happenings spoken of, *are not.* Derrida has already constructed a Heideggerian text *out* of Nietzsche. The event or happening of Being resonates throughout this brief text, but at a *distance* (*in die Ferne*). That which *is* does *not* seem to be present, *because* it takes place in the distance—and, *distancing* is the very operation inscribed *in* this text, this text which speaks about six things, six events in the distance.

Fine. This is interesting, and it is an effective way of opening a discourse about *woman* (indeed, the letter is addressed to Malwida von Meysenbug). But it is also a text about Nietzsche, about his many-voiced and polyvalent style, as well as about the Heideggerian concept of Being (as *Ereignis*). Woman-style-Being. These three topics will be the concern of Derrida's text, *Spurs: Nietzsche's Styles.*

But what of Derrida's *own* operation so far? Several possibilities of interpretation already present themselves to us, when we think ahead to the larger text *en bloc.* We could say that this text is simply meant to be an explication *of* the three themes just mentioned. Or, that this is a *justification* of Nietzsche's complex attitudes towards women. Or, we could say that this text may well be an imputation. Perhaps, by a judicious or injudicious editing of Nietzsche's remarks concerning women, Derrida projects or imputes one or several values *of* woman into the tapestry of Nietzsche's own text. Such a concept of woman may appear to describe a heterogeneous *or* a homogeneous quantity. And, what Nietzsche's text may well admit Derrida's will force upon it. According to such a view as this, what emerges will be Derrida's valuation of woman.

To determine *the* interpretation, i.e., *one* interpretation, or the motivations for a polyvalent interpretation—which may well devolve to a decidable or undecidable resolution about woman (and this either for Nietzsche's text or for Derrida's text)—all this requires our attention. Especially to Derrida's own operation. Derrida everywhere claims that the text exceeds the author. Knowing this, he also writes; presumably with a second order claim of control. Derrida writes and he writes about writing, about its control, its excess, its indebtedness, and its wanderings.

Wandering, i.e., an erratic exergue. Let us say, once again, that marginality (or in more Heideggerian terms, horizonality) is forever being introduced into the text and its subject matter; to the extent that marginality becomes central. This has to be qualified, of course. If horizon is simply exchanged for figure, it no longer operates as horizon: rather, it becomes figure. Thus, while the marginality of woman, style, being, etc., will be of central concern to Derrida, it is inevitable that his own discourse must be an *oblique* one. Two indications, already, of this oblique character of the text: (1) Derrida writes across Nietzsche. Indeed, across his letters and a variety of texts. (2) He introduces what he wants to discuss without really mentioning it: in an exergue, which serves as a kind of preface, a space outside the text, a *pre-face.* A margin.

We already have a rather precise notion about *what* is said in that exergue, about its positive content, about what is presented to us, and about what that might lead to, in the distance. But let us not forget that the exergue itself is in Nietzsche's own hand.

Nietzsche *writes,* Derrida *snips: "Je découpe."* I cut up, I cut out, I cut off—I also make a sort of collage with what remains, i.e., I make a *découpage.* At once, Derrida suggests that *he* is castrating the text of Nietzsche. He performs a kind of violence to it, that is, he *excises* a part of the original text—and in the first instance, this is the text of a letter. But by doing this, Derrida at the same time privileges what remains. And what is it that remains after an excision? Two things: that which is cut off, and that from which something is cut off. Immediately after the so-called exergue, Derrida tells us: "The title for this lecture *was to have been* the question of style. *However*—it is woman who *will be* my subject." By wielding the knife upon Nietzsche's text, already in the exergue, the subject matter *becomes* woman. The subject was to have been style. Indeed, the title of Derrida's text still remains that: "Nietzsche's Styles." It should have been style—however—it is woman who will be my subject. *However,* here corresponds to *exergue:* and what is excised by the exergue results in the question of woman. As Derrida remarks later on in the text, "If style were a man (much as the penis, according to Freud, is the 'normal prototype of fetishes'), then writing would be woman" (*S,* p. 47).

Not only, then, does the space of the exergue *suggest* a kind of castration, it *performs* one. But what is *altered* in and by this exergue? Derrida is attentive enough to insert a series of *ellipses* into the exergue—to stand in for what was taken out. When we examine the content of this excision, by comparing the exergue with Nietzsche's original letter,[9] we find some surprising indications, namely, remarks that would appear to have a strong bearing on *any* analysis of sexuality or style in Nietzsche. Let me cite what Derrida *omits* or cuts off in his transcription of this letter.

The first ellipsis is practically negligible: "Respected Fraulein"—that is, *Verehrtestes Fräulein*—a common form of address, made from the past participle of the verb "to respect." That Nietzsche the philologist or Derrida the grammalogue fails to note the alliterative latin term for testicles is not clear. Especially when addressed to Malwida von Meysenbug, the political activist and ardent feminist, the spinster author of *Memoirs of an Idealist.* Derrida also fails to note the name of this famous dentist—his name itself is curious, especially since Derrida makes so much of the dentist figure—that is, of extirpation, castration, excision. The name of the dentist in question was Dr. *Marter,* which in German means torture or torment, and is the root word for the tortured believer, the martyr. It is to this dentist (in double quotes) that Nietzsche *owes* a *debt* of gratitude. The debt, whatever it is, reinforces the economic and numismatic character of this "exergue." This will not only point up the questions of debt, exchange, circulation, etc., but also those of sexual identity and conventional moral value. Aristotle himself established the etymology: *nomos* comes from *numis.* Thus, the value and the very identity of woman will *also* be a conventional moral or social issue, and this will be caught up in the classical dispute between a natural origin or identity (*homo natura, vita femina,* primary nature) and a conventional origin or identity (second nature, social being, Christian and bourgeois moral evaluation).

Following the sentence about the celebrated dentist, there follows another ellipsis, where Nietzsche himself introduces the agency of the *spur,* which term, of course, figures in the very title of Derrida's text. Nietzsche says, "You will certainly not yet know the apologia by professor Rohde of Kiel, which he has written with *sword as well as pen,* and with great superiority over his opponents."

Such a sword *or* pen wields superiority over his opponents, yet stands in as an *apologia*—it speaks for Nietzsche, pro- Nietzsche, apo-Nietzsche. As sword, it is a parrying threat, as pen it is a defense—or the reverse, or both. A defense *for* Nietzsche, all the while *at a distance,* i.e., from Kiel. Warlike, apologetic, distant, acting at a distance, peaceful, sword, and pen: all this, Derrida argues, will constitute the issue of woman. Yet *none* of this is cited here in the exergue, by Derrida. Nietzsche closes this letter, incidentally, by saying, "Dearest Fräulein von Meysenbug. . . . Who knows *how much like your life mine may become? . . .* And here I think of you and am heartily glad to have met with you, dearest Fräulein von Meysenbug, who are a lonely fighter for the right. . . ."

So far, we have examined a *snippet* of some 20 lines or so, which stands at the margin, outside Derrida's text, yet which is orchestrated by him. Why does Derrida excise what he does from this letter? Why does he not comment on what he could well draw out of this text? Does what he snip off constitute an axis of interpretation? One less favorable to Derrida's explicit interpretation? Or, if it *were* a preface or pre-text, does this excised fragment itself direct and guide Derrida's interpretation? And is this interpretation pointed, that is, univocal, or is it heterogeneous? Is Derrida's interpretation, whatever it is, veiled and obscured, as is the excised fragment? Is this excised fragment silent by its absence? Or, is this removal the very *operation* of interpretation? Troubling questions, due precisely to their Derridean cast: how does it stand, then, with these marginal, silent non-inscriptions, and their mysterious agency in the distance?

III

First, let me review what Derrida advances, what he claims or argues *for,* in his text. More or less, we could say that Derrida defends or discusses three topics:

The first topic occupies the first third of the text (pp. 31-59). There, Derrida is ostensibly concerned with the figure or appearance of *woman* in the text of Nietzsche. He argues that for Nietzsche, the term "woman" is the name for a dimension of truth. Specifically, it signifies the non-truth *of* truth, the negative, dissimulating, reserved aspect of truth. Here, non-truth conditions that which emerges *as* truth. By a complementary process, it is precisely what is obscured by the emergence of truth. Granted, such a discussion is somewhat obscure itself. It owes what coherence it has to Heidegger's interpretation of the Greek concept of truth as *alētheia,* i.e., truth as the process of *unconcealment.*

Such a notion of truth is bound to the Greek naturalist understanding of *Being* as a process of growth, presentation, standing-forth, subsistence, and passing-away. Thus Heidegger argues that the presocratic Greeks understood Being according to the process of nature—*physis*—of coming-to-be, growth, endurance, and passing. To speak of Being, then, means to understand that which *is,* insofar as it presents itself to us and sustains itself in itself. Thus Being manifests itself, shows itself forth, as a general process of nature. The truth of Being, then, is for Being to reveal itself; that is, to come forth, to e-merge, to un-cover, un-veil, or un-conceal itself. To come to be, to come to pass, etc., it must stand forth, it must be at work, it must come out of its cover, its sleep. Thus the *negative* aspect of truth is already inscribed at the start of the Western tradition of understanding: *a-lētheia,* to wake *up* from sleep, to come out of forgetfulness, away from concealment, to shed its veil. What comes into sight, then, necessarily obscures something else. And that something else, that which is removed or concealed, permits what *is* to appear as such; i.e., to present itself to us, in the present.

As Nietzsche had already suggested, and as Heidegger will develop it, this notion of non-presence, of absence, or difference—which initially belonged to the truth of Being—this becomes forgotten by the metaphysical tradition. Once Being is reduced to the image, to the *view* of beings, and becomes understood as *idea* or *ousia,* it gets interpreted as simple presence. And this, in turn, will be the principal axiom for understanding Being as reality or objectivity, or, as the immediate certitude of subjective Being, i.e., of self-presence or *parousia.* It is the latter conception, self-presence, that will find its strongest formulation in Descartes, with his assertion that the *cogito* or consciousness is the ground of our knowledge of Being: what is real and true must present itself as clear and distinct to the intuiting cogito. This tradition of subjective and objective idealism extends through Hegel and is finally brought into question by Nietzsche. Thus, it is Nietzsche (followed by Marx and Freud) who will assault this privilege of presence, whether as objective Being or as truth. What is, what is true, will henceforth admit the unclear, the non-verifiable, the subconscious, the distant, dissimulating, and complex. Such a state of affairs will *not* divulge itself to the clear and distinct inspection or to the simple register of intuitive certainty. It will continually defer and distance itself—as *woman.*

The second issue Derrida concerns himself with is Heidegger's interpretation of Nietzsche, and this occupies the second third of the text (pp. 59-95). By failing to take the *heterogeneity* of Nietzsche's text seriously, Heidegger is led to condemn Nietzsche as a metaphysical thinker; indeed, as the last metaphysical thinker, he who brings the traditional metaphysics of presence to a close, by reversing or inverting its doctrines and operations. In an extremely forceful reading of Heidegger's *Nietzsche* volume, Derrida points to an omission on Heidegger's part, namely, his failure to analyze a section from *Twilight of the Idols,* where Nietzsche makes the explicit identification of woman and truth. In discussing the evolution of the concept of truth, Nietzsche states, "it [the idea] *becomes female*—it becomes Christian."[10] This *omission,* Derrida argues, testifies to the very limits of Heidegger's project of interpretation, of hermeneutics, since it cannot assign a discrete value to such a concept as woman. It is because philosophy is already *taken up* in the historical project ("The History of an Error") which Nietzsche describes, and because Heidegger's project to uncover philosophical truth within this movement is likewise *bound* to this epoch—it is for these two reasons that Derrida claims that such a philosophic-hermeneutic *decoding* of this or any stage of historical development is necessarily incomplete and inadequate. Such a hermeneutic analysis is precisely caught up in an argument pro and contra, subject to the binary oppositions of conventional metaphysics itself.

For Nietzsche and Derrida, however, it is just such a heterogeneous concept of *woman* which *escapes* this kind of classification, of metaphysical subsumption and valuation. "Hence," as Derrida claims, "the heterogeneity of Nietzsche's text"—*and* his style, and his women. There is no master sense to such concepts as style, text, truth, woman, Being. Thus, the hermeneutic interpretation which claims to speak about *the meaning* of Being encounters its limits at the point where its categories are *transgressed,* and not merely inverted. No master sense: this means, no single truth of Being, or, in short, no single meaning of Being—much less, of woman. Consequently, there is no simple, discrete counter-term. This is why Derrida will argue that woman *or* truth escapes and confounds the logic of castration. The meanings of these terms, *the* meaning of the text, all this overflows the conceptual and categorial control of the philosophic-hermeneutic code: for such a code is itself caught up in the logic of castration, that is, ultimately, in the discourse of presence. Thus Derrida will argue,

> The question of woman suspends the decidable opposition of true and non-true and inaugurates the epochal regime of quotation marks which is to be enforced for every concept belonging to the system of philosophical decidability. The hermeneutic project which postulates *a true sense of the text* is *disqualified* under this regime. Reading is freed from the horizon of *the* meaning or truth of Being, liberated from the values of the product's production or the present's presence. Whereupon the question of *style* is immediately unloosed as a question of writing. (*S,* pp. 83-85; emphases added)

Derrida goes on to excuse himself by saying matters are not quite so simple with any invocation of Heidegger. Thus, once Heidegger comes to understand Being in terms *of* appropriation (of *Ereignis*), he has by that token advanced *beyond* the hermeneutic analysis: beyond the analysis which limits itself to *the* truth and thus, to the circumscribed history of Being. That kind of analysis perforce remains metaphysical.

What then is Derrida's issue with Heidegger? At the time of the *Nietzsche* volume (1940 is the date for the section in question), Heidegger failed to see the necessarily indeterminate character of woman, that is, of truth. Thus, he claimed that the Nietzschean doctrine as a whole, was conventionally metaphysical—that it could be submitted to the question of Being, to the hermeneutical analysis of Being which establishes the truth and meaning of Being. Only some twenty-two years later, with the appearance of *Time and Being,* did Heidegger realize the importance of *Ereignis*—of the *happening,* the *event of* Being, that is, of appropriation, of the giving and the abyss of Being. This, in turn, dictates and thus subverts the very truth of Being. Derrida sees the later account of *Ereignis* precisely *as* the feminine operation itself. In which case, the entire reading of Heidegger's *Nietzsche* work has to be completely rethought.

The third and final discussion (pp. 95-110) concerns a specific posthumous fragment of Nietzsche's, which his editors have dated as belonging to the period of *The Gay Science.* An apparently trivial fragment such as this would at best evoke a smile of knowing recognition from the archivist or chronicler. The fragment is brief. It simply states: "I have forgotten my umbrella." Is this but a shard or scrap? Or, is it a fragment of an initial draft? Or, is it a piece of coded writing, and thus significant? Derrida argues that it is *structurally impossible* to resolve this question. For Derrida, this scrap or fragment stands as a model for *any* text. Which is to say, *no* text is ever fully comprehended, *or* does it ever fully express the intentions of the author. It may mean more, it may mean less. It may depend on context, circumstance, or the events of the time in which it was written or read (or, indeed, the weather: " *C'est une question du temps*"). Or, it may not. It may be intentionally subversive, divisive, unintelligible. It may or may not take account of its audience—unlike speech.

IV

We find ourselves cast back to the initial framing of the subject matter which we saw in the exergue: woman-truth-style. Three motifs which inter-penetrate as do the three figures of Nietzsche-Heidegger-Derrida. Let us pursue this relationship by raising one or two manageable issues. What is the *value,* for example, of woman, and what does the question of woman have to do with truth? And how does the issue of truth bear on the style or styles of Nietzsche's writing? Finally, what comprehension does such a text—Nietzsche's text—admit of?

One thing *is* clear: Derrida begins his analysis by immediately overdetermining the term "woman." He tells us that his reading of woman-style-Nietzsche belongs to an affirmative and contemporary project of deconstruction. Thus, we shall find out what it is that has come to be known *as* woman, or, how woman has been understood, used, abused, etc., as a topic or agency in Nietzsche's thought. When I say that woman is overdetermined, I mean that Derrida will at once deny a simple—or following the numismatic metaphor—a reverse essence to woman, yet he will find these two senses as well as a multitude of significant tracings within the nominal unity of this term. Consequently, the term "woman" explodes under Derrida's pen. Within the course of the first three pages alone, we can construct a metonymic chain to carry the plural values of woman: woman, style, pen, sword, pointed object, spur, prow, headwall, elytron, language, tongue, veil, sail, wake, trace, indication, mark, word, umbrella, Nietzsche himself. What conceptual unity or identity is to be found here, in this *Musterrolle* of designations? What essence? What *whatness?*

By overdetermining the signifier—"woman" can point to practically anything—Derrida has cut off a word from its *natural* meaning, its given concept or reference, which we all *know,* is quite simply one gender of the human species. *Une femme est une femme: plus jamais.* By Derrida's operation, woman now becomes *transitivized,* and this according to at least three models *other* than Nietzsche's own: First, the operation follows the late Heidegger's account of *Ereignis;* Second, according to Derrida's concept of the sign; Third, according to the dynamic model of psychoanalytic interaction. By the folding-back of each of these models upon the other, *the* question of "woman" becomes irrecuperable.

In the simplest terms, by identifying the question of woman with that of truth, Derrida effectively removes woman from *the* truth *of* woman. Thus, the *nature* of woman precedes the metaphysical discourse of logos. Or, in other words: the question of woman precedes the metaphysical discourse of *nature* itself, of essence, quiddity, or whatness; hence, of Being and the truth *of* Being. At every turn Derrida will avoid the fetishizing discourse of logocentrism when it comes to submit woman to its imperious and imperializing logic of nomination, classification, and ordination. "Woman" is neither an essence, nor a being, nor simple Being itself or truth itself (herself). Hence Derrida's overdetermination of woman: woman, who escapes the trap of metaphysical discourse. We should be aware that this is precisely Heidegger's operation at the moment he tries to thematize the post-metaphysical doctrine of *Ereignis.* In *Time and Being,* we read the following passage—the passage which precedes Derrida's own citation of the same text (*S,* p. 121n):

> How about this convincingly justified and candidly posed question: *What is* Appropriation [*Ereignis*]? The question asks for whatness, for the essence, it asks how Appropriation becomes present, how it presences. Our seemingly innocent question, What is Appropriation? demands information about the Being *of* Appropriation. But if Being itself proves to be such that it belongs to Appropriation and from there receives its determination as presence, then the question we have advanced takes us back to what first of all demands its own determination: Being in terms of time. This determination showed itself as we looked ahead to the "it" that gives [*es gibt Sein*], looked through the interjoined modes of giving: sending and extending. Sending of Being lies in the extending, opening and concealing of manifold presence into the open realm of time-space. Extending, however, lies [or rests] in one and the same with sending, in Appropriating. This, that is, the peculiar property of Appropriation, determines also the sense of what is here called "lying" [i.e., resting, reposing]. What we have said now allows and in a way even compels us to say how Appropriation must *not* be thought. What the name "event of Appropriation" names can no longer be represented by means of the current meaning of the word: for in that meaning "event of Appropriation" is understood in the sense of [an] occurence and happening—not in terms of Appropriating as the extending and sending which opens and preserves. (*T&B,* p. 20; emphases added)

A few lines further, and this *is* included in Derrida's citation, we read:

> Appropriation is not the encompassing general concept under which Being and time could be subsumed. Logical classifications mean nothing here. For as we think Being itself and follow what is its own, Being proves to be destiny's gift of presence, [i.e.,] the gift granted by the giving of time. [But] the gift of presence is the property [*Eigentum*] of Appropriating [*Ereignens*]. (*T&B,* pp. 21-22; *S,* p. 121n)

Granted, one could pursue Heidegger's labored account of *Ereignis* at great length; something we could perhaps be spared, for the moment. What is decisive in any case is that Derrida finds a model for stating the privilege of *woman* in Heidegger's text about *Ereignis.* Like *Ereignis,* woman will be the "abyss," the *Ab-grund* of Being and hence, of truth. She constitutes its gift and its reserve: she is its giving and its withholding, she is her own giving and her own withholding. Moreover, she is conceived before the advent of metaphysics, before the Being of beings. She operates at a distance from things, precisely by opening, extending, and concealing their realm. Woman, like *Ereignis,* "can no longer be represented by means of the current meaning of the word."

The second model for the question of woman stems from Derrida's analysis of Husserl. In *Speech and Phenomena,* Derrida found that Husserl had submitted the order of signification—of signs—*to* the order of truth and Being. In this sense, Derrida was able to show the conventional metaphysics of presence at work in determining Husserl's distinction between two kinds of sign: indication and expression. There, Derrida went to great lengths to show how the very notion of sign has to precede the truths of any metaphysics or ontology, precisely in order to give them any claim to truth at all. If Husserl failed to reflect on "the essence" of signs in general, this suggested their *priority* over essence and objectivity—where essence and objectivity at least require the being of a reiterable identity. The closest Husserl came in ascribing an essence or unity to the sign was in saying that "signs are always *of* something" (or for something: für Etwas). Yet this is enough for Derrida: such a generalized and functional notion of the sign could embrace an extraordinary variety of operations—e.g., presentation, representation, indication, expression, ostensive reference, speech, writing, depicting, tracing, suggesting, pointing, gesturing, iteration, reiteration, identification, etc.,—and once again, escape *essentialization* or categorial identity.

The second stage in Derrida's critique of the sign (which he carries out in *Grammatology, Ecriture et différence,* and elsewhere) was to revise Saussure's concept by denying the essential opposition between the signifier and signified. The important thing is to see the *system* of language and to recognize the differential or diacritical value each term possessed. Thus, the discrete concept or meaning—the signified—is replaced with a coherent set of signifiers, which are in turn set off from the rest. The ontological consequences for such a view are immense. The rigid metaphysical distinction between empirical signifier and ideal signified becomes obliterated in a generalized circulation of signs, i.e., in the *play* of signifiers (—and were we to retain the value which separates signifier and signified, we would say Derrida turns the signified into a signifier; but by crossing out the line between them, by crossing over the line, let us call this signifier "sign"—quite simply).[11]

Like Heidegger, both Husserl and Saussure are to all appearances silent about woman. Neither *Being and Time,* the *Logical Investigations,* nor *A General Introduction to Linguistics* could be viewed, precisely, as a feminine or feminist tract. Indeed, there is total silence. Yet, once one performs a deconstructive analysis on these texts, a certain kind of liberation does emerge: precisely a liberation from the hierarchical oppositions which constitute the very Being of metaphysics—signifier/signified, empirical/ideal, body/soul, absence/presence, etc. Henceforth, the significance of a term—a term such as "woman"—derives from its circulation, from its active employment as well as from its negative distance of phonic and semantic differentiation.

We could, however, say the same for *any* term, for any term other than "woman." Hence, the strategic necessity for Derrida to invoke the third model, namely, the Freudian psychoanalytic model. Freud recognized that sexuality achieves its significant stages and determinations only through the dynamics of circulation and interaction, or what he calls the "economic-dynamic system." Hence *Derrida's* repeated stress on the psychoanalytic sense of the term "position": my libidinal impulses attain their progressive psycho-sexual stages of organization only by taking up a *position* with regard to myself and my body, with regard to others and their bodies, and with regard to the external forms of prohibition and approbation.

What role, then, does Freud play in Derrida's text? Surely the question of woman is elaborated across the central metaphor of castration, that is, of the phallus and its castration. Yet the phallic stage takes place and is resolved within the Oedipal complex; the most universal of complexes for Freud. Indeed, it is only through a resolution of the Oedipal complex that one can fully attain the final stage of psycho-sexual organization, the genital stage—whereby the individual can *resolve* his or her sexuality, where masculine and feminine are differentiated at the onset of puberty. Also, the phallic stage is preceded by the earlier forms of organization, i.e., by the oral and anal stages, which are respectively characterized in the Freudian schema by the oppositions between biting and being bitten—or, by eating and being eaten, and between active and passive. Again, all these terms designate the progressive evolution of sexuality *per se.*

But by advancing to the Freudian analysis, however, it seems as if we have compounded our difficulties. It seems as if the problem of logocentrism were in fact compounded by phallocentrism. Or, to borrow a Derridean neologism, it seems that the question of woman is trapped within what he calls "phallogocentrism." How does this most conventional of sexual logics work? For Freud, the schema active-passive is reproduced within the Oedipal complex to structure the opposed values phallic-castrated. This in turn anticipates the final resolution, masculine-feminine. Thus, passive-castrated-feminine is the *reverse* of active-phallic-masculine. The *only* positive term, the only master sense here, is *phallus,* the term which designates masculine sexual identity and mastery by pointing to a positive anatomical term, the penis—the only positive anatomical term.

Hence, there would seem to be, at least for Freud, a *natural* foundation for the genesis of sexual identity, namely, the penis. Consequently, there would be a natural bond between the penis and the phallus—and, ultimately, of a fixed meaning to all sexual identity. But, Derrida reads Freud in the same fashion as he reads Saussure. There *is no* master meaning, no simple phallus so naturally defined. Therefore, there is no natural hierarchy, no simple meaning of sexual being, or as he would say to Lacan, no transcendental signifier.

If Derrida castrates the text of Nietzsche and Heidegger, he also does this to the text of Freud. Thus, what is important is the exchange value, the differential value of the terms, and not the substance of any single term. Let us assume that he follows Melanie Klein here, as elsewhere; that he follows her analysis: that the penis is a partial object, significant of sexual and bodily identity, but that it finds its equivalent at the oral stage with the breast of the mother, or at the anal stage with the feces, with gifts, with teeth, with the umbrella—as *detachable objects.* There seems to be an abundance of textual evidence to support this, even in the brief exergue. Also, we know that Freud disallowed any positive value to the vagina or to its specifically sexual sensations—this need not be commented on. Melanie Klein suggests that woman can afford to be modest in this respect. Her pleasure and knowledge need not be manifest. Indeed, they are not—except to herself. Let us follow our assumption and conclude that it is on the basis of an anatomical parity that the real issue arises: not castration, but the castration *complex.* This is the apotropaic anguish or anxiety that Derrida continually speaks of and that he finds everywhere in the text of Nietzsche. Where do I turn? What use, end, function must I make of my phallus in order to properly retain it? For it to be, and me as well? What position must I assume in order to resolve it? Here, the dream imagery sown throughout Nietzsche's texts—of the father, of the mother, of the silent ship with its billowing sails, with the beckoning and call at a distance, with flight and wandering.

Perhaps Nietzsche himself had such an anxiety complex. One could, as Derrida suggests at the end of his text, make a conventional psychoanalytic reading of Nietzsche's writing. Two citations from Nietzsche might suggest such an Oedipal path. The first passage was written in 1888, and it opens up the first chapter of *Ecce Homo:*

> The happiness of my existence, perhaps its unity or uniqueness (*Einzigkeit*), dwells in its fatality: to express this in the form of an enigma: "As my father, I am already dead; as my mother, I am still alive and growing older." This double origin which so to speak, extends to the highest and lowest level of life—at once decadence and beginning—this, if anything were ever able, explains my *neutrality*, my free impartiality in relation to the whole problem of my life; this perhaps distinguishes me.[12]

The second passage was written in 1858, when Nietzsche attained the unlucky and troublesome age of thirteen—i.e., the onset of puberty. In it he recounts a dream that took place at the age of six, in which he dreams of his dead father and of the death of his young brother—who was to die the very next day:

> At this time, I dreamed I heard the sounds of organ music coming from the church, during a funeral. As I sought to see what the cause of this was, suddenly, up rose a tombstone. And out of the tomb came my father, wearing his funeral shrouds. He hurried into the church and quickly came back out, carrying an infant in his arms. The grave opened up, he descended into it, and the headstone once again closed over the opening. Immediately, the organ groaning stopped and I awakened. The next day, little Joseph suddenly fell ill with cramps and died within several hours. Our grief was immense. My dream was completely fulfilled. To make matters worse, the small cadaver was placed in the arms of my father.[13]

When Nietzsche recounts this dream three years later, in 1861, he twice substitutes, in place of his father, the term "a white form." A premonition, a dream, and no doubt, ruthlessly traumatic. He anticipates the death of his infant brother, he identifies himself with his father, who is already dead, and with his mother, who is alive. The ill health and decadence Nietzsche suffered from, was tortured by, all his life, was inherited, he thought, from his father. Yet the means of transfiguration and overcoming stem from his mother, who he is and who is yet alive. Hence, we might say, Nietzsche undergoes a masculine *and* feminine resolution of the Oedipal complex. I am decadence and *beginning!* And, as my brother, that little cadaver, I too am taken out of the church. I can now be free, neutral, and impartial. Once more, the language of the ship: sailing over its apotropaic anguish.

But all this is only a perhaps—as is the umbrella. As in the letter to Malwida von Meysenbug, all the traces of psychosexual development are to be found here, in these two citations: their stages and their characterizations—and this from both a masculine and feminine viewpoint. Which is to say, they are confounded in their conventional, their purported authority. As Nietzsche remarked in the first passage, "the unity of my existence," its *Einzigkeit,* dwells in its fatality, and this can be expressed as an *enigma.* I have a double origin: and this distinguishes me, this *explains* my neutrality.

There is an apocryphal story told about Nietzsche that might—if true—lend confirmation to the neutral, if not neuter character of this resolution. It seems that on one of his frequent visits to Triebschen, Wagner's estate on Lake Geneva, Nietzsche fell somewhat ill. Wagner (who many critics perhaps too easily see as a father figure for Nietzsche at this period) recommended his own physician. Some weeks later, again at Triebschen, a banquet was held; and Wagner, cackling, urged his physician to make a toast to the young Nietzsche. The physician did so, and in the course of his toast, he recounted the event of Nietzsche's physical examination to the assembled guests. In an extremely rude form of humor, the physician pronounced that he had never, in his professional experience, seen such a miniscule penis. Nietzsche was of course mortified. He fled Triebschen *and* Wagner, never to return: an action that, *perhaps,* brought about to his own mind, the death of a *second* father. He realized afterwards, again perhaps, the excess of narcissism, his own fetishistic narcissism, that led to this humiliation. A neutral fatalism, a double origin, an enigmatic sexuality would henceforth characterize his texts.

The overvaluation of the phallus results from a misplaced importance attributed to the penis; the intensity of this valuation is a manifest form of narcissism. Woman *knows* this because she is told. Nietzsche knew this and felt this in direct proportion to his humiliation. Woman knows this but does not *believe* it—for she, too, has her own erogenous narcissism, her own intense sexual sensations—and is thus loath to concede to herself the value of sexual negativity; that is, of a kind of reverse or merely receptive identity.

Nonetheless, woman answers or resolves man's castration complex by allowing herself to replace the Oedipal mother—which role or function she may or may not choose to assume. She may take up *any* attitude towards this: castration, penis-envy, childbirth, or, the allure, the promise of completion, of satisfaction and sexual fulfillment, by which *she* resolves the decision *of* sexuality. Or, she may withdraw; beckon from a distance, act at a distance—all the while knowingly enigmatic, playful, tempting. Thus *she escapes* subsumption, classification, all the while confounding the logic of phallogocentrism. Derrida calls her logic, her silent logic, that of the *hymen.* Let me cite a brief discussion of this, from *La Dissémination:*

> Hymen signifies first of all the fusion, or consummation, of marriage, the identification or confusion between two. *Between* two, there is no longer any difference; rather, an identity. In that fusion, there is no longer any distance between desire . . . and the fulfillment of presence, between distance and nondistance; no more difference between desire and its satisfaction. Not only is the difference abolished . . . but the difference between difference and nondifference equally. . . . The hymen, confusion between the present and nonpresent . . . "has taken place" in the between; it is the spacing between wish and fulfillment, between perpetration and memory. . . . Hymen—consummation of differents, continuity and confusion of coitus, marriage—becomes confused with what seems to be its place of derivation: hymen as protective screen, casket of virginity, vaginal partition, thin and invisible veil that, for the hysteric, maintains itself *between* the inside and the outside of woman—hence between the wish and its fulfillment. It is neither the desire nor the pleasure but between the two. It is the hymen that the desire dreams of piercing, of bursting, with a violence that is (either both or between) love and murder. If the one or the other had taken place, there would be no hymen—but even if they had not occurred, there would still be no hymen. Hymen, with its completely undecidable meaning, hasn't happened except when it has not happened, when nothing *really* happens, when there is consummation without violence or violence without thrust, or thrust without mark, mark without mark (margin), etc., when the veil is torn *without being* torn; for example, when someone is made to die of laughter or happiness.[14]

Finally, we are brought back to the issue of *truth.* But now, truth is in double quotes: "truth"—so-called, by Nietzsche. As the truth of Being is suspended in *Ereignis,* as the truth of sexuality is suspended by the exchanges of the "feminine operation"—which operation *is* the exchange, the difference, the distance, the giving and withholding *of* resolution—so woman is also suspended. She *is* the suspension of the quotation marks, of truth. Specifically, for Nietzsche's text, this is the epoch, the *epoché,* the parenthesis or suspension of truth from its simple origin and simple possession. Truth, Nietzsche says, "becomes more subtle, more insidious, incomprehensible—*It becomes female.*" Such truth becomes traced out as Derrida finds it, in the graphics of the hymen, the *pharmakon,* or, of differance. The veil can no longer be simply lifted to *expose* woman-truth, or woman *to* truth—for it is not that kind of veil, nor is it any longer a question of simple presence. Rather, truth belongs to woman as *hymen:* subtle, insidious, incomprehensible—it *is* just as much as it *is not.* Its value is undecided and undecidable.

Likewise with the text of Nietzsche. That Derrida finds a threefold operation of woman within Nietzsche's text; that the operations are neither assimilable to a generic concept, nor to a simple affirmation or negation, nor to a dialectical resolution. This is perhaps what Nietzsche already knew when he wrote:

> If anything signifies our *humanization*—a genuine and actual *progress*—it is the fact that we no longer require excessive oppositions, indeed no opposites at all.[15]

> A "world of truth" that can be *mastered* completely and forever with the aid of our square little reason. What? Do we really want to permit existence to be degraded for us like this—reduced to a mere exercise for a calculator and an indoor diversion for mathematicians? Above all, one should not wish to divest existence of its rich *ambiguity. . . .* Whether existence without interpretation, without "sense," does not become "nonsense"; whether, on the other hand, all existence (itself) is not essentially, actively engaged in *interpretation—that cannot be decided. . . .* Rather, the world has become "infinite" for us all over again, inasmuch as we cannot reject the possibility that *it may include infinite interpretations.*[16]

By the same token, whenever one attempts to interpret and definitively resolve the written text, one always finds "a more comprehensive, stranger, richer world beyond the surface, an abysmally deep ground behind every ground, under *every attempt to furnish* 'grounds.' "[17]

SUNY-Stony Brook

NOTES

1 Jacques Derrida, *Spurs: Nietzsche's Styles,* trans. Barbara Harlow (Venice: Corbo e Fiore, 1976). (Hereafter cited as *S.*) This text originally appeared in *Nietzsche aujourd'hui* (Paris: Union Générale d'Éditions, 1973), and has been partially reproduced in *The New Nietzsche,* ed. David B. Allison (New York: Delta, 1977). A shorter version ("Becoming Woman") has since appeared in *Semiotext(e),* 3, No. 1 (1978), 128-37; as has also a new French version, *Eperons: les styles de Nietzsche* (Paris: Flammarion, 1978).

2 Martin Heidegger, *On Time and Being,* trans. Joan Stambaugh (New York: Harper & Row, 1972), p. 82 (hereafter cited as *T&B*).

3 For an important analysis of recent Nietzsche criticism, see R. Kuenzli, "Nietzsche und die Semiologie: Neue Ansätze in der französischen Nietzsche-Interpretation," in *Nietzsche-Studien,* 5 (1976), pp. 263-88.

4 Paul de Man, "Genesis and Genealogy in Nietzsche's *The Birth of Tragedy,*" *Diacritics,* 2 (Winter 1972), 44-53 (hereafter cited as *GG*); and "Nietzsche's Theory of Rhetoric," *Symposium,* 28 (Spring 1974), 33-51 (hereafter cited as *TR*).

5 See the "Introduction" to *The New Nietzsche,* pp. XI-XXVII.

6 "Letter to Carl von Gersdorff," June 28, 1883. Cited in *Nietzsche: A Self-Portrait from his Letters,* ed. and trans. Peter Fuss and Henry Shapiro (Cambridge: Harvard Univ. Press, 1971), p. 74.

7 Friedrich Nietzsche, "Thus Spoke Zarathustra," §6, *Ecce Homo,* in *On the Genealogy of Morals and Ecce Homo,* ed. and trans. Walter Kaufmann (New York: Vintage Books, 1969), pp. 304-05.

8 Jacques Derrida, "Structure, Sign, and Play in the Discourse of the Human Sciences," in *The Languages of Criticism and the Sciences of Man: the Structuralist Controversy,* ed. Richard Macksey and Eugenio Donato (Baltimore: The Johns Hopkins Univ. Press, 1970), pp. 247-65.

9 "Letter to Malwida von Meysenbug," November 7, 1872, in *Friedrich Nietzsche, Werke in drei Bänden,* ed. Karl Schlecta, 3 vols. (Munich: Carl Hanser, 1954-1956), III, pp. 1077-79. English trans. in *Selected Letters of Friedrich Nietzsche,* ed. and trans. Christopher Middleton (Chicago: Univ. of Chicago Press, 1969), pp. 107-09.

10 Friedrich Nietzsche, "How the 'True World' Finally Became a Fable (The History of an Error)," *Twilight of the Idols;* in *The Portable Nietzsche,* ed. and trans. Walter Kaufmann (New York: Viking, 1954), p. 485.

11 For an extended discussion of the concepts of "game" or "play" in language, see David Allison, "Derrida and Wittgenstein: Playing the Game," in *Research in Phenomenology,* 8 (1978). Forthcoming.

12 See Schlechta, ed., *Werke,* II, p. 1070. My translation.

13 Friedrich Nietzsche, "Aus meinem Leben (Die Jugendjahre 1844 bis 1858)," in Schlechta, ed., *Werke,* III, p. 17. My translation. The passage in question is discussed by Pierre Klossowski in his *Nietzsche et le cercle vicieux* (Paris: Mercure, 1969), pp. 255 ff.

14 Jacques Derrida, *La Dissémination* (Paris: Editions du Seuil, 1972), pp. 237-41. Trans. Teuben Berezdivin, in Allison, *The New Nietzsche,* pp. 188-89n.

15 Nietzsche, *The Will to Power,* §115, ed. Walter Kaufmann; trans. Kaufmann and R. J. Hollingdale (New York: Vintage Books, 1968), p. 70.

16 Nietzsche, *The Gay Science,* §§ 373-74, trans. Walter Kaufmann (New York: Vintage Books, 1974), pp. 335-36.

17 Nietzsche, *Beyond Good and Evil,* trans. Walter Kaufmann (New York: Vintage Books, 1966), p. 229.

Forgetting the Text: Derrida's Critique of Heidegger

David Couzens Hoy

The history of philosophy, perhaps like the history of poetry, has often changed, although not always progressed, as a result of one thinker's interpretation and criticism of a major precursor. Familiar examples are Aristotle on Plato, Berkeley on Locke, Kant on Hume, Hegel on Kant, and Heidegger on Husserl. Whether the newcomer's reading of his predecessor is a misreading, and whether misreadings are inevitable, would be difficult to ascertain unless such a judgment were itself absolutely certain. The task confronting a post-structuralist and post-modern theory of reading is to explain misreadings without generating ontological commitments of the same sort that caused previous distortions. One such commitment is the "metaphysical" belief that the current reading has grasped the indubitable truth while the prior misreading erred because it failed to grasp the essence of the matter.

Whether Derrida's interpretation and criticism of Heidegger is the latest development in the history of philosophy is itself an important philosophical question. The answer depends partly on whether the post-structuralist theory of reading is accomplishable, for Derrida's theory of *écriture* is actually an attempt at such a theory. Unlike Heidegger whose "destruction" of the history of ontology as originally announced in *Being and Time* is to result in a more fundamental ontology that would overcome this tradition, Derrida's method of "deconstruction" aims to dismantle a style of writing and thinking to see how it works (or in the case of traditional philosophy, to see how it does not work) without any intention of replacing it by a more proper one. The prescriptive thrust of Heideggerian destruction purportedly veils an ontological commitment to the "truth of Being" when this is the very sort of thing that should have been destroyed. Derrida's deconstruction is not to be yet one more ontology that will in turn be superseded. A form of playful irony, it remains nonprescriptive and merely allows previous metaphysics to destroy itself.

Of Derrida's many deconstructions of philosophical and literary writings, none is more significant than that of deconstruction's own parent, Heideggerian destruction itself. Furthermore, since the major precursor for the project of an *Überwindung* of metaphysics is Nietzsche, the paradigmatic problem for Derrida is to deconstruct Heidegger's destruction of Nietzsche. Any post-Freudian can see that the successful resolution of this problem would have the effect of removing a threatening parent and replacing him with a less reproving and more playful grandparent. No one is more aware of this, of course, than Derrida himself.

Since a good psychoanalyst would be suspicious of a subject's self-analysis, I do not think the immanental strictures of deconstruction will be violated by challenging Derrida here. I thus propose to go back to Derrida's essay, *Spurs: Nietzsche's Styles,*[1] which David Allison's commentary has greatly illuminated, and question those points that are directed against Heidegger and the philosophical position called hermeneutics. Subsequently, I intend to defend hermeneutics against this deconstruction and to suggest instead that deconstruction is simply one moment, although an important one, in the hermeneutical circle of understanding and interpretation. My aim is to translate Derrida's ambiguous, indirect discourse into theses that will be provocative both for those who defend Derrida, and for those who, if my translation manual is appropriate, may now wish to oppose him.

I. The Deconstructive Ideal: No Decidable Meaning

A footnote in *Spurs* reminds us that this is not the first time that Derrida has addressed the question of Heidegger's reading of Nietzsche as the thinker who in the very act of attacking the epoch of metaphysics remains unconsciously trapped in it. *Of Grammatology* suggests that Nietzsche can be freed from Heidegger's reading not simply by defending Nietzsche, but by letting this reading reach its own limits, beyond which the unique strangeness of Nietzsche's text will appear in its own right.[2] Heidegger's failure to perceive this strangeness is itself said to be due to the inability of Heidegger's destruction to transcend the metaphysical epoch. Despite Heidegger's efforts to avoid any commitment to an ultimate metaphysical reality, Derrida thinks that Heidegger's talk about the presencing of Being and its appropriation involves such a metaphysical metaphor. In fact, it is Heidegger's theory of language that reveals his entrapment. *Of Grammatology* intends to show that any theory of the sign as consisting of an irreducible dualism between signifier and signified is based on the metaphysical illusion that a sign must be a sign *of* something and that language needs this referentiality to be capable of expressing truths.

Derrida's critique of Heidegger in *Grammatology* is thus that Heidegger and hermeneutics are wrong in thinking that a theory of language must involve a theory of truth and of reference, and that Nietzsche is the one who in fact sees this. It will be a "difficult thought," Derrida tells us,[3] to think of an alternative theory (as he will try in working out the notions of trace and *différance*). *Spurs* takes up the implications of this thought for Heidegger's method of reading Nietzsche, and in so doing generates not only a theory for the reading of all texts, but furthermore, a theory of the conditions for the possibility of any act of understanding, interpretation, and communication.

Hermeneutics is precisely the area of philosophy that concerns itself with such theory, yet Derrida makes a point of opposing it. He emphasizes this opposition by selecting from Nietzsche's *Nachlass* a paradigm text that he thinks will inevitably frustrate the hermeneutic interpreter. This "text" is simply a scrap of paper, found with other apparently unrelated jottings, on which Nietzsche wrote, "I have forgotten my umbrella" (*S.* pp. 94 ff.).

The interesting feature of this passage for Derrida is that the words are entirely translatable and unambiguous, and yet its interpretation is completely indeterminate. It necessarily escapes the hermeneutic circle of interpretation and the attempt to bring the totality of a text into an intelligible reading because it has, in Derrida's words, "no decidable meaning."[4] He also suggests, furthermore, that this lack of decidable meaning may hold for all of Nietzsche's writings, both individually and as a corpus. The play with this possibility is part of the "difficult thought" that is to take both Nietzsche and Derrida beyond the confines of the metaphysical epoch.

Derrida is fully aware of the paradoxical character of his suggestion, of course, and avoids any outright assertion that this is what Nietzsche does mean. Nevertheless, he makes the implications of his thought sufficiently clear, saying that there is no such thing as a "totality" to Nietzsche's writing, and "no measure to its undecipherability" (*S.,* p. 105). Heidegger's attempt to show that the meaning of Nietzsche's writings amounts to a failed destruction of metaphysics thus does something that is proper only to a philosophical order, and this is indeed, says

Derrida, "the very order that Nietzsche's operation should have otherwise *put out of order*" (*S.*, p. 65).

Derrida rarely speaks in his own voice, but here in *Spurs* it is apparent that what holds for Nietzsche's text also holds for Derrida's own. He raises the question whether *Spurs* itself has any decidable meaning. To tell the truth, he says, it does not, but this information will not help a reader in his interpretive search for the presence or absence of such meaning, since the best way to lie and dissimulate is precisely to say that one is telling the truth (*S.*, p. 107). The paradoxical theory of truth at stake is clearly both Derridean and Nietzschean:

> there is no such thing either as the truth of Nietzsche, or of Nietzsche's text. . . . Indeed there is no such thing as a truth in itself. But only a surfeit of it. Even if it should be for me, about me, truth is plural. (*S.*, p. 80)

Similarly, the umbrella passage can be read coherently in any number of ways, and the serious hermeneutic reader who thinks that a text cannot be interpreted unless the surrounding context or the underlying reference can be discovered is defeated. The possibility of a text with no decidable meaning would show that the limits of hermeneutics are only the beginnings for deconstruction. In fact, the poverty of hermeneutics is demonstrated by the ability of deconstruction to "play" with all texts, even those that hermeneutics cannot take seriously.

At the risk of being accused of lacking a sense of humor, however, hermeneutics must resist thinking that Derrida is right in saying that it is an intelligible possibility that texts could have the status suggested by his playful paradigm. There is nothing wrong with play, but even play would seem to be impossible for a text having "no decidable meaning"—unless, that is, there is a sense in which this phrase does not imply the Pyrrhonism Derrida appears to be advocating.

If Derrida is a skeptic, he is not a naive one, and cannot be refuted in the usual way by showing that he tacitly accepts the very beliefs he denies. The claim that there is no decidable meaning is purposefully vague, and Derrida knows that it will be almost impossible to decide what he means by it. He thus cannot be accused of attaching a special epistemic status to the claim, since he himself does not purport to *know* what Nietzsche's fragment means. The point of the passage, and of Derrida's essay, may very well be to bring the whole enterprise of epistemology to an end, but the deconstruction that brings this about does not itself make any knowledge claims and does not pretend that its own standpoint is epistemologically privileged.

The hermeneutical project of deciphering Derrida's and especially Nietzsche's works is bound to try to penetrate this obscurity, however, and will inevitably be dissatisfied with the implied conclusion that no one can know what these works mean. The first point to clarify, then, is what might Derrida mean by "meaning?"

There are at least three related terms that should be distinguished: (a) "meaning" strictly speaking, or sense; (b) meaningfulness, or significance; and (c) reference. The first is merely a syntactical matter, and since Derrida himself says that "everybody knows what 'I have forgotten my umbrella' means" (*S.,* p. 99) and that it can be translated "with no loss" (*S.,* p. 101), he could not be talking about decidable meaning in this respect. Similarly, Derrida could not simply have significance in mind (although that is clearly part of what he means) since it is true for many texts that there is no such thing as the unique or ultimate significance of the text, and there are usually many possible implications or connotations that might be relevant, but might not. Of course, the umbrella passage is peculiar in that there is no available evidence for deciding whether it is significant at all. This makes it inaccessible in practice only, however, and Derrida is claiming that it is inaccessible in principle (*S.,* p. 97).

Since nothing so far would either explain such an inaccessibility in principle or be likely to thwart hermeneutics, Derrida's slogan will only be of interest if some views about reference and about truth are also implied. These views are difficult to pin down precisely, though, because Derrida's strategy is to find these implications buried in the figurative way Nietzsche speaks of women. The need for figurative language is not merely coincidental, however, if the conclusion at stake is the negative one that no theory of reference or of truth will be viable. It is also appropriate, then, that the paradigm sentence itself have no decidable referents or truth value. By extending this point analogically to Nietzsche's entire corpus, Derrida apparently intends to say both that Nietzsche does not have a metaphysical commitment to a "transcendental signified," and that there is in any case no way to determine the ultimate reference for a language, presumably not even in such general terms as "the True or the False," "the World," the "fact of the matter," or even simply "the facts."

Whether Derrida can make this analogical inference depends, however, on a point that he mentions but does not analyze sufficiently. As the sentence "I have forgotten my umbrella" stands in the original, it is already in quotation marks. In this particular case it is also true that the quotation marks do prevent the identification of the referents of the terms, and the extension of the indexical or token-reflexive "I" is in fact undecidable (although its intension is not). The consequence of treating Nietzsche's entire work as if it were also in quotation marks and thus also had an undecidable truth value is that philosophy becomes like fiction, at least according to a common theory of fictional statements as being propositions that are uttered in tacit quotation marks and thereby not asserted to be true. Sir Philip Sidney's line about the poet, that he "nothing affirmeth and therefore never lieth," would also characterize the philosopher.

This provocative thesis is vitiated, however, insofar as quotation marks do not always function as Derrida implies, and do not necessarily block all possibility of reference. Scarequotes, for instance, may still imply a referent. Speaking of somebody ironically as a "real athlete" does not deny that there are athletes in reality, but on the contrary presupposes that there are. Furthermore, even if an entire text were in quotes, the possibility of truth and falsity would still not disappear, since there would be, for instance, sentences about the textual lines or the fictional facts that are true or false. Finally, if the umbrella sentence had the status Derrida attributes to it, then it would not be an actual sentence in a discourse, but only the name of a sentence in a natural language. In the very act of trying to interpret the meaning of the sentence further, Derrida would be guilty of a mention-use confusion. Since the requisite causal chain or historical explanation behind the actual use of the sentence is entirely lacking, it may well be part of the wisdom of hermeneutics that it does not try to interpret the fragment.

Overlooking these features of quotation marks, Derrida dramatizes his opposition to Heidegger's conception of philosophy by claiming Heidegger fails to understand that Nietzsche is the very thinker who undercuts philosophy in this sense through his institution of what Derrida calls the epoch of quotation marks:

> The question of the woman suspends the decidable opposition of true and non-true and inaugurates the epochal regime of quotation marks which is to be enforced for every concept belonging to the system of philosophical decidability. The hermeneutic project which postulates a true sense of the text is disqualified under this regime. Reading is freed from the horizon of the meaning or truth of being, liberated from the values of the product's production or the present's presence. . . . The stylate spur rips through the veil. (*S.*, pp. 83-85)

In this epoch it becomes a characteristic of textuality as such to be in quotation marks, and thus methods of interpretation, like deconstruction itself, must resist trying to dig behind texts to find their "hidden meaning," that is, some causal relation to an aspect of the real world.

Derrida is not alone in contrasting this theory of textuality and of reading with a hermeneutical one. Like Derrida, Foucault criticizes hermeneutics and says historical discourses should be examined to see what is said, and not what might be meant.[5] He also maintains that descriptive terms in scientific discourses do not refer to theory-independent objects, and that such discourses are incommensurable. In yet a different context, Ian Hacking also stresses the need in writing a historical account of philosophy to avoid what he describes ironically as the commentators' assumption that "it would be uncharitable, and indeed inhumane, if they did not interpret the greatest minds of the seventeenth century as discussing the problem in what are now known to be the right ways."[6] Speaking not of Heidegger's hermeneutics but of nineteenth-century biblical exegesis, he contrasts his own procedure with this older hermeneutical one:

> The hermeneuticist tries to re-experience the ancient words in terms of his own life and problems, thereby uncovering the profound and hidden meanings that lie beneath the text. . . . Writing as I do in the heyday of the sentence I reverse the procedure of hermeneutics, charity, or humanity, and read only what is written on the surface, for there is nothing else.[7]

The procedure of charity or humanity that Hacking mentions along with hermeneutics is precisely what *Spurs* must also be rejecting. "Charity" is actually a technical term in current philosophy of language for the methodological principle that the beliefs expressed in a language foreign to us must be for the most part similar to our own, and thus the correct translation or interpretation will be that with the maximal number of truths, or the least number of falsehoods or contradictions, as determined from our point of view.[8] Since the Derridean quotation marks around texts would presumably cut off all questioning about common causal referents underlying them, and thus make texts incommensurable with one another, Derrida can be located in contemporary philosophical space by identifying his opposition to realists who insist on the principle of charity.

Within the hermeneutical tradition this point has been argued in terms other than those of semantic theory. One of the first to defend something like the principle of charity as an explicit hermeneutical maxim is Schleiermacher—the "veil maker" of the Derridean allusion to a way of veiling all differences by spreading one's own manner of thinking over other peoples and times. The hermeneutical bridge over the historical gap between text and interpreter is said to be formed by making the strange familiar. In wanting to hear precisely the strangeness of Nietzsche's voice, and in thinking of deconstruction as the process of letting this strangeness appear, Derrida is correct in resisting Schleiermacher's pontification. Yet he is wrong in supposing that this critique of nineteenth-century hermeneutics will also be valid against the more recent hermeneutic theories of Heidegger, Gadamer, and others. Derrida's deconstructive spurs are not the first to tear Schleiermacher's veil.

Post-structuralists like Derrida and Foucault thus picture even contemporary hermeneutics as the interpretive project of making the strange familiar, and of finding present beliefs and interests in what are actually incommensurable discourses or conceptual frameworks. Hermeneutics is believed to make the mistake of an overzealous application of the principle of charity due to a misunderstanding of the nature of textuality, one that leads to the illusory attempt to decode the text in terms of a hidden, underlying meaning. A text without such causal connections to the world would thus be the downfall of hermeneutics both practically—since this text could not be deciphered—and theoretically—since the unquestioned, and presumably unjustifiable, ontological presuppositions of hermeneutics would thereby be revealed.

This picture attributes at least four theses to recent hermeneutic theory incorrectly. First, hermeneutics since Heidegger has not advocated bridging the gap between text and interpreter by translating all that is strange into familiar terms. On the contrary, contemporary hermeneutics is based on a thoroughgoing criticism both of the Enlightenment assumption that everyone everywhere thinks essentially alike and of Schleiermacher's and Dilthey's tendency to presuppose the universal validity of their own beliefs, interests, and psychology. Heidegger's theory that the history of metaphysics is the history of the forgetting of Being, despite its many problems,[9] does recognize the discontinuities or paradigm shifts in this history, and thus has as a central tenet (which Heidegger himself unfortunately violates in some cases) that the interpretive reading recognize the unique strangeness and perhaps even the incommensurability of these various moments. Gadamer also argues against reducing or collapsing the horizon of the past into the present horizon. No elaborate argument is required, though, to make the point that just as poetry makes the ordinary appear extraordinary, so must interpretation be able to perceive the unique strangeness of a text, no matter how familiar it may seem. If this is achieved through a deconstructive reading, then deconstruction may well be an essential moment of the hermeneutic circle, no point of which can claim to be the inevitable starting point, the origin, center, or beginning that will thereby have a special epistemic or ontological status in the interpretive understanding that results.

The post-structuralist picture of hermeneutics is also incorrect in attributing to it the methodological belief that there must be one right interpretation capturing *the* meaning of the text. There are contemporary proponents of an objectivist hermeneutical tradition going back to Schleiermacher who do accept this ideal, but they are precisely the ones who attack Heidegger and Gadamer for being historical relativists. In another place I have argued that hermeneutic theory can avoid the paradoxes of relativism without committing itself to the belief that there is only one right interpretation for any given text.[10]

A third feature of Derrida's picture to be reconsidered is his claim that hermeneutics must attribute a totality to a text or corpus, even when deconstruction can show that such a structure does not exist. While it is true that for hermeneutics there is a tendency in all interpretive understanding to posit a unity or coherence to a work, this positing is only a regulative ideal that does not rule out the possibility that a work may fail to satisfy it.

In "The Origin of the Artwork" Heidegger describes interpretation as a preservation of the work, and also says that preservation must be creative. He therefore holds a reception theory of artworks according to which no interpretation or reading is ever final. Gadamer complements this point with his theory that a work of art or literature only comes to be in an act of understanding or reading and is thus constituted by the history of its effects, its *Wirkung.* The literary text is thus for hermeneutic theory not an independent and autonomous object, an interpretation is not a representation, and the relation between text and interpretation cannot be one of correspondence. These points obviate Derrida's now irrelevant fourth criticism, which is that hermeneutics has an unquestioned ontological commitment to a metaphysics of presence since it presupposes an independent signified behind any significant discourse, no matter how indirect and elusive.

Heidegger's metaphors often do make him vulnerable to Derrida's criticisms, though, and there is no point in defending his opaque language too ardently, especially since Derrida often only corrects misreadings of Heidegger (including, however, Heidegger's own misreadings of himself). Although hermeneutics does not require anything like the metaphysics of presence mentioned above (and is entirely unmetaphysical in this sense), the implications of this fourth criticism for Heidegger's programmatic destruction of the history of ontology are worth considering further.

III. The Destruction/Deconstruction of the History of Philosophy

However much Derrida may wish to deconstruct the methods of his philosophical parent, are the effects of his manner of reading the history of philosophy all that different from Heidegger's? The fourth criticism raises the question whether Heidegger's frequent references to a still hidden truth of Being commit him to an ontology of a dualist or realist sort when he wishes to avoid ontology in the traditional sense altogether. The very project of a destruction of the history of ontology may even imply such a commitment since, as Heidegger himself says in a late work, "On Time and Being,"

> To think Being without beings means: to think Being without regard to metaphysics. Yet a regard for metaphysics still prevails even in the intention to overcome metaphysics. Therefore, our task is to cease all overcoming, and leave metaphysics to itself.[11]

Heidegger's strategy of carrying out this destruction by showing that the history of philosophy is the history of the forgetting of Being thus appears only to catch him in the use of "Being" as yet another metaphysical name for the ground of everything, including language. In contrast, Derrida argues that "there never has been and never will be a unique word, a master name . . . not even the name of Being."[12] He accordingly bases his deconstructions on a conception of language as a play of differences between signifiers, presumably on a purely syntactic level with no need for a "transcendental signified" that comes to presence in language and grounds it.

Heidegger and Derrida do differ on whether language has built into it a transcendental need for referentiality, but this disagreement should not lead to the misconstrual of Heidegger as a metaphysical dualist with a correspondence theory of truth. Heidegger, in this respect like Derrida, is quite effective in showing the emptiness of traditional philosophical dualisms. Furthermore, there is no such thing as *the* meaning of Being, according to Heidegger, and one suspects that he gradually comes to realize that "Being" is merely a metalinguistic notion resulting from a transcendental deduction based on the *need* for something to which language could refer. Although this result still puts Heidegger at odds with Derrida, it is a much weaker conclusion than would follow if he were actually presupposing the metaphysics of presence.

To worry about the term "Being" at this point, however, is to get on the wrong *Holzweg* and to forget that the history of metaphysics is the history of the *forgetting* of Being. Does *Spurs* itself forget this forgetting? Is "forgotten" only by coincidence the central word in "I have forgotten my umbrella"? Of course not, but nevertheless Derrida waits until a second postscript (as if he had twice forgotten) to begin explicating it, and then says merely, "Let us not pretend to know what it is, this forgetting" (*S.,* p. 109). He could have explained, although we perhaps all know, that Heidegger owes his special understanding of the word to Nietzsche. Derived from the Platonic doctrine of recollection, forgetting is not a derivative state occurring only after a prior instance of conscious knowledge (since knowledge involves deliberation and reasoned justification). It is also not a negative phenomenon, and in the second "Untimely Meditation" Nietzsche makes it an essential precondition for transcending the despair of nihilism and becoming truly creative.

Much of this explication occurs in Heidegger's "Zur Seinsfrage" (a crucial background text for *Spurs*), and in the postscript on forgetting Derrida cites the following passage (which he maintains he had forgotten while writing *Spurs* although he had quoted it in an earlier essay): "Thus, the 'forgetting of Being' has frequently been represented as if Being were, figuratively speaking, an umbrella that had been left somewhere through the forgetfulness of a philosophy professor."[13] The forgetting of Being, properly understood, would thus not be a phenomenon that could lead

Heidegger to claim that his destruction of metaphysics puts him in a more privileged position than previous thinkers by enabling him now to "remember" Being, and to represent and name it as it truly is. Another passage that Derrida may have forgotten inveighs against the superficial misunderstanding of destruction either as a demolition of metaphysics that smashes it to bits only to pick up and use the pieces again in a new way, or even as "a deconstruction (*Abbau*) of familiar but now empty representations in order to win back the original experiences of Being in metaphysics."[14] Derrida probably intends his exposition of the umbrella fragment to prevent similar misunderstandings of his own conception of deconstruction.

With these misunderstandings aside then, there is no reason to chide Heidegger for searching for a single meaning underlying this history of otherwise discontinuous discourses. When Derrida in "White Mythology" deconstructs the various metaphors of presence from Plato to Hegel, he is also inserting an interpretive principle of continuity into this history. Derrida is not committed, of course, to the belief in a single thing called presence, since the metaphors are only illusions and are necessarily multiple. But neither does Heidegger have to think the forgettings of Being are alike, and he can speak of the necessary plurality of ways in which this forgetting manifests itself without asserting that Being could possibly not be forgotten.

Whether Heidegger formulates and practices his theory of destruction as consistently as he should, however, is a different question. In this regard there is another work by Heidegger that Derrida could also have recalled, for it is one that is perhaps in many respects like his own commentary on the Nietzsche fragment. "The Anaximander Fragment"[15] is also a notorious case of the overinterpretation of a single sentence fragment with an irretrievable context. It should not be overlooked that this essay is not a direct reading of Anaximander, but of a reading of Anaximander by Nietzsche (in *Philosophy in the Tragic Age of the Greeks*). Anaximander and Nietzsche are, moreover, the beginning and the end of the history of metaphysics, and Nietzsche's entrapment in this history is shown, Heidegger thinks, by his unimaginative blindness to the Anaximander fragment.

If Derrida forgets Heidegger's text, he also forgets Nietzsche's book, where his own notion of "ontological undecidability" could be rooted. In an illuminating study Sarah Kofman points out that Nietzsche here revives the notion of an indemonstrable, undecidable philosophy, a conception he attributes to Heraclitus, who goes even beyond Anaximander, the philosopher of the "indefinite," in saying that everything is both itself and its opposite and thus denying the principle of noncontradiction. In contrast to Aristotle, Heraclitus is said to prefer a philosophy based on the metaphor rather than on the concept, the concept being simply a forgetting of an original metaphor. Furthermore, Nietzsche's book is, Kofman argues, an attack on Aristotle's reading of the history of philosophy as a continuous process of evolution: "Instead of considering pre-Socratic philosophy to be a simple and impedimented speech that was gradually smoothed out by later Greek thought—as Aristotle does—Nietzsche finds a veritable break between the dawn of philosophy and its later development: the pre-Socratics belong to a rare type; they are irreducible to any other."[16] Both Derrida and Heidegger may thus have been anticipated by Nietzsche's criticism of Aristotle's use of the principle of charity, and in particular, Derrida's critique of Heidegger's project of destruction may have been presaged in Nietzsche's reading of Heraclitus' critique of Anaximander.

By heightening the undecidability of *Spurs* itself through the hint that the essay is only a "parodying graft," however, Derrida tantalizes the hermeneutic reader who prefers to think that the issues between them, while not necessarily decided, are not undecidable. To claim that the essay is a parodying graft on these forgotten texts of Heidegger and Nietzsche would be to fall into Derrida's trap by searching for hermeneutical keys and hidden allusions that are as farfetched as his own playful readings of the umbrella fragment. Nevertheless, a parody must be a parody of something, and without the parodied text it would not even be amusing. Both the destruction and the deconstruction of the history of philosophy have the effect of leading not to a forgetting or an overcoming of it, but to an increased preoccupation with it. Nietzsche and Heidegger recognize this and, regretting that this concern with overcoming inhibits creativity, wish to abandon the overcoming in favor of another kind of philosophy altogether.[17] Derrida comes to the same recognition, but concludes that there is no other kind of "philosophy." The objection that his critique of Heidegger thus comes down merely to an undecidable disagreement about the meaning of a word should, of course, not disturb him. In the epoch of philosophy-in-quotation-marks nothing more is to be expected.

Barnard College, Columbia University

NOTES

1 Jacques Derrida, *Spurs: Nietzsche's Styles,* trans. Barbara Harlow (Venice: Corbo e Fiore, 1976). (Hereafter cited as *S.*)

2 Jacques Derrida, *Of Grammatology,* trans. G. C. Spivak (Baltimore and London: The Johns Hopkins Univ. Press, 1976); see especially Part I, Chapter 1, section 3. See also *L'Écriture et la différance* (Paris: Seuil, 1967), p. 427.

3 Derrida, *Of Grammatology,* p. 24.

4 "Structurellement émancipée de tout vouloir-dire vivant, elle peut toujours ne rien vouloir-dire, n'avoir *aucun sens décidable,* jouer parodiquement au sens, se déporter par greffe, sans fin, hors de tout corps contextuel ou de tout code fini" (*S.,* p. 102 [my emphases]).

5 Michel Foucault, *The Archaeology of Knowledge,* trans. A. M. Sheridan Smith (New York: Harper and Row, 1972), p. 162.

6 Ian Hacking, *Why Does Language Matter to Philosophy?* (Cambridge: Cambridge Univ. Press, 1975), p. 168.

7 Hacking, *Language,* p. 168.

8 Hacking discusses the principles of charity and humanity in Chapter 12, "Donald Davidson's Truth," especially pp. 146-150; he cites Richard Grandy who defines his principle of humanity as follows: "So we have, as a pragmatic constraint on translation, the condition that the imputed pattern of relations among beliefs, desires and the world be as similar to our own as possible" (p. 149). Hilary Putnam calls this the Principle of Benefit of the Doubt and makes it an important ingredient, along with a causal theory of reference and a Tarski- "correspondence" theory of truth, in his scientific realism, which is captured succinctly in the following rhetorical question in "What is 'Realism?' ": "Given the Quinian Predicament (Kantian Predicament?) that there is a real world *but* we can only describe it in the terms of our own conceptual system (Well? We should use *someone else's* conceptual system?) *is it surprising* that *primitive* reference has this character of apparent triviality?" (p. 192).

9 See my "The Owl and the Poet: Heidegger's Critique of Hegel," in *Martin Heidegger and the Question of Literature*, William V. Spanos, ed. (Bloomington: Indiana Univ. Press, 1979).

10 For a critical comparison of the objectivist hermeneutics of E. D. Hirsch and E. Betti with the hermeneutic theory of Heidegger and Gadamer see my book, *The Critical Circle: Literature, History, and Philosophical Hermeneutics* (Berkeley, Los Angeles, London: Univ. of California Press, 1978).

11 Martin Heidegger, *On Time and Being,* trans. Joan Stambaugh (New York: Harper and Row, 1972), p. 24.

12 Jacques Derrida, "Differance," in *Speech and Phenomena, And Other Essays on Husserl's Theory of Signs,* trans. David B. Allison (Evanston: Northwestern Univ. Press, 1973), p. 159.

13 *Spurs,* pp. 110. My translation is taken from "Zur Seinsfrage," in Martin Heidegger, *Wegmarken* (Frankfurt: Vittorio Klostermann, 1967), p. 243.

14 *Wegmarken,* p. 245.

15 Published in Martin Heidegger, *Early Greek Thinking,* trans. D. F. Krell and F. A. Capuzzi (New York: Harper and Row, 1975).

16 Sarah Kofman, "Metaphor, Symbol, Metamorphosis" (trans. David B. Allison), in *The New Nietzsche: Contemporary Styles of Interpretation,* ed. David B. Allison (New York: Delta, 1977), p. 212.

17 See *On Time and Being,* p. 24, 41.

Ater nos
ter qui es
in celis
sanctifice
tur nomē
tuum Adveniat regnū
tuum Fiat voluntas
tua sicut in celo et in ter
ra Panem nostrum quot

The Art of Theology and the Theology of Art: Robert Penn Warren's Reading of Coleridge's *The Rime of the Ancient Mariner*

Homer Obed Brown

Coleridge as "a weak and lisping old man" reported, according to *Table Talk:*

> Mrs. Barbauld once told me that she admired *The Ancient Mariner* very much, but that there were two faults in it—it was improbable, and had no moral. As for the probability, I owned that that might admit some question: but as to the want of a moral, I told her that in my own judgment the poem had too much; and that the only, or chief fault, if I might say so, was the obtrusion of the moral sentiment so openly on the reader as a principle or cause of action in a work of such pure imagination. It ought to have had no more moral than the *Arabian Nights* tale of the merchant's sitting down to eat dates by the side of a well, and throwing the shells aside, and lo! a genie starts up, and says he *must* kill the aforesaid merchant, *because* one of the date shells, it seems, put out the eye of the genie's son. (Quoted by Warren, p. 199)[1]

I have chosen to discuss Robert Penn Warren's essay on Coleridge's *The Rime of the Ancient Mariner,* "A Poem of Pure Imagination: An Experiment in Reading,"[2] for a number of associated reasons: because of the centrality of Coleridge's thought for the question of Modernism, for modern criticism in general and the New Criticism in particular,[3] and because of the way Warren's essay opens onto that thought and those questions. Warren's essay is itself one of the finest examples of New Critical explication, while at the same time it places Coleridge's poem in the larger context of his literary, philosophical and theological theory. Although he expresses occasional discomfort about moving outside the poem, Warren's strategy in appealing to this larger context is clear: by means of both poem and theory he is able to argue and demonstrate his version of the New Criticism's most important tenets. To paraphrase Warren, like Coleridge's theory, Warren's essay expresses a point of view about both the poem and about poetry in general and, as an "experiment in reading," a point of view about literary criticism. Warren's essay has a historical importance in its opening up a complex relationship between the *two* Coleridges of traditional scholarship, poet and thinker, and it is still a necessary point of departure (acknowledged or not) for any study of the poem. Finally, the issues it raises are still relevant to critical discussion today, and although the terms have changed somewhat (only somewhat), the battle it engages is still being fought.[4]

In general, Warren's purpose was to remove discussion of the poem from the welter of source-hunting studies, biographical (semi-psychoanalytic) interpretations, and narrowly didactic readings it was receiving at that point. More particularly, using the Mrs. Barbauld anecdote as a point of departure, his targets were the warring notions of the poem that on the one hand it is too didactic (focusing on the Mariner's homily at the end) and on the other hand, it has *no* meaning other than itself, that it is "pure poetry." It is as if, he says, the notion that a poem should not "mean" but only "be" implies "that the 'be-ing' of a poem does not mean." Additionally he sets out to attack a specific version of the "pure poetry" argument by contending with the idea that "we accept illusion only when in some fashion it bears the semblance of truth," that meaning is only a "structural device for creating illusion." In short, Warren attacks the notions that either the poem is "arbitrary"—has no "relevance to life" or that, on the other hand, its moral statement is arbitrary—that is to say, unearned, not embodied formally and structurally in the poem. "Arbitrary" is a word he worries about a great deal in his essay, as I will in mine, and it obviously lurks in the Arabian Nights story with which Coleridge answers Mrs. Barbauld. The question of arbitrariness is also central in the controversy Warren's essay raised almost immediately. There is a curious symmetry in the relationship of that response to the positions Warren attacked, although many of the attacks on him, as one critic put it, make use of his own methodology and even his own ideology. Most of the attacks focus on Warren's too rigid and sometimes contradictory reading of the light symbolism in the poem—the sun/moon, day/night oppositions. And most notably, since in his essay Warren makes much of Coleridge's famous symbol/allegory opposition and embraces the symbol as his main argument for the mode of meaningfulness in the poem, many of the responses to his essay accuse Warren of *allegorizing* the poem.[5] Quite obviously he does allegorize it in the sense that he makes his reading of it a fable of all critical reading, just as he finds the poem a model for the structure of the universe, and the Mariner's dark voyage and fate a fable of the poet. In Paul de Man's sense, Warren's essay reaches toward allegory as it reaches toward total understanding of the poem, toward totalization. The essay is also curiously allegorical in relationship to the poem in a more superficial sense. Like the poem, Warren's study is divided into seven parts and just as he finds the crucial turning point in the poem in its fourth part, the fourth part of *his* essay demonstrates what he calls the "symbolic fusion" of the poem's themes.

Warren's justification against these charges would, of course, be Coleridge's definition of the symbol—both the poem and the essay "participate" in the greater whole which they represent. Like the symbol, they can be "characterized by a translucence of the special in the individual, or of the general in the special, or of the universal in the general . . ." (quoted by Warren, *SE,* p. 217). At any rate, part of what is at stake in Warren's reading of Coleridge and in any close reading *of* that reading will be the instability of the symbol/allegory opposition.[6]

In his essay Warren will argue (1) that the poem has meaning—he calls it "theme" which he defines variously as "some significant relation to the world" (*SE,* p. 199), "relevance to life" (*SE,* p. 200), "comment on human conduct and values" (*SE,* p. 201); (2) he will argue that this meaning is *intended* (and intention he will define in a special sense); (3) that this meaning or theme is *"embodied"* formally and structurally—that is to say, in the relationship between all the elements of the poem, including overt statement, and (4) finally, he will argue that the poem is a "document of very central and crucial issue of [Coleridge's] period: the problem of truth and poetry," obviously a crucial issue still in our own time, the particular New Critical version of it, however, being poetry versus science and the problem of the historic "dissociation of sensibility."

While at every point Warren's explication of the poem consists of elucidation of the text by reference to Coleridge's critical and philosophical prose, it is important that the terms Warren draws from the prose—imagination, symbol, organic or organicism, and will—not only allow him to accomplish his claim—that the poem has meaning, that this meaning is formally embodied—"organic," and that this organic meaning is "intended"—*willed,* but these terms also allow Warren to make his own statement about the nature of poetry, of literary criticism, of life, and of the relationships between them.

To make his first point, Warren offers Coleridge's famous definition of the primary and secondary imaginations. Warren argues that Coleridge in his use of the term "pure imagination" would hardly have "tossed away that sacred word which stood for the vindication of his most fundamental beliefs as irresponsibly as the merchant in the story of *The Arabian Nights* tosses away the 'date shell' " (*SE,* p. 206). Far from it, Warren believes that "Coleridge's concept would redeem works of pure imagination from the charge, amiable or otherwise, of being in themselves meaningless and nothing but refined and ingenious toys for an idle hour" (*SE,* p. 206).

Here is Warren's comment on the passage: "It is the primary imagination," he notes, "which creates our world, for nothing of which we are aware is given to the passive mind. By it we know the world. . . . We know by creating, and one of the things we create is the Self" (*SE,* p. 207). "Even here," Warren notes, "we can observe that when 'the imagination is conceived as recognizing the inherent interdependence of subject and object (or complementary aspects of a single reality), its dignity is immeasurably raised.' But when we turn to his interpretation of the secondary imagination, that dignity is further enhanced. For here we leave creation at the unconscious and instinctive level and define it as coexisting with, and in terms of, the conscious will; here it operates as a function of that freedom which is the essential attribute of spirit" (*SE,* p. 207). Possibly most important for Warren in this comment and the passage from the *Biographia* is the analogy between poetic making and structure and Divine Creation. For Warren and other New Critics, as well as for Coleridge, poem and world have analogous structures—each is conceived as a dynamic unity of differences.

In his introduction here, however, of the question of the will, Warren is looking forward to the way he explains poetic intention, and he is also setting up his argument against the one voiced by Wordsworth, and others since, that the Mariner is passive and not free. The question of will is preparation against the accusation of necessitarianism or fatalism and an argument for the importance to the poem (and to Warren) of the concept of original sin. The association between poetic intention and willful assertion proves to be problematic, however, in some not yet apparent senses. In his comment on Coleridge's definition Warren has introduced the crucial idea of self—"and one of the things we create is the Self."

Making a poem is also making the self. Beyond even that—more explicitly than Coleridge, Warren in later work will identify poetry with self-assertion,[7] but this idea is already implicit here as a troubling shadow in Coleridge's definition: "The primary Imagination I hold to be . . . a repetition in the finite mind of the eternal act of creation in the infinite I Am." There is, one might say, a fatal ambiguity here, productive of unacceptable consequences. God utters himself in his *I Am* and thereby creates the world. The finite mind repeats the divine and primary act and re-creates the world and the poem. What is the status of that finite and human "I am"? "In Xanadu did Kubla Khan/A stately pleasure-dome decree." That Coleridge was bothered by the troubling implications of this idea might be reflected in the fact that late in life he allegedly expunged the phrase from a copy of the *Biographia,* but other evidence could be offered for that uneasiness.

At any rate, Warren's immediate purpose now is to justify and clarify his own notion of "intention"—his claim that Coleridge "intends" the "theme" or "statement" the poem "embodies." The passages to which Warren refers to explain poetic intention involve also moral accountability for even unconscious and instinctive acts. "Does Coleridge imply," Warren asks, "that the poet in composing his poem acts according to a fully developed and objectively statable plan, that he has a blueprint of intention in such an absolute sense?" (*SE,* pp. 207-8). No, Warren answers, he does not mean intention in so simple a sense—creativity always involves unconscious activity. He goes on:

> Perhaps the answer could be found in an application of Coleridge's discussion of the Self, Will, and Motive. The common idea of will, he says, is the power to respond to a motive conceived of as acting upon it from the outside. But what is motive? Not a thing, but the thought of a thing. But all thoughts are not motives. Therefore motive is a determining thought. But what is a thought? A thing or an individual? Where does it begin or end? 'Far more readily could we apply these questions to an ocean billow. . . . As by a billow we mean no more than a particular movement of the sea, so neither by a thought can we mean more than the mind thinking in some one direction. Consequently a motive is neither more nor less than the act of an intelligent being determining itself. . . .' But will 'is an abiding faculty or habit or fixed disposition to certain objects,' and rather than motive originating will, it itself is originated in terms of that predisposition or permanent will. (*SE,* p. 208)

It is this concept later that explains the Mariner's murder of the albatross as a "motiveless" act (and hence a representation of original sin)—that is to say, an *originating* act, a self-determining act and not a determined one. The question of pre-disposition is a complicated one, though logically and doctrinally—there cannot "originally" have been a "pre-disposition" to original sin. At any rate, the self-determining of the permanent will is both a self-creation and a self-assertion. Man says "I am"— and creates a poem or murders an albatross.[8] However if the will is *permanent,* then any particular act according to its predisposition becomes determined and necessary. For example, near the end of the essay, Warren says the poet "cannot do otherwise than "intend" what his poem says, any more than he can change his past as past" (*SE,* p. 269).

Anything then enacted by that permanent will can be said to be "intended" in however complicated a way. Warren says, "It seems clear that the secondary imagination does operate as a function of that permanent will, but the particular plan or intention for a particular poem may be actually developed in the course of composition in terms of 'unconscious activity' . . . and may result from a long process of trial and error" (*SE,* p. 208).

Warren's image for that long, mostly unconscious creative process of trial and error is Coleridge's image—the natural growth of an organism, usually a plant. This easy association, of course, is based on a contradiction (or several) whose tensions will never be far from the surface of the argument. Here Warren brings in Coleridge's formula as explanation: "The organic form is innate; it shapes, as it develops, itself from within, and the fulness of its development is one and the same with the perfection of its outward form." Warren also links this organic development, as is traditional, with dialectical movement: "in other words, the plan and meaning of the work may be discovered in the process of creation. But it is to be remembered that this process is a function of the permanent will which constantly moves to fulfill itself in consciousness" (*SE,* p. 209). It is the continuity of the notion of organic development that grounds the "abiding"ness of the permanent will in the "process of trial and error" which might otherwise suggest all sorts of discontinuities and it is that borrowed continuity which conserves intention and redeems, in a sense, both poem and world as meaningful structures—objects. The same can be said for Warren and some other New Critics. One of the statements persisting through four editions of *Understanding Poetry* is: "If we must compare a poem to the makeup of some physical object, it ought to be not to a wall but to something organic like a plant." In Coleridge's words, "the good poem must 'contain in itself why it is so and not otherwise.' Or as Shelley said, it must 'contain the principle of its own integrity,' by which Shelley meant that the parts of the good poem are unified, are 'integrated' in an expressive whole in which all parts by their interrelation participate."[9]

Organic form is not simply the metaphor for the poem, neither for Brooks and Warren nor for Coleridge; it is also the metaphor for the structure of mind, of world, of life—for what Warren calls later in the essay "the unity of being." Moreover, the primary imagination not only creates the world of perception, it is also for Warren as well as for Coleridge a guarantee of the meaningfulness of what is perceived. It is value-producing.

Now, having demonstrated that a poem, particularly a Coleridge poem, not only can but must have formal meaning—Warren can address himself to the particular theme *The Ancient Mariner* embodies. It should be clear that this preliminary discussion pretty well sets up the meanings he will educe from the poem—he has asserted from the outset the coherence of the poem's themes with "Coleridge's basic theological and philosophical views as given to us in sober prose" so it is no surprise that the two themes he sets out to explore and relate are outgrowths of the themes he has already introduced. Warren's "primary theme" he calls that of the "one life," a phrase from Coleridge's "Eolian Harp," or the "sacramental vision" or "sacramental unity," and says that it is the "issue," or "outcome of the fable taken at its face value as a story of crime and punishment and reconciliation" (*SE,* p. 214). On the other hand, the "secondary" theme, which he calls "the theme of the imagination," is "concerned with the context of values in which the fable is presented and which the fable may be found ultimately to embody, just as more obviously it embodies the primary theme." After exploring the operation of each in turn, Warren says, he will "then attempt to define the significance of their final symbolic fusion in the poem" (*SE,* p. 214).

The logic of Warren's division of themes is at first glance a bit puzzling. His statement obviously suggests the operation of a dialectic which in turn suggests that we are dealing with oppositions that can be dialectically organized. In their very statement, however, there is already from the outset a subtle exchange of terms that will make mediation or "fusion" possible: the primary theme deals with "vision" as well as "the One Life", and the secondary theme of the imagination (or vision) is already embodied in a "context of values." Moreover, the fusion is already claimed in the Coleridge definition of the imagination, which Warren has given. But the immediate logic of the division would seem strategically related to the attitudes toward the poem Warren is refuting. In effect, Warren seeks to find a point of union for the two major traditionally conflicting readings of the poem.

The primary theme, Warren says, is not quite overtly stated but "receives only a kind of coy and dramatically naive understatement which serves as a clue—'He prayeth best, etc.' " (*SE,* p. 214). He complicates the notion of the simple and obtrusive moral that readers had objected to, while at the same time he attempts to recuperate the idea that moral asserted. His explication of the secondary theme of the imagination will involve the improbabilities, the supernatural atmosphere, images, and machinery, which had always seemed irrelevant and disproportionate to the simple moral of the fable. In other words, the secondary theme addresses the argument that the poem is pure art without moral meaning or pure art only to the extent it survives the naive moral tacked on at the end. In a sense, this dichotomy repeats the old division in aesthetics between art's double function of teaching and pleasing which is made to overlap another opposition between the rational or motivated and the arbitrary or unmotivated. The primary theme is concerned with the moral universe (or ambiguously, moral vision) and the secondary theme is aesthetic and, ambiguously, "the imagination in its value-creating capacity." The "fusion" would consist of the integration of the two.

Before exploring these themes and their integration into a unified whole, however, Warren must introduce two more distinctions—between these themes taken together which he calls "objective" and "another type of theme"—which he calls the "personal" theme—and a further distinction between symbol and allegory. The personal theme results from the idea "that the poem is 'an involuntary but inevitable projection into imagery' of his [Coleridge's] own inner discord"—Warren cites and grossly reduces Kenneth Burke's elaborately developed treatment in *The Philosophy of Literary Form* "of the sexual and opium motives" (*SE,* p. 215). But Burke, Warren says, is interested in "the psychology of the poetic act" and is too "sensible" to make the mistake that such readings of personal themes and motives usually make which is confusedly to identify the basic material with what is made from it.[10] We must remember, according to Warren, "that the poem, even regarded in this light, is not an attempt merely to present the personal problem but an attempt to transcend the personal problem, to objectify and universalize it" (*SE,* p. 215). This division between objective themes and personal themes repeats the first division of the objective themes into primary and secondary and begs the same resolution. The personal theme consists of arbitrary and accidental particulars which must be "normalized"—transcended, objectified and universalized in order to have significance or moral meaning.

Warren now introduces the famous Coleridgean distinction between symbol and allegory to justify his finding the source of the poem in multiple thematic motives rather than one. A single theme or motive, according to Warren, would produce simple, naive two-dimensional allegory, while the symbol involves and integrates many levels of meaning and is "perfectly consistent with Coleridge's emphasis on diversity within unity" (*SE,* p. 216). This division, however, again repeats the one between the objective and the personal themes and represents a further elucidation of the necessity of transcendence or sublation. Warren quotes Coleridge: "A poet's heart and intellect should be *combined,* . . . intimately combined and unified with the great appearances of nature, and not merely held in solution and loose mixture with them, in the shape of formal similes" (*SE,* p. 217). Again, the attempt is to "combine" or integrate—fuse, the objective with the subjective (those familiar terms of Romantic and Coleridgean criticism and philosophy), the self and nature. Tropologically what is desired is identity—but an identity that at once erases and conserves difference (metaphor as symbol) and what is rejected is the mechanical identity of resemblance—simile. Simile is characterized by the loose and given or "accidental" association of resemblance. Allegory, in the Warren-Coleridge formulation, is also "mechanical" and "arbitrary." On the other hand, "The symbol is not arbitrary—not a mere sign—but contains within itself the appeal which makes it serviceable as a symbol"

(*SE,* p. 218). The "symbol is rooted in our universal natural experience," the symbol "partakes of the reality which it renders intelligible," it is "sacramental." Allegory is only a "mere translation of a discursive sequence" while "a symbol" implies a body of ideas which may be said to be fused in it" (*SE,* p. 218). It is "the condensation [in the psychological sense] of several themes and not a sign for one" (*SE,* p. 218).

All this is familiar material. What I want to underline is the way Warren's primary division seems always to necessitate the proliferation of all sorts of new divisions between literal and metaphoric, true religion and false religion, the symbol of necessity and the symbol of congruence, between "bad" metaphor and "good" metaphor, "bad" allegory and "good" allegory. These dichotomies in turn reflect or repeat all the divisions or oppositions mentioned so far, those I have called attention to, those I have not, and those which are generated throughout the rest of Warren's essay: for example, the opposition in the imagery between moon and sun, and even in the sun between "good sun" and "bad sun," and ultimately in the poem, the opposition between marriage of two and "going to church in a goodly company" and between the exiled Mariner and the universe of love and communion. And in the essay itself, between the poem conceived of as an organic totality and the critic-reader, between critical system and what Warren calls "divisive, vindictive internecine voices," and also between the integral self and self-division. I have no doubt that these oppositions are in the Coleridgean text along with the attempt to resolve them dialectically. As far as I know it, they seem to be repeated in Warren's own novels and poems, and quite probably they inhere in the culture and in the metaphysical designation of the terms of the opposition. In fact, to suggest that this is so is merely to *repeat* the oppositions on another level, rather than to resolve them, and that in turn suggests to me part of the mechanism of their opposition. The attempt to explain or rationalize the opposition, to contain one in the other—that is to say, to remove, integrate, or transcend the fugitive arbitrary element—always seems to result in the repetition of the oppositions on another level. The recurrence of the problem of the arbitrary is the failure of meaning to close, to be recuperated.

Perhaps that recurrence, among other things, is related to the problematic nature of allegory—both in the Warren-Coleridgean sense of the term and in the de Manian sense—a repetition of difference that can never reach identity. De Man states, "It remains necessary, if there is to be allegory, that the allegorical sign refer to another sign that precedes it. The meaning constituted by the allegorical sign can then consist only in the *repetition* (in the Kierkegaardian sense of the term) of a previous sign with which it can never coincide, since it is of the essence of this previous sign to be pure anteriority . . . whereas the symbol postulates the possibility of identity or identification, allegory designates primarily a distance in relation to its own origin and, renouncing the nostalgia and the desire to coincide, it establishes its language in the void of this temporal difference. In so doing, it prevents the self from an illusory identification with the non-self." One would note here possibly Warren's and Coleridge's employment of "a defensive strategy that tries to hide from this negative self-knowledge."[11] But that doesn't seem to be the point—and may not be the case since the text acknowledges (de Man would say) the failure of the search for identity or identification without surrender of the nostalgia. The point would be, further, the inability to avoid the repetitions of allegory and the irredeemable arbitrariness that adheres to the allegorical.

The arbitrary ordinarily is what is capricious or unreasonable, what is despotic and absolute, not bound by rules, arising instead from accident. This sense can characterize the external world. Yet the word also implies what is subject to *individual* will or judgment without restriction. There is an obvious duplicity in the concept that haunts Warren's and Coleridge's use of the word and that points ultimately to an irreducible duplicity in the poem and the theory. The word can refer both to an unmotivated or accidental event that "happens" to the individual, mariner, poet, or reader and also to the act he commits. The arbitrary is at once extraneous and determinative. In short, one is tempted to say, the problem of the arbitrary is the problem of *The Ancient Mariner.* But there is another complication that must be explored.

It is not a case of simple oppositions. The problem is the ambiguous interdependence of the two sides of the opposition or the intermittent or arbitrary intersection of one by the other. In a sense, the problem is the symbol as *synecdoche*—a term hidden in Brooks and Warren, but one understood very well by Kenneth Burke. In fact, most of the oppositions I have mentioned can be thought of as part-whole oppositions. In his discussion of the symbol, Warren quotes Coleridge's famous distinction from *The Statesman's Manual* which I cited earlier:

> It is among the miseries of the present age that it recognizes no medium between literal and metaphorical. Faith is either to be buried in the dead letter, or its name and honors usurped by a counterfeit product of the mechanical understanding, which in the blindness of self-complacency confounds symbols with allegories. Now an allegory is but a translation of abstract notions into a picture-language, which is itself nothing but an abstraction from objects of sense. . . . On the other hand a symbol . . . is characterized by a translucence of the special in the individual, or of the general in the special, or of the universal in the general; above all by the translucence of the eternal through and in the temporal. It always partakes of the reality which it renders intelligi-

ble; and while it enunciates the whole, abides itself as a living part in that unity of which it is the representative. (Quoted by Warren, *SE,* p. 217)

The Mariner's murder of the albatross may be, as Warren shows, a crime against the laws of man, god, nature, and the imagination. It may also repeat or be a version of original sin, but it isn't symbolic, in this sense, because it "combines" or "fuses" all of these crimes—that would be metaphoric and Coleridge, unlike the New Critics, recognizes the metaphor as a "fragment of allegory."[12] The Mariner's crime against the bird is a crime against the "symbol"—that is the individual, not as divine messenger, but *as* individual—because the albatross has value in itself. In this sense, the Mrs. Barbauld anecdote with which Warren opens his essay is more meaningful and more problematic than he admits, but I will come to that in a moment.

It is to Warren's credit that he suggests more openly in this essay than most critics who make use of the Coleridgean concept of the symbol its ultimate recourse to theological "mystery." He introduces the passage I have just quoted by saying that Coleridge is here contrasting "true" and "false" religion and he will elaborate the "mystery" of original sin, as Coleridge was forced to do, in order to explain the antinomies of the poem. I do not mean to telescope as difficult a problem as the complexity of Coleridge's thought by pointing out the theological nature of the Coleridgean symbol. The symbol is ultimately the Eucharist as consubstantial, as the passage suggests. The adoption of it for critical purposes without analysis of its theological implications or even of its rhetorical operations is problematical at best. It is also worth noting that this much quoted definition of the symbol is introduced by Coleridge specifically in the context of scriptural interpretation—reading with the aim of preserving Biblical meaning against the onslaught of textual and historical research. The Higher Criticism would reveal the historical or "accidental" and thus arbitrary nature of the text. Coleridge's desire is to preserve its universality. Warren's impulse is the same with regard to *The Ancient Mariner.*

There still remains the problem of understanding "the translucence" of the whole in the part or the part in the whole. The problem is the relationship of part—not as part but as whole in itself, as *end*—to a larger whole. Such a relationship never escapes the shadow of the arbitrariness which is part of synecdoche's uneasy association with metonymy. For an example of both his proliferation of divisions and his problem with the symbol, immediately after defining the symbol Warren sub-divides it into a new difference with itself—into "necessary" symbols and symbols "of convergence." The first are necessary because they are "natural"—part of the universal experience of mankind—and are therefore imposed on poet and reader alike. The second are the result of the poet's manipulation of materials and context. The tropological slide should be obvious. It is only

Warren's subtle manipulation of symbol as metaphor, rather than as synecdoche, which allows him both to preserve and erase difference and to read the text or symbol as translucence and transparency.

The question of context suggests another way of stating the problem. Near the beginning of the essay Warren distinguishes his multiple themes from a plurality of meanings derived from looking at a work of art from different perspectives—namely intrinsic and extrinsic perspectives. At the end of the essay, he describes a relationship of *force* between the two sides of the opposition. Without "a blue print" of the poet's intention, he asks, "on what basis may a poem be interpreted?" "The first piece of evidence," he answers, in New Critical fashion, "is the poem itself."

> And here, as I have suggested earlier, the criterion is that of internal consistency. If the elements of a poem operate together toward one end, we are entitled to interpret the poem according to that end. Even if the poet himself should rise to contradict us, we could reply that the words of the poem speak louder than his actions.
>
> But the application of the criterion of internal consistency cannot be made in a vacuum. All sorts of considerations *impinge* upon the process. And these considerations *force* on the critic the criterion of *external* consistency. First, in regard to the intellectual, the spiritual climate of the age in which the poem was composed. Second, in regard to the over-all pattern of other artistic work by the author in question. Third, in regard to the thought of the author as available from non-artistic sources. Fourth, in regard to the facts of the author's life. (*SE,* pp. 269-70, my italics)

Both the necessities and theoretical difficulties of such work are sufficiently commonplace and do not require comment. Let me point out merely that this ever widening circle of context has no logical, but only a theological and transcendental end. Second, that each relationship necessarily involves what is contingent, accidental, and arbitrary. Third, that just as these "considerations *impinge* upon the process" and "*force* on the critic the criterion of external consistency," the "context" imaged is that of a tight causal web in which the authority of each detail, image, action, or individual—its arbitrariness or its integrity—is molested by the arbitrary causal links in which it is caught up and by the totalizing authority of the whole. Perhaps it is now appropriate to return to the Mrs. Barbauld anecdote.

The more one ponders this anecdote the more the Arab merchant's world seems the nightmarish extension of the world of the Mariner. It is a vision of "the universe of love," "the organic whole," become a nightmare of minute causal connections and reverberations.[13] Sardonically, by extension an ecological nightmare—one should not indifferently throw away date shells. For that matter, the date shell would be just as important *in itself* as the albatross or the water-snakes or the genie's son's eye, or, as both Burke and Empson have suggested, the maggots the sailors feed to the albatross before its murder in the first version of the poem. The accidental intersection of radically heterogeneous levels suggested by the story of the merchant and its minute invisible causality are also repeated in the epigraph from Burnet which Coleridge gave the poem. And one can also see this vision as Coleridge's own nightmare (as for example, in "The Pains of Sleep"), his nightmare of reason—of a world so rational that no act, however minute or trivial, could escape the web of causality and endless consequences, a world in which *no* intention is relevant

The history of *The Ancient Mariner* can be seen as one of a series of revisionary or supplementary representations beginning with Coleridge's early reported desire to write a poem about the origin of evil in the world, then Cain's murder of Abel and subsequent wandering, to the 1798 version of the poem, and then through successive revisions such as the introduction of the subtitle—"A Poet's Revery"—of the epigraph from Burnet and of an interpreter/editor with his marginal prose glosses. Each revision is an apparent attempt to define and control the wandering meaning—in a sense the reading—of the poem. In this way, Mrs. Barbauld's anecdote is possibly the last of Coleridge's serial supplements. But as Warren's essay and possibly his own novel—*All The King's Men*—testify, each version repeats the problem in the form of a new narrative. The poem, like its protagonist and teller,—or perhaps the poetic impulse—seems indeed doomed to "pass,"—to wander—like night, from land to land, repeating its tale of problematic and arbitrary crime and punishment. And each version of this tale is allegorical in relationship to the one prior to it, as the oppositions of Warren's essay are allegorical in relationship to each other and to the problem of the poem as Warren's novel may be allegorical in relationship to his essay.

At this point, we can usefully, I think, discuss the necessary breakdown of the allegory of redemption or symbolic "fusion." Warren announces "the regeneration of the Mariner" in this way: "In the end, he accepts the sacramental view of the universe, and his will is released from its state of 'utmost abstraction' and gains the state of 'immanence' in wisdom and love" (*SE,* p. 233). One could easily translate this into Coleridge's definition of the symbol, allegorizing it in the process: the Mariner who "enunciates the whole, abides . . . [himself] as a living part in that unity of which . . . [he] is the representative." The problem, of course, is that he doesn't. The Mariner is finally excluded from the living harmony he enunciates and so is possibly the Wedding Guest. I called attention earlier to the identification of the organic development of the poetic process with dialectical movement. In the terms of the poem, it is impossible to see the Mariner's repetitive penance—which is the poem itself—as a dialectical fulfillment.

In the Warren-Coleridgean dialectic there is always something left over. I want to avoid the temptation of saying, though I cannot fully, that what is left over is what is specifically literary.[14] Certainly, one of the things left over here is the Mariner. However brilliant and convincing Warren's explication of the Mariner's redemption in his blessing of the water snakes, he cannot explain the necessity of the Mariner's continued alienation after it *within* the terms of the poem. He has to acknowledge that "alienation," which in fact is his word, but has to resort to another level of discourse for explanation—the "peculiar paradoxical situation" of the Mariner is the situation of the poet in Coleridge's age and ours. He can only justify the fate of the Mariner by recourse to history and the Romantic myth of the *poète maudit,* which in turn reflects "the dissociation of sensibility." This is one of those arbitrary extrinsic contexts mentioned earlier and also one of the points where his reading of the poem touches upon his own allegory. One could say in this regard that what is left over is both the "personal" and the historically contingent. This still cannot, of course, explain why the Mariner or the poet is excluded from "the organic whole" or "the unity of being."

But there are also a number of other significant things "left over" in Warren's reading of the poem. He cannot deal with the poem's excessiveness—by that I do not mean simply the disproportionate and arbitrary weight of the punishment in relationship to the crime. I mean the other disproportions of the poem—its exorbitant and possibly unmotivated detail, its supernatural machinery, its redundancy of ambiguously redemptive moments. The blessing of the water-snakes—the turning point—the decisive act—takes place slightly less than half way through the poem.

There is also an emphasis on chance in the poem that Warren must either ignore or discount. He ignores the dice thrown by Death and "The Nightmare Life-in-Death" for the Mariner's punishment and he discounts the ambiguous suggestion of chance in the Mariner's choice of audience for the agonizing repetitions of his tale.

Perhaps the most spectacular effort Warren makes to save the universe of love is his treatment of the argument (made by Burke, among others) that "the Mariner repudiates marriage, contrasting it with . . . religious devotion" (*SE,* p. 255). Warren argues, instead, that "human love, which the guest presumably takes to be an occasion for merriment, must be understood in the context of universal love" (*SE,* p. 256), one of the repetitions of the scheme of oppositions I noted above. One is, he says, an image of the other. In order to qualify the emphasis in the Mariner's clear statement—

> O sweeter than the marriage-feast
> 'Tis sweeter far to me,
> To walk together to the kirk
> With a goodly company!—

Warren sets up a *scale* of values to redeem the marriage-feast and concludes rather perversely with the claim that "the Mariner now sees the chain of love which gives meaning to the marriage feast. In one of its aspects the poem is a prothalamion" (*SE,* p. 256).

Here, one might also consider the complaint about the rigidity and contradictions in Warren's reading of the sun/moon oppositions. One problem is that of who actually is punishing the Mariner in the poem: the Polar Spirit or the Moon, the symbol of the Imagination, since the Mariner has sinned against both, according to Warren. But the larger problem is, as some critics have pointed out, that in his philosophical works Coleridge, more traditionally, identifies the sun with Reason (capital R) and thus with the Imagination which would not then be symbolized by the Moon. However, it should be noted that the harsh light of the *physical* sun (as opposed to the symbolic Sun of Reason) reveals things in their apparently irresolvable differences. Sunlight by making everything visible insists on the externality of the things of the world in their separateness from the subject and therefore non-transparent or "translucent." The physical sun subjects the mind to what Wordsworth called "the tyranny of the bodily eye." Moonlight, on the other hand, or twi-light or half-light, is conducive to the imagination in that it *blurs* differences and separations. In this way, as reflective light, rather than being associated with the merely reflective and death-like faculty of the understanding, moonlight can be associated with the *mediating* and reconciling function of the imagination and of art. The problematic ambiguity, however, remains. It would seem significant that *in* the poem the sun (and the Mariner) can only be "redeemed" by way of the sun's spectral double—the moon—the mimeme which reflects it.[15] In his essay, Warren admits the disturbing ambivalence of the moon/imagination which is both a curse and a blessing. But although Warren grants what he calls this "doubtful doubleness of the imagination" (*SE,* p. 257), he does not seem to want to consider further the troubling implications about the nature of poetry that these passages and the effect of the story on the Wedding Guest suggest. He hints at those implications by saying that the end of the poem offers "another [counter] fable of the creative process" and a fuller statement of Coleridge's concept of the poet" (*SE,* p. 258), but he leaves it at that. He seems almost on the verge of a de Manian suggestion that the poem allows two totally correct, but totally incompatible interpretations.

There are also similar patterns concerning the exclusion of the subject from the whole he envisions, perhaps more hidden however, in other Coleridge texts, even before the Dejection ode and the late, terrible notebook poems. For example, the so-called "conversation poems" in which the speaker usually moves through stages of self-effacement or sacrifice towards identification with another, who is blessed like the water snakes. In the end, the harmony envisioned by the speaker for another either subtly excludes him or remains conjectural, as for example in "This Lime Tree Bower."

In part, as I suggested earlier the problem has to do with the nature of the organic metaphor. It is precisely this point which engages Paul de Man in his battle with both the Coleridgean Romantics and the organicist New Critics. "Is not this sense of the unity of forms being supported by the large metaphor of the analogy between language and a living organism, a metaphor that shapes a great deal of nineteenth-century poetry and thought?"[16] In several essays, de Man has argued the distinction between the intentional structures of language and hence poetry and the organic wholeness of a natural object. A person may be considered an organism, but a subject or consciousness cannot be, nor can a poem. In his most famous formulation, de Man charged Romantic poets such as Coleridge and their critics of succumbing by means of the organic metaphor, to the temptation "for the self to borrow, so to speak, the temporal stability it lacks from nature."[17] The Mariner may be included in an organic cosmos inasmuch as he is a piece of nature. Inasmuch as he has a consciousness of self, inasmuch as he is a "poet," using language, he necessarily stands apart from that wholeness. De Man extends his argument in relation to the New Critics, who have obviously influenced him a great deal:

> The ambivalence reappears among modern disciples of Coleridge, in a curious discrepancy between their theoretical assumptions and their practical results. As it refines interpretations more and more, American criticism does not discover a single meaning, but a plurality of significations that can be radically opposed to each other. Instead of revealing a continuity affiliated with the coherence of the natural world, it takes us into a discontinuous world of reflective irony and ambiguity. Almost in spite of itself, it pushes the interpretive process so far that the analogy between the organic world and the language of poetry finally explodes. The unitarian criticism finally becomes a criticism of ambiguity, an ironic reflection on the absence of the unity it had postulated.[18]

There still, however, remains the sense of guilt that seems to haunt almost everything Coleridge wrote and the obsessive concern with reason and cause, (the "why me?" cry of "The Pains of Sleep") reflected even in the Barbauld anecdote, the constant paranoid attention to signs as portents, for example, the motif of superstitious weather signs. The sense of guilt cannot of course be explained and, as we have seen, explains nothing in itself. But the guilt would seem to be part of another pattern having to do with usurpation (a note Coleridge struck, remember, in regard to the "counterfeit" of allegory in the passage quoted from *The Statesman's Manual*). For example, "Kubla Khan." The logic of the poem is that *if* and only *if* he could or would dare to reclaim the vision of the maid with the dulcimer and build the Khan's pleasure palace in air (words), *if* he did this:

> All should cry, Beware! Beware!
> His flashing eyes, his floating hair!
> Weave a circle round him thrice,
> And close your eyes with holy dread,
> For he on honey-dew hath fed,
> And drunk the milk of Paradise.[18]

I am aware of the allusion to Plato's *Ion* in this passage but the argument still seems to be that if he were capable of the poem, he would be *exorcised*—"weave a circle round him thrice"—as a satanic usurper. Hence, just possibly, the disclaimers of the note with which Coleridge prefaced the publication of the poem. It is not a poem, but a "fragment," "a psychological curiosity." He did not write it—it was given to him in a dream, and he didn't want to publish it, Lord Byron *made* him do it. I have already mentioned this poem in relation to the passage about the primary imagination as a repetition in the finite mind of the infinite I AM. One of the troubling implications of that definition is the possibility that repetition of what is creative utterance on the part of the Divine may be blasphemous, usurping self-assertion on the part of man. The same "peculiar paradox" inheres in Coleridge's concept of the will. In his discussion of the Mariner's crime and the problem of original sin, Warren quotes Coleridge:

> Though the act which re-enacts the mystery of the Fall is appropriately without motive, the sin of the will must be the appropriate expression of the essence of the will. And we shall turn to a passage in *The Statesman's Manual.* Having just said that, in its "state of immanence or indwelling in reason and religion, the will appears indifferently as wisdom or love," Coleridge proceeds: "But in its utmost abstraction and consequent state of reprobation, the will becomes Satanic pride and rebellious self-idolatry in the relations of the spirit to it-

> self, and remorseless despotism relatively to others . . . by the fearful resolve to find in itself alone the one absolute motive of action." (*SE,* p. 227-28)

One might add that unless it finds "in itself alone the one absolute motive of action" there is no possibility of original sin—yet inasmuch as the paradoxical exercise of the freedom of will is "of the essence of the will" it is necessary and determined.

At any rate, as in the anecdote of the Arab merchant, the ambiguity of action in such a universe could render one either immobile or render any act that suggested self-assertion—as for example, writing a poem—damning.

Allow me one more example of this ambiguity before turning back to *The Ancient Mariner* and Warren's essay. It is a question much too complicated to discuss fully here, but consider the nagging problem of Coleridge's plagiarism. Coleridge's thought aims for universal truth, as does poetry according to Warren. If it were universal truth it would belong to everyone and we could all live in its unity—it could not be "signed" by Schlegel or Schelling or Coleridge. There could be no problem of plagiarism. Coleridge almost seems aware of his difficulty in just these terms when he makes this remark in the *Biographia* concerning the relationship of *his* argument to that of Fichte and Schelling and the possible charge of plagiarism: "I regard truth as a divine ventriloquist: I care not from whose mouth the sounds are supposed to proceed, if only the words are audible and intelligible."[20] Such a disclaimer unfortunately has failed to satisfy many critics. A world requiring of truth an individual signature, however, presents a fairly dramatic instance of contradiction in the system. In Coleridge's work, "plagiarism" becomes a *pointed* case of self-assertion and usurpation.

The Ancient Mariner grabs an innocent Wedding Guest and mesmerizes him with a tale of murder that quite possibly alters his life. "A sadder but wiser man," the Wedding Guest, "who cannot choose but hear," quite possibly will remain celibate and therefore isolated all his life—the poem is possibly a "fable" of the consequences of the *fascination* of art, a fable of usurpation. Moreover, the tale the Mariner must repeat until the end of his days to free himself from periodic and agonizing convulsions—he himself is usurped by the tale—is *first* told in answer to the hermit's fearful question, "What manner of man art thou?" The story he tells is sub-titled by Coleridge "A Poet's Revery." The hermit's question of identity is similar to the Wedding Guest's question at the moment the Mariner reaches his murder of the albatross in his narration. And that is also the first instance of the Mariner's use of the first person singular—"I shot the albatross"—before the crime he speaks only of "we."

The tale that repeats the crime "repeats" it in a double sense: it tells the story which identifies the self-assertion of the crime with the self-assertion of the telling—the killing of the albatross with the usurpation of the Wedding Guest.

The poet's act of composition is a repetition of the Mariner's crime, both involving the paradox of necessity and will and the problem of intention. As Warren says:

> And the only thing he, in the ordinary sense, may "intend" is to make a poem. In so far as his process of discovery has been more than a rhetorical exercise, he cannot do otherwise than "intend" what his poem says, any more than he can change his own past as past, but he does not fully know what he "intends" until the poem is fully composed. (*SE,* p. 269)

Neither, of course, does the Mariner know what he "intends" until he has committed the act—not when he kills the albatross, not when he blesses the water-snakes, nor when he seizes the Wedding Guest. Nor can he "do otherwise than 'intend' " his acts of violence and blessing "anymore than he can change his own past as past." These acts are all responses to the question "What manner of man art thou?" Acts of violence, acts of blessing—not symbols for but manifestations of the ambiguous poem with its duplicitous gift to and constraints on wedding-guests, readers, and critics alike. A legacy that requires repetition of its blessings and violences on another level of discourse, a constantly belated but apparently inevitable translation and allegorization.

Paradoxically, it seems that the power of Warren's essay resides precisely in its repetition of this pattern and the thematization of that repetition. Robert Penn Warren set up the issues for future criticism, but, what is more, he provided the basis for, indeed a solicitation of further attempts at interpretative totalization, for the necessity of reading it in some sort of integrative and structurally unitary way. I am tempted here to repeat his final words: "And *The Ancient Mariner* is a poem on *this* subject." By taking up and repeating in a different, but compelling form the problem set by the poem itself, Warren's reading seemed to draw the capacity to collect or frame or generate supplementary and even contradictory meanings. Finally, and more generally, Warren's reading and those of the other New Critics, following Coleridge, confirmed the cultural institution of a certain discourse about poem and intellectual/philosophical context, a discourse *in* literature that is (to use the phrase of Lacoue-Labarthe and Nancy) the "production of its own (*propre*) theory."[21]

By means of a reading of Robert Penn Warren's essay on Coleridge, I have found three separate but tangled questions that now have to be untangled for future exploration. One, of course, is the relationship between *The Ancient Mariner* and the rest of the Coleridge canon as well as Romantic poetics in general. Work here could receive fresh guidance from investigation of the other two problems: one is the question of the relationship of the Coleridgean symbol and other tropes to modes of modern signification. Beyond that is the much larger question of the relationship of Romanticism to Modernism in general. Of course, it is *not* a matter of *reopening* this question—for a long time now, it has never ceased being re-opened, like a wound that refuses to heal.

University of California, Irvine

NOTES

1 Robert Penn Warren, "A Poem of Pure Imagination: An Experiment in Reading (1945-46)," in *Selected Essays* (New York: Random House, 1958), pp. 195-305, hereafter cited as *SE.* See Frances Ferguson's valuable "Coleridge and the Deluded Reader: *The Rime of the Ancient Mariner," Georgia Review* 31 (1977), pp. 617-35, for comments on this anecdote in relationship to Mrs. Barbauld's own writings. Her point (pp. 624-26) that Mrs. Barbauld's morality is the sort that most readers (including Warren) try to impose on the poem is a useful one. Ferguson's study of the problem of reading *as* the problem of moral interpretation and as the problem the poem takes up *not* to close (as most Barbauldian readers want it to do) follows a somewhat different path than I pursue in what follows, though we touch on several similar issues.

2 Warren's essay was first published in the *Kenyon Review* in 1946 and then later that year in expanded form with critical notes in an edition of the poem. The *Selected Essays* version is again revised and expanded with additional notes, some added as discussion of various criticisms (chiefly Humphrey House's) of the earlier versions. *Selected Essays* begins with Warren's important "Pure and Impure Poetry" essay and ends with "A Poem of Pure Imagination," the two essays providing the theoretical (and somewhat dialectical) "framing" for the volume.

3 The importance of Coleridge and, indeed, of romanticism for modernism and the New Criticism may seem a commonplace now, but it was not always taken for granted. Some of the crucial early texts were T. S. Eliot's quotation of the wit in his 1921 essay on Andrew Marvell, I. A. Richards' study *Coleridge on* Coleridgean imagination as the reconciliation of opposites to define "good" *Imagination* (1934) and Cleanth Brooks's remarks on Coleridge in *Modern Poetry and the Tradition* (1939), but the relationship was there even earlier—see Murray Krieger's *The New Apologists for Poetry* (Minneapolis: Univ. of Minnesota Press, 1956), especially the first chapter on the anti-romanticism of T. E. Hulme; Richard Foster's *The New Romantics: A Reappraisal of the New Criticism* (Bloomington: Indiana Univ. Press, 1962), especially pp. 134-36; Frank Kermode's *Romantic Image* (London: Routledge & Kegan Paul, 1957); and, of course, the New Critics' own retrospective history—William K. Wimsatt, Jr. and Cleanth Brooks, *Literary Criticism: A Short History* (New York: Alfred A. Knopf, 1964). For some of the other texts dealing with the controversy, see the surveys by Frank Jordan (pp. 62-65) and René Wellek (pp. 257-58) in Frank Jordan, ed., *The English Romantic Poets: A Review of Research and Criticism,* Third Revised Edition (New York: The Modern Language Association of America, 1972). The introductions and essays in Kathleen Coburn, ed., *Coleridge: A Collection of Critical Essays* (Englewood Cliffs: Prentice-Hall, 1967) and James D. Boulger, ed., *Twentieth Century Interpretations of "The Rime of the Ancient Mariner": A Collection of Critical Essays* (Englewood Cliffs: Prentice-Hall, 1969) are also useful in regard to Coleridge's contemporary reputation.

4 The questions are ubiquitous, but I could cite as examples relevant to my inquiry Paul de Man's "Intentional Structure of the Romantic Image" (1960, 1968), rpt. in Harold Bloom, ed., *Romanticism and Consciousness: Essays in Criticism* (New York: W. W. Norton, 1970)—in fact, this whole volume; "The Rhetoric of Temporality: Allegory and Symbol, Irony" in *Interpretation: Theory and Practice,* ed. Charles S. Singleton (Baltimore: The Johns Hopkins Press, 1969); and his chapter on the New Criticism in *Blindness and Insight: Essays in the Rhetoric of Contemporary Criticism* (New York: Oxford Univ. Press, 1971); Murray Krieger's *Theory of Criticism: A Tradition and Its System* (Baltimore: The Johns Hopkins Univ. Press, 1976); and the recent work of Philippe Lacoue-Labarthe and Jean-Luc Nancy for these issues in the context of German romanticism—see particularly their *L'absolu littéraire: Théorie de la littérature du romantisme allemand* (Paris: Editions du Seuil, 1978.) One should also mention here E. S. Shaffer's important work, *'Kubla Khan' and The Fall of Jerusalem: The Mythological School in Biblical Criticism and Secular Literature, 1770-1880* (Cambridge: Cambridge Univ. Press, 1975).

5 The attacks on Warren's reading are usefully summarized by Max Schulz and Thomas Raysor in Frank Jordan, *The English Romantic Poets,* pp. 176-77. One might single out for special attention Elder Olson's review in *Modern Philology* in 1948, reprinted in *Critics and Criticism,* ed. Ronald S. Crane (Chicago: Univ. of Chicago Press, 1952); E. E. Bostetter, "The Nightmare World of *The Ancient Mariner, Studies in Romanticism"* (1962) rpt. Coburn, ed., Coleridge; and his *The Romantic Ventriloquists* (Seattle: Univ. of Washington Press, 1963); and the more sympathetic criticisms and supplementary interpretations of Humphrey House, *Coleridge* (London: Rupert Hart-Davis, 1953); J. B. Beer, *Coleridge the Visionary* (New York: Macmillan, 1959). Indeed, the hegemony of Warren's reading, in the face of the cogency and even the savagery of some of these attacks or responses, is an interesting question. I mean the pattern I will analyze here to suggest, in part, some reason for its success.

In regard to the issue of Warren's essay as allegory here and in the lines that follow, see Richard Foster, pp. 38-39.

6 See Wimsatt and Brooks, p. 400, n. 3; Hans-Georg Gadamer, *Truth and Method,* no translator identified (New York: The Seabury Press, 1975), pp. 64-73; Walter Benjamin, *The Origin of German Tragic Drama,* trans. John Osborne (London: New Left Books, 1977), pp. 159-67; and de Man, "The Rhetoric of Temporality."

7 See his *Democracy and Poetry* (Cambridge: Harvard Univ. Press, 1975), pp. XV-XVI.

8 See Michael Cooke's valuable analysis of these paradoxes and problems in *The Romantic Will* (New Haven: Yale Univ. Press, 1976), and particularly his interesting and rather perverse reading of *The Ancient Mariner* (pp. 29-39) which reaches conclusions similar to those I suggest below. For an equally interesting reading of these same texts with somewhat different conclusions, see Leslie Brisman's excellent chapter "Coleridge and the Ancestral Voices" in his *Romantic Origins* (Ithaca: Cornell Univ. Press, 1978). Brisman deals with the latter half of *The Ancient Mariner* within Warren's terms better than most later readers.

9 I am quoting the most recent, the fourth edition (New York: Holt, Rinehart and Winston, 1976), pp. 11, 13.

10 Reduced in this way, and in a sense Burke makes this reduction possible, his reading of the poem seems to have had more influence than Jonathan Arac seems to think in his response to my paper. Admittedly, however, the influence has often been an unacknowledged one, and the reduction is a telling one. The point about Burke's reading as a shadowy "other" to Warren's seems to me to be this: in his pursuit of the structure of the poem by means of a richer sense of the notion of "motive" than Warren allows for, Burke analyzes suggestively (and not extensively) five different strands—the aesthetic, marital, political, drug, and metaphysical problems—as essentially discontinuous "motives" (he calls them "disrelated"). That is to say, whatever their differing and uneven relationships, these strands cannot be resolved into oppositions or into a totality. This irresolution may account for the revival of interest in Burke recently and to his earlier eclipse by Brooks and Warren. There is a curious sense in which Burke rather resembles Coleridge with his rangings over a vast realm of ideas, his flashes of insight, quick sketches of interpretation, sudden transitions, sometimes apparent rambling. He even defers analysis at one point with the parenthetical remark: "that would require much quotation, and I plan to do this at length in a monograph on 'The Particular Strategy of Samuel Taylor Coleridge' on which I am now engaged," *The Philosophy of Literary Form,* third edition, (Berkeley and Los Angeles: Univ. of California Press, 1973), p. 95.

11 These quotations are from "The Rhetoric of Temporality," pp. 190-91.

12 For example, see Thomas M. Raysor, ed., Coleridge's *Miscellaneous Criticism* (London: Constable, 1936), p. 28. Symbol and metaphor are too easily identified by Warren and the New Critics—for Coleridge, they were clearly distinct, as in the definition of the symbol, quoted above, where the symbol, apparently, is at once literal *and* metaphorical or mediates between them. Again, in the same text, *Lay Sermons,* ed. R. J. White, *The Collected Works of Samuel Taylor Coleridge,* Vol. 6 (Princeton: Princeton Univ. Press, 1972), p. 79: "True natural philosophy is comprized in the study of the science and language of *symbols.* The power delegated to nature is all in every part: and by a symbol I mean, not a metaphor or allegory or any other figure of speech or form of fancy, but an actual and essential part of that, the whole of which it represents." The problem of the Coleridgean metaphor is a thorny one and clearly needs to be re-thought. The metaphor usually, wherever he speaks of metaphor *as such,* is based on resemblance, not difference, and thus on association and the fancy or understanding. It is then arbitrary—in either of the senses of that word.

The logic of this suggests another problem perhaps inherent in the concept of the symbol, but at least a danger risked by Warren with his subdivision of natural symbols and symbols of convergence or context (see below). If simile and metaphor are devalued because they depend on the mechanical associationism of resemblance, what is their difference from a symbol that is "rooted in natural experience" and therefore a *given* for the mind? To put the question another way, is there *other* than a theological difference? To push these questions would ultimately lead to the whole question (which Coleridge found uncomfortable) of the arbitrary nature of language—see the passage from his letters quoted in Arac's response, n. 26. One of the significant things about this letter of excited questions is that it is addressed to William Godwin and full of appeal to the "great man" to come and theorize those questions away. The tone of the letter and the series of questions make it another example of Coleridge's constant urge to escape the shadow of the arbitrary. For extensive comments on this question (and the letter), see Gerald Brun's *Modern Poetry and the Idea of Language* (New Haven: Yale Univ. Press, 1974).

As he does with the question of metaphor, Coleridge also tends to depreciate *wit* conventionally as belonging to the fancy and having to do with the arbitrary association of contradictory or opposite entities, qualities, or ideas. For this problem in the larger context of Romanticism, see the important work of Philippe Lacoue–Labarthe and Jean-Luc Nancy, *L'absolu littéraire: Théorie de la littérature du romantisme allemand,* particularly the chapter on "L'exigence fragmentaire," and Nancy's essay, "*Menstruum universale* (Literary Dissolution)," trans. Paula Moddel, "Literature and its Others," *Sub-stance* 21 (1978), p. 21-35.

13 Curiously, because Warren wants to redeem the universe of love and wisdom in *The Ancient Mariner,* the world of the Arab merchant in the anecdote resembles nothing so much as the images of the web in Warren's novel *All the King's Men,* a novel which is also concerned with the paradoxes of system and individual accountability:

> Cass Mastern lived for a few years and in that time he learned the world is all of one piece. He learned that the world is like an enormous spider web and if you touch it, however lightly, at any point, the vibration ripples to the remotest perimeter and the drowsy spider feels the tingle and is drowsy no more but springs out to fling the gossamer coils about you who have touched the web and then inject the black, numbing poison under your hide. It does not matter whether or not you meant to brush the web of things. Your happy foot or your gay wing may have brushed it ever so lightly, but what happens always happens and there is the spider, bearded black, and with his great faceted eyes glittering like mirrors in the sun, or like God's eye, and the fangs dripping. (New York: Bantam Books, 1959), pp. 188-89.

The novel was first published in 1946. Another curious way the essay seems to reflect Warren's preoccupation with the issues and patterns of his novel is his apparently casual reference to Shakespeare's *Julius Caesar* as his example for discussion of the relationship of extrinsic and intrinsic perspectives on a literary work. While the play concerns massive and questionable self-assertiveness, its murder is certainly a motivated, if not over-determined, act.

14 I do not want to say this because it merely repeats the implied oppositions in the argument about "pure" poetry. It might be useful here to reconsider Kenneth Burke's point about the "note alien to the perfect harmony . . . 'Transcendence' is the solving of the logical problem by stretching it out into a narrative arpeggio, whereby a conflicting element can be introduced as a 'passing note,' hence not felt as 'discord'." (*The Philosophy of Literary Form,* pp. 99-100). Cf. the final lines of "This Lime Tree Bower, My Prison."

15 I did not take up the question of the sun/moon opposition in the lecture given at the Binghamton conference. My brief suggestion here I offered during the discussion. I find extremely useful the reading of the problem suggested there by Jonathan Arac and presented more fully in his response in this issue.

16 de Man, *Blindness and Insight,* p. 27.

17 de Man, "The Rhetoric of Temporality," p. 181.

18 de Man, *Blindness and Insight,* p. 28.

19 *The Poems of Samuel Taylor Coleridge,* ed. Ernest Hartley Coleridge (London: Oxford Univ. Press, 1957), p. 298.

20 *Biographia Literaria,* ed. J. Shawcross (London: Oxford Univ. Press, 1962), I, p. 105.

21 It is not my intention to provide simply another repetition of that pattern—though this perhaps is at least partially inevitable—but to question the mechanism and operation of that pattern.

There is, of course, importance in the investigation of the lines of force governing canon formation and the academic institutionalization of the New Criticism, as Bill Warner and Jonathan Arac suggest (see the latter's response). What interests me at the moment, however, is the repetition and thematization of that repetition in the discourse itself. To posit simply an "outside," or set up an opposition between Warren and Burke, between the New Critics and a sociological (or historical or psychoanalytic) criticism eclipsed by them is further to succumb to the repetition of the oppositions I try to explore in this paper. There *are* larger cultural issues at stake, of course—Raymond Williams has long since provided a valuable beginning for the study of the institutional and cultural power of the Coleridge tradition.

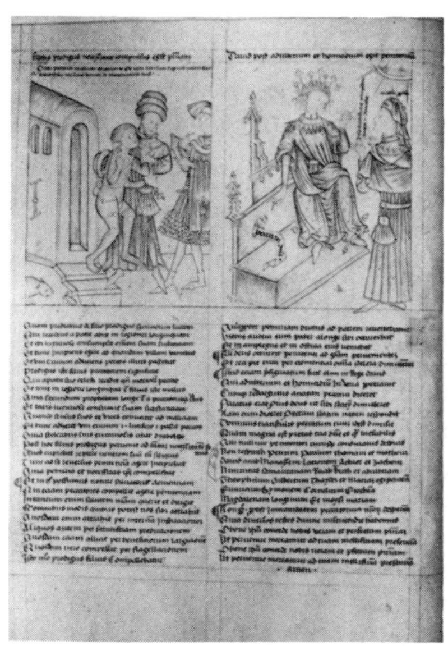

Repetition and Exclusion: Coleridge and New Criticism Reconsidered

Jonathan Arac

In "The Art of Theology" Homer Brown elucidates repetition and exclusion as the basic operations that determine Robert Penn Warren's reading of *The Rime of the Ancient Mariner.*[1] Warren constantly repeats variants of the opposition between too much and too little meaning, while excluding from sight those elements of Coleridge's text that fall through the meshes of this network of oppositions. Brown's essay itself is marked by these basic operations, by which it too joins, as a representative instance, the larger history in which our reading and writing work. Those processes of (repetitive) emphasis and (exclusive) selection involved in reading a text pertain to the whole problem of cultural reproduction, the formation of textual canons and institutional elites that determine—both constrain and enable—the critical practice of a given time and place. We attend now to Warren's essay because of his place in New Criticism and our sense of all that we inherit from that way of reading, writing, and teaching: the burden of its repetitive concerns from which we must free ourselves, the absence we wish to make good of texts and methods it excluded.

Through reading Warren's essay and rehearsing its critical strategies, Brown wishes to liberate some of the excess in Coleridge's text that Warren has excluded, but that now appears peculiarly and valuably "literary." But in his close attention to Warren's essay Brown repeats the most significant exclusion effected by Warren, that of establishing the domination of his discourse over the discourse of other critics. A liberation of poetry and criticism from what we take as excessively limiting in New Criticism can not come from merely looking *through* New Criticism, poring over its texts so intensively that we see daylight, or the abyss, through the weave, however tight its texture may have been drawn. We have to look *around* it as well.

In opposing Lowes and Griggs, Warren's essay is a crucial document in the struggle that allowed criticism to supplant scholarship as the major activity by which even academic teachers and students of literature defined their relation to the texts they read. The victory belonged, however, not simply to criticism, but to New Criticism, and even that of a specific variety. In 1938, when Warren and Cleanth Brooks, both teaching at Louisiana State University, published *Understanding Poetry,* they were far less important representatives of New Criticism than William Empson, Kenneth Burke, or R. P. Blackmur. By twenty-five years later (when I entered college), *Understanding Poetry* was in its third edition, Brooks and Warren had long been at Yale, and their sober pedagogical effectiveness had displaced the willfulness of Empson, the preciosity of Blackmur, the playfulness of Burke. For the classroom, or even for comfort, those three were too disturbingly brilliant (like the sun in *The Ancient Mariner*). Furthermore, from the thirties to the sixties Blackmur, Burke, and Empson were all proving themselves ever more clearly critics in the larger, Arnoldian sense that Edward Said noted last night, while the students and disciples of Brooks and Warren were working to refine a more exclusively *literary* criticism.

Homer Brown has scrutinized the *discourse* of Warren, but his project thus far remains at the stage that Marie-Rose Logan this afternoon ascribed to Hayden White's *Metahistory,* still far from any practice beyond discourse. Even the rhetorical subtlety of Paul de Man, to which Brown has turned, may remain as partial a tool as Logan finds Northrop Frye, or we find the New Critics, in its restriction to discourse, in its attempt to deny the possibility of any other realm than that of the text. Indeed, literary history as defined (repeatedly) by de Man—the shift in rhetorical registers within the small space of a short text, or few pages of a longer text—seems too exclusive to achieve the larger scope we want. We want both to take in more than a few pages of Rousseau or a sonnet of Mallarmé and to put out more, to write books as well as essays of literary history. One such book would be, as William Warner suggested last night, a study of New Criticism that undertook to chart its effect, to place it not only intellectually but also institutionally (in relation to such issues as textbooks, graduate schools, job placement). We also need thoughtful attention to the readers of New Criticism, represented in Brown's essay only by himself and de Man. How did an intellectual movement that received so much bad press, so many serious attacks, as did New Criticism, somehow prevail?

I don't want, however, to continue to exclude Homer Brown's essay from my discourse; instead, I now repeat its movement and join it in turning to Warren's essay.

II

I begin with Warren's most striking exclusion, which leads to Coleridge and repetition. Despite his wish to show the consistency between his interpretation of *The Rime of the Ancient Mariner* and Coleridge's "sober prose" (*SE,* p. 203) (an oddly ironic way of describing Coleridge's theology and metaphysics), Warren mentions only once, briefly and early, Coleridge's most crucial term, the Reason, the power of transcendent intuition, Coleridge's master word for the unity he so constantly sought, and at which Warren aims also (*SE,* pp. 210-11).[2] Warren instead establishes the imagination, for Coleridge a "mediatory" power, as the dominant operative term of his reading.[3] He finds in the poem an opposition of moonlight to sunlight, symbolizing the opposition of imagination to understanding. It is hard to establish clearly the relations among Coleridge's major terms. (This is why he is so fruitfully available to some readers and contemptuously dismissible for others.) Nonetheless, without elaborating in detail the curious logic that mobilizes these terms, I find little warrant in Coleridge for the opposition of understanding to imagination, and even less for the alignment of concept with image (understanding-sun) that Warren proposes.

In Coleridge's later prose the sun is regularly aligned with the Reason: "Reason and religion are their own evidence. The natural Sun is in this respect a symbol of the spiritual."[4] Ignoring the Reason drives Warren into what seems unintentional antiphrasis, when he makes the sun symbolize the "reflective faculty" (*SE,* p. 241), although the sun's power is projective. Furthermore, in discussing the symbol by "necessity" (*SE,* p. 219), the natural symbol, Warren fails to note the natural dependence of the moon, which *is* reflective, upon the sun for its light. (The imagination of course could not similarly depend upon the understanding.) For all its attempt to contextualize, Warren's essay achieves its reading in a way exemplary of New Criticism, through fidelity to the poem's independent contours, *despite* its difference both from Coleridge's "sober prose" and from nature. A distance remains between the poem and the origins with which Warren wishes it continuous: the world of nature (with which it should be integral by the theory of the symbol) and the poet's prose (with which it should be developmentally coherent—cf., *SE,* p. 273).

This distance enables Brown to read Warren's essay in terms of de Man's concept of "allegory" and to show the remainder, the excess left over (the *self* above all) that prevents the perfect fit that Coleridge wanted and that Warren claims.

What conditions might determine Warren's misreading, his neglect of the Reason and its associations with religion and the sun? First, there is the *problem* of religion. As Brown notes, Warren importantly renewed our understanding of the theological bases of Coleridge's criticism. Warren, however, will not recognize that for Coleridge's writing religion is not just the base, the point of departure, but is even more the center and ultimate goal. Such recognition would raise the question of religion as displacing Coleridge's poetic activity and would have necessitated thinking through the notorious fact that Coleridge's most productive years as a prose-writer were extremely lean poetically. To be sure, the revisions of *The Ancient Mariner* for *Sibylline Leaves* (1817) (notably the gloss) are contemporary with his activity in speculative prose and succeeded in "connecting . . . the chief poem of Coleridge, with his philosophy."[5] They may well also, however, have afforded a haven from which Coleridge was unwilling or unable to set out again. We may acknowledge the 1817 *Ancient Mariner* as "Coleridge's one great complete work, the one really finished thing, in a life of many beginnings," and still find this completion the terminal domestication of Coleridge's poetic wanderings, the ultimate correction of error through revision.[6] Such considerations would all have compromised Warren's hope for the peaceful coexistence of religion and poetry.

We arrive then at a second area of determination. By ignoring the Reason and its relation to the sun, Warren harmonizes poetry and religion but sets in opposition imagination and understanding. He thus repeats the characteristic New Critical dichotomy of poetry and science, echoed at about the same time by Cleanth Brooks in *The Well-Wrought Urn.* "Myth is truer than history," explained Brooks in discussing Keats's "sylvan historian," repeating yet another version of this opposition and suggesting some of the function of such oppositions.[7] Myth keeps you out of the tangled web of history that Brown has already mentioned in relation both to Coleridge and Warren. Myth promises a unifying clarity; it holds together what falls apart into distinction in the harsh sunlight of history or science or understanding.

Within the poem such an archaizing move toward unity and away from history governs the function of the word "cross." In his prose speculations on language Coleridge noted a historical tendency to "desynonymize" words with multiple meanings.[8] Such words split into different words, each bearing a single meaning of the original plurality. A word like "cross" accordingly takes on different meanings in its historical evolution. But its sequence of uses in *The Ancient Mariner* suggests a unity that overrides any possible historical distinctions or any logic that would analyze the uses as mere homonymity.[9]

The climax of the poem's second section relates the albatross to "cross" in a specifically Christian context:[10]

Instead of the cross, the Albatross
About my neck was hung.
(141-42)

The force of this moment derives in part from the two earlier uses of "cross," each of which links "cross," the albatross, and religious language in a way that appears merely casual:

At length did cross an Albatross,
Through the fog it came;
As if it had been a Christian soul,
We hailed it in God's name.
(63-66)

"God save thee, ancient Mariner!
From the fiends, that plague thee thus! —
Why looks't thou so? "—With my cross-bow
I shot the ALBATROSS.
(79-82)

The third instance ("Instead of the cross . . . ") reveals the system behind these chance appearances. The arbitrary, metonymic links of poetic syntax prove instead meaningful, metaphoric, paradigmatic. The earlier references to "God" and "Christian" are now packed by implication into the "cross," to which the albatross is shown as equivalent, holding the same place. For Coleridge such unity derives from Reason, but for New Critics like Warren, from experience. In terms of Warren's distinction between two types of symbol, this usage for Coleridge would be of "necessity," from the pre-existing divine unity that establishes correspondences in the nature of things, in which words participate. For Warren, however, "cross" would function as a symbol of "congruence," based on our experience of the poem, which succeeds in establishing an order otherwise unavailable (*SE,* pp. 219-20).

I find finally a third area of contradiction that Warren avoids by not recognizing the Coleridgean Reason in its full force and its association with the sun. Warren saves himself from having to puzzle over the negative value he finds accorded to the sun in *The Rime of the Ancient Mariner.* Such a reversal of value would have forced Warren to question his premise that the poem must be "truly the poet's," that it "expresses him" and therefore "involves his own view of the world" (*SE,* p. 203). Or if it did not shake that premise, then it would change the "view of the world" ascribed to Coleridge. It would suggest an incoherence in Coleridge's Christianity (and William Empson has read the poem in this light) that might in turn lead to the "personal" themes of Kenneth Burke's inquiry, which Warren ruled out of his concern (*SE*, pp. 214-16). Coleridge could no longer have served so effectively as the normative figure of a sensibility unified on the basis of religion.

In pursuing further ramifications of this problem with the sun, I will not myself explore the "personal" but will assume the context of western religious experience (the wish to mediate the distance from an excessively omnipotent father-divinity) and western rhetorical practice (the inevitable interruption and displacement of philosophic discourse by metaphoric vehicle).[11]

III

Despite the supreme value accorded to the sun of Reason in Coleridge's prose, the sun characteristically does not—as Warren notes—figure affirmatively in his poetry. Homer Brown even speaks, paradoxically in this context, of Coleridge's "nightmare of reason." The sun's power is too overwhelmingly great. There is no return possible to the sun, no reciprocity. It pours ever forth a light that man can only receive; in its immediacy the sun is blinding, stunning. Coleridge prefers mediated systems that allow the recipient to give something back. Thus we reach the positive function of the moon in Coleridge's poetic world. At night the sun remains a hidden source, known in its absence, like the divine creative I AM that we know only through its repetition in the primary imagination. The earth may then further echo the moon, as the secondary imagination the primary. The moon is both mirror and lamp, source and recipient of light, as in the earthlight evoked in the epigraph to "Dejection," as in the echoings of sound and light in "The Nightingale" and the icicles at the end of "Frost at Midnight," "Quietly shining to the quiet moon."[12] In his poetry Coleridge gains intimacy and identity in distancing himself from the direct presence of the origin and symbol of totality. Thus for Coleridge, as for Paul de Man whom Brown cites, man's effective relationship to nature begins with a loss of immediacy, the recognition of a power different from the self.

In the terms of Roman Jakobson's communications model, the addresser (the source, God, the sun) is displaced into the message.[13] So in "Hymn before Sun-Rise, in the Vale of Chamouni" all the landscape is called upon to "Utter forth God" (l. 69). This ecstasy is summoned, however, only before the sun emerges, while the divine I AM is held off. Appropriately Coleridge wrote this poem as if spectator at a scene he in fact never visited but knew only through the mediation of other literary texts. When Shelley actually visited the scene, "Mont Blanc" enacted a very different experience.

In investigating the "nightmare of reason," Homer Brown considers the possible guilt of the human I AM as an originating self-will that threatens to usurp the power properly belonging only to the sun or God. Coleridge offers a possible resolution to this problem in a letter highly relevant to the subject and form of *The Ancient Mariner:*

> The common end of all *narrative,* nay, of *all,* Poems is to convert a *series* into a *Whole:* to make those events, which in real or imagined History move on in a *strait* Line, assume to our Understandings a *circular* motion—the snake with it's Tail in it's Mouth. Hence indeed the almost flattering and yet appropriate Term, Poesy—i.e. poiesis=*making.* Doubtless, to *his* eye, which alone comprehends all Past and all Future in one eternal Present, what to our short sight appears strait is but a part of the great Cycle—just as the calm Sea to us *appears* level, tho' it be indeed only a part of a *globe.* Now what the Globe is in Geography, *miniaturing* in order to *manifest* the Truth, such is a Poem to that Image of God, which we were created into, and which still seeks that Unity, or Revelation of the *One* in and by the *Many,* which reminds it, that tho' in order to be an individual Being it must go forth *from* God, yet as the *receding* from *him* is to *pro*ceed towards Nothingness and Privation, it must still at every step turn back toward him in order to *be* at all—Now a straight Line, continuously retracted forms of necessity a circular orbit.[14]

Coleridge images "individual being," human identity, as a suspended fall. One is always falling away from God, in order to be differentiated from the totality, yet always also falling back toward the source, being held in orbit, in order not to become the satanic reduction of pure self-will that has fallen to the bottom. My I-ness exists in a distanced relation that avoids both the career into outer space of atheism and the engulfment in the undifferentiated source.[15] This conversion of "a series into a whole" takes up as well another issue Brown raised: it gives a model for the systematization of the "arbitrary," or in Brooks's terms, the transformation of history into myth.

To specify further Coleridge's preferred condition for life, we might pursue the notion of "response," raised earlier today for us by Marie-Rose Logan. Despite the danger he fears in satanic origination, Coleridge recognizes a constant need for a *responsive beginning.* In "To William Wordsworth," Coleridge is at first overwhelmed by hearing *The Prelude* read aloud to him. He finds in the poem Wordsworth's "inner Power" (l. 16), a solar energy that "streamed from thee, and thy soul received / The light reflected, as a light bestowed" (II. 18-19). Coleridge recognizes in Wordsworth's imagination the "strength of usurpation"[16] that makes Wordsworth himself the origin, which like a star "shed[s] influence" (l. 52). Wordsworth's power, however, arouses in Coleridge only self-regarding pain over his own waste. Finally Coleridge succeeds in moving out from himself into a state of "prayer" (l. 112). He motivates himself through revising his solar, stellar figures for Wordsworth, at the same time revising Wordsworth's poem, repeating it with a difference:

> My soul lay passive, by thy various strain
> Driven as in surges now beneath the stars,
> With momentary stars of my own birth,
> Fair constellated foam, still darting off
> Into the darkness; now a tranquil sea,
> Outspread and bright, yet swelling to the moon.
>
> (96-101)

In this scene the vagaries of will (as in the passage on will and ocean billows cited by Brown and Warren) are "constellated," given a beautiful order by what they reflect; its "surges" then are tranquillized, organized into a totality of response, as the quiet ocean gravitationally swells toward the moon that makes it "bright." Wordsworth becomes the moon, and Coleridge can feel at rest in a "sweet sense of Home" (l. 92) rather than in a "coffin" (l. 75) as earlier. This climactic passage in Coleridge's poem echoes and revises the climactic scene of moon and sea at Snowdon in *The Prelude.* And Coleridge fully succeeded in giving something back to Wordsworth, for I find in Wordsworth's own revision of the Snowdon scene a significant Coleridgeanizing of his experience and comprehension of imagination.[17]

Through pursuing "response," we reach another area that Brown rightly points to: *The Ancient Mariner* as an allegory of reading. The Wedding Guest, Brown's "innocent" reader, figures the naiveté of response that can say nothing back and is merely "stunned" by the poem as the Mariner was by the noon sun and Coleridge by *The Prelude.* Not to be annihilated, to respond, one needs some distance from the object: one must diminish the object, "miniaturing in order to manifest" it. Following Warren's observation that "the poem is the light and not the thing seen by the light" (*SE,* p. 212), the reader must turn the poem from a sun into a moon, as Coleridge had done with Wordsworth. The gloss functions as Coleridge's own, responsive, beginning to the process of diminishing the poem, distancing it into a manageable moon, closing the annihilating gap across which power had first streamed only in one way. In speaking we sometimes make a "glottal stop," a constriction at the top of the throat by which we prevent hiatus, a choking to keep from gaping (as "in the middle of saying 'No' by going *unh-unh*").[18] We (physically) draw a bar to make a difference. The glottal stop involves a "momentary complete closure" followed by an "explosive release" (*American Heritage Dictionary*). So, as Pater claimed and Lawrence Lipking has shown in more detail, what we may call Coleridge's "glossal stop" makes a whole of the poem by closing it off.[19] Yet from that model of reading have streamed forth all the many further readings of the poem, like Warren's repetitive proliferation of the differentiating closure begun by Coleridge.

A further element of responsibility and imaginative responsiveness joins *The Ancient Mariner* to the tale from the Arabian Nights in the anecdote of Mrs. Barbauld with which Warren and Brown begin their essays. The full version of the tale involves not only a gratuitous act and dreadful consequence, but also a circular journey (the merchant defers his end for a year but must return to pay his penalty to the genie) and a focus on fabulation (the merchant is saved when three mysterious old men buy off the genie with ever more marvelous stories—all of which concern transformations between man and beast, magic versions of the theme of "one life"). The tale (the very first of the series) thus immediately echoes the framing situation of Scheherazade and her life-preserving power of narration. A sufficiently marvelous response may control even the most extravagant arbitrariness.

But we may follow Warren to ask what kind of control we achieve through our response. Warren opens "Pure and Impure Poetry," his most programmatically new-critical essay, with an analogy that joins criticism to the world of fable: "The poem is like the monstrous Orillo in Boiardo's *Orlando Innamorato.*" (Orillo's powers of regeneration resemble those of the hydra that Brown cited from Paul de Man.) No critical method, Warren argues, can take care of the poem as dexterously as the hero managed to deal with the monster. For us critics, "There is only one way to conquer the monster: you must eat it, bones, blood, skin, pelt, and gristle." But this strategy limits the mastery of the critic over the poem: "Even then the monster is not dead, for it lives in you, is assimilated into you, and you are different, and somewhat monstrous yourself, for having eaten it" (*SE,* p. 3). Warren thus recognizes the place of repetition in the critical relationship. The principle of contagion that Warren figures forth recalls the sober prose of Cleanth Brooks arguing that paraphrase only begins to succeed as it becomes itself poetical.[20] There is no metalanguage for criticism, only repetition and variations of the poem. Warren recognizes, therefore, that the founding criticism of the poem, the gloss itself, hardly does all that one would hope. The gloss "should have made the structure of the poem clearer" (*SE,* p. 262), but failed. "Apparently the Gloss needs a gloss" (*SE,* p. 231). Repetition solicits repetition.

At this point we may leave Warren. He found in the poem "lags and lapses" that block its "pervasive logic" (*SE,* p. 262); he discerned the "meaninglessness" (*SE,* p. 303), the "over-lays" and "undigested chunks" (*SE*, p. 288) that are the meat of much modern criticism, but his interest lay elsewhere. One task that still awaits the student of modern criticism is to define that interest, to locate New Criticism from the distance that we now hold from it.

If Warren discovers, but avoids, the impasses many critics now seek, he did not avoid them enough for Elder Olson. In one of the most important early responses to Warren, Olson raises issues that are still very much with us. He defines *The Ancient Mariner* as "one of those poems the interpretations of which have rather illustrated the different methods of interpretation than explained the poem," and he finds Warren's essay "valuable principally as exhibiting what happens to poetry in interpretation"—the use to which we have put it today. For Olson this is no praise. He dismisses Warren's project as fundamentally flawed. "The words have a meaning; they mean the poem; but why should the poem itself have any further meaning? What sense is there in asking after the meaning of something which is itself a meaning? . . . Shall we not have further meanings still, and so on *ad infinitum,* so that interpretation becomes impossible, as being an infinite process?"[21] Thirty years ago Olson saw opening up in New Criticism the abyss that his fellow Chicagoans in *Critical Inquiry* are still trying to cover. Are we then so distant from New Criticism?

IV

Finally I would like to leave the chain of displacements I have been pursuing through Coleridge and his critics, end this cycle of repetition, and ask (again!) after an exclusion upon which Warren's essay, and Brown's critique, made me meditate. The ideological function of Coleridge for New Criticism need not be further elaborated at this time, but why are we—post-New Critics—still so fascinated by Coleridge as to allow him to dominate our discourse, even if we are speaking of him in order to refute, or expose, him?

Consider instead for a moment Shelley, a theorist who like Coleridge tried to harmonize Plato and Bacon; like Coleridge focused on the imagination; indeed, who offers everything Coleridge does except the theology. Pater defined "two ways of envisaging those aspects of nature which seem to bear the impress of reason or intelligence." One takes them "merely as marks" and "separates" nature from any ultimate source. The other "identifies the two" and "regards nature itself as the living energy of an intelligence" like man's.[22] Coleridge takes the latter way; his speculative world offers smooth closures, echo and participation. If we cannot be *at* the divine origin, he offers the hope of being *with* it through his systems of mediations and repetition. Shelley instead *opens* gaps: "It is infinitely improbable that the cause of mind . . . is similar to mind."[23] For Shelley the "footsteps" of imagination "are like those of a wind over a sea, which the coming calm erases, and whose traces remain only as on the wrinkled sand which paves it."[24] This complex process of transmission and inscription makes the source so different as to be unimaginable from its traces. And even if we could think our way back to it, the source would no longer be there. Shelley's history runs forward without return. As opposed to Coleridge's organic notion of language, Shelley considers language not divine, natural, or vital: "Language is arbitrarily produced by the Imagination and has relation to thoughts alone."Shelley derives his highest values (love, beauty, truth, virtue) from the fact that people live among other human beings, from the principles by which "the will of a social being is determined to action, inasmuch as he is social."[25]

In the nineteenth century both Coleridge and Shelley were read by poets and those who cared deeply for literature, but there is an instructive divergence in their wider readerships. Crudely, Coleridge was read by Anglican divines and Tory politicians; Shelley by workers and radicals. New Criticism banished Shelley's poetry and appropriated Coleridge's theory. What should we make of the continuing exclusion of Shelley from serious consideration as a thinker, even as his poetry is now regaining the attention it deserves?

Princeton University

NOTES

1 Robert Penn Warren, "A Poem of Pure Imagination," in *Selected Essays* (1958; rpt. New York: Random, 1966), pp. 198-305 (hereafter cited as *SE*).

2 "The REASON without being either the SENSE, the UNDERSTANDING or the IMAGINATION contains all three within itself, even as the mind contains its thoughts, and is present in and through them all; or as the expression pervades the different features of an intelligent countenance," *The Statesman's Manual* (1816), *The Collected Works of Samuel Taylor Coleridge* (Princeton: Princeton Univ. Press and London: Routledge, 1969-), VI, 69-70.

3 The imagination is "the completing power which unites clearness with depth, the plenitude of the sense with the comprehensibility of the understanding," "that reconciling and mediatory power . . . incorporating the Reason in Images of the Sense, and organizing . . . the flux of the Senses by the permanence and self-circling energies of the Reason." *Statesman's Manual,* pp. 69, 29.

4 *Statesman's Manual,* p. 10. See also, "The light of religion is not that of the moon, light without heat; but neither is its warmth that of the stove, warmth without light. Religion is the sun whose warmth indeed swells, and stirs, and actuates the life of nature, but who at the same time beholds all the growth of life with a master-eye." *Statesman's Manual,* p. 48.

5 Walter Pater, "Coleridge," in *Appreciations* (1889; rpt. London: Macmillan, 1897), p. 100.

6 Pater, "Coleridge," p. 101.

7 Cleanth Brooks, *The Well-Wrought Urn* (1947; rpt. New York: Harcourt, n.d.), p. 213.

8 Samuel Taylor Coleridge, *Biographia Literaria* (1817), ed. J. Shawcross (1907; rpt. London: Oxford Univ. Press 1962), I 61 (ch. IV).

9 On homonymity see Richard A. Rand, "Geraldine," *Glyph,* 3 (1978), 84-85, 96.

10 All my quotations from Coleridge's poetry refer parenthetically to line numbers in *The Poems of Samuel Taylor Coleridge,* ed. Ernest Hartley Coleridge (1912; rpt. London: Oxford Univ. Press 1964).

11 On rhetoric see Jacques Derrida, "La mythologie blanche: la métaphore dans le texte philosophique," in *Marges de la philosophie* (Paris: Minuit, 1972), pp. 247-324. From Derrida's observations on the ship (p. 288), the sun (esp. pp. 298 ff.) and the home (pp. 302-3) as figures of metaphor, one might go on to read *The Ancient Mariner* as the narrative transformation of a theory of metaphor.

12 On the moon as mediator between earth and sun see Aristophanes' myth in Plato's *Symposium,* 190b.

13 Roman Jakobson, "Linguistics and Poetics," in *Style in Language,* ed. Thomas A. Sebeok (1960; rpt. Cambridge: M.I.T. Press, 1966), p. 353.

14 *Collected Letters of Samuel Taylor Coleridge,* ed. Earl Leslie Griggs (Oxford: Clarendon, 1956-71), IV, 545 (March 7, 1815).

15 See also *Statesman's Manual,* p. 60.

16 William Wordsworth, *The Prelude,* ed. Ernest de Selincourt (1926), 2d. ed., rev. Helen Darbishire (Oxford: Clarendon, 1959), Bk. VI, ll. 532-33 (1805 text).

17 Wordsworth, *The Prelude* (1805), Bk. XIII, ll. 52-65; (1850), Bk. XIV, ll. 50-62. In revision the extremes of power and isolation are moderated; the scene is filled out (e.g. "stars" are added); and reciprocal interrelations are established. Briefly, consider the following changes: "single glory" vs. "encroachment none / Was there, nor loss"; "the homeless voice of waters" vs. "the roar of waters"; the addition of "felt by the starry heavens." The passage from "To William Wordsworth" revises a text Coleridge began writing en route to Germany (with Wordsworth) in 1798. See *The Notebooks of Samuel Taylor Coleridge,* ed. Kathleen Coburn (London: Routledge, 1957-   ), I, entry 335; and *Letters,* I, 416 (offering a debunking earthly source: "What these Stars are, I cannot say—the sailors say, that they are the Fish Spawn which is phosphorescent.")

18 Morton W. Bloomfield and Leonard Newmark, *A Linguistic Introduction to the History of English* (New York: Knopf, 1967), p. 38.

19 Lawrence Lipking, "The Marginal Gloss," *Critical Inquiry,* 3 (1977), 613-21.

20 Brooks, *The Well-Wrought Urn,* p. 198.

21 Elder Olson, "A Symbolic Reading of the *Ancient Mariner*" (1948), in *Critics and Criticism,* ed. R. S. Crane (Chicago: Univ. of Chicago Press, 1952), pp. 138, 139.

22 Pater, *Appreciations,* p. 75.

23 Percy Bysshe Shelley, "On Life" (1819), in *Shelley's Poetry and Prose,* ed. Donald H. Reiman and Sharon B. Powers (New York: Norton, 1977), p. 478.

24 Percy Bysshe Shelley, "A Defence of Poetry" (1821), *Shelley's Poetry and Prose,* p. 504.

25 Shelley, "A Defence of Poetry," pp. 483, 481. Contrast Coleridge, "Is *thinking* impossible without arbitrary signs? &—how far is the word 'arbitrary' a misnomer? Are not words &c parts & germinations of the Plant? And what is the Law of their Growth? —In something of this order I would endeavor to destroy the old antithesis of *Words & Things,* elevating, as it were, words into Things, & living Things too." *Letters,* I, 615-26 (Sept. 22, 1800). The concept of the "arbitrary," so important here and in Brown's essay, is immensely tangled. For a start at analyzing the confusion see Margaret W. Ferguson, "The Exile's Defense," *PMLA,* 93 (1978), 279; and for rich information, Gerard Genette, *Mimologiques* (Paris: Seuil, 1976) and Tzvetan Todorov, *Théories du symbole* (Paris: Seuil, 1977).

Vom werck des funfftē tags

Am fünfften tag hot got gesprochē. die wasser sollē bringē kriechēds ding lebendiger sele vñ geflügel auff die erden vnder dē firmamēt des himels. vñ got hat beschaffen groß walfische. vñ alle lebendige vnd bewegliche sele. die sye vasser brachten in ir gestalt. vñ alles geflügel nach seinē geschlecht. vñ got sahe das es gůt was. vñ hat die gesegnet sprechende. Ir söllet wachssen vñ gefilfeltigt werdē vñ erfüllen die wasser des meers. vñ die fogel vilfeltigend sich ob dem ertreich. darúmb hat got an disem tag dē lufft vñ das wasser gezieret. den luft mit dē geflügel. vñ die wasser mit den schwimmēdē dingē: Es werdē groß walfisch vñ wasser thier swunderlich vñ auß vberflüssigkeit irer feüchtigkeit grössere in dem mere gefundē. vñ was in einichem teil der natur geporñ wirt das ist auch als man gemainlich helt in dez meer. kund vñ offenbar sind die ding die vō geberūg ð thier hernach folgē. dañ noch den pflantzē sind geselte ding die in bewegnus vñ empfintlichkeit gemainsamē wie wol die pitagorici den pflantzē auch ein vnbrūfende empfintlichkeit zuschreyben. vñ die selben geseleten ding werden hie von moyse. vnd in Thimeo in dreyerlay getailt. als in dez lufft in wassern vñ auff der erden wonende. ob man anders sprechen mag das das geflügel im luft wone. wir wollen vermeiden die disputatioñ. in was gestat die lieb der thier auß den elementen oder wie die besamungē den naturen ð ding vō got eingepflantzt seien. oder ob das lebē ð vnuernünfftigen thier vō der materi. oder ob alles lebē vō gotlichem anfang her kome. als plotinus gar vestiglich helt. welcher mainung moyses an dem ort villeicht zufallende geschen wirt. dañ nach dē er gesprochen hat. die wasser sollen kriechends ding lebendiger sele bringē. do setzt er darnach hin zu. vñ got hat beschaffen alle lebēdige selē. do möcht ymant nit allain das haltē. das die wasser auß gottes geheyß geperen vnd das darnach auch got gepere. sunder auch das. das an dem ort do vō dē werck gottes meldung geschicht geschriben steet. Got hat beschaffen ein lebendige sele. wo aber ð wasser gedacht wirt do steet das nit. die sele. sunder ein kriechends lebentiger sele herfürgepracht werden sol. vñ wiewol moyses vō dreyerlay thiren ð erdē in dē nachfolgenden tag meldung thut so sind doch die allermaisten vñ größisten thier in dē meer ð indier. vñ zuuor werden in dez meer grosse wūder thier an dem ort do sich die suñ wendet: gesehen. vñ daselbst durch die grossen wellen vō den hohē pergen in das mer fallende auß tieff des mers vbersich auff den menschen zugesicht getriben. vñ vil wunderperlichē ding von den naturen ð fogel vnd fisch an mancherlay enden teglich erfaren.

Semiology and Critical Theory: From Marx to Baudrillard

Mark Poster

In the twentieth century several groups of social theorists have labored to unlock the Marxist paradigm from the grip of economic reductionism in which it was held by the Second International and Stalinism. The Italian Communist, Antonio Gramsci, the theorists of the Frankfurt School, Adorno, Horkheimer and Marcuse, independent critics such as Ernst Bloch, Walter Benjamin and Karl Korsch, Eastern European Communists, Georg Lukacs in Hungary, Adam Schaff in Poland, the *Praxis* group in Yugoslavia and Karel Kosik in Czechoslavia, and finally the existential, phenomenological and even structuralist Marxists in France and Italy have all argued that the concept of the superstructure must account for the relative autonomy of culture. They have made this argument on both epistemological and historical grounds. The epistemological arguments are by now well known and need not detain us. The reflection theory of consciousness upon which Second International and Leninist Marxism rests is clearly false and was not maintained by Marx.

Although the rejection of reflection theory leaves many questions unanswered, the historical arguments are equally important and lead directly into a discussion of the problem of culture. In the twentieth century, certain transformations have altered the shape of capitalist society. The system of production has changed from one of small, decentralized units to one of leviathan international corporations. The international system has changed from one in which the capitalist states of Western Europe enjoyed unchallenged hegemony to one in which large socialist states and third world nations limit and even deter the play of capital. Within each capitalist state, the political system intrudes upon the economy much more forcefully than in the nineteenth century. These structural transformations in the political economy of capitalism have been matched by additional changes in the organization of culture. Local popular cultures have been destroyed by the corporate system of distribution and marketing, producing the strange new phenomena of mass culture. The family, once embedded in networks of kinship and sociability, is increasingly isolated and subject to severe tensions. In the twentieth century capitalism increasingly attempts to colonize everyday life, organizing leisure time and family life into the process of accumulation. Jürgen Habermas, perhaps the last important thinker to be associated with the Frankfurt School, has argued in *The Legitimation Problem of Late Capitalism* that the major contradictions threatening the system no longer derive from the organization of work but from the organization of culture.[1] For Habermas the question of values and motivation threatens the survival of capitalism. In the advanced nations the material benefits of labor seem to outweigh the oppressiveness of exploitation. But the psychic consequences of labor and consumption no longer provide the basis for adherence to the system. For Habermas the weight of the contradictions of capitalism has shifted from the base to the superstructure.

In this historical conjuncture, efforts have been made to scrutinize the media, which can be considered an important new mediation in the play of forces which account for the stability of the system. I will argue that radical criticism of the media must rely on semiological theory and that the best recent effort to develop such a theory has been the writing of Jean Baudrillard. The need for semiology can be demonstrated by looking briefly at analyses of the media which employ older models of liberal and Marxist theory.

In the 1960s optimism dominated the discussion of the media. Reacting against the elitist condemnation of mass culture of the 1950s (Reisman, *et. al.*), the liberal Marshall McLuhan and the radical Hans Magnus Enzensberger celebrated the new media (such as television) as the basis for in the one case a sensory transformation into a tribal village and a radically democratized society in the other. Basing himself none too firmly on a questionable theory of perception, McLuhan rejoiced in the waning of the linear, hot age of print and the birth of a cool, involving age of visual media.[2] Enzensberger looked to the technical possibilities of electronic media and predicted that the TV receptor could easily become a transmitter. In this way the voice of the people could be heard accurately by the simple flick of a switch or push of a button.[3]

Such sanguine theorizing has not sold well in the 1970s. In both liberal and Marxist circles, the image of the media has suffered. The new liberal position is expressed by John Phelan in *Mediaworld: Programing the Public.* Phelan returns to the classical theory of John Stuart Mill in which democracy depends upon a rational, informed and independent public. In Phelan's words, "Mill's ideal traditional forum for public opinion was peopled by free, rational, particular individuals who engaged in debate within a commonly accepted universe of discourse toward the realization of moral values through public policies."[4] Because of the evil machinations of advertising executives and corporate directors, the benign world of John Stuart Mill has become, in Phelan's eyes, the irrational world of the media. Phelan continues:

> American assumptions of instrumentalism, the mechanisms of mass marketing, the economic necessities of the news and information business, the multi-cultural awareness of internationalism, the vast complexities of high technology have created the transitional forum. Free individuals are being replaced by predictable types, publics are becoming audiences, issues are assigned topics for harmless comment. The will of the people is now the mood of the mass; methods of communications are subverted to techniques of propaganda.[5]

For a liberal such as Phelan the media have produced in democratic America the same irrationalism that Hitler produced in authoritarian Germany, without some of the hysterics. No doubt there is more than a grain of truth in the liberal's somewhat high-strung lament. Yet his argument has numerous flaws. First, Mill's utopia of rational individuals never existed, not even for the bourgeoisie in the nineteenth century. So this is a case not of the simple destruction of a rational world but the production of a new structure of communications which Phelan cannot explain. Second, Phelan attributes the horrors of mediaworld to the unfortunate influence of the corporate elite as if a different group, with more enlightened purposes, might avoid the nefarious effects of the media. By placing the blame where he does, Phelan does not really grapple with the necessities of the system of capitalism that directs the hands of the managerial elite. Finally, Phelan does not account for the success of mediaworld: how is it that a free, rational populace has accepted such irrationalism? In Phelan's account the public is the passive receptor of change from above. This position assumes a model of behavioral conditioning which is at odds with Phelan's premise of rational individuals.

The weaknesses of Phelan's account are only partially overcome by the Marxists, who are best represented by Stuart Ewen in *Captains of Consciousness: Advertising and the Social Roots of the Consumer Culture*.[6] Unlike Phelan's moral essay, Ewen presents an account of the historical origins of advertising, showing how it was initiated as a response by capitalists to concrete contradictions in the economic system. Mass production beginning in the 1920s required mass consumption. The greatly expanded productivity of the economy required new consumption patterns. Ewen outlines the process through which large national corporations systematically destroyed local distribution and market systems along with the local cultures that accompanied them. Rural towns and urban ethnic communities had to be nationalized and Americanized. A new social character had to be created—the modern consumer—whose desires and needs were geared not to local traditions but to the exigencies of mass production.

For Ewen the crucial mediation in this process was the capitalists themselves. Many of them realized, as the book demonstrates through quotes from trade journals and books by capitalists such as Filene, that consumption was a social process which required deep changes in the habits of Americans. The captains of industry became captains of consciousness. New methods of advertising drew upon the fears generated by the system and presented them as needs that could be satisfied by the products of industry. Yale locks were touted as guaranteeing security and peace of mind in a society plagued by poverty and hence by crime. Soap became more than an aid in removing dirt: it was a sign that the individual was competing successfully for a career. Anxiety over success in business was allayed by the right purchase of a commody. Newspapers, magazines, radio broadcasts and later television carried these messages to the masses, influencing profoundly the culture of advanced industrial society. Ewen's achievement is to have shown how the birth of modern advertising was part of the general transformation of society, how it was initiated self-consciously by industrialists and how it worked to transform family and leisure patterns. In Ewen's hands historical materialism is applied successfully to an important phenomenon of modern society.

Yet there are some major drawbacks in Ewen's account which derive both from his use of Marxist theory and from his lack of a semiological theory. *Captains of Consciousness* views the spread of advertising and mass culture as the child of the bourgeois elite. Capitalists *manipulate* the masses: it is as simple as that. Unfortunately this is not so. The success of mass culture depends on more than that. One must be able to explain how and why the working class and the petty bourgeoisie, the ethnic communities in the cities and the farmers in the mid-West, were won over to the new system. In Ewen's presentation the agent of history is the elite bourgeoisie; one must also show the popular classes as active in this process, however alienated that action might be.

More fundamentally, Ewen reduces the new system of commodities to the manipulating intention of the capitalist. The structure of communication, the new logic of commodities does not emerge from his account. Consumer culture is not dissected to reveal what it has most to show: a new mode of signification. Because the process of creating a mass culture is reduced by Ewen to the mode of production, consumer society does not appear as a relatively autonomous phenomenon, with an articulated complexity of its own. Critical semiology alone can reach into the logic of the new mode of signification and reveal its hidden structure. The value of semiology for such an analysis is indicated by Umberto Eco in *A Theory of Semiotics.* Eco states the argument this way:

> Thus a theory of codes (which looks so independent from the *actual* world, naming its states through signs), demonstrates its heuristic and practical power, for it reveals, by showing the hidden interconnections of a given cultural system, the ways in which the labor of sign production can respect or betray the complexity of such a cultural network, thereby adapting it to (or separating it from) the human labor of transforming states of the world.
>
> This transformation cannot be performed without organizing such states of the world into semantic systems. In order to be transformed, the states of the world must *be named* and structurally arranged. As soon as they are named, that system of sign systems which is called 'culture' (which also organizes the way in which the material forces are thought of and discussed) may assume a degree of extra-referential independence that a theory of codes must respect and analyse in all its autonomy.[7]

These remarks, which come unforunately at the end of Eco's study and indicate a task which he does not carry out, remind Marxists that culture cannot be analysed solely through the categories of the mode of production. The structure of codes requires its own theory and its own independent analysis.

The work of providing such a critical semiology has been carried furthest by Jean Baudrillard, a sociologist at Nanterre. In general Baudrillard has attempted to establish the limits of Marxist theory for analysing critically advanced society and to offer elements of a new social theory which can reveal the deep structure of corporate capitalism and point to its contradictions. In this sense, Baudrillard may be classified in that group of French theorists who can be called post-structuralists, and include most notably Michel Foucault, Gilles Deleuze and Jacques Derrida.

In his early books—*Le Système des objets* (1968); *La Société de consommation* (1970); and *Pour une critique de l'économie politique du signe* (1972)—Baudrillard developed his critical semiology within the context of Marxism. Both Roland Barthes and Henri Lefebvre, Baudrillard's teacher, had earlier pioneered the critique of the media. In *Mythologies,* Barthes illuminated the hidden, ideological significations of various communications systems. A cover of *Paris-Match* advertised the solidity of imperialism by showing a black man in a French army uniform. The surface signification was innocuous; but beneath it, at the unconscious level, the reader of *Paris-Match* imbibed the important message of ideological legitimation. For Barthes, semiology revealed how simple, rational information became mythic supports of the social system.[8]

The Marxist humanist Lefebvre, always critical of structuralism, was willing to employ semiological categories to expand the analytical power of Marxism to encompass the experiences of everyday life. Lefebvre contended that advanced capitalism spread its oppressive tentacles beyond the workplace to the world of leisure and the family. The contradictions of capitalism had infested language itself, of which structuralism was a symptom not an analytical theory. Saussure's separation of the sign from the referent was not a scientific advance but an ideological cover for what Lefebvre called "the collapse of the referentials." At the turn of the twentieth century the capitalist system became so irrational that the classical symbols of the liberal world-view—reason, progress, freedom—no longer coherently explained the world. Words became detached from things in society before structuralists adopted that separation as an analytical tool. In addition to the collapse of the referentials, the structure of language underwent a shift from signs to signals. The sign embodied a dialectic of word and mental image, a split between signifier and meaning. This gap allowed the individual to question their correspondence as, for example, in the statement "France is a free nation." Increasingly, however, with the advent of modern advertising the signal took over. The semiotic structure of the signal collapsed word and image, conditioning the individual to accept the correspondence without the mediation of critical reason. In an analysis of an advertisement for an after shave lotion Lefebvre unveiled a new level of social terrorism. The message of the ad demanded the use of the product at the risk of social ostracism. At an unconscious level the reader's fear was manipulated to produce an immediate identification of the product with social acceptance. In this way, Lefebvre integrated semiology with Marxism.[9]

These exploratory investigations of the media were encouraged by the events of May '68. For many social critics, including Baudrillard, May '68 provided testimony for the possibility of altering radically the mode of communication. Against the bureaucratic, unidirectional messages of the media, both print and electronic, the rebels of May '68 opposed *la parole,* the spoken word. In the halcyon days of May people spoke with each other directly; social communication was no longer mediated by the commodity and the media. In May '68, "the street . . . was the alternative and subversive form to all mass media."[10] At least for a while, anyway. The lesson of May seemed to be that the structure of language was not inalterable. Structuralist semiology had to account, therefore, not only for synchrony but for diachrony. In short, language and the media were part of history and the logic of their transformation had to be conceptualized.

In *The System of Objects* and *Consumer Society,* Baudrillard deepened the work of Barthes and Lefebvre by analyzing consumer objects in terms of a code. Commodities were socially significant not so much as material objects which were produced by labor but as signs, as a mode of signification that was independent of the mode of production. In contemporary society consumer objects bear signs which have meaning as part of a structure. The signifiers associated with commodities are autonomous from the labor process that produced the commodities materially. Today, commodities no longer function as use values, as things which serve the needs of the rational individual, rather they are part of the social system of the exchange of meanings. The consumption of an object has more semiological than material significance. According to Baudrillard, "the social logic of consumption . . . is not at all that of the individual appropriation of the use value of goods and services; nor is it a logic of satisfaction. It is a logic of the production and manipulation of social signifiers."[11]

A few examples from advertisements will illustrate the point. Pepsi Cola promises participation in a generation; drinking Pepsi means having a community. The use of certain toothpastes provides one with sexual attractiveness. Splashing Brut cologne on one's body magically produces an aggressive personality. For Baudrillard the problem raised by the media is not that of the collapse of the moral individual nor of the proof of the machinations of the capitalists. Instead, it suggests that the social field has been infiltrated by a new semiological structure which must be analysed in its own terms. "The media . . . prohibit responses, which make impossible all processes of exchanges. . . . This is their true abstraction. And in this abstraction is founded the system of social control and power."[12] This new structure Baudrillard terms the sign as distinct from the symbol of precapitalist times.

In *Toward a Critique of the Political Economy of the Sign* Baudrillard formalizes his earlier semiological critique and relates it directly to Marxism. The Marxist concept of the commodity serves as the mediating link. For Marx, the commodity consists of a double determination; it is both use value and exchange value. It is created by labor for use by a consumer and it is produced for a market and exchanged for money. For Marx the secret of capitalism is that exchange value functions to mystify use value. On the market, the labor process disappears from view leaving a pure object of consumption determined solely by a price. Thus the human relation of laborer to consumer is reified and the material relation of product and money is "humanized." As Lukács points out, under capitalism relations between men take on the character of relations between things and vice versa.[13]

Baudrillard supplemented this analysis with the concept of the sign. In relation to Marx's analysis, the signifier corresponds to exchange value and the signified to use value. Semiology reveals that in addition to the reversal of subject and object, the commodity also reverses the normal pattern of communications. The signifier is detached from the signified just as exchange value is detached from use value. Like the price, the signifier floats in the social space of consumer capitalism, mystifying the whole relation of man to man and man to thing. Community, sexiness, aggressivity—these signifiers constitute a semiological level of capitalist exchange. The question Baudrillard left unanswered in this book, however, is to what extent is the semiological level independent of the mode of production. In short, is critical semiology compatible with the critique of political economy?

In the *Mirror of Production* Baudrillard turned to face Marx head on, concluding that Marx's categories were too conservative, too rooted in the liberal notion of production and therefore were inadequate to a radical critique. Marx's notion of use value, which stood behind exchange value and provided the basis for the future socialist world, was, to Baudrillard, still grounded in the liberal notion of economic man. Marxism relied on an anthropology of man the laborer who created use values. It was apparent, however, that the same social system that created exchange value also created the notion of use value. Only in a market system, Baudrillard contended, is it necessary to distinguish between the two forms of value. Consequently, the critical function of the notion of use value is reduced by its implication in the system of political economy.

The reliance of Marxism on an anthropology of laboring man also reduces all forms of practice to labor. In part against himself, Marx presents labor as a natural necessity (*The German Ideology*), a status which he is unwilling to grant to language, sexuality and other activities. But this is precisely the liberal position in which man is above all a tool-making animal (Benjamin Franklin). Baudrillard chides contemporary French radicals who see production as the only model: there is Althusser's theoretical production; Kristeva's textual production, Deleuze and Guattari's libidinal production. If everything is viewed through the mirror of production, the logic of the mode of signification is obscured. Burdened by an anthropology of labor, Marx regresses to classical liberal dualities. As in liberalism, Marx posits nature in opposition to reason. Nature is a realm to be conquered; it is necessity as opposed to freedom.

Not only is the concept of the mode of production rooted in conservative liberal doctrine: it is used by Marx and Marxists in an imperialist manner. Whereas liberals extend the laws of supply and demand backwards and forwards throughout history, Marx applies his doctrine to "primitive societies" where it is inappropriate. According to Baudrillard these societies are governed by symbolic exchange, not by the sign. The prominence of kinship structure means that all exchanges are reciprocal. Private property and accumulation are absent. Society operates through gifts, gifts from person to person and man to nature. There are no floating signifiers because each exchange is a total act, with a complete shift of meaning back and forth between people.

Like liberalism, Marxism views these societies as inferior since they do not generate a surplus. Looking through the lens of production, these theories cannot focus on the radical difference of primitive society which relies on a mode of signification bearing no resemblance to our own. In defense of the application of the concept of the mode of production to primitive society, Emmanuel Terray, a Marxist anthropologist, agrees that economic determinism cannot account for kinship society. Nor, however, is he willing to grant validity to the alternative of allowing for reciprocal autonomy between kinship and economy. He turns instead to Althusser's notion of kinship, in which the economy merely determines which level is *dominant* in any society. Thus in primitive society kinship is dominant because human beings are the only source of labor or energy. Hence the rules that govern the production of men—kinship patterns—must be the dominant level.[14] Attractive as this logical twist might appear, it is faulty for the following reasons: it would lead one to conclude that when machines are the major source of energy, technology is dominant, thus going against Marx who showed how the social relation of capitalism determined the direction of the means of production; and it still does not account for symbolic exchange as the mode of signification in primitive society.

In another context, Marx presents a stadial view of the rise of exchange value which allows Baudrillard to outline the limits of the notion of the mode of production. In the first stage only the surplus of production is exchanged; the rest is consumed by the producer. In the second stage, which witnesses the birth of capital, all industrial production is exchanged. Baudrillard is willing to allow the concept of the mode of production some validity during this period. In the third stage, virtue, love, knowledge—the elements of the superstructure, come under the market system. Marx denounces this development as the corruption of human values. In Baudrillard's view, Marx cannot account for the shift from stage two to stage three. Instead, he reduces it to the mode of production. Stage three witnesses not a simple prostitution of all values, but a new structure of control. In Baudrillard's critical semiology, there is a shift from one form to another, from the commodity to the sign, which results in the destruction of symbolic exchange by the code. In stage three there is a radical transformation in the mode of signification with the signified and the referent being abolished in the communication process.[15] In stage two labor was controlled by capitalism; but in stage three capitalism extended its reach far deeper. It now controls meanings. Looking back on the entire history of capitalism, Baudrillard asks if the dominance of the sign was not capitalism's true meaning from the start. The rational abstraction inherent in the commodity was perhaps part of a more profound process, begun during the Renaissance, in which the sign replaced symbolic exchange. And this process requires a radical critique.

Critical semiology provides, according to Baudrillard, a true basis for a radical critique of capitalism. It indicates the importance of transcending the code and it points to new groups—minorities, youth, women—as the bearers of the revolution. The zone of disaffection is drawn around those who are "non-marked terms", those who are outside the dominant code. In his most recent major book, *L'Echange symbolique et la mort* (1976), Baudrillard locates the model for protest in death. In death there is a form in which the determination of the subject and value is lost to the system. In capitalism the dead are excluded from the circulation of meanings in society. The ancestors no longer function, as they did in primitive society, in continuity with the living. In a fundamental sense, then, the dead provide a model for the living and the radical basis for the overthrow of capitalism.

There are several material deficiencies in Baudrillard's attempt to construct a critical semiology. Most obviously, the concept of praxis is weak or absent. Baudrillard can see only a repetition of May '68: a sudden explosion of the people which, in its intensity, overthrows the code. Also, he separates exchange from production too sharply. Ewen has demonstrated the interconnection of the mode of production with the new system of signification. Baudrillard wants to look at society as a system of exchange only, refusing to grant any validity to the concept of labor. When pushed, he argues that we need to theorize production in new ways that bring it under a structuralist notion of signification. Consequently, Baudrillard can be accused of the same crime he accused Marx of: the mode of signification in Baudrillard is as reductionist and imperialist as the mode of production in Marx. Given Baudrillard's radical pretensions, it is strange that he does not account for relations between the core and the periphery, between the industrial world and the third world, between the world of the sign and the world of the symbol. This is certainly a deficiency in his theory. With the advent of communication systems designed by capitalist powers for distribution in the third world, much could be done with a critical semiology in this area. The success of Coca Cola and *I Love Lucy* in Africa needs to be explained.

Perhaps the most striking flaw in Baudrillard's thought is his concept of symbolic exchange. As an analytical vantage point from which to criticize the dominant mode of signification—somewhat like Habermas' notion of the ideal speaking situation—it is useful. But in Baudrillard's writing it forms the metaphysical horizon of both the past and the future. Symbolic exchange romanticizes primitive society and utopianizes the revolution. It is an abstract concept that juxtaposes too sharply the good, archaic past from the bad present. Certainly there are differences between the mode of signification in primitive society and that of a liberated future, as Baudrillard sees it. But he has not discussed these differences or accounted for them at all.

The charge is sometimes made against Baudrillard that things are not so different today than they were in the period of classical capitalism in the nineteenth century. The floating signifiers of the contemporary media which Baudrillard conceptualizes so well in structural terms might also have accompanied the commodity in earlier times. This charge is unfounded. The great value of a critical semiology is to enable us to analyse the specificity of advanced capitalism. In the nineteenth century proletarians were certainly not subject to the mystifications of the code. The few purchases they did make were too basic for that. Even when they consumed so-called non-essentials like gin, one hardly needed to advertise this product as the essence of manliness or whatever. The bourgeoisie certainly did engage in Veblenesque consumption. An elaborate social code determined which fashions provided social status and which did not. But again these determinations were generated within bourgeois exchanges and remained part of everyday life. The proper hat or coach kept its use value, its referent and its signified. One purchased a chair not, as we find in ads today, for the ultimate realization of peace and contentment, but for its craftsmanship, its utility, its style and its fashion. As Ewen has shown, it was not until the twentieth century that local markets were destroyed and mass distribution took over. Within the context of local markets, the symbolic meaning of commodities was still determined within systems of social exchange and hence the mode of signification was not determined by the code.

The one example from the past century that comes close to the contemporary system is that of the huckster or charlatan who sold patent medicine. In this case the commodity embodied promises that were unrelated to its contents. Sound health could not be derived from the concoctions hawked in towns throughout America. The semiotic structure of these commodities was still different from what is seen today. Some relation still existed, however remote, between the product and its significations.

The example of charlantry raises a major question for the semiological analysis of the media. Baudrillard's theory remains at the objective, structural level. The spectre of subjectivity, which is anathema to contemporary French theory, cannot be dismissed so easily. Ewen and Lefebvre locate the basis for advertising in the negative needs—fears, anxieties, insecurities, discontents—that are generated by capitalism itself. It is possible to argue also that the absences of capitalism—friendship, community, love, self-respect—are also at stake. Ads play not only upon fears of social rejection, as in all the body odor products, but also upon desirable features of social life that are incompatible with capitalism. In this way, ads reveal inadvertently the critical negation of the system. Ads function as false promises, as substitute gratifications for the real inadequacies of the capitalist system. Hence the empirical application of critical semiology can reveal not only the deep structure of the contemporary mode of signification, but also the phenomenology of the masses, the concrete discontents of women, workers, minorities which form the program for a better world. It can allow us to see that consumers who participate actively in the code are not simple fools. Rather, they are trying to find something that is worthy of attaining, and they are seeking satisfactions in substitute ways only because these are the only means permitted or possible under the present circumstances. Thus, critical semiology needs to be supplemented by a phenomenological level of analysis which addresses the subjectivity of the consumer.

The major criticism that Baudrillard's work must bear, one that suggests the most pressing need for further theoretical work, is that the concept of the mode of signification has not been developed enough to capture historical differences and therefore remains unconvincing. The notion of the sign, with its absent referent, its detached signifier and its one-directional communication, remains too crude. A seventeenth-century priest, reciting the mass in Latin to his illiterate rural parishoners, was certainly engaging in one-directional communication which included floating signifiers (the Latin words) and absent referents (God, Providence, heaven). If the concept of the mode of signification is to take its place beside the concept of the mode of production, much more theoretical elaboration is called for which can enable us truly to write a critical history of communication systems.

University of California, Irvine

NOTES

1 Jurgen Habermas, *Legitimation Crisis,* trans. Thomas McCarthy (Boston: Beacon Press, 1975).

2 Marshall McLuhan, *Understanding Media: The Extensions of Man* (New York: McGraw-Hill, 1965).

3 Hans Magnus Enzenberger, "Constitutents of a Theory of the Media," *New Left Review,* 64 (November-December, 1970), 13-37.

4 John Phelan, *Mediaworld* (New York: McGraw-Hill, 1977), p. 56.

5 Phelan, *Mediaworld,* p. 57.

6 Stuart Ewen, *Captains of Consciousness* (New York: McGraw-Hill, 1976). Cf. also Herbert Schiller, *The Mind Managers* (Boston: Beacon Press, 1974), and *Mass Communications and the American Empire* (Boston: Beacon Press, 1971).

7 Umberto Eco, *A Theory of Semiotics* (Bloomington: Indiana Univ. Press, 1976), p. 297.

8 Roland Barthes, *Mythologies,* trans. Annette Lavers (New York: Hill and Wang, 1972), p. 116.

9 For an examination of Lefebvre's position see Mark Poster, *Existential Marxism in Postwar France: From Sartre to Althusser* (Princeton: Princeton Univ. Press, 1975), pp. 253-259.

10 Jean Baudrillard, *Pour une critique de l'économie politique du signe* (Paris: Gallimard, 1972), p. 218.

11 Jean Baudrillard, *La Société de consommation* (Paris: Gallimard, 1970), pp. 78-79.

12 Jean Baudrillard, *Pour une critique,* p. 208.

13 Georg Lukács, *History and Class Consciousness,* trans. R. Livingstone (Cambridge, Mass.: MIT Press, 1968), p. 83 ff.

14 Emmanuel Terray, *Marxism and "Primitive" Societies,* trans. M. Klopper (New York: Monthly Review Press, 1972), p. 144 ff.

15 Baudrillard, *La Société de consommation,* pp. 191, 194 and *The Mirror of Production,* trans. Mark Poster (St. Louis, 1975), p. 119.

Ad matut. invitat. allã:
Spiritus domini repleuit orbẽ
terrarum: Venite adoremus allã:
Ps. Ven. Hy. Iã xpo astra:
Ad noc: aña: Factus ẽ repente
de celo sonus aduenientis spũs

A Response to Mark Poster on Jean Baudrillard

Michael Hays

I would like, first of all, to thank Mark Poster for offering this brief introduction to Jean Baudrillard's critical theory. And since he himself has begun a critique of Baudrillard's work, I would like to continue in that vein, but with a little less sympathy for what appear to be fundamental weaknesses in Baudrillard's analysis.

Baudrillard's basic assertion seems to be that Marx and Marxist theoreticians have failed to recognize the difference between the system of exchange circumscribed by capitalist political economy and the symbolic exchange which Baudrillard claims governed primitive societies. It is interesting to note that in making this assertion, Baudrillard fails to credit those anthropologists from Mauss to Levi-Strauss who *have* discussed this question. At the same time he often borrows great snatches from the results of work by both Levi-Strauss and Bataille. And when Baudrillard deals with Godelier's Marxist anthropology he misquotes and misrepresents both Godelier and Marxist anthropological theory in general.

Marxist economic theory is also much more complex than Baudrillard would have it. So he creates and then attacks a caricature of some "common sense" or "vulgar" concepts which have come to be associated with Marxist economics.[1] I do not have the time here to go into a detailed discussion of theory—that would not be relevant to the goals of this symposium in any case—so instead I will make two observations:

Marx assumed that societies produce themselves by organizing their productive effort. In this theory, exchange has the function of creating social solidarity. Commodities, however, are only one form of exchange. Marx and Marxist theorists recognize the existence of other forms.

Furthermore, Marxist theory does not view primitive societies as inferior. And Baudrillard is himself wrong when he asserts that primitive societies do not generate surpluses. He seems not to know the difference between surplus and surplus value. Marxist and non-Marxist economists and anthropologists alike have long pointed to the surpluses produced by societies in order to support monastic orders (in Tibet, for example) or in order to make possible the construction of temples and other monumental architecture such as we find in South and Central America.

I will return to the question of primitive societies in a moment. Before doing so I would like to clarify the relationship between Baudrillard's theory of floating signifiers and Marx's most fundamental assertion about capitalist exchange. Marx claims that the real nature of commodity exchange—the functional structure of interpersonal exchange—is hidden. This, by the way, is also a fundamental principal of psychoanalysis. Both attempt to reveal the real rapport between what appear to be objective conditions and the structures they mask. Price, for example, seems to be a natural aspect of the commodity just as behavior and attitude seem to be natural fixed attributes of the individual. It is not surprising then that Baudrillard attacks psychoanalysis with as much vehemence as he attacks Marxist theory. I think Mark Poster should have mentioned this connection, so that the implications of Baudrillard's position would have become a little clearer. Baudrillard rejects the notion of production of the individual or society because he thinks that notion is a by-product of the mental structures of the nineteenth century. Only by doing so can he clear the field for his own semiotic notion of the sign and the mode of signification. But Poster is wrong when he says that this notion is "as reductionist and as imperialist as the mode of production in Marx." It is *more* so. Baudrillard has applied the notion of fetishism to use value. This in itself is an extension of Marxist analysis, not a revolution away from it. He then magnifies this idea as a total explanation of the mystified relationship between the consumer and the commodity caused, supposedly, by media advertisements.

The problem with this part of Baudrillard's work and with Mark Poster's discussion of it resides in the lack of a definition of commodities which is as complete as that given by Marxist theory. Put in another way, Marxist theory gets short shrift because Baudrillard does not understand or simply ignores the full scope of Marxist (and I should add Freudian) analysis. In Baudrillard, a commodity appears to be simply an object which can be acquired. This kind of "common sense" definition is hardly sufficient to the subject, however. Commodities, says Marx, first enter the world in the form of use values or commercial materials such as iron, cloth, wool, etc. That is simply their natural form. They only become commodities when they are two things at once, objects of utility and carriers of value. They cannot enter into circulation as commodities until they are present in this double form. In other words, a commodity is always the non-material effect of a certain kind of social organization as well as a physico-technical event.[2]

What Baudrillard calls floating signifiers (and are actually part of the fetishization of the exchange process as represented by the commodity) certainly existed before the advent of media advertising. One of the examples Mark Poster gives makes this point for me. He suggests that in the nineteenth century a chair was bought for reasons of fashion and not because it represented peace and contentment. But is fashion somehow more real than peace and contentment? Isn't it rather that they are the same? Fashion contains within it an aspect of mythic fulfillment—only the image of that fulfillment changes. And if we look at the nineteenth century attitude in England towards rum or in France toward absinth it is clear that they carried with them a male mystique of power. As to the suggestion that some relation existed between patent medicine and its significations, I can only add that people *do* brush their teeth, they do not just buy toothpaste to attract the opposite sex. I would also suggest that the man with the expensive car *does* get the girl. As Marx suggested in another context, there is a prosaic reality to this aspect of mystification.[3] Only if the total linguistic and actional structures of such "events" are analyzed in terms of their concrete manifestations, can they be understood and overcome. Actually, Baudrillard's analysis of publicity itself offers little more than that already contributed by Barthes, Lefebvre, and the Frankfurt theorists.

A corollary argument of Poster's needs to be dealt with here. What he refers to as local markets destroyed in the twentieth century had in fact been infiltrated by larger market forces long before that: mail order and pattern catalogues, for example, and, of course, international trade in grain, timber and other natural resources. In *The Age of Reform,* Hofstadter gives the following description of midwestern farmers in the nineteenth century: "There was among them little attachment to land or locality; instead there developed the false euphoria of local "boosting" encouraged by railroads, land companies, and farmers themselves; in place of village contacts and communal spirit based upon ancestral attachments, theirs was professional optimism based on hopes for a quick raise in values."[4] What the media add in the twentieth century is quantitative, not qualitative, change.

Finally, semiotics itself turns against Baudrillard. He assumes the existence of primitive exchange systems but cannot account for the way in which these systems were organized, that is produced, on the social level. He probably does not care, though, since his real desire is to project this primitive world into the future as an ideal model. But as both Umberto Eco and Lévi-Strauss have pointed out, semiotic and structural analysis, although they may serve to establish the historicity of certain conceptual or communication patterns, *cannot* be used to predict. In addition, the quotation that Poster uses in his presentation indicates that Eco incorporates a notion of production into his theory of the development of semiotic systems.

If Baudrillard would apply himself to the task of analyzing concrete semiotic events or texts he might be of more interest to us. Had he, like Walter Benjamin, worked on the double connection, positive and negative, between the masses as a political force and the technical reproducibility of art as a social manifestation of mass culture, he might have contributed to our understanding of the interaction which formulates cultural change. Or, if he would analyze in the concrete the historical "situation" of language and text (I think here of Peter Szondi) as parts of the aesthetics of literary productivity he might make a valuable contribution to our knowledge of the way in which texts signify. As it is his vague abstract analyses seem to offer little more than a hidden but virulent anti-intellectualism which leads him to misrepresent rather than to criticize and idealize rather than analyze.

In his most recent work, *Oublier Foucault,* he writes that "challenge creates an ineluctable, non-dialectical space. It is neither means nor end. It opposes its own space to that of political space. It knows neither middle nor long term. Its only term is the immediacy of response or of death. Everything that is linear, including history, has an end. It alone is without end since it is indefinitely reversible. It is this reversibility that gives it its fabulous power" (pp. 77-78). And he closes by saying that "power is an illusion, truth is an illusion" (p. 87).[5]

In response to this I will quote from Baudrillard's teacher Henri Lefebvre. In speaking about certain anarchist-idealists he says:

> [Their] analysis of concrete oppression and the forms this oppression takes in the consciousness is done in the name of an ideal—and against society in general—against all institutions in the name of "revolt." This anarchist analysis, although it is not completely false, remains abstract. Rejecting the past as absurd and imagining that all oppression is the result of brute constraint, anarchism puts all institutions in the same category, on the same "inhuman" level. It seems to suppose that one day . . . "men" will understand each other, deliver each other,

destroy violence and enter singing into the kingdom of joy. These criticisms are naive, utopian and unhistorical: Very sincere—but incapable of explaining the real movement of history or of acting upon it.[6]

Columbia University

NOTES

1 The degree to which Baudrillard oversimplifies economic theory can readily be seen if one compares his notions of "value" and "commodity" in *The Mirror of Production,* trans. M. Poster (St. Louis: Telos Press, 1975) with those discussed by Michel de Vroey in his recent book, *La théorie de la valeur de Marx: I, Valeur et marchandise dans la production marchande* (Louvain-la-neuve: Institut d'Économie, Université de Louvain, 1978).

2 Karl Marx, *Capital,* trans. S. Moore and E. Aveling, vol. 1 (1887; rpt. Moscow: Foreign Language Publishing House, N.d.), p. 47 ff.

3 See Karl Marx, *A Contribution to the Critique of Political Economy,* trans. S. W. Ryazanskaya (New York: International Publishers, 1970), pp. 34-35.

4 Richard Hofstadter, *The Age of Reform* (New York: Knopf, 1956), pp. 42-43.

5 Jean Baudrillard, *Oublier Foucault,* (Paris: Editions Galilée, 1977), pp. 77-78; 87.

6 Henri Lefebvre, *La conscience mystifiée* (Paris: Gallimard, 1936), p. 80.

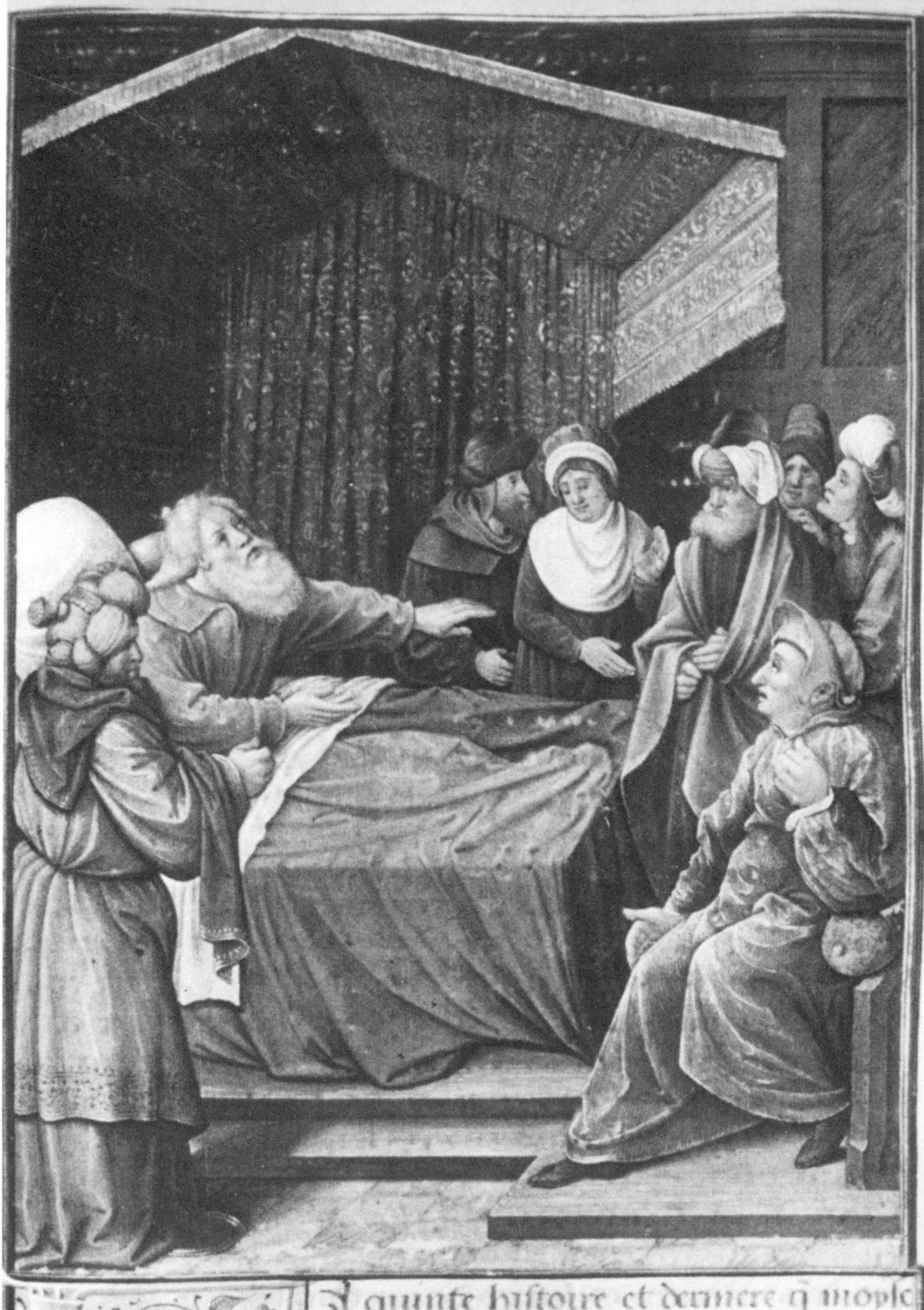

La quinte histoire et derniere q̃ moyse
escript en grec est appellee deuterono
me: cest a dire la seconde loy: car
deuteron vault autant comme se
cond et nomma comme loie: si est
a dire deuteronome seconde loy pour
ce que ce livre est appelle seconde loy. Aucuns ont este
qui disent quilz furent deux loix au temps des hebrieu

The Demiurgic Imagination In Art and Experience

Stephen Crites

According to the so-called cosmogonic myth, the world of our experience took shape when a craftsmanly god, such as the *demiourgos* (artificer, craftsman) of Plato's *Timaeus,* gave form to primordial chaos. I am referring, of course, to the myth of creation we find with many variations throughout the ancient Near East, and even turning up independently but recognizably in geographically remote cultures. There are other types of creation myth, but this one in particular has enough resonance in human experience that we need not be surprised to find people inventing or discovering it afresh.

One of the things that is so handsome about this myth is that it exemplifies the very process it describes. It tells a story, and such storytelling is one of the prime devices through which our world of experience is constituted. In this sense it is a myth about the myth-making process itself. Telling a story *about* giving form to the chaos is in fact an act by which the chaos is *given* form.

But that is a point to which we will return. First I would like to offer an interpretation of the myth. I have no idea whether this interpretation is original. I don't suppose I can have made it up myself, and anyhow originality is cause for suspicion in interpreting a myth. For me, at any rate, the interpretation presented itself a few semesters ago in conversation with a student of lively intelligence named Deborah Malamud. A student like Debbie can get a teacher to saying things he never thought he thought or knew he knew. So as we were thinking out loud together, I found myself explaining that the prosaic name for the primal chaos out of which the gods formed the world is: the future.

I was surprised to hear myself saying that, because the myth seems to present the primal chaos as a kind of ultimate past. It was there first, and then in some sort of sequence came the shaping and forming that produced a cosmos. But that is an inversion that is characteristic of myth, and is essentially a concession to narrative form. It is a matter of perspective. If one stands outside a story, as a hearer who grasps it from beginning to end as a completed whole, the beginning necessarily appears as a specious past for all that follows. But from the point of view of a character in the story, such as our demiourgos, what he is to make or to do presents itself first as "in the future." The beginning, that is, of the thing that is in the making or in the doing, is that peculiar state in which it is not yet made or done at all, but is still unformed, just as our myth suggests. It is still, as we say, "in the future." For so it is with any event in our experience. Its future is what comes first, its beginning, when it does not yet exist.

In our naive experience, the thing or event seems gradually to gather itself together and take shape as it moves "toward" us, as we say, "out of the future." It has been suggested to me that a photograph taken by an instamatic camera provides a good image (though not an instance) of this process: as we watch the exposed print it first appears a muddy-colored blank, in which the picture that has just been taken gradually takes clearer and clearer shape before our eyes. Just so, an object of experience materializes out of the inchoate blank of the future, becoming determinate as it moves into our present, which is the instant of its vivid reality, so full of presence that we hardly know what to make of it. Typically, we can only give it a name, classify, understand, explain it, as it recedes again—into the past, taking its place among the familiar furniture of an articulated world. Now we who are experiencing it are not in fact so passive as this description suggests, but we will come to that point presently. In my naive sense of myself as a fixed, positioned consciousness, things seem to approach and recede from me in this manner, steadily taking form out of their inchoate futurity as they do. Augustine adopts this naive standpoint for the moment when he says that the mind (*anima*) "anticipates and attends and remembers, so that what it anticipates passes through what it attends into what it remembers" (*Confessions* XI:xxviii).

It is the same, according to our myth, with the cosmos itself. In the beginning it is purely future, unformed, still a chaos and not yet a cosmos at all. So the *demiourgos,* or the spirit brooding over those waters, in Genesis I, must have regarded it. Then it began to take form, but only gradually, usually in quite definite stages such as the six days recounted in that first chapter of Genesis. By and by it actually exists, in its pristine freshness when the Creator in Genesis pronounces it good; but then, alas, it gradually recedes into the past. For the real movement of that story, like all stories, is from the future into the past.

The story itself, of course, is a thing made. Once it is made it is past. Even that myth that represents all making, the cosmogony, must present the whole process as something that happened once upon a time. But what it represents as the beginning, which in truth *is* the beginning of every thing, presents itself in experience as the yet unmade. It is a myth of the myth-making process, including the making of *this* myth, because it is the myth of all making and of all experiencing.

The movement is from the indeterminate future through the living present into the determinate past. Such, too, is the movement of world-making, from the point of view of the *demiourgos,* the craftsman, who makes it. But we must remind ourselves of what we remarked about the experiencing subject generally: the *demiourgos* is not in fact passive in this process. He it is who wrestles and shapes a cosmos out of the chaotic future. This prodigious activity is precisely what we mean by the present, in all making and experiencing. It is the critical pass between fluid possibility and the definiteness of things made. Your own activity is always present in this sense, and in your act of making or experiencing something you form yourself afresh as well, emerging from the struggle along with it, still wet with the future. In our myth this critical pass is occupied by a god, who pulls and moulds everything, makers and all, out of that fluidity into a cosmos. And when he lets it go it sinks, a thing made, into the past.

For to be past is to be part of a nameable, classifiable environment. It is still in flux in the sense that what has been given one meaning can be reinterpreted, can be placed in a new context of meaning, or simply reassessed through hindsight; an old ailment gets a new diagnosis, a different physics is applied to the physical objects we've lived with all our lives, a hoary classic yields up new secrets, a marriage turns out to be the beginning of big troubles rather than the end of small ones. A new interpretation of the past comes to us, like everything new, out of the future. Still, for all this hermeneutical relativity, with the past it is a matter of reinterpreting or even discovering something already there to be pondered, and usually already understood in a certain way. When things have sunk into the past we are able to discriminate, say, between human beings, articles of furniture, animals, works of art, gods, and so forth.

But I do not in this sense know exactly what I shall be contending with in the future. A horizon of possibility appears, not a world of things, for only what is actual is definite. No doubt that horizon of possibility contains a play of powers, among which I may find myself: or more precisely, among which I may gather together something that I shall identify as myself. The "I" that will emerge will not be in simple identity with the "I" that enters the contention, indeed it may be constrained to identify itself, as well as the other things with which it contends, quite differently than it does now. For they will not *be* the same, and neither will I. Even that past with which I identify myself may thereby require a new interpretation.

It is not merely, as we say, that "things" will "change," an expression that seems merely to attribute to definite items collected out of the past some capacity to alter their condition or situation while remaining essentially what they were. That common-sense view, in which one can recognize the echo of a traditional metaphysics, offers a plausible enough approximation of what seems to happen a good deal of the time. For a certain ontic inertia perpetuates, for instance, the physical structure of the past, placing at least temporary limits on what can take shape out of the future. As things continue to slip into the past they may resemble those things we have known before, giving us the comfortable illusion that they haven't changed much. More important for our purposes is the fact that human activity has a momentum that projects it into the future, either in the effort to change what is or in the effort to give what will be a shape to which we are already accustomed. We scheme and plan and shore up, and to the extent we succeed we impose the structure of pastness on what is coming to be. But these projects are not often a total success; even when the state of affairs that emerges is the direct result of our activities it is not generally quite what we had in mind when we launched the project.

In any case the ordinary way of speaking about things changing does not prepare us to confront a future ventilated with possibility. For in the future as such there are neither tables nor hens nor human beings nor gods, as we know them. In the future are the mighty deeps and all-devouring Leviathan, the sheer formless energy of existence. It is the water that nourishes all that is, in which all that now exists will perish, or undergo a sea-change, or a purifying baptism. What "I" shall be, I who articulate the order of my environment by addressing and naming and classifying and thinking it over, this "I" will itself emerge anew from the play of powers in that still unformed future, and will have to think again!

That is more or less what Debbie and I pieced out between us in considering the cosmogonic myth a few semesters ago.[1]

I

Now the "world" to which I wish to apply this interpretation of the cosmogonic myth is specifically the world of our experience, the world that is formed imaginatively, through language, through visual constructions, through patterns of sound, and the like. That may seem inclusive enough. But there is no doubt a silence that precedes all speech and remains independent of it, a molecular and galactic silence constituted by the sheer, dense thatness of things, which we can perhaps abstractly conceive but cannot experience. To this silence we can attribute neither time nor eternity. Human beings, on the other hand, inhabit the world linguistically, imaginatively, and can experience only what they have the imaginative resources to form. We experience actively: we do not merely hear, but listen; we do not merely see, but look at. Looking and listening, speaking and thinking (inner speech), we carry on all our conscious dealings with things, and our own conscious lives are ventilated by imagination through and through.

Yet imaginative beings are not altogether porous. They too have their densities, their opacities. I refer not only to our physiological densities, that we must haul about from place to place, but those densities that are formed by the temporal tensions of our demiurgic experiencing itself, between past and future, which gives rise to the tenses of language. Language, for instance, constitutes its own silence within and among those who speak, the silences of the not-spoken, the secrets that are kept precisely in speech.

But that would be the subject of another lecture. I mention it here only to forestall the misunderstanding that what is imaginatively formed has simple transparency, and can be manipulated at will. There are necessities, and also common decencies, to which the demiurge must submit.

What I wish primarily to suggest, however, is that the demiurgic imagination functions in parallel ways, through employment of the same formal media, in art as in experience. To speak of imagination is to think first of all of those artificers among us we call artists. But the exercise of imagination in literary or graphic or musical composition is rooted in the way we experience, represents in fact a refinement of the formal qualities integral to experience itself. The human significance of art depends on that parallel. For the influence of the two is bilateral. The demiurgic activity of experiencing is the common human source of every work of art, and the cultural significance of art consists not only in presenting us with purified objects of experience but also in expanding and refining the imaginative resources of ordinary experience.

In an effort, however, to clarify this parallel and this bilateral influence, I want to present, and then expound, a general thesis on the aesthetics of experience:

We do not undergo experience; experiencing is neither passive nor instantaneous. In every formation of experience the imagination actively strives to achieve a unity of form and content, and a correlation of subject and object, akin to that of a work of art. This imaginative activity, furthermore, is positioned by the practical activity in which the subject engages as a socially constituted organism in a particular cultural situation.

That is the thesis. Now a bit of commentary:

Unity of Form and Content—The imagination strives to give the sensory and emotional contents of experience an aesthetic shape in which they will achieve coherency. We do not usually notice how active imagination is in the formation of experience, just because its demiurgic energy is so integral to the process; just as we do not notice our eyes when we see, precisely because we could not see anything without them. But without this prodigious activity there would be no experience at all, but only what James called the "whirling, buzzing confusion" of sights and sounds and feelings etc. The process of experiencing perhaps typically begins in that confusion, and that is why it often takes awhile to give it shape, through making a story of it, for instance, or a clear enough visual image to lodge it in memory. Sometimes we need others to help us complete the experience, for instance through telling them our story. For we do not generally experience anything all at once, nor is our experiencing sorted out into atomically discrete "experiences." The imagination, demiurgic, must steadily tend its garden, weeding, watering, staking, letting things grow together at their own pace.

For the imagination does not necessarily impose a ready-made form on the confusion. It lets what is given in experience take whatever shape it has the resources to find in it. In every coherent formation that takes shape there is a fresh synthesis of form and content that renders the form and content inseparable, a whole: the content exists only in *this* form; the form, in its full articulation, is peculiar to *this* content, though it may belong to a general type. As in a completed work of art, the form and the content come into concrete existence together, and until they do the form is only an abstract adumbration, the content an indistinct fluidity.

Correlation of Subject and Object—The subject and object of experience also take form together, in what phenomenologists call an intentional act. Only in this synthesis is either the experiencing or the experienced concrete and whole, the conscious subject of just this object, the formed object of just this experiencing subject. This synthesis, too, is a work of imagination, at heart the same work of imagination in which form and content coalesce. For that coalescence constitutes precisely the object of the experience for this subject, in which subjective affect or feeling diffuses its tone through what is given to the senses. The subject for which just this object exists is also formed by its experience of that object, the person or persons involved becoming changed in the experience. The shape "I" give my experience also reshapes this "I."

Approximation to the Work of Art—Since experience does not take form all at once, since it achieves completeness only to the extent that imagination achieves the synthesis we have described, it seldom, indeed, succeeds in completing this act of unification entirely. A successful work of art, or a ritual act, achieves this completeness to an extent rarely possible in the more volatile medium of experience. Only occasionally, in a kind of ecstasy, does experience become transparent and fully formed. But when we summon the energy to experience a work of art we enjoy that same ecstatic transparency, which is also available in a religious liturgy for those who can enter it fully. That is why the ritual or the work of art is so satisfying: not because it is entirely different from the sort of synthesis for which we strive in experience, but precisely because it does so fully satisfy that same striving. The rite or the work of art is an ideal paradigm of experience, in which, indeed, demiurgic anthropos, weary in his struggles with the recalcitrant stuff of experience, finds rest, and illumination for his task.

Action and Experience—We are positioned toward experience by our active projects, or more generally by our life-activity. The agent of the act becomes the subject of experience as well, of the particular sort of experience toward which his act positions him. The mode of praxis in a well-defined social situation not only situates experience, but also mobilizes the particular imaginative resources that yield any particular synthesis of experience. That is why people in different social situations will not only experience different things, but will experience them differently. A typical bank clerk and a revolutionary activist will not even experience the same scene in the same way.

II

So much for systematic exposition of our thesis. In many ways it is not new, but there would be no point in tracing its lineage in post-Kantian continental philosophy. The basic demiurgic model, in fact, seems to me to be implicit in the ancient cosmogonic myth itself. Rightly understood! But by way of bringing out what is distinctive in it we might briefly contrast it with another model, also a hardy perennial, namely the realistic or mimetic model, which is also a model of both art and experience. There does tend in general to be a rough correlation between theories of art and theories of experience, even if the one does not logically imply the other.

The mimetic theory of art, for instance, is generally persuasive to people who hold realistic or mimetic views of experience. In this view, experience registers a kind of mental copy of what is really already *there,* in the world, independent of experience. In the terms we have established, the real world stands forth in a state of *pastness,* already articulated into beads, bottles, boulders, bosoms, and boards, and we make mental copies of them, either spontaneously or with some labor. Present experience registers the pastness of the world. The relation is in fact generally conceived to be causal: what *is,* already sorted out into the many things in the mode of pastness, causes our experience of it. To conceive things this way is already to consider that relations among them are causal, and the experiencing subject is actually one of those discrete things, so that his experience will consist in mental images caused by other things.

Now this so-called realistic view of experience is at least congruent with a realistic aesthetic or a mimetic theory of art, and proceeds from similar premises, so it is not surprising that they often go together. Representational painting, on this theory, "re-presents" what has already presented itself, in the mode of pastness, in nature. The realistic novel attempts to reproduce concrete social relations as they actually exist, often with a strong underlying assumption of causal determinism, rooting social relations in quasi-"natural" relations governing the material conditions of life and the social class relations resulting from their production and exchange. Here the "present" of the writer or artist conveys to "future" readers or viewers the pastness of real things as they exist, in their causal relations. But even that present and future are really modes of pastness, as causal consequences necessarily following from what has been.

I think it would not be difficult to suggest a similar congruence between expressivist theories of art and idealistic theories of experience. Only in that case the past and future would be specious modes of that presentness constituted by the inner state of the experiencing subject or the artist. Something like this correlation has in fact been revived in recent years under the appropriate banner of "Nowism."

Of course aesthetic theories are one thing and what artists in fact do is another, even if an artist himself understands what he is doing in terms of one or another aesthetic theory. A realistic novelist, for instance, might intend to be reconstructing, in words, the material pastness of a concrete social situation, in its causal relations. But I do not think that is in fact what he is doing at all. His work is an exercise of the demiurgic imagination in spite of his intentions: wresting a particular image of the past, articulated on certain assumptions about social dynamics, out of the great void of the future. For whatever its relation may be to what has been, it is an *account* of the past that has never existed before.

III

Now the *demiourgos* has got to begin his work by establishing the great frame within which his universe of order can be formed, and such framing is also a fundamental necessity of the demiurgic imagination generally. Only for us mortals the frame is an enclosure that sets something apart from everything else: from all those totalizing systems in which the past predetermines the future. The cause and effect system of the physical world, for instance, and the economic system of supply and demand, and the eternal circles of family conflict, and so on. These systems seem perfectly global, encompassing everything a person has got to understand to get on in the world: they seem to contain the whole world, in the mode of pastness.

But a frame creates a crack or fissure in that world of pastness, setting its contents apart from all that sound and fury. What exists within the frame constitutes its own little microcosmic system, with all its elements related integrally to one another and essentially to nothing else in the great world outside. Kant speaks of a work of art as being characterized by *Zweckmässigkeit ohne Zweck,* that is as having an interior teleology, a self-contained purpose in itself, not determined either by theoretical constructions or by practical aims in the great world outside. Presenting something inside the frame signals this interior teleology to the beholder: don't expect what goes on in here to behave as if it were part of the plenary system outside. It is something special.

But the frame does not merely enclose. Its much more important function, which the enclosure serves, is to create the opening of which we have spoken. The frame does not enclose in order to seal its contents in, but on the contrary in order to provide an unobstructed space through which they can pass out into the world of our experience. The frame, after all, is open front and back. Something pours through it that is precisely not subject, say, to covering-law models of universal reiteration.[2]

So there is a paradox in this matter of framing: we keep what is framed free of the plenary space and time outside, not just to amuse ourselves with it, but in order to gain fresh purchase on our experience in the great world outside. We suspend the pastness of the plenary space and time, the better to occupy the world of experience in a manner that is illuminated and disciplined by our concentration within the frame. That may be especially evident in the case of the sort of framing that takes place in religious rites and disciplines, to which I will refer presently. But works of art function that way as well, whether we expect them to or not. I will want to claim that we employ the device of framing in experience itself, furthermore, in a way that is susceptible to the influence of these more artfully constructed frames.

For the frame makes precisely that opening in the totalizing circle of pastness through which the demiurgic imagination pulls, wrestles, and shapes the great void of the future. Through this passageway into the void, typified by the untouched canvas or the blank piece of paper in the typewriter or the empty stage, demiourgos conjures the unseen powers of the fluid deeps into visible form.

But now I must get my speculative enthusiasm under control a little, to try more soberly to explain this phenomenon of framing.

Sitting in the choir loft of a Sunday morning, as is my habit, with my mind wandering a little, which also happens, I could not help noticing how carefully framed the service is, in time and space. When my mind does not wander I am too thoroughly inside the frame to notice: all the more evidence of how sturdy the frame really is. I should mention, too, that this particular church is of the Yankee Congregationalist sort, not one of your temples of high liturgy. No clouds of incense fill the sacred space, no ancient rite inscribed in black leather organizes the sacred time, no eunuch prances before the sacred altar. Yankees worship their maker with the same grave informality with which they address their pot roast. Religion, after all, is supposed to be of a piece with Real Life. Yet our puritan determination to purge all nonsense has not succeeded in introducing so much as a crack in that frame. We try. Our young minister opens the service with a hearty, Good Morning! as if he were hailing us in front of the post office. But we do not respond by nodding, waving, or saying "H'are ya." No. The congregation intones the echo of his very words, in unison! We do other strange things. We in the choir parade up and down the aisles with our hymn books, wearing black bags from which only our extremities protrude. At regular intervals, and on signal, everybody stands and sings in full-throated chorus; for we are an enthusiastic congregation. At regular intervals, and on signal, we bow our heads in silence, each member of the congregation joined with the others only through the ears, by the unseen tissue of the minister's voice. Throughout that hour we indulge in behavior that would seem quite mad in any other place or during any other hour of the week. For that hour is set apart; everything that happens then is framed.

Our critics, and our own clerical scolds, are often heard to complain that we do not behave the rest of the week as we do on Sunday mornings. There can be a serious point in that complaint, but taken literally it is pretty silly. If we did break into psalms and such when our paths chance to cross in the supermarket, we'd have to do something else on Sunday morning—if they didn't lock us up first!

This phenomenon of framing, at any rate, besides being universal in religious observances, public and private, is one of the things religious rites share with the arts. To speak of frames, in fact, is first of all to think of paintings. The frame of a painting is integral to it as a work of art, in a sense that has nothing to do with whether the frame is plain or ornate, gilded or black. For the painting stands forth as a work of art only by being demarcated by clear boundaries. It differs from the play of color and form that exists everywhere in our environment because of this deliberate act of placing a frame around it, or choosing to paint within a frame. This space is different, not part of the plenary space of the universe at large, and to look at the painting is to concentrate our attention purely on this plane, as if nothing else existed, for its tensions and dynamics are internally related. The time of our attention to it, furthermore, is detached from our other times as the painting is from all other spaces, as detached and as complete in itself.

With a piece of music, on the other hand, the framing is primarily temporal, and only incidentally spatial. Like the temporality of the painting, the space of the piece of music is relative to those attending to it. Still, the music can generally be listened to only within a limited space, and even within that space it is set off in our attention from all the extraneous sounds, coughing, cars going by, that are within earshot. We hear all these sounds, but we do not listen to them, for even when they do intrude into the physical space in which the music is heard they do not share its aesthetic space. We filter out the infernal coughing and rustling of programs, letting the piece form its own space in our attention. But this spatial dimension is subordinated, in music, to the temporal one, and really is constituted by it. Within the twenty-five minutes, say, that elapse in the ordinary time the piece takes up, there is a unique temporality formed by the piece itself. This temporal frame is generally both harmonic and melodic, enclosing both a synchronic tonality and a diachronic succession of pitched sounds, rhythmically arranged, that begin and end. Framed off from the normal tempo of social life, the temporality of the piece is intrinsically related to its harmony, melody, and rhythm, but only incidentally related to the twenty-five minutes. Cosmic, organic, social time left to recede to the periphery of our attention, we keep time to the music.

Those examples may be sufficient both to suggest the general significance of framing in religion and the arts, and also to suggest that the frame is differently constituted according to the nature of the medium in question. It would not be difficult to extend our analysis to stories, to drama, to poems and other literary texts, in each case making the relevant distinctions in the way the frame is formed. It is worth mentioning that religious usages share with works of art not only the phenomenon of framing, but also the same aesthetic forms that are employed within the frame, formalized movements, music, narrative, lyric, and so on. That is my special professional interest in the matter, as a philosopher of religion, but I won't elaborate on its strictly religious implications here. In general I'd say simply that from a formal standpoint there is no difference between the arts and the religious employment of the same media, but there is a difference in the mode of participation. In a religious act the participant enters bodily into the frame: his movements, his voice, his physical presence, are incorporated into the very medium. For those who are under the sacred canopy the narrative will express a myth or scriptural story linking his life to the acts of the gods, the dramatic form will be employed in its liturgical re-enactment, the visual representation will be a holy icon, and so forth. People pray to icons, not to paintings.

However that may be, I want finally to suggest, consonant with the general thesis of this lecture, that the phenomenon of framing functions in ordinary experience, as well as in religion and the arts. Experience does not transpire in an undifferentiated and boundless cosmic soup. In fact, an entirely unframed experience is unimaginable. Until an event in your life achieves some servicable frame you do not yet experience it at all. That is why, when things seem unsettled and chaotic, the imagination struggles to provide the frame, sometimes trying one and then another, to bring what is happening into some aesthetic coherence. The frame is seldom quite so clearly delineated, or the aesthetic forms within it so refined, as in liturgies or works of art. But we do insist on seeing and hearing quite highly organized spaces and times, and daily life is full of little rituals. We see what we can bring into the organized visual frame of our attention, leaving many things out or relegating them to the periphery of our vision. Similarly with our lived time: the confusing flow is full of episodes, long and short, that we may *experience* as having quite definite beginnings, middles and ends.

Just how confining this framing activity may be will depend, really, on our aesthetic resources. It is a question of the most fundamental moral consequence. For the frame, spatial, temporal, or linguistic, is the enclosure in which *demiourgos* struggles with the fluid energies of the future. If he can do no more than try to impose the familiar forms of pastness on them, he will at best succeed only in damming up their mighty onrush until they break through and overwhelm him. But if he can summon the originality to let these energies assume forms that are answerable to their own demands, he will be performing his true task. To do so, however, he must also have the courage to face great risks to his own sense of identity.

The artist, I think, and also the prophet, takes these risks. In this sense he presents us with an ideal model of experience itself, of rich complexity and yet completed and whole, a model of genuine beauty and sacred possibility at the roots of experience itself. To speak of beauty and sacred possibility in this way may lead to misunderstanding. What appears in the frame may not be pretty. What takes shape may be ugly or horrifying, a Guernica or a terrible fairy tale or a crucifix, and the frame may force us to look at it steadily rather than turning our eyes away as we usually do. Precisely the formal intensification induced by the frame gives the imagination the resources for grasping the terrible rather than evading it, and that too may open experience to its sacred sources.

For the frame suspends the pastness of routine flux and flow in the social environment with which we busy ourselves. It introduces a break in that routineness, opens up a kind of aesthetic black hole in the pastness of our tight little cosmos. We peer into this hole, or even disappear into it for a while, like Alice down the rabbit hole, and what we find there is not necessarily either pretty or empty. As the example of Alice suggests, we may find ourselves in a region of wonder, in which the latent psychic content of the world we live in is placed in the foreground, full of playfulness and terror. Upon our return out of this particular frame we may find even the pastness of the world transformed, and ourselves with it.

For the frame is the passageway of revelation from the unbounded future. It does not necessarily provide you with some discursive truths you can write down in your notebook—which is in any case a fairly trivial notion of revelation. Rather, the formal purity that is achieved in the frame in-forms the imaginative structuring of experience generally, giving it the elasticity to cope with the powers of possibility with which the future confronts it. To end this lecture with a snappy slogan: We enclose in order to disclose.

Wesleyan University

NOTES

1 I think the Plato of the *Timaeus* understood all this, but there are at least apparent differences between his classic interpretation of the cosmogonic myth and the one sketched here, and it may help clarify the intent of our interpretation to comment a little on the most important of these apparent differences. We have adopted his name for the god who occupies the critical position which, in our rendering, is always the present. But Plato introduces a playful ambiguity into the portrayal of his *demiourgos:* he is certainly a god, yet he is engagingly anthropomorphic, in some ways even more so than the classical Olympians. He is the very image of the busy craftsman, with a job he can scarcely manage. With his eye cocked on the eternal archetypes, the demiurge moulds and shapes the formless stuff into their very imperfect copy, which is the cosmos of our experience. But he can never quite get the stuff to conform to the archetypes. It keeps squirting out or slopping over, and things seem in constant need of repair. The job is endless, the task of the perpetual present.

What Plato's rendering of the myth does not seem to accommodate is the possibility that the demiurge, who does the shaping, must himself constantly emerge from the watery flux in order to sustain his hold on the present. The demiurge, after all, is a god, not only immortal but essentially unchanged by his activity, in spite of being otherwise so human. Also, the fact that the god has a kind of blueprint before him in conducting his handicraft, namely the eternal forms or ideas, gives the impression that the god is steadily imposing a kind of ideal pastness on things as they emerge from the chaos.

Still, Plato's rendering of the myth does splendidly bring out the essentially active role of the demiurge. The eternal ideas merely subsist, while he has the job of contending with the chaos, by prodigious labor moulding the recalcitrant elements into some semblance of order. Furthermore, I think it would not be difficult to show that Plato intended us to understand that we are ethically and aesthetically the imitators of the demiurge, that indeed we share the task of the great artificer, for instance in the ethical shaping of our personal lives and in the political shaping of our shared social life. For with us, at least, Plato is clear that the shaper also needs reshaping: that we who give such form as we can to the chaos are ourselves of its very stuff, our lives a constant emergence from a great formlessness. However it may be with the demiurge himself, that is the paradoxical situation of his child, the demiurgic *anthropos.*

2 That is why I found point-missing the suggestion of some colleagues with whom I discussed this notion of framing, that the frame ought to be broken, or open on one side. In that case, "nature" abhorring a vacuum, the frame would simply be inundated with that plenary space it is designed to hold at bay. There is indeed always the danger that our making and experiencing will be so clogged by that stale and fetid smog that nothing fresh can pass through it. The frame is needed in order to keep the opening clear.

An innocent in the literary-critical wars, I had not been aware of the minefield I was passing through in this lecture. The term, "framing," in particular turned out to be a particularly active mine. I had forgotten about its use by an earlier generation of critics, who seem to me, however, to have drawn quite different implications from it.

Much more relevant to my use of the term, I discover, is that of Erving Goffman in *Frame Analysis: An Essay on the Organization of Experience* (New York: Harpers, 1974), which I had unfortunately not yet read when I prepared this lecture.

Insinuations of the Word: Irony in Stephen Crites's "The Demiurgic Imagination In Art and Experience"

Daniel O'Hara

Given the general drift of the symposium so far, I want to begin on what I guess will sound like a dissonant note, with a quotation from a poet who was also a great critic:

> The music of a word is, so to speak, at a point of intersection: it arises from its relation first to the words immediately preceding and following it, and indefinitely to the rest of its context; and from another relation, that of its immediate meaning in that context to all the other meanings which it has had in other contexts, to its greater or less wealth of association . . . it is only at certain moments that a word can be made to insinuate the whole history of a language and a civilization. This "allusiveness" is not the fashion or eccentricity of a peculiar type of poetry; but an allusiveness which is in the nature of words, and which is equally the concern of every kind of poet.[1]

I want to use this quotation from T. S. Eliot's "The Music of Poetry" to sound the central theme of my response, which now will be gradually unfolded.

I

Before I raise possible objections to Professor Crites's paper, I would like to give you my understanding of his position. Although Professor Crites began his philosophical career with significant studies of Kierkegaard's ironic pseudononymous authorship and a monograph on Hegel and Kierkegaard, he has now apparently returned to a more purely Kantian position on the human imagination. Of course, Professor Crites's respect for and use of Kant could already be seen in his comparison and contrast of Hegel and Kierkegaard, to be found in his work, *In the Twilight of Christendom.* What he argues now—and I am oversimplifying for polemical purposes—is that because the human mind is constituted as it is it tends to see experience in terms of narrative schemas. And although ordinary human experience in society does not afford the opportunity for perceiving the perfect harmony of subject and object, form and content which we find in the best or highest works of art and the most representative ritual acts—nevertheless it is appropriate and just, even necessary, to conceive of ordinary human experience as always potentially a perfect work of narrative art, always capable of expressing, in an ecstatic moment, a certain radiant fullness and distinctive clarity (Professor Crites's 1971 article, "The Narrative Quality of Experience," supplements his views presented in this talk).[2]

The means by which the work of art or the ritual act achieves this kind of transcendental unity of apperception and understanding is what he calls the "frame" of the work of art or the ritual act: the "frame," I take it, is the Kantian schema writ large. For it is that which separates off and isolates a kind of resonant, almost sacred space, in which we discover at times the vision which our demiurgic imagination has made. "We enclose in order to disclose," as Professor Crites concludes. In other words, like the creator-figure in the cosmogonic myths studied by Mircea Eliade and other comparative-minded phenomenologists of religion and myth, the human imagination does actually create the future it envisions.

I think this is a generally fair if obviously incomplete summary of Professor Crites's position. What I want to do now is to suggest three lines of possible questioning which may be of some help in furthering discussion later. The first line has to do with what might be called the genealogy of the word "demiurge." The second concerns the apparent change in the history of philosophy and critical theory from the idealistic Romantic concept of the imagination to an ironic modern one. The third line of questioning involves Kant's own sense of the philosophical and critical inadequacy of what he termed "aesthetic ideas." In short, I plan to raise questions that arise from my own concern with literary and cultural history.

But before I turn to my lines of inquiry, I would like to raise another possible objection, if only to banish it almost immediately from your minds again. It would be possible, for those of you familiar with Professor Crites's earlier work, to read into some of the illustrative imagery that he uses here to dramatize his philosophical concepts, the description of the ironic consciousness from Søren Kierkegaard's *The Concept of Irony With Constant Reference to Socrates.* There, you will recall, Kierkegaard criticizes the ironic consciousness for attempting to escape the apparent fragmentation of the world of experience by dreaming nostalgically of ideal images suggestive of an ultimate transcendental unity behind experience. I am thinking especially of Kierkegaard's interpretation of Plato's *Symposium* and its movement from conflicting opinion through ironic questioning to mythic truth. This kind of unwitting dialectic appears to develop from a sense of the pure fragmentation of experience through the construction of an ironic poise of antitheses to a mythic image of harmony, and it is a clear case of self-mystification. (Whether Kierkegaard is completely right about Socrates and Plato is another question.) Such self-mystification, of course, can have no place in a truly self-conscious and sophisticated philosophical enterprise as Professor Crites's clearly is. You may ask, then, why bring it up at all? The reason is that I want to forestall any attempts to hoist Professor Crites on his own petard.

II

Now that I have framed Professor Crites's paper with my historical perspective, let's see if I can create my first space of significant questioning.

This first line of questioning can be summed up by the phrase "let the Archive speak." That is, why not let the standard lexical meanings, the etymology of the key word "demiurge," open a doorway of possible questioning.

The *Oxford English Dictionary* says that "demiurge" comes from the Greek word that was formed from the words *demios* and *ergos* and that it means literally "public or skilled worker." The *Oxford Dictionary of English Etymology* supplements this entry by noting that *demios* comes from the Greek word for people, *demos,* from which we get one half of our word democracy. And this word *demos* is related to the Old Irish *dam* and *damh* meaning tribe, family. And, as well, it is related to the Gaelic word *daimh* which means relationship. So it seems that there is a family of language relationships just in the history of the meaning of the word "demiurge."

But let's return to the *O.E.D.* for a few further meanings. The next one is familiar: "a name for the Maker or Craftsman of the world, in the Platonic philosophy; in the Gnostic system, conceived as a being subordinate to the Supreme Being, and sometimes as the author of evil." And the last meaning is from Greek political history rather than from philosophy: "a magistrate in certain Greek states, and in the Achaean league; hence creative." (This conclusion is perhaps the most paradoxically appropriate *non-sequitur* I've seen yet.) I find all this word-play and these language games extremely fascinating since it suggests that at the center of Professor Crites's arguments stands a word which is part of a network of fluctuating meanings and ironic resonances: that is, at the center of the paper is *différance,* as a rabid Derridean would now say. But for me this *différance*—if it is that—is radically historical and social, tied to the discourse and the situation of a people at certain moments in their history and informing, like the subliminal memory of an apparently forgotten tune, the later uses of the word "demiurge," even when those uses are part of different contexts. But I'll hurry on now, since I'm not sure that every one shares my fascination with the historical adventures of mere words, however great their resonances.

But I need to make one more entry on our list of meanings. Consulting a classical dictionary, I found that the original form of the word "demiurge" is given as the plural Greek word *demiourgoi,* a form of the word that goes back to the root meaning of "pressing down and against," from which we get our words organ and orgasm. The word *demiourgoi* means literally "public workers," but listen to what the archive has to say about them:

> "public workers" are in Homer such independent craftsmen as metal-workers, potters, and masons, and also seers, doctors, bards, and heralds (though not beggars!). Plato and Xenophon use the word thus. But in pre-Solonian Athens they comprised all who gained their livelihood other than from the soil, perhaps including wage-earners. They enjoyed a short-lived right of supplying two of the archons (580 B.C.). They do not subsequently appear as a separately organized class. As the highest, often eponymous officers, demiourgoi appear in several States; though perhaps of the greatest antiquity in Elis and Achea, they are most often mentioned in Dorian records. Their exact function varied from State to State. In the Achaean Confederacy they formed a council of ten who assisted the general . . .[3]

I regret having to read all this at you, but I do have a point to make. I find it very curious that, despite Professor Crites's conscious intentions, the key word that he uses in his paper discloses this particular history that involves not only philosophy but politics and the rise and fall of a social class originally identified with the founders and name-givers of a culture. More significantly, even though Professor Crites refers initially in his paper to the universal cosmogonic myth in which some kind of creator—figure or other appears to shape the primeval, or should I say, apocalyptic chaos, the word "demiurge" itself is steeped in Greek thought, in Greek politics, in Greek life.

In fact, one could construct a little history or genealogy of the word from its concrete origins in Homer where it describes a certain class of artisans separated from the martial heroes, to its use as a term to designate a much larger class of wage-earners, government functionaries and administrators, all of whom came to have a purely formal or academic role in the affairs of the city-states. Of course, the word's final home comes to be philosophy where it is used to refer both to the well-intentioned but clumsy mechanic-god who jury-rigs this world and to the author of evil himself, the greatest *Daimon* of them all. But now there is the further history of the word as this play of associations generates its own idealized image as traced by Professor Crites's use of the word "demiurge" to designate the shaping spirit of the imagination—what used to be called the Romantic ideal of imagination or the transcendental imagination, and then came to be called the transcendental ego, and which now we might just name "the technological imagination," especially if we think of Heidegger's "The Question of Technology," "The Age of the World Picture," and "The Word of Nietzsche," three recently translated essays from his later work.[4] I find it strange that a word so culturally-bound as "demiurge" has been taken by Professor Crites as the most appropriate word to designate that innate power of the human mind to give shape to experience. After all, perhaps in other cultures people don't *quite* conceive of the relation between the imagination and experience in *precisely* this fashion, having as they would a very different history. I realize that this reservation of mine goes against the grain of our comparative religion people like Mircea Eliade, but so what? I'm in English literature. Besides it is fascinating, isn't it, to watch how the messy historical and political associations of a word are erased from it until it stands in all its mock-pristine purity reverberating as a philosophical paradigm of universal import and application.

III

The second line of possible questioning which I would like to suggest arises from my desire, apparently not shared by Professor Crites, to let the post-Kantian tradition in philosophy have its say. Let's see what has happened to this *concept* of the demiurgic *imagination* in the nineteenth century alone. Just a contrast between two writers in that tradition, one from the beginning and one from the end of the century, should suffice to make my point.

Samuel Taylor Coleridge, English Romantic poet and critical theorist, defines the creative imagination in chapter 13 of his *Biographia Literaria.* Shortly before doing so, he invokes the guiding spirit of his master in these things, Immanuel Kant, "The venerable sage of Koenigsberg." Then he goes ahead and defines the imagination himself—in words borrowed from Kant, Schelling, and Milton's commentary, in Books 5 and 7 of *Paradise Lost,* on the opening of St. John's Gospel.

> The imagination then I consider either as primary, or secondary. The primary imagination I hold to be the living power and prime agent of all human perception, and as a repetition in the finite mind of the eternal act of creation in the infinite I am. The secondary I consider as an echo of the former, co-existing with the conscious will, yet still as identical with the primary in the kind of its agency, and differing only in degree, and in the mode of its operation. It dissolves, diffuses, dissipates, in order to recreate; or where this process is rendered impossible, yet still, at all events, it struggles to idealize and to unify. It is essentially vital, even as all objects (as objects) are essentially fixed and dead.[5]

I think that with only a few, very slight modifications this definition of the creative imagination could be taken as a description of Professor Crites's essential position.

But what I want to do now is to show what happened to this idealized view of the creative imagination in the nineteenth century. I don't even want to suggest that Beckett and company, the dramatists of the absurd, should now get into the act. Let's look, instead, at the retrospective "Preface" Friedrich Nietzsche provided for his first book, *The Birth of Tragedy,* about fifteen years after its initial publication in 1872.

You will recall that in *The Birth of Tragedy* Nietzsche argues that all human experience, in so far as it can be justified, (i.e., made conceivable for humankind), must be seen as a work of art, particularly as a work of tragic art. For in tragic drama the aesthetic phenomenon arises out of the fraternal conflict between two interrelated gods—mirror images of one another, viz., Dionysius, the spirit of music, suffering, orgy, dance, and tragic insight; and Apollo, the principle of individuation, form, dream-vision (as opposed to Dionsyian intoxication), and the sculptured image. You will remember also that in one passage in this later "Preface," Nietzsche sums up his second thoughts and suspicions of the idealized Romantic version of the creative imagination, a version which derives from Kant, Schelling, and the Protestant religious tradition and which haunted

Nietzsche's earlier thinking, especially his youthful enthusiasm for art for art's sake as expressed in *The Birth of Tragedy.*

> In the book itself the most suggestive sentence is repeated several times, that the existence of the world is justified only as an aesthetic phenomenon. Indeed, the whole book knows only an artistic meaning and crypto-meaning behind all events—a "god," if you please, but certainly only an entirely reckless and amoral artist-god who wants to experience, whether he is building or destroying, in the good and the bad, his own joy and glory—one who, creating worlds, frees himself from the distress of fullness and overfullness and from the affliction of the contradictions compressed in his soul. The world—at every moment the attained salvation of God—is the eternally changing, eternally new vision of the most deeply afflicted, discordant, and contradictory being who can find salvation only in appearance.[6]

Nietzsche is quite willing to accept this image of the creative imagination, since it prefigures his later vision of it as the latest form of the will-to-power over existence and of the purely artistic conception of the imagination. For the truth about this conception of the imagination is that it still rather directly derives from the religious view of the world inherited from the Judeo-Christian tradition, especially from Genesis. In fact, this artistic or aesthetic idea of the imagination and its relation to the world is this religious view of things stripped of its moralizing masks and idealizations and reduced to what is essentially a human, perhaps all-too-human horizon. What I want to suggest is that any use of the demiurgic concept of the imagination in art and experience cannot escape all the implications—including those of the will-to-power and mastery—insinuated by the very terms and ideas used to articulate this concept.

My point is that Professor Crites's view of the creative imagination, a view deeply embedded in the history of the West and its exercise of the will-to-power over experience and other cultures and peoples, has been seriously questioned and undermined: it has been exposed as a hollow idol of absurd authority. In fact, as Paul Ricoeur (among others)[7] has brilliantly shown, the entire history of our culture since the nineteenth century at least has been a struggle between those who are suspicious of this Romantic image of the creative imagination and who would deconstruct it by tracing its secret genealogy and those who blindly subscribe to the understanding of man's relation to the world built into this image from the very beginning of Western culture by the different words and discourses used to realize this image in our history. I don't want to say that no one now can possibly hold Professor Crites's view of the human imagination, because history has refuted it. Nor is the issue simply a question of whether the work of art frames a tragic or a comic experience, or a beautiful or an ugly one, or a pleasant or an unpleasant one—or even whether it can be conceived with equal validity as a mimetic and an expressive project. Rather the issue, for me, is how the work of art can open up the question of the historical injustice and untruth at the basis of any interpretation of human experience that arises within a particular culture at a particular time. In other words, the issue is how the work of art, perhaps, indeed, as a further refinement of experience, provokes a kind of critical reflection of or ironic dialogue with its culture, a dialogue whose language or discourse is similar to that of the work of art itself. What I want to suggest, then, is that all of us, victims of blindness all, must be engaged in an open and explicit dialogue with what Ricoeur calls the masters of suspicion: Marx, Nietzsche, and Freud. I would argue that this list needs some updating now to include the names Heidegger, Derrida, and Foucault, among others that could come to mind. But the point is that all of us now, whatever our orientations, must engage in active dialogue with these thinkers and we must find a language, a discourse complex, flexible, and concretely historical enough to do justice to each others' critical situations.

In order to give you a sense of what I mean by such a critical language, I'll now read to you a passage from T. S. Eliot's 1928 "Preface" to *The Sacred Wood,* his famous collection of essays which was originally published in 1920, in which I find hints of just such a language. In this passage, Eliot uses irony to hollow out the different definitions of poetry inherited from the Romantic and Victorian periods. More significantly, he turns that irony also on himself by adopting a revised version of Oscar Wilde's pose of the aesthete as he gives us his own openly inadequate definition of poetry:

> Poetry is a superior amusement: I do not mean an amusement for superior people. I call it an amusement, an amusement *pour distraire les honnêtes gens,* not because that is a true definition, but because if you call it anything else you are likely to call it something still more false. If we think of the nature of amusement, then poetry is not amusing; but if we think of anything else that poetry may seem to be, we are led into far greater difficulties. Our definition of the use of one kind of poetry may not exhaust its uses, and will probably not apply to some other kind; or if our definition applies to all poetry, it becomes so general as to be meaningless. It will not do to talk of "emotion recollected in tranquility," which is only one poet's account of his recollection of his own methods; or to call it a "criticism of

life," than which no phrase can sound more frigid to anyone who has felt the full surprise and elevation of a new experience of poetry. And certainly poetry is not the inculcation of morals, or an equivalent of religion, except by some monstrous abuse of words. And certainly poetry is something over and above, and something quite different from, a collection of psychological data about the minds of poets, or about the history of an epoch; for we could not take it even as that unless we had already assigned to it a value merely as poetry.[8]

Eliot goes on in this vein, but we need not follow him now. I think you can see the finest approximation of Socratic irony in this passage—I am thinking of the kind of irony that pervades the greatest of Plato's dialogues, the *Symposium.*[9] For this kind of restless, ever qualifying irony permeates Eliot's poetry in the same way that it informs his criticism. Eliot's criticism thus becomes as "poetic" and "creative" in its way as his poetry is.

Consider how Eliot's irony here anticipates our dissatisfaction with his own definition of poetry. Eliot uses his irony to lay out three definitions of equal vacuity in a spatial plane, in a differential configuration, a system of ironic impressions. Eliot does not construct a hierarchy of progressively more satisfactory definitions. If anything, he begins with the most unpalatable if least false of false definitions and then proceeds to the most false: Arnold's. Eliot naturally stops by the way to notice Wordsworth's earlier definition. It is thanks to Arnold that criticism has become so god-awful serious and inflated, always pronouncing on the fate of mankind and turning to its own distorted notions of literary language as a solution or at least as a diversion. Eliot's "Preface" here thus seems to be a parody of criticism. It is as if his definition of poetry were just a convenient critical fiction pointing to a shifting center of critical judgment for which no one name or set of definitions would be adequate, except perhaps the musical resonances of his own name, "Eliot." My point is that perhaps even we "post-modern" thinkers can learn much from such "modernist" poet-critics. Perhaps we can learn to employ a deft irony to negotiate the exchanges between our own masters of suspicion and their diverse rhetorics and those victims of a beautiful eloquence we are all too ready to become.

IV

Finally, now that I have framed Professor Crites's master, Immanuel Kant, with Coleridge, Nietzsche, and Eliot, I would like to throw out the last line of possible questioning, one suggested by some remarks of Kant himself from the *Critique of Judgment.* At one point Kant pauses in his efforts to enumerate the faculties of the mind which constitute imaginative genius to remind us of what he thinks of *aesthetic ideas,* or ideas of experience found in and formed solely on the model of the work of art and its apparent processes of creation. And I quote: "by an aesthetic idea I mean that representation of the imagination which induces much thought, yet without the possibility of any definite thought whatever, i.e., *concept,* being adequate to it, and which language, consequently, can never get quite on level terms with or render completely intelligible."[10] I will read this quotation again, since Kant's own style is so oblique, it is as if he suffered from an acute case of writer's cramp while possessing a mind that had subtle fingers for nuances. . . . I suppose that this line of possible questioning, suggested by Kant's ironic reservation concerning aesthetic ideas, should provoke the most serious consideration for any of his disciples.

I would like to conclude my response by recalling Paul Valéry's ironic gloss on our dilemma as modern writers facing the sphinx of history as it is disclosed by language. In what otherwise is generally a whimsical little piece of his entitled "Man and the Sea Shell," Valéry introduces his *jeux d'esprit* in the following way: "All we have to do is leaf through a dictionary or try to make one, and we will find that every word covers and masks a well so bottomless that the questions you toss into it arouse no more than an echo."[11]

Temple University

NOTES

1 T. S. Eliot, "The Music of Poetry," *On Poetry and Poets* (New York: Farrar, Straus and Giroux, 1957), pp. 25-26.

2 Stephen Crites, "The Narrative Quality of Experience," *JAAR,* (December, 1971), 291-311.

3 C. T. Onions, ed., *The Shorter Oxford English Dictionary On Historical Principles* (Oxford: Clarendon Press, 1933), p. 478; C. T. Onions, ed., *The Oxford Dictionary of English Etymology* (Oxford: Clarendon Press, 1966), p. 268; N. G. L. Hammond and H. H. Scullard, eds., *The Oxford Classical Dictionary* (Oxford: Clarendon Press, 1969), p. 327.

4 Martin Heidegger, *The Question of Technology and Other Essays* (New York: Harper and Row, 1978).

5 Samuel Taylor Coleridge, *Biographia Literaria,* ed. George Watson (New York: E. P. Dutton, 1975), p. 167.

6 Friedrich Nietzsche, "Preface," *The Birth of Tragedy,* trans. Walter Kaufmann (New York: Random House, 1966), p. 9.

7 See Paul Ricoeur, *Freud and Philosophy,* trans. Denis Savage (New Haven: Yale University Press, 1970). See also Gerald L. Bruns, *Modern Poetry and the*

Idea of Language: A Critical and Historical Study (New Haven: Yale Univ. Press, 1974).

8 T. S. Eliot, "Preface," *The Sacred Wood: Essays on Poetry and Criticism* (London: Methuen, 1950), pp. viii and ix.

9 Søren Kierkegaard, in *The Concept of Irony,* trans. Lee Capel (Bloomington: Indiana Univ. Press, 1968), pp. 128-140, has the best reading of Plato's irony in this dialogue.

10 Immanuel Kant, *The Critique of Judgment,* trans. James Creed Meredith (Oxford: Clarendon Press, 1928), p. 177.

11 Paul Valéry, *An Anthology,* ed. James R. Lawler (Princeton: Princeton Univ. Press, 1977), pp. 108-109.

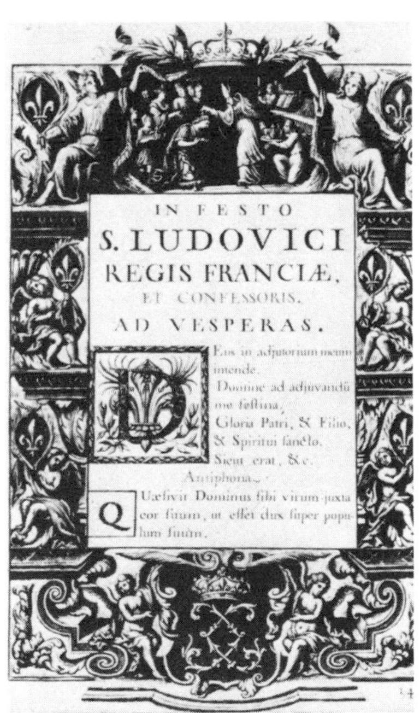

IN FESTO
S. LUDOVICI
REGIS FRANCIÆ,
ET CONFESSORIS.
AD VESPERAS.

D Eus in adjutorium meum intende.
Domine ad adjuvandũ me festina,
Gloria Patri, & Filio, & Spiritui sancto.
Sicut erat, &c.

Antiphona.

Q Uæsivit Dominus sibi virum juxta cor suum, ut esset dux super populum suum.

A weroan or great Lorde of Virginia. III.

THe Princes of Virginia are attyred in ſuche manner as is expreſſed in this figure. They weare the haire of their heades long and bynde opp the ende of theſame in a knot vnder thier eares. Yet they cutt the topp of their heades from the forehead to the nape of the necke in manner of a cokſcombe, ſtirkinge a faier lõge pecher of ſome berd att the Begininge of the creſte vppun their foreheads, and another ſhort one on bothe ſeides about their eares. They hange at their eares ether thicke pearles, or ſomwhat els, as the clawe of ſome great birde, as cometh in to their fanſye. Moreouer They ether pownes, or paynt their forehead, cheeks, chynne, bodye, armes, and leggs, yet in another ſorte then the inhabitantz of Florida. They weare a chaine about their necks of pearles or beades of copper, wich they muche eſtee me, and ther of wear they alſo braſelets ohn their armes. Vnder their breſts about their bellyes appeir certayne ſpotts, whear they vſe to lett them ſelues bloode, when they are ſicke. They hange before thẽ the ſkinne of ſome beaſte verye feinelye dreſſet in ſuche ſorte, that the tayle hangeth downe behynde. They carye a quiuer made of ſmall ruſhes holding their bowe readie bent in on hand, and an arrowe in the other, radie to defend themſelues. In this manner they goe to warr, or tho their ſolemne feaſts and banquetts. They take muche pleaſure in huntinge of deer wher of theris great ſtore in the contrye, for yt is fruit full, pleaſant, and full of Goodly woods. Yt hathe alſo ſtore of riuers full of diuers ſorts of fiſhe. When they go to battel they paynt their bodyes in the moſt terible manner that thei can deuiſe.

Beyond Logocentrism:
Trace and Voice Among the Quiché Maya

Dennis Tedlock

. . . I don't know where to begin this story. Quiché Maya stories occur naturally in conversation. People do not set aside an occasion for story-telling, where all other kinds of talk come to a stop. It is true that stories are likely to be heard at wakes, but people don't die just so someone can tell stories at their wakes.

When an anthropologist asks a Quiché, "Tell me a story," chances are that he or she will be unable to think of a story, given no reason to tell a story other than that someone wants to hear a story, any story. At least one anthropologist decided that there were no stories among the Quiché Maya.[1]

A Quiché story does not begin with a series of formal opening announcements that call a halt to conversation and point only into the story, and it does not end with a series of formal closures that call a halt.[2] The story may include or refer back to bits of the previous conversation, and when it is over, bits of the story are caught up in the conversation that follows.

The Quiché hearer does not remain silent, or merely affirm from time to time that he is listening. Rather, the listener may ask a question, or else echo the words of the story now and then.[3] The Quiché story of the creation, like Genesis, tells of creation by words, but the words are a dialogue, not a monologue.[4]

A Quiché story does not carry us away into another world or another aeon, a separate reality that has no connection to the world of the conversants. It does not go on for an hour, or even half an hour, but lasts only five or ten minutes, and once in a great while twenty.[5] The story does not move strictly forward along the path of its events, but always gets a little ahead of itself here and looks back on itself there.[6]

I do not know where to begin this story. It has one root that runs backward into the conversation that immediately precedes it, with runners that connect it to conversations of previous days, and it has another root that runs forward into the rest of its own day, with further connections to following days. On what grounds do I introduce such a story into my statement here, to you? If it is to be truly an example of Quiché story-telling, it must be connected, as something more than an isolated object held up for examination, to the rest of the conversation of our conference here. What is there about the present occasion that calls for this story? The story has to do with being in jail. In terms of the world of the body, as the Quiché see it, being in jail is like being caught in someone's armpit. It's not quite as bad as being at the bottom of that canyon behind the folded knee: that is the grave itself. There is some talk that we are all, all of us here, caught in the armpit just now, not knowing quite how to get out. One name we give to our prison is language. Jacques Derrida calls this prison "the Western metaphysic," "God," "logocentrism," "phono-centrism," "logo-phonocentrism," "phono-logocentrism," and he doesn't know how to fight his way out without getting a further sentence for attempted escape.[7] The problem, as he sees it, is that we in the West are trapped by the voice. Trapped by our alphabetic writing, which follows the voice. The voice is linear, in his view: there is only one thing happening at a time, a sequence of phonemes. On a larger scale, the unidimensional march of the voice is replicated in our linear view of history, what Derrida calls "the epic model" (*OG,* pp. 72, 85-87). The bars of the prison, then, are made of speech and of oral poetry, and the way out, in Derrida's thinking, is through a writing and a literature that finally realize their full potential by severing their connections with the voice.

While our hero goes on seeking escape through an examination of the spaces between the bars, the rest of us might do well to take a second look at the prison itself, to see how the bars were set into the wall, and what they are made of, and whether they are substantial. First of all, does alphabetic writing, or the refined alphabetic writing that linguists call phonemic—is this writing in servitude to the voice? Derrida himself, toward the end of the *Grammatology,* touches here and there on the fact that writing slights what he calls, or Rousseau calls, "accent," and to that we could add features like pausing, tone of voice, and amplitude.[8] As Derrida puts it, writing writes only that part of the voice which is already most inscribable, the so-called articulations, the one-at-a-time sequence of items that interrupts vowels with consonants. The entire science of linguistics, and in turn the mythologics (or larger-scale structuralism) that has been built upon linguistics,[9] are founded not upon a multidimensional apprehension of the multidimensional voice, but upon unilinear writing of the smallest-scale articulations within the voice. The *purest* linguistic transcription, in fact, (*here, speak in a monotone*) has only lower-case letters of a single style, (*here, exaggerate stress accents*) includes only such accents and tones as occur at the level of isolated words, (*here, run the words together*) only grudgingly admits spaces between words, (*monotone*) and excludes all punctuation. It is sheer (*pause*) alphabet. On this everything else is built. The grammatology, the science of writing Derrida calls for, already exists—for the alphabet, at least—and it is called (*pause*) linguistics. Even glimpsing this, as he does at the end of the *Grammatology* (*OG,* p. 315), we find him ten years later still blaming the voice and seeking freedom in writing, still looking at the holes in the enclosure he has described for himself (*LI,* 220, 249).

And what of that unilinear poetry of the voice, the epic? Just as we questioned whether the alphabet is in servitude to the voice, so we may ask this question of the epic, with its long march through events in hexameter time. Is this the voice of the preliterate Greeks we hear? Or is it oral *literature:* written literature meant to be recited aloud, as all literature was up to the time of the Renaissance? When we look at the earliest written literature, that of the Sumerians, we find no such verse epic. When we look at cultures known to have been free of alphabetic or syllabic writing, not only African and Amerindian but also Chinese, we find no epic. Wherever we find epic today, in Islamic Africa, in Central and Southeast Asia, in the Balkans, it always exists within a literate tradition that uses alphabetic or syllabic writing, and the oral versions, though sometimes performed by individuals who are themselves illiterate, always exist in close proximity to written versions.[10] This was in fact the case with the Homeric epics as they existed in classical Athens, where upperclass schoolchildren were taught to recite a written Homer but not to read it.[11] For all we know, this epic, this genre we have enshrined as the quintessence of oral poetry, was born within writing, literature indeed. This question cannot be finally settled: the Greeks, for their part, did much of their writing on perishable surfaces, something most historians of the alphabet would say they were already doing at the time of—let us call it the Homeric—war,[12] and for our part, there is no way we can take a tape-recorder into antiquity. It might still be that the epic came *before* the alphabet, as part of the same tendency of mind that produced the alphabet in Greece, while other minds in other places went their own ways. What matters here is that the epic, far from typifying the oral poetry of illiterate peoples, in fact typifies the oral poetry of alphabetic and syllabic peoples. I, for one, have no objection to calling the epic oral *literature,* in the strict sense of that word: made of *letters.* Even when sung, the epic tends toward the univocity of alphabetic writing: the varied spacing of spoken accents or vowel quantities is reduced to a totally predictable meter, and the varied contours of spoken pitches are reduced to a single melodic line, repeated over and over, line after line. The epic is a marvel of mechanical engineering, and its perfection, and perhaps even its invention, were greatly facilitated by alphabetic writing.[13]

Yet for all this, Derrida is right in saying that writing writes something that was already written in the voice, it writes articulations, traces, differences that are missing when the voice simply cries out without talking. We can extend this and say that the epic writes something that was already written in oral narrative, something that is missing when talk tells no story. We cannot escape our enclosure simply by reversing Derrida and saying that the name of the bars is writing, and that the name of the spaces between them is the voice. We do not wish to choose between writing articulate but endless letters from prison, as David Antin does—it is true that he speaks, but his voice is the voice of the typewriter before the tapes are even transcribed.[14] We do not wish to choose between talking without a shift key and roaring like a tiger in a cage, as Michael McClure did in his beast-language poems.[15]

But here I've gone too far again. The bars, the stripes that Antin wears are at least sawn through: he puts in blank spaces, the breaths as they occur, and the spacing of these blanks is anything but a marvel of engineering. McClure, for his part, articulated his cries with alphabetic transcription, even if he did it all in caps and with his own hand. If we could only navigate the difference, the dif-ference between them,[16] we could speak with articulate passion, and write with passionate articulation.

Well then.

Perhaps it's time to begin the story, that Quiché Maya story I promised you. But I still don't know where to begin. But the story does have a jail in it, and writing, and the voice. And animals. We had been talking, in a town in Guatemala, with a person who is a weaver and a diviner by profession. We had been learning about omens. You may wonder what an American Indian diviner will have to teach us about "Problems of Reading in Contemporary American Criticism." The answer is already partly there in the word "reading." At its Teutonic root, that word means "to make clear what is obscure," and it still has that meaning when we say things like, "What's your *reading* of the situation? " The Romance (and German) words for reading have, at their root, the meaning "to collect, to gather," as when one recognizes words in groups of letters. Now *sortilege,* as a technique of divination, contains this same root and has this same meaning, it is a gathering. What a diviner does, as a profession, is to make a gathering that renders clear what is obscure.

Well then, we are conversing with a diviner. For some reason we were talking about quail, and he said that just as people have chickens, so the *Mundo,* the Earth-deity, the Mountain has quail. We had been learning about omens, so we asked whether it was good luck to come across a quail in the woods. He said that it was a question of whether the quail crossed one's path, and in which direction:[17]

> A movement to the right is good
> to the left is evil.

That seems a clear enough way to read the quail, and it even corresponds to our own valuation of the right and left hands. He goes on:

> The Mundo sends it
> as an announcement it is sent.

So omens are sent not by God, but by the World, the Earth, the Mountain, the owner of the quail. The missionaries attempted to teach the Quiché, as they succeeded in teaching our own ancestors, that those who read omens are deceived by the devil, that nothing but ill can come of it.[18] But the Quiché say that it is not the devil who sends an omen:

> The Mundo sends it
> as an announcement it is sent.
> Since animals don't talk
> they pass by
> almost in one's path.

So the Mundo, or the animals it sends, don't *talk.* They articulate by making a *mark* in the path ahead, leaving a *trace.* This is what Derrida would call writing (*OG,* pp. 9, 55, 62, 65, 70; *LI,* p. 190), but it is not delivered in words. The Word, we may guess, belongs to God, that voice from the sky. God speaks only the Good, but the Mundo writes of both good and evil. The Mundo writes *boustrophedon,* like the pre-imperial Greeks,[19] moving back and forth across our field of vision rather than always one way.

At this point our diviner thinks of a story, but the first sentence of his story in no way interrupts the conversation: it half belongs to the conversation and half to the story, it's like a title for the story. He says, about these announcements of the Mundo:

> It's like the squirrel

it happened to a guy from just above here
he's almost a neighbor of ours.

So we're not in for any excursion into some far off fantasy land, some "other world" to be projected for us by the text, a world that exists only because of this text: the hero is *almost* our neighbor.[20] All the more reason for us to be afraid.

Now this guy
in the time of Ubico
in '36 or
'37
when all kinds of papers were asked for—
certificate, identification
summons, I don't know
how many papers—

We're under a Central American dictator, everywhere we go we have to show our papers to the authorities.

now this guy
didn't take his papers with him
he didn't remember
when he took the road to San Francisco, he went to sell
his blankets
but when he left his house, he was now about a
league and a half, or two leagues
from his house—

The distance is a league and a half, or two leagues. The time is '36, or '37. We need a certificate, or an identification, or a summons, or all of these, we don't know. Diviners stay close to "the rift of difference," as Heidegger calls it, even a small difference. They leave us between two points, or *at* both of them, and sometimes three.

but when he left his house, he was now about a
league and a half, or two leagues
from his house—
then a squirrel came out
it crossed the road
to the left
it went inside a
tree—
because there are trunks of massive trees
that have holes—

So our diviner stops the flow of the story here to remind us that massive trees have hollows in them, the trees we all know, not just the tree occurring in this story, he strikes a chord here rather than just playing the melody. Having done this, he goes on:

> and the squirrel went inside there

We've already heard that a few lines ago, but he has to get the story back on the track again after his lecture about trees.

> and the squirrel went inside there
> lllooooooking at this guy as he came along

This lllooooooking makes the voice do more than one thing at a time. It has no place in phonology or grammar or a structuralist analysis except as just plain "looking," but lllooooooking tells us that the squirrel is looking continuously at our hero, looking from a distance and through a time, looking in a way that should've gotten his attention, that gave him every chance to think, to read what had already been written there,

> but the guy didn't think about what it announced, this
> this animal
> then
> he went down to San Francisco el Alto
> he just handed himself over.

Our diviner doesn't keep us from what's obviously going to happen in the next moment: he announces it in advance. We already knew that our hero didn't have his papers, and we already knew that a movement to the left is evil. Now we're told he handed himself over. But it hasn't quite happened yet:

> They were looking at the
> tickets

Tickets? They were looking at the—(pause)—*tickets,* our diviner has carefully chosen this word. We've already heard about papers, certificate, identification, summons—*summons? That* sounds ominous—and now it's *tickets.* Where is our oral repetition of formulas? Of one thing we can be sure, this story is no epic. But let's get on with it:

> They were looking at the
> tickets
> the poor guy went for a stay in jail.

Because he didn't have the tickets, he ended up in jail. People who have tickets get somewhere, they move on; people without tickets have tickets for jail, they move nowhere. I've just made a classic structuralist move here, or was it me? Could it have been our diviner, about to put the hero in jail, while he hesitated long enough to choose the word "tickets"? Do I have the right to say, with Lévi-Strauss, that our storyteller is an unconscious structuralist, while I am the literate discoverer of the workings of his mind? Could it be that our diviner spéaks with the wíles of a wríter? But there's more:

> Now he didn't sell
> his wares
> he just handed himself over.

This doesn't move the story forward, but dwells on what we already know. The pauses here have no place in writing and therefore no place in linguistics or mythologics, but they do describe a form. In their relationship to the words, they echo the structure of the previous sentence. Here are both sentences in juxtaposition:

> They were looking at the / Now he didn't sell
> tickets / his wares
> the poor guy went for a stay in jail / he just handed
> himself over

We've heard that last line before: "he just handed himself over." It's the only exactly repeated line in the whole story. But it doesn't have the weight of those epic formulas, it's not clunky. It's something one might say in conversation. *Is being said* in conversation. In the present context, it takes on a fuller meaning:

> Now he didn't sell
> his wares
> he just handed himself over.

He didn't "sell," but instead "just handed over," and it wasn't his wares he left there in San Francisco, but himself. "He just handed *himself* over." Now, if there is any remaining thought that the "civilization" of our Mayan diviner is merely lying dormant in a "savage" mind, waiting to be excavated, the next sentence should take care of that. He now looks back over the story:

> This was the announcement the animal gave
> looking at him here as if he were already in jail there.

So the hero failed to see himself, there in the hollow of the tree; he did not meet the gaze of the squirrel's Illoooooooking. To paraphrase Heidegger: If we could only see, for once, just where we are already.[21] And who's "we"? What is said here is not only between the hollow in the tree and the jail, but between the story and the rest of our conversation. "Where we are *already":* we can wait for more, but our diviner never *will* tell us that this story is the *origin* story of omens, the starting point even of this particular *kind* of omen. *That* would have to take place long before '36 or '37, and it certainly couldn't have happened to our next-door neighbor. If the omen *has* an origin in any other way than just being *seen.* Already.

But now that I've managed to get us into the story, I don't know how to get us out of it. Our diviner already seems to be done with it, to have summed it up, but now he will go right on. It is not only squirrels who make announcements, but—

Such are all the animals
the quail, rabbits
and the jays—
the *jays:* when
one
goes on the road

And we're on the road again, but this time it's not a story about some neighbor, it's when *oneself* goes on the road, there's no hero unless it's us.

Now, our diviner got through quail and the rabbits, but he lit up when he got to the jays. He told us before that animals don't talk, but now he comes again to the rift of difference with these jays:

they suddenly whistle:
"SHAOwww [*whistling*] shiiiieww"
then, there is
evil
in the road
since the jays are whistling.
And when they just sing:
"SHAOww SHAOww SHAOww"
it doesn't mean anything
but when it's, "SHAOwwww [*whistling*] shiiiieww"
there's
a problem in the road
yes.

So when the jay merely sings, repeating itself, its voice has no meaning, but when it cuts from its song to a whistle, then something is written in its voice, something which asks to be read. It moves sharply from full voice to a closing down of the voice, to something like a sigh or a gasp. I don't know whether the Mundo here has a voice after all, or whether jays are sent by God. Or whether this is an intelligent question.

At this point our diviner pauses for several seconds, expecting us to speak. He has now held the floor for some fiiiive minutes. Now we will ask him about the coyote that ran across the road in front of our car, yesterday. The coyote is the dog of the Mundo, and this one went *left.* But did he go up the mountain after that, or down in the canyon? He went up, so this is good, even though he went to the left. And so we go on talking about omens, today and again on some other day, and I do not know where to end this story.

But there is a loose end from back at the beginning, and that concerns Derrida: we have left him in jail, a prisoner of logocentrism, of God: God, the First Cause, that would-be monologue artist of creation whose Name, let us remember, is written only in consonants, only in articulations, and must never be pronounced out loud. God, whose own words have been written down once and for all. But are we sure he's in there? Derrida, I mean: is Derrida inside the enclosure, scratching away at the mortar? We can say this much: he engages in dialogues with his texts, quoting them in their entirety in the process;[22] no monologue artist he. Stanley Cavell resents having read the *Grammatology* and says he would have to give Derrida a B- in undergraduate philosophy at Harvard. I think that's because Derrida uses too many rhetorical questions, too many exclamation points, too much underlining, too many parenthetical remarks: those things our grammar school teachers beat out of us. The same teachers who earlier made us stop moving our lips (and our bodies) when we read. What I'm saying is, Derrida has put a lot of *voice* into his writing. He hypostatizes writing with the voice. I have never *heard* his voice, but he signed his name in public,[23] and we can just as well divine through graphology what we could have divined from his voice. If the voice has writing in it, then handwriting has voice.

According to the Quiché, God and the Mundo, Heart of Sky and Heart of Earth, Hurricane and Greenfeather Serpent, created "everything here where we are."[24] There were always already two of them, there was no beginning from one. No beginning at all, as we understand that. They talked,

> then they thought, then they wondered, then they agreed
> they joined their words, their thoughts
> then they conceived, it came to them
> it dawned on them and they conceived man.

So they are described as speaking with one another rather than sending their papers to one another in advance. They speak with the voice, but their breath is full of the writing of difference:

> it was just like a cloud, like a mist
> that grows then comes apart.

Their act of creation is "only by cutting an opening." The Quiché word here is *puz,* which means to butcher, or to cut a sacrifice open. That is all that is needed, because the creation is already all there:

> all is contained, all is stilled
> not one thing moves

Through their dialogue they find the rift of difference, they cut open the enclosure:

> then is the dawn, then is the brightening

and all of this takes place

> *pari k'ekum, pari ak'äb*
> in the blackness, in the early dawn.

We have to translate with two words, "early dawn," because English has no monolexemic way of referring to the time that is called in Quiché *ak'äb,* when it is still night but there is a trace of light in the east, very very early, or else the morning star has already risen. In this creation it is already early dawn then, always already dawn. "We would like only, for once, to get to just where we are already. . . ."

Boston University

NOTES

1 Sol Tax, "Folk Tales in Chichicastenango: An Unsolved Puzzle," *Journal of American Folklore,* 62 (1949), 125. This has everything to do with the fact that the "dialogical anthropology" perceived by George Quasha in "DiaLogos: Between the Written and the Oral in Contemporary Poetry," *New Literary History,* 8 (1977), 485, is only barely emerging now.

2 For examples of formal openings and closures, see Dennis Tedlock, "Pueblo Literature: Style and Verisimilitude," in *New Perspectives on the Pueblos,* ed. Alfonso Ortiz (Albuquerque: Univ. of New Mexico Press, 1972), pp. 222-24, and "Verbal Art," in *Handbook of North American Indians,* ed. William C. Sturtevant (Washington: Smithsonian Institution Press, n.d.), I, ch. 50.

3 The Zuni audience is limited to periodically saying *eeso,* which has the effect of "yes, indeed"; see Dennis Tedlock, *Finding the Center: Narrative Poetry of the Zuni Indians* (New York: Dial Press, 1972), pp. xxv, 3, 11, 27, 28. Here is

an example of Quiché echoing:

> Narrator: . . . he slept beneath the trees. There, in that place. In the summer.
> Respondent: In the summer?
> Narrator: Yes, in the summer. . . .

4 *Popol Vuh: The Sacred Book of the Ancient Quiché Maya,* tr. Delia Goetz, Sylvanus G. Morley, and Adrián Recinos (Norman: Univ. of Oklahoma Press, 1950), pp. 80-84; tr. Munro S. Edmonson, Publications of the Middle American Research Institute, Tulane University, 35 (1971), 7-14. See Dennis Tedlock, "The Story of Our Darkness, The Vision of the Light of Life," *Alcheringa,* (in press) for my own translation of this passage, excerpts from which are quoted elsewhere in the present talk.

5 Zuni stories, by contrast, last from half an hour to well over an hour, even in their ordinary hearthside versions.

6 This is true even in the *Popol Vuh,* which was written down (using the Latin alphabet) by a Quiché. See Tedlock, "The Story of Our Darkness," for numerous examples. In some *Popol Vuh* episodes, the course and outcome of a story are announced, in brief, before the narrative even begins, as in Goetz et al., 96.

7 Jacques Derrida, *Of Grammatology,* tr. Gayatri Chakravorty Spivak (Baltimore: Johns Hopkins Univ. Press, 1976), pp. 3, 11-12, 43, 71, 78-79, 99; (hereafter cited as *OG*) "Limited Inc," *Glyph,* 2 (1977), 220, 224, 236, 249, (hereafter cited as *LI*).

8 For discussions of nonalphabetic features of the voice, see Dennis Tedlock, "On the Translation of Style in Oral Narrative," *Journal of American Folklore,* 84 (1971), 114-33; "Oral History as Poetry," *boundary 2,* 3 (1975), 707-26; "Toward an Oral Poetics," *New Literary History,* 8 (1977), 507-19. The classic critique of what I like to call "alphabecentrism" in linguistics is that of J. R. Firth, "Sounds and Prosodies," in his own *Papers in Linguistics, 1934-51* (London: Oxford Univ. Press, 1957), pp. 121-38.

9 "Mythologics" is of course a direct translation of Lévi-Strauss's *mythologiques,* with its deliberate retention of the suffix (surname) of its claimed parent.

10 For a discussion of the verse epic and its distribution, see Ruth Finnegan, *Oral Poetry: Its Nature, Significance and Social Context* (Cambridge, Eng.: Cambridge Univ. Press, 1977), pp. 9-10. The epic she mentions as occurring in China is Central Asian, not part of indigenous Chinese tradition. Throughout my own discussion here, I use "epic" in the strict sense, meaning a heroic narrative with a metrical, sung text.

11 Eric Havelock, "The Preliteracy of the Greeks," *New Literary History,* 8 (1977), 369-91.

12 Berthold Louis Ullman, *Ancient Writing and its Influence* (Cambridge, Mass.: MIT Press, 1969), p. 21. Havelock would disagree with this, because in "The Preliteracy of the Greeks" he wants to picture preliterate Greece as lasting much longer, teeming with people who are veritable storehouses of memorized hexameter and only waiting for the opportunity to write it down. He ignores

the entirety of the ethnographic literature on the "preliterate" world, which discloses no metrical verse at all in the absence of alphabetic or syllabic writing.

13 David Antin, in "Notes for an Ultimate Prosody," *Stony Brook,* 1-2 (1968), 173-78, asserts that the marvel of engineering that is the *Beowulf* meter is entirely the creation of nineteenth-century scholarship, having no existence in the text. He also suggests that meter has been largely visual, rather than auditory, in its effects on poetry, but what I am arguing here is rather that an early purpose of written meter was to create a mechanical (and memorizable) *sound.* See Tedlock, "Toward an Oral Poetics," p. 507.

14 David Antin, *Talking at the Boundaries* (New York: Dial Press, 1976).

15 For examples of Michael McClure's work, see *Caterpillar,* 6 (1969), 40-46 and cover.

16 In matters of "dif-ference," I follow Martin Heidegger, *Poetry, Language, Thought,* tr. Albert Hofstadter (New York: Harper and Row, 1971), pp. 202-205.

17 Transcribed and translated from field tape Q50, side 1, in the author's possession. Line changes correspond to definite pauses.

18 I am thinking here of the seventeenth-century Catholic catechism in Ernesto Chinchilla Aguilar, *La Danza del Sacrificio y otros estudios* (Guatemala: Minesterio de Education Publica, 1963) pp. 65-76, but its frontal attack on omen-taking, dream interpretation, and divination has been repeated many times around the world. One could not want a purer expression of the "Western metaphysic," including those parts of it which have become implicit for most of its adherents, than is found in missionary catechisms.

19 See Ullman, *Ancient Writing and Its Influence,* pp. 27-28, on the direction of ancient alphabetic writing.

20 Paul Ricoeur's notion of a "world" created by texts, lying "beyond" or "in front of" texts which are "freed" from a "dialogical situation" to pursue the true "destination" of discourse in *Interpretation Theory: Discourse and the Surplus of Meaning* (Fort Worth: Texas Christian Univ. Press, 1976), pp. 36-37, 88, seems foreign to the present text in its violence of directionality. Ricoeur is at pains in this work to free himself from what Derrida would call the metaphysical "enterprise of returning to an origin" (*LI,* p. 236), but in the process he seems to have simply moved the "other world" from behind the text to a position in front of it.

21 Heidegger, *Poetry, Language, Thought,* p. 190.

22 In his reply to John R. Searle's earlier criticisms (*LI,* pp. 198-208), he quotes every (copyrighted) word Searle wrote.

23 Jacques Derrida, "Signature Event Context," *Glyph,* 1 (1977), 196.

24 The passages quoted here are from Tedlock, "The Story of Our Darkness."

A cheiff Ladye of Pomeiooc. VIII.

About 20. milles from that Iland, neere the lake of Paquippe, ther is another towne called Pomeioock hard by the ſea. The apparell of the cheefe ladyes of dat towne differeth but litle from the attyre of thoſe which lyue in Roanaac. For they weare their haire truſſed opp in a knott, as the maiden doe which we ſpake of before, and haue their ſkinnes powncеd in theſame manner, yet they wear a chaine of great pearles, or beades of copper, or ſmoothe bones 5. or 6. fold obout their necks, bearinge one arme in the ſame, in the other hand they carye a gourde full of ſome kinde of pleaſant liquor. They tye deers ſkinne doubled about them crochinge hygher about their breaſts, which hange downe before almoſt to their knees, and are almoſt altogither naked behinde. Commonlye their yonge daugters of 7. or 8. yeares olde do waigt vpon them wearinge abowt them a girdle of ſkinne, which hangeth downe behinde, and is drawen vnder neath betwene their twiſte, and bownde aboue their nauel with moſe of trees betwene that and thier ſkinnes to couer their priuliers withall. After they be once paſt 10. yeares of age, they wear deer ſkinnes as the older ſorte do.

They are greatlye Diligted with puppetts, and babes which wear brought oute of England.

The Need for an Audience: A Response to Dennis Tedlock

Neville Dyson-Hudson

If responses need or deserve a title, then the title for this one would be, the need for an audience. It seems particularly appropriate at 9 o'clock this morning. Tedlock is an anthropologist, though an unusual one. Any man who can persuade a private university in these financially tight times to publish a journal like *Alcheringa,* which is guaranteed to make typesetters whimper in their sleep, and even to slip recording discs in the back of it, must be considered unusual. But I am a less unusual anthropologist. It would, therefore, have been possible to give an anthropological response to this paper. And such anthropological responses come in many varieties. The first variety says: well it's interesting that Quiché Maya tell that sort of story in that sort of way. Indeed, it is not at all surprising when you consider the kind of houses that they live in or the way they calculate their kinship or the political system they have to stumble along with, or the religious beliefs they manipulate. In fact, the whole thing is so Quiché Maya, it's quite astonishing. And then there is the second variety of anthropological response. This says: well, Quiché Maya may tell stories like that in that possible way, but the Bongo Bongo don't. And, in fact, the Bongo, Bongo, whom I happened to have been privileged to study, would have said something else altogether, and in a different way entirely—and there you are!

You will, I hope, be happy to know that I propose to inflict on you neither the constipated essentialism of the first approach, nor the sour Sears-Roebuckery of the second. Regrettably, I know no more about the Quiché Maya than the rest of you and I have happily forgotten such Bongo, Bongo tales as I may once have collected. So, I shall, instead, address the issues which my peculiar perspective shapes from Tedlock's paper: literature as performance, literature as conversation, and in each case, the need for an audience which raises firstly, the question of how much an audience needs to know, and, secondly, the associated Heisenbergian problem which this paper presents of how a "critic-listener" can be an "interactive listener."

"I don't know where to begin this story," says Tedlock. Not once, but with enough repetition that we must accept it as his major ordering device, as his message. Tedlock shares this problem, this device, this message, it seems to me, with at least two other people. He shares it analytically with Foucault, who, you may remember, began his institutionally constrained discourse on language at the College de France in 1970, with the comment, "I would really like to have slipped imperceptibly into this lecture. . . . I would have preferred to be enveloped in words, borne way beyond all possible beginnings. At the moment of speaking, I would like to have perceived a nameless voice long preceding me. . . . There would have been no beginnings: instead, speech would proceed from me, while I stood in its path." Tedlock shares this problem analytically with Foucault, he shares it instrumentally with his particular, and from what he says, apparently every other Quiché story teller who "would be unable to think of a story given no reason to tell a story, other than someone wants to hear a story, any story." The Quiché problem, and maybe Tedlock's problem, and maybe even Foucault's problem is that there is no way "to begin with a series of formal opening announcements that call a halt to conversation and point only into the story or to end with a series of formal closures that call a halt, preceding conversation and subsequent story, preceding story and subsequent conversation," Tedlock notes, "which are not disjunctive." Tedlock's insistence on the difficulty of beginning as an ordering device is matched, indeed, only by his insistence on its companion, its mirror image: "But now that I have managed to get us into the story, I don't know how to get us out of it! " And if he cannot stay true to his first dilemma, of not knowing where to begin without giving us a paper which is merely a succession of false starts—and surely this one is not—he can and does remain true to his second dilemma, whether he wishes it or not, whether he knows it or not, because we make a Cheshire cat exit, slipping by the low key mechanics of Quiché lexicology into a drifting Heideggerianism. Like old soldiers, Tedlock's paper does not die, it merely fades away.

In between the elaborated, delayed, italicized, almost caesarean nature of his entry and the diminuendo of his ghostly exit, Tedlock gives us a story so brief and exiguous that it is understandable that at least one anthropologist decided that there were no stories among the Quiché Maya. Anyway, in short—and that does seem the proper phrase—in short, about 40 years ago, a Mexican merchant left home to sell some blankets in San Francisco but finished in jail because he lacked the necessary papers and also because, in Sherlock Holmes's famous words, he saw, but did not observe, that a squirrel crossed his path from right to left just a few miles from home. In one sense, this could be a most unfair collapse of Tedlock's minor tale; a similar collapse might render *Romeo and Juliet* as boy sees girl, boy gets girl, boy loses girl. But, not really, not really. The Quiché tale occupies only a short paragraph or, if we follow Tedlock's contention from his earlier articles that oral prose literature is perhaps more sensibly approached as poetry, it occupies about 45 lines. Surely, this is no accident; it is not an embarrassing example of a narrated, near non-event. If Tedlock's earlier exposition of Zuni material is a reasonable prelude to this paper, then paralinguistics is the issue that he has in mind; the need to see text as performance, the insistence that "that's all she wrote" is an inadequate guide unless we know quite how she said it. And what better instance of reaffirming that repetition is no accident, that silence is 40 percent of speech, that narrative is but a pale representation of narration, that primitive prose is but native poetry, than to present for our inspection an item which preoccupation with content cannot easily be an obstacle to perception of form.

At this point, I conclude that not only does Tedlock have two companions in his quandary, Foucault and the Maya tale-teller, he also has two extra problems. How to begin and how to end are epiphenomenal problems which arise from the problems of what to put in and what to leave out. And these primary problems of inclusion and exclusion are common problems for both Tedlock and his Maya story-teller. Now, in Tedlock's case, we can solve the problem by returning to his writings elsewhere in the *Journal of American Folklore* and *Alcheringa,* for example, and there we can discover his overriding concern with paralinguistics as an essential element of oral literature, with *how* things are said as well as, and if necessary, *rather than,* with what things are written. This is an established tradition to be sure, which stretches from Buffon's 18th century observation that the style is the man himself, to McLuhan's 20th century insistence that the medium is the message by way of whatever post-Buffon pre-McLuhan writer noted that it "t'aint what you do, it's the way that you do it."

In the Maya story-teller's case, the problem resolves itself into the question of audience. It is this construct of audience which I find both necessary and missing in Tedlock's rendering of Maya renderings of stories. This construct may be the key to why some anthropologists supposedly thought there were no Maya stories. The question is not the situational question of the audience; we all know that unless any person is to be derided and ultimately committed, they require an audience before they tell a tale. It is the functional or operational question of audience, that is, how much does an audience need to know if, that is, it is to understand a given story and, thus, to allow a person to be recognizably a story-teller. Audience, in fact, seems to me to be the crucial question posed by Tedlock's paper: are the problems of reading, like the problems of hearing, questions of what is a requisite or perceived or available audience? How far are the functions of critic and audience commensurate; and, what happens to an artist who searches for an audience but finds only critics? Is this statement unfair to critics? And, do artists create audiences or is it only that critics, by interposing, create audiences? The issue of audience is posed by Tedlock because he insists that the manner in which things are said is a significant parameter of their existence, and, in that sense, he notes that the structuralist assumption that any translation will serve, is very disturbing: things are not said; people say things. In this way, statements of any sort must be seen as performative utterances. They are manifestations of performance. This, reassuringly, touches a major concern of the behavioral sciences, especially of social anthropology, for a choice between the act as given, standardized, homogenized, artifact and the act as performance—better or worse, more or less relevant or convincing or effective.

Presumably, in the telling of a tale, the act is audience influenced in the same way that in a performance of a role, the performance is audience influenced. Narrative, then, through the act of narration, becomes a form of behavior, rather than a form of literature, and, in its use of or need for an audience, it becomes an interactive form of behavior, a conversation. In that sense, literature in its contemporary written form has only an audience as victim, the audience gets told; it cannot, Tedlock reminds us, even move its lips. It has no audience as respondent, as participant and to that extent the problem of reading must be solved not just by readers, but by writers in deciding what the people they write for need to know. So, insofar as literature, at least in the form of Maya narrative is a vector of outcome of three things, an author, a message and an audience, what we still need to know about is the audience and how the performance changes with the audience and how much the fact that the audience is a Heisenbergian Tedlock and not just another Maya makes this performance of the narrative what it is. That is, how much what the narrator needs to narrate is a function of what the audience needs to know.

SUNY-Binghamton

Wilhelm Worringer and the Polarity of Understanding

W. Wolfgang Holdheim

1. Worringer Revisited

Abstraction and Empathy, the young Wilhelm Worringer's doctoral dissertation of 1908, is very much a classic now. Written as a strictly scholarly attempt to correct the one-sidedness of the aesthetics then current, propelled into prominence overnight, it soon found itself in the position of a manifesto heralding the powerful modern trends towards abstract art. The monograph's influence became ever more pervasive and also spread to the Anglo-Saxon world, where it had an impact, among others, on literary theorizing. This impact, in fact, is what mostly concerns me here.

Let me nevertheless start by returning to Worringer himself—a movement I propose to execute again and again in the course of these deliberations. A classic, unfortunately, is cited more than read. A manifesto, on its part, tends to be simplified and distorted for the glory of a cause. Imagine then what it means to have written a classic manifesto! Of course it has lately become a commonplace that parricidally adaptatory misreading is the earmark of creativity. I would, therefore, be content with leaving this early-century work to its distortedly canonized fate, were it not for my sneaking suspicion that it still looms larger than many a recent world-shaking opus. Worringer's fruitfulness has simply not been exhausted by his progeny, and he comes closer to certain overriding modern problems than many of his successors, semi-successors, anti-successors. Beyond them, we have to reach back to the ancestor; the creative parricide should for once be matched by a liberating infanticide. The ideas of this classic bear interpretation and expansion in ways that have hitherto not been sufficiently noticed. But first, let us effect a brief *retour aux sources.*

The duality proclaimed by the title is by now well-known and self-explanatory; we also speak of idioplastic as against physioplastic art. On the one hand, there is the urge to naturalistic, lifelike, organic creation—on the other, the impulsion towards non-naturalistic, even non-figurative and linear-geometric patterns, tending to the inorganic and devitalized. In 1908, the naturalistic ideal had been dominant ever since the Renaissance, so that its concomitant aesthetics of empathy (of human self-recognition and participation), then most prominently represented by Theodor Lipps, had come to consider itself as the quintessence of all aesthetics. Non-naturalist art had sunk to the status of an as yet imperfect approximation, vitiated by deficient technical know-how. Worringer followed his compatriot Alois Riegl in rejecting this naïve materialistic determinism: know-how is less a cause than a result, is itself the expression of an "absolute artistic intention." Abstract art is not an aberration or a deficiency but reflects a positive impulse to abstract, devitalize, distantiate. Two radically opposed artistic intentions have been active in the history of art.

What we have, then, is a polarity. Worringer was not, as he is sometimes made out to be, a fervent proponent or a propagandist of geometric linearity. Naturally, its restoration to autonomous significance could not go without some emphasis. Yet he kept his balance, and even a refreshingly undogmatic uncertainty, reflected in the unsure historical status assigned to the abstracting urge. Is it in the first place the universal beginning of art, to be replaced by naturalism in the normal course of development? Or is it on principle an alternative to empathy at all times? We sense a peculiar vacillation here. To be sure, Worringer was well aware that the impulse to create geometric forms is not a specialty of primitives: we have had Egypt and Byzantium, and some rather odd ultra-moderns as well. The question was how such revivals of the anti-vital are to be evaluated. One thing on which this art historian never ceased insisting is the irremediably pristine character of primitive art. In his preface to the re-edition of 1959, he violently defended his thesis of the abstract origins of art against the discovery of seemingly naturalistic cave drawings from the Ice Age.[1] And in an essay of 1954 he took issue with the modern penchant for adopting the archaic, which cannot be properly revived in a contemporary context.[2] On the other hand, Worringer had great admiration for the civilized variants of the abstract style. He tried to avoid the potential conflict between an evolutionary and a radically polar conception by shifting the problem to the level of religion and epistemology, where the two perspectives could be accorded in an ultimately polar sense. Naturalistic, organicizing art is that of men who follow immanent religions, who feel at home in the world and at ease as to its knowability. The urge for abstraction comes to those who live in a disquieting world they do not understand. Worringer describes their anguish as a "spiritual dread of space" [*geistige Raumscheu*], comparable to the physical state of agoraphobia.[3] This is the instinctual state of mind of the primitive, but it also characterizes the wisdom of the Oriental which transcends mere rational knowledge: here lies the link between primitivism and mystical sophistication. And a similar insecurity is bound to recur in the epistemological skepticism of a post-Kantian age (*AE,* pp. 29-30, 122 ff.; *G,* pp. 75-76, 167 ff.).

In his desire for spiritual security, the epistemological skeptic seeks to fixate the data of experience, stripping them of everything uncertain, contingent, temporal. We should note that this, for Worringer, entails a suppression of spatial representation, whereas Anglo-Saxon literary theory has on the contrary seen space as the quintessence of the abstracting urge. The contradiction, of course, is largely terminological. For the art historian, unconcerned with literature, the opposition does not run between a sequence of words and a contiguity of images, but (*within* the realm of images) between three-dimensional space and the two-dimensional plane. Three-dimensionality involves a succession of perceptory moments that need combining; it suggests time values, depth dimensions that call for an active, subjective, in fact an empathizing participation of the viewer (*AE,* pp. 21-22; *G,* pp. 56-57). Worringer would speak of "planification" where Joseph Frank refers to "spatial form." At least this should make us question, from the outset, the conceptual precision of the widespread spatial metaphor.[4]

As for empathy, it does not represent (as is sometimes mistakenly assumed) an impure mixture, an influx of non-artistic values and impulsions. Naturalism (Worringer is categorical on that point) is genuinely artistic. He never tires of warning us against confusing it with imitation. Its purpose is not to approximate organic reality, but to provoke the joy which we derive from vitalizing the lines and rhythms of living organicity. The empathy which organic art invites is described by Lipps as "objectified self-enjoyment" (*AE,* p. 28; *G,* p. 63).

The term, admittedly, sounds suspect to a contemporary ear. It smacks of subjectivism. Still worse, it dangerously skirts a widespread definition of cheap art: Kitsch throws us back upon our self-enjoyment, functions as a pretext for the delicious ruminations of our private feelings. But this is not Worringer's meaning at all. The naturalistic work does not invite passive sentimentality: it *demands* from us ("mutet uns zu") a markedly dynamic, voluntaristic activity. Self-enjoyment is "inner motion, inner life, inner self-activation," it is (in Lipps's words) "volitional activity, striving or willing *in motu* (*AE,* p. 5; *G,* p. 37). Indeed in Worringer's conception (and let us keep this firmly in mind!), viewer participation is the exclusive characteristic of the aesthetics of empathy. He would never dream, for example, of relating the increasing modern insistence on the reader's collaboration to the abstractive urge, which by definition favors a contemplative stance. Nor is that "objectified" self-enjoyment meant to be subjectivistic. What I project into the object (life, striving, inner dynamism) is general in nature, and I grasp and enjoy it through the object alone. There is, in fact, an element of self-alienation here which briefly leads to a new artistic monism: both in the vitalism of empathy and in the anti-vitalism of abstraction we free ourselves from our individual being, so that all art is ultimately a way to lose ourselves (*AE,* pp. 23-25; *G,* pp. 58-60). No doubt Schopenhauer loomed so large in 1908 that he had to pop out at some point. But the monistic temptation remains a passing remark—luckily, for the importance of Worringer's thought lies in his *polarity* of artistic forms.

Still the Schopenhauerian strain should remind us that Worringer wrote at a certain period and has to be evaluated in its context. He wrote in an overall tradition of historicism, committed to the concept of period styles, at a moment when materialism in art history had begun to be thoroughly shaken by Riegl's theories on artistic intentions. He also moved in the giant shadow of Wilhelm Dilthey. In his late preface of 1959, he described his enterprise (very much in Diltheyan terms) as "a method of cognition primarily oriented towards the psychology of forms and the history of ideas" (*G,* p. 18; my translation). The latter orientation is easily spotted in those global connections made with world views and religions, in those huge ramifications (always thought-provoking but often too sweeping) to which *Geistesgeschichte* has accustomed us. The other aspect is perhaps more interesting from our perspective. The very epithet "form-psychologisch" seems to imply an objective dimension which removes the taint of "psychologism." Does a spearation between the subjectively psychological and the objectively formal, between the subject and object of knowledge, in fact still seem adequate here? "The form of an object is always its formation by me, by my inner activity. *It is a fundamental fact of all psychology,* and most certainly of all aesthetics, that an 'object given as a sensory datum' is strictly speaking an absurdity—something that does not and cannot exist. In existing for me—and such objects alone can be at issue—it is permeated by my activity, by my inner life." Thus Lipps as quoted by Worringer, who adds: "This apperception is therefore by no means random and arbitrary but is necessarily connected with the object" (*AE,* pp. 6-7; *G,* p. 39; italics mine). Lipps and Worringer were not epistemologists, but they here seem to be groping for a new conception of knowledge in which the putative "givenness" of the object is inseparable from the intentionality of the cognitive act. Did Worringer know Husserl's early work? The term "phenomenological" seems not to have been at his disposal. But it occasionally happens to the great (and to them alone—the epigones invariably have the opposite problem) that the implications of their thought outstrip their vocabulary. Let us remember this next time we stumble over Worringer's determination of empathy as "enjoyment," lest we be deterred (to our disadvantage) by the old-fashioned narrowness of the term.

2. From Abstraction to Spatialization

A re-emergence of abstractionist tendencies characterized the modernist movement in the arts, and in literature as well. An exhaustive account of this development is out of the question here. I shall concentrate on a very limited number of theorists influenced by Worringer, mainly in the Anglo-Saxon tradition, who exemplify how a master's thesis can be inflected and modified.

It is unavoidable to mention the publicist T. E. Hulme, the first in England to discover Worringer (whom he met in 1913). While primarily concerned with the fine arts and philosophy, he was also the first to see that the new perspective might have implications for literature. Also, Hulme stood strategically in the middle of diverse consequential movements: imagism in literature, modernism in art, right-wing antiromanticism in the history of ideas. It is the centrality of his position, not its depth or cogency, which induces me to discuss him here. Like most polemicists a *terrible simplificateur,* he was never able to weld his various interests into a coherent whole. Of course he was still young when he was killed in World War I, and one can only speculate whether his work (had he been permitted to live) would have been less fragmentary and immature.

Symptomatically, some of Hulme's most finished studies are résumés of the thoughts of others. He himself describes his essay on "Modern Art and Its Philosophy" as "practically an abstract of Worringer's views."[5] Such it is, and a very lucid one. Hulme only adds the diagnosis of an abstracting trend in modern art, the harbinger of a change in sensibility. He predicts that archaicizing tendencies will prove to be a mere stage in this development, and that the geometric art of the future will approximate the mechanical principles of modern machinery.

In "Humanism and the Religious Attitude" (1915), the tone changes. The point of departure is Worringer's thesis that post-Renaissance art (as distinct from certain abstract pre-Renaissance styles) has been naturalistic, and that this distinction reflects radically different views of life. But this discovery now becomes a challenge to take sides. The post-Renaissance *Weltanschauung* is humanistic, and humanism believes in man's goodness and perfectibility and would give him freedom to develop. This view, however, is quite simply wrong. The re-emergence of abstraction heralds the end of Western humanism and the return of religion, which (knowing about Original Sin) insists on the necessity of geometric order and discipline.

Of course this essentially political anti-humanism is miles away from Worringer. With hindsight, we can relate it to a number of still rather playful authoritarian and proto-fascist trends that emerged at that time. It was the period of right-wing condottieri such as T. E. Lawrence and Ernst Jünger. If in fact we connect Hulme's anti-humanism with his admiration for the abstract charms of machinery, we could find some affinity with Jünger's book *Der Arbeiter* (1932), that immediately pre-Nazi annunciation of a new post-humanist, post-bourgeois and pseudo-Nietzschean mechanical man. The ironically inclined student of intellectual history might be amused that a quite similar pseudo-Nietzschean anti-humanism now rears its head, convinced that it represents the last word of left-wing revolutionism! But these are filiations that might have lain in Hulme's unfulfilled future. The politico-literary masters he chose for himself in his present were Pierre Lasserre and Charles Maurras, of *l'Action française,* who considered themselves as humanists. Hulme made some efforts to relate their duality of "Romanticism and Classicism"[6] to the one he adapted from Worringer. Romanticism is damp, sloppy, neurotic; it sees man, foolishly, as a reservoir of great possibilities: we recognize the anti-romanticism of a period which is also that of Irving Babbitt. But how to equate this recent movement with the entire humanist epoch? It is humanism in its definitive horror, when it no longer flaunts elements of greatness that still spilled over from an earlier religious era: Michelangelo was destined to turn into Greuze. But the other pole, that of abstraction, defies even such Procrustean arrangements. How to relate classicism to the mosaics of Byzantium or the pyramids of Egypt, and how to get around the fact that it is (on the contrary) the very soul of the *non*-geometric humanist tradition? [7] Hulme does not as much as try. Classicism is dry, hard, and accurate; it is aware of man's finiteness and of the need to subject him to discipline: that is the vague and disappointing upshot of his views. The disciple of Worringer cannot merge with the disciple of Lasserre.

It seems only fair to cite a more effective exponent of committed abstractionism, whose manifesto on the subject has become a classic in its own right. I am referring to Ortega y Gasset's "Dehumanization of Art" (1925).[8] The new art is unpopular in its essence: the right-wing perspective is less virulent than Hulme's but occasionally takes on an unfortunate snobbish hue. The references to those clever young people under thirty whose tenderly barbarous sensibility can no longer bear the romantic-realist heritage are sometimes a little hard to take. But the polemical simplification of Worringer here acquires an unequaled cutting edge.

It is evident in the very title. For all its Spenglerian suggestion of rejuvenating barbarism, the term "dehumanization" contains the true essence of Worringer's abstraction. It means distancing, deforming and stylizing reality, wrenching it out of human measure. It means annulling vital spontaneity, destroying the subjective, replacing unconscious emotion by intellectual lucidity. Dehumanization is the quintessence of the aesthetic, "a seeing pleasure."[9] Ortega finds it in art, in literature, even in music, where Debussy represents the *nec plus ultra* of aesthetic purity. In Wagner, on the contrary, we have the peak of melodrama—but precisely that peak is toppling over into its opposite: "the human voice has already ceased to be the protagonist and is drowned in the cosmic din of the orchestra." The observation points forward to Adrian Leverkühn, that coldly distant incarnation of modernism, rejecting the "cow warmth" of the human voice! [10]

Even Ortega, however, does not entirely come to terms with the status of romantic-realistic art. Ideally it seems to be an aberration of taste based on psychic contagion, essentially non-artistic, so that geometric aestheticism would be simply a return to art as such.[11] But this monistic tendency alternates with the reaffirmation of an artistic polarity. The vacillation causes a certain amount of unclarity at times. Ultimately, it is the polarity which prevails, and this in a peculiarly dialectical form that gives an important new twist to the question. Ortega suggests a historical dialectic in which abstract art is essentially an iconoclastic reaction against a preceding art of organic forms—a view which comes close to contemporary Formalist theories of defamiliarization and which actually makes Ortega contradict Worringer by affirming the historical primacy of naturalism.[12] Elsewhere, even more interestingly, Ortega insists that even the individual work is an act of dehumanization rather than a representation of inhumanity, implying an active tension between the two poles of artistic experience.[13] There is, then, no complete absence of human substance; it is there to be neutralized.

In the Anglo-Saxon tradition, the abstractive tendency in literature culminates in Joseph Frank's essay on "Spatial Form in Modern Literature" (1945). Frank starts by arguing that the distinction in Lessing's *Laokoon* between the "time art" of literature and the plastic "space arts" is too rigid. Just as Worringer has shown time values to emerge in three-dimensional plasticity, literature can (and modern literature does) transcend the sequential character of its linguistic medium in a movement towards "spatial form." The space-time duality has here been elevated into a universal category, expanding and replacing the polarity of abstraction and empathy. This expansion is singularly tempting. Does it not conjure up memories of Kant and Bergson, and transport us into untold depths of philosophical discourse? Let us, however, determine from the outset that this impression is illusory in the present case. Lessing's distinction runs between words sounding in succession and images coexisting in simultaneity, and Frank merely liberalizes the possible localization of these poles but leaves them untouched in their definition. "Time" remains mere succession, "space" mere contiguity—and both are skeletal abstractions, ideal gauges without claim to existential reality, as formal and schematic as Rousseau's natural state or Condillac's statue, very much in the analytic manner of the 18th century. Even in everyday life, we continually undercut the formal sequentiality of speech, and our visual perception is never quite simultaneous. Confusion must result if such rudimentary notions of time and space are applied to the realities of modern literature!

Yet literature does tend to counteract sequentiality in a more intensive way than everyday speech, and to that extent Frank's demonstration is potentially valuable. It first centers on imagist poetry, but what interests me here is its truly original contribution: Frank finds the quest for spatial form in the very novel, the realm of narrative itself and therefore (one would say) of time. His pages on *Madame Bovary, Ulysses* and Proust's *Temps perdu* are well-known. Has it ever been noticed, however, that his conclusions on Joyce and Proust simply do not follow from his demonstration, that what he proves differs markedly from what he thinks he proves?

Frank shows how Flaubert, in the country fair scene of *Madame Bovary,* cinematographically cuts back and forth between three juxtaposed levels of simultaneous action. He considers this a spatialization of form, since the temporal flow is time and again displaced by a reflexive interplay of relationships between separate units of meaning. Of course these are merely interruptions of an overall coherent sequence, so that Frank is actually describing a dynamic tension between narrative progression and "spatializing" reflexivity. He knows this without emphasizing it, for what matters to him is the second pole alone: the emergence of a "spatializing" trend that will (so he thinks) gain out completely in Joyce and Proust.

Ulysses is a huge collection of chronologically unconnected cross-references, a total fragmentation of narrative sequence. Flaubert's new technique has here become universal, contiguity has triumphed over the last remnants of "time." This at least is the superficial conclusion, and it is adopted (I am afraid) by Joseph Frank. And yet he knows that the chaos is not meant to remain untouched. The reader is supposed to weave the disjected fragments into a coherent whole. Is this reconstruction perchance "spatial" in nature? This seems to be what Frank would have us believe. The reader tinkers like a mechanic, assembles the parts of the puzzle until he attains a "unified spatial apprehension" of the totality.[14] But here we run into the almost infinite obscurantist potentialities of the concept of "space." Let us discard it for a moment. For Worringer, as we recall, the viewer's (for us: reader's) collaboration always pertains to empathy, never to abstraction. In *Ulysses,* the reader is forced to active empathy, and Frank unwittingly states this in the strongest terms. Does he not actually inform us that "at the conclusion of the novel, . . . Joyce literally wanted the reader to *become* a Dubliner"?[15] Only in this way can he acquire that knowledge of the whole which is needed to understand the parts. Reading *Ulysses,* therefore, is an accretion of experience. This is not mechanical tinkering but hermeneutic understanding! The whole which the reader gets to know (which he grows into) is not an abstract geometric structure but a concrete configuration, a *Gestalt,* an organism.[16] It is the living organism of *Ulysses* with its nuances of time and narrativity, quite irreducible to such a thing as sheer succession; the *Gestalt* of Dublin with its historical perspectives, quite irreducible to such a thing as pure chronology. What Frank actually demonstrates is that the tension between "time" and "space" (between the organic and the inorganic) is even more extreme here than in *Madame Bovary,* since Joyce's technique of contiguity goads the reader into an aggressive temporalizing, organicizing role. How could there be a "unified spatial apprehension" of such a long and complex work? It has been said about the *Zauberberg* that it evolves in time even though it aspires to entire presence at every moment. Frank would have been well advised to discuss the *Zauberberg*—but it will probably remain forever impossible to bring home to an Anglo-Saxon critic that any comparison between Joyce and Proust should include Thomas Mann as *tertium comparationis.*

Frank's account of Proust exemplifies his fallacy even more clearly. Proust supposedly "spatializes" by juxtaposing snapshots of characters from various periods, culminating in the party in *Le Temps retrouvé* where the narrator (meeting his acquaintances after many years) encounters images which bear Time on their faces like a visible mask. But isn't it quite obvious that this alienating presentation of discontinuity jolts the narrator (and the reader) into an explicitly temporalizing act of empathy—restoring the line of narration that has been interrupted, the lapse of time that has been skipped?[17] There is still more imprecision to come! It appears that Marcel's quasi-mystical experiences of the "petite madeleine" type, in which the past is revived in the present, are somehow of the same kind (viz., spatial) as those passages where past and present are juxtaposed. Having conquered time, Proust wants the reader to repeat the process.[18] An uncontrollable fusion is equated with a deliberate juxtaposition, a lyrical experience of timelessness grounded in the involuntary memory is identified with a voluntaristic restoration of the narrative lapse of time. Decidedly, confusion cannot go much further, and the concept of "spatiality" can accommodate any contradiction at all! In reality, of course, Proust's work is built on the ironic contrast between a passive lyrical experience and a narrativity reinforced by the fact that it is partly a challenge to the reader. Abstraction (in the sense of discontinuity) functions as a spur for an exacerbated empathizing, temporalizing effort. We have the same dialectic as before.

Frank is not any more convincing when, at the end of his essay, he reaffirms the "spatiality" of *Ulysses* from a completely different perspective: juxtaposing the ancient and the modern, Joyce (like Eliot and Pound) robs history of its historicity and propels us into the timeless world of myth.[19] I am not certain if such a happy result can accrue from a museum-like accumulation of past objects. Nietzsche warned us against decadent historical antiquarianism, and it might be some distance between the fatigue of decadence and the pristine youth of myth. Of course we are here touching upon a pervasive modern nostalgia, a quest for "private myths" (formulated by the German romantic critics) which are struggling to emerge in the midst of contemporary reality. But it would be rash to speak of "spatialization," for every dialectic cuts two ways. The appearance of the timeless in the contemporary is not only a mythologization of realism, it is also, conversely, a temporalization of myth.

3. The Reaction of Temporality

In Joseph Frank's essay, influential despite its contradictions, inspirations that ultimately came from Worringer have shrunk into spearheads of a "spatializing" modernism. One could expect a reaction of injured temporality, as radical as the provocation, emanating from the modern philosophy of existence. And this attack, indeed, has been vigorously pressed by William Spanos. My account, unfortunately, cannot do full justice either to the complexity of the philosophical issues or to the evolution of Spanos' position which—starting under the impact of French existentialism—has developed into a systematic expansion of Heideggerian ideas, in a veritable *retour aux sources.*[20]

Spanos's point of departure is the existential analytic of *Being and Time* which shows how *Dasein* deals with its radical temporality, revealed to it in the anguishing experience of uncanniness or homelessness (*das Unheimliche*), in the sense of being thrown into a boundless world. *Angst* is dread of *nothing,* and "nothing" is time; *Dasein,* therefore, is here thrown back upon the state of potentiality that characterizes its authentic being-in-the-world. Fear, on the other hand, is transitive: one fears *something,* the nothingness of time is solidified into a determinate thing. This transformation of dread into fear is paradigmatic for the way in which *Dasein* evades its temporality. Absence is reified into presence, a *telos* is from the outset imposed upon the boundless flux. And this inauthenticity of everyday existence is paralleled by the development of metaphysics in the Western tradition ever since the classical Greek philosophers. Man is the animal endowed with *logos*—but "logos" (originally the living fluidity of "speech") soon hardened into such determinations as "judgment" or "reason." The conception of truth implied by "judgment" is one where the mind corresponds with the object of knowledge. "Knowledge," then, has here contracted into an "object" (an autonomous presence cut off from all existential temporal contexts) viewed from a distance by an observer. Thus the primary mode of experiencing entities (that of *Zu-*

handenheit, availability) is replaced by a derivative ontology of sheer presence (*Vorhandenheit*), which sees entities as being simply and neutrally there. A logic of propositions reflects that triumph of neutral presence. Behind it all, there comes to stand the concept of *logos* as Divine Word, God, *nunc stans,* permanent presence—guarantor of a reality where things can be viewed teleologically from the end. Spanos contends that this entire complex of contraction, hardening, objectification, reification is in effect a spatialization of time, its planification into an image as in the visual arts. The Cartesian radicalization of this development shows it clearly: the Divine Word there becomes the aggressive *logos* of human subjectivity; the duality of subject and object is pushed to the utmost; and the world is flattened into a "world picture" (*Weltbild*) of objects existing in a contiguity of sheer presence, manipulable as a system of mathematically determined coordinates.[21]

Now Spanos posits a parallel spatialization of literary criticism since the Greeks. It proceeds, roughly, in two stages. The first, effective into modern times, is that of Aristotelianism: dread is exorcized by catharsis; the plot, adopting the teleological perspective of Western philosophy, proceeds according to a detective mentality which views everything in terms of a pre-known *telos.* Thus time is spatialized, reality reassuringly transformed into an autotelic whole.[22] The modernist movement (from symbolism and imagism to neocriticism and, finally, structuralism) merely radicalizes this spatializing trend.[23] It constitutes the end, the fulfillment of the Western literary tradition, parallel to the end of metaphysics diagnosed by Heidegger—and the German philosopher's move to transcend spatial metaphysics should in its turn be paralleled by a post-modernist literary hermeneutic of temporality.[24]

Note that Spanos follows Frank, whom he reverses but unfortunately takes very much by his word. He even reaffirms Lessing's original, purely medial distinction, defending it against Frank's prudent criticism: literature *is* temporal by virtue of its medium. Isn't it really quite a jump from Lessing's formal sequentiality of language to Heidegger's ontological temporality of *Dasein?*[25] The categories are space and time, not abstraction and empathy, and the entire Western tradition has become one of covert or overt spatiality. Such a global conception is well served by Frank's generously imprecise conceptuality. Forgotten is Worringer's demonstration of an alternation of styles, and the fact that he wrote (after all) against the domination of a classical aesthetics which in Spanos' perspective would have to be inverted into a "spatial" one. But Spanos does not acknowledge this shift from Worringer to Frank. He treats their two polarities as identical and blames the art-historian for his commitment to an antitemporal Gnostic-Platonic prejudice—an over-interpretation due, I think, to an overly Hulmean perspective. Above all, however, he criticizes both authors for ignoring a third option which cuts across the other two and goes as far back as Shakespeare, Dürer, Dostoevsky: man's urge for a head-on encounter with the temporality of his existence.[26] A triad is supposed to replace the polarity of artistic intentions.

Originally, Spanos views this third possibility in the terms suggested by Sartre's essays around 1940: the work draws in the reader, makes him partake in its own tormented time. Increasingly, this process is seen as hermeneutic in the specific sense—as a dialogue of the reader with the text.[27] Spanos's attack against spatiality here runs parallel to Gadamer's exhaustive critique of the aesthetic differentiation. Then more and more, Spanos has come to view absurdist literature as the alpha and omega of Heideggerian temporality: it disorients the reader, throws him back upon his uncanny homelessness, and forces him to take upon himself the potentialities (the nothingness) of his dreadful freedom.

Let me object, first of all, to erecting the "existential option" into a third autonomous artistic urge. The ultimate fruitfulness of Worringer's thought lies precisely in his discovery of an artistic polarity, and we should not discard it simply because we no longer agree with all its details. This is, rather, where he should be updated—in accordance, I submit, with the deeper implications of his thought. We should correct the *geistesgeschichtliche* oversimplification which makes him relate abstraction alone to existential homelessness. His conception of empathy (taken over from Lipps) is too harmonious, too enjoyable, too Winckelmannian. But Worringer's own work contains the germs of an extension. Empathy is connected with temporal depth dimensions and demands active efforts on the viewer's part. I was able to trace it in the dynamic restoration of narrativity to the modern novel. Expanded in accordance with its inherent possibilities, "empathy" is broad enough to accommodate temporality, even in the more or less tormented form of the existential option. Worringer's polarity is ultimately that of abstracting distantiation and concretizing participation.

In choosing our favorite mode of participation, let us not overstress the literature of the absurd. Is it really the ideal "dialogue" to be incessantly prodded, jolted, and provoked? Clarifying an issue amongst equal partners—that is the model of hermeneutically fruitful discourse, and I fail to see how it is best served by transforming the text into an *enfant terrible.* The latter's task, for one thing, is terribly easy. How do I know if he is authentic and not merely snotty? Spanos himself suggests that the line between genuine and false absurdism is sometimes hard to draw.[28] What, in effect, is "temporal" and what is "spatial" here? Thus Georg Lukács attacks the modernistic theater and novel as decadent, descriptive, immobilizing (i.e., spatial), in the name of an aesthetics of temporal empathy. The parallel with Spanos's position is patent, although the latter would reject Lukács's kind of temporality because of its Aristotelianism. But what about Brecht's insistence that his "epic theater" jolts the spectator into critical activity? Isn't this a case of the absurdist procedure working in markedly distantiating, abstracting, "spatializing" ways? And what essential difference is there, really, between the absurdist's prodding and Joyce's "spatial" efforts to goad us into cooperation?

Possibly these questions could be answered, though with the aid of taxonomic exertions so infinitely subtle as to be almost unmanageable. Let us concede, therefore, the ideal existence of a genuine absurdist literature, however hard to define, appealing to a reader's temporality. But what kind of temporality is here presupposed? Only the bare outline of a Heideggerian one. We never live in a state of sheer dread, in the unadulterated mode of "being thrown" (*Geworfenheit*) to which the true absurdist would reduce us. *Angst, Unheimlichkeit, Geworfenheit* are limit concepts, non-transferable in their pure form to the ontic domain in which literature operates, in fact partial even on the ontological level. We never revolve in an aimless void. Surely the mode of instrumental availability (*Zuhandenheit*) is suffused with finalism. The future towards which we live is contingent but not vacuous, our possibilities are never empty but have the shape of partly realizable and partly unrealizable projects. Rejecting metaphysical teleology should not lead to the fallacy of denying the authenticity of all *teloi.* Being-in-the-world is not *Geworfenheit* but *geworfener Entwurf,* and only heuristically can the two be separated. There is no disorientation without orientation, just as the very notion of absurdity makes sense only in terms of understanding. Authentic dread is not a fixed point of departure but something that shines through our purposive activities, as a pervasive *idée de derrière.*[29] Absurd literature seems to split this unitary complex into a mechanical two-step process: the text takes care of the *Geworfenheit,* the reader is requested to supply the *Entwurf.* As an experiment this is justified, though it resembles a philosophical demonstration—but it remains an enterprise of a very specialized kind. And this simplifying anatomical division of temporality may prove to be more prone to clichéification than Aristotelianism ever was.

Let us, for that matter, not be too hard on the detective mentality of the Aristotelian plot. It has proved subject to automatization but cannot be rejected from the outset. The detectory schema is, after all, a metaphor for understanding, that basic mode of our being-in-the-world. It may reflect a teleological metaphysics because the work is written from the end—but isn't this the very essence of literature? The literary universe is theistic, teleological, has a godlike author, even when he tries to conceal the fact.[30] Praxis is an interaction of form and chaos (if must be: of "space" and "time"). So is the literary work—only that form is primary. Life is a constant effort to shape the flux of things; in literature, the recreation of that experience always has an element of make-believe. Reality is a continual formalization of chaos; literature even at its most existentially "temporal" has something of a deliberate chaotization of form. This is revealed in the process of rereading, a possibility not given in the realm of praxis, and an experience that a radical existentialist aesthetics of temporality usually has trouble accounting for. Spanos tries to equate rereading with the comprehension of first reading and even of oral discourse, which also involve a tentative prevision of the whole.[31] But there is a qualitative difference between hearing and rereading, between the modifiable whole of hermeneutic fore-understanding and the gradually clarified organism of artistic form. Each expert rereading brings deeper insight into the artificial organism's complex workings. A great work will never be reduced to complete transparency, it will always maintain a tension between recognition and surprise. But that tension will shift its emphasis, become more knowing with each increase in recognition, and (with its growing sophistication) more acute. To be sure, the reader is to let the text speak to him—but every dialogue presupposes a correct evaluation of its context, and the good critic knows that literature invites a dialogue of a special (and an especially complex) kind.

Again we encounter a dialectic of participation and distantiation, foreshadowed in some way by Ortega's notion of a dehumanization of the human. Nor would Worringer be startled by such an idea—didn't he view Gothic art as an empathizing of the abstract? I think that his polarity still passes the test of validity and usefulness. In fact I believe that it cuts still more deeply than has hitherto been indicated, reaching (beyond art and literature) into the problem of knowledge and understanding itself.

4. The Polarity of Understanding

Correlating art and knowledge is nothing new. There is, of course, the perennial question whether history is a science or an art. On the other hand, it is almost a commonplace to speak of the elegance of the formulae of science, of the economy and even imaginativeness of its explanations. These perceptions, however, do not go far. The aesthetic side of scientific knowledge is viewed as an ornamental admixture, or perhaps as a purely psychological premise for discovery. The debate on historical cognition takes place on a more systematic level but usually stops short of the depth dimensions into which it should be pushed. Ultimately, Hayden White's recent *Metahistory* is just another example of that fact.[32] It relates the various ways of conceiving history (even the extra-narrative ones) to literary and linguistic models, thus establishing (so it seems) a perfect coincidence of the cognitive and the aesthetic, of the quest for truth with that for form. But upon closer examination, the cognitive urge is not exhausted by the models. In actual fact it is split in two. Behind the knowledge that coincides with the linguistic-rhetorical taxonomies, there lurks an unthematized norm of pure truth, an unacknowledged ideal of supra-aesthetic knowledge, in whose perspective all that carefully classified historical cognition is nothing but literature. The result is a skepticism overcome only, most questionably, by a deliberate self-transcendence of irony.

The reason is that the aesthetic-literary aspect is conceived on a surface level—not as a vital impulsion but very much as a dead butterfly which, pinned to the carton, can be expected to hold still. Those rhetorical and linguistic schemata are reified detriti of literature and language, rigidified into pure objects of perception and description. This, of course, implies an equally pure cognitive subject who transcends the schemata, as the supreme though unexamined norm of truth. Essential discourse does not operate on the level of such derivative abstractions, it is not an object of knowledge but is equi-original with the act of knowing itself. And so is the "aesthetic," which should not be confused with the "artistic."[33] It is the ground in which the artistic can occur and, having occurred, can be rhetorically classified. The homology of art and knowledge is situated in the aesthetico-cognitive ground, not on the taxonomic surface. And Worringer's expert concern with "absolute artistic intentions" has made him penetrate to that depth dimension, his polarity of empathy and abstraction is one of "absolute cognitive intentions" as well.

In abstract art, for example, the experiential datum is stripped of every suggestion of subjectivity, uncertainty, or depth, and depicted as a sheer object, statically autonomous in its material individuality. It is removed from all its contingent natural contexts and shaped or submerged into an inherently necessary geometric form (*AE,* pp. 6-7, 20-21, 22; *G,* pp. 50-51, 55-56, 57). In this particularization and decontextualization, we can hardly fail to recognize the very procedures of theoretical knowledge. Scientific method painstakingly isolates phenomena for the sake of experimental manipulation, transforms them into pure objects of cognition. The fitting Husserlian term for the world of "natural contexts" is *Lebenswelt*—not itself an experience but the ground of all experiences. Its structure is that of a horizon, a shifting and non-thematic background in which specific perceptions are embedded—the very dimension of depth and uncertainty which abstract art wants to abolish and which science would transform into the sum total of thematized objects of experience, ultimately reduced to a system of abstract coordinates. The *Lebenswelt* is also the all-embracing ground of familiarity (*Vertrautheit*) which renders experience possible. But abstract art, born from disorientation, is defamiliarizing, and we immediately see its relation to formalist techniques of estrangement. Now we can also relate it to the horizon-destroying, experience-unhinging stance of theoretical knowledge. Artistic defamiliarization and methodical estrangement have an essential affinity, grounded in the aesthetic polarity's abstractive pole.[34]

Obviously, "empathy" is historical understanding viewed as *Nacherleben,* the imaginative recreation of human experience, expressed in the narrative process of following events as they unfold in time. Against this, there stands an attempt to subject even history (and in fact all "human sciences") to the theoretical mode of knowledge by reducing phenomena to abstract universal laws. Or (in a radicalized but essentially identical effort, a heady mixture of Descartes and Freud) phenomena are dissolved in supposedly underlying unconscious abstract patterns. This conflict in historical epistemology has been going on for many generations and shows no sign of abating. No wonder: it expresses a polarity of understanding ultimately equivalent to Worringer's duality of artistic intentions. Positivist explanation and structuralist reduction are pitted against hermeneutic comprehension, the abstract against the concrete. Etymologically, "concrete" refers to *concresco, concrescere:* "to congeal" or (more originally) "to grow together." Time as it were slows down, various strands of occurrence temporarily grow together, standing in relief (*Hervorhebung*) as meaningful organic configurations called "events."[35] Theoretical knowledge works through *construction* of the abstract, hermeneutic comprehension through *Hervorhebung* of the concrete. Theoretical abstraction is obtained by an *application* of method that is mechanical, manipulatory—*applico, applicare* means to "bring near" or "join to," to move together in space what is spatially apart. Hermeneutic empathy is based on temporal concrescence, and accretion of experience is its aim.

Louis O. Mink speaks of a "theoretical" and a "configurational mode" of comprehension. But he adds a "categoreal mode" which, he insists, is not to be confused with the theoretical: theory "enables us to infer and coordinate a body of true statements about [a] kind of object," whereas "categories . . . determine of what kind those objects may be."[36] I submit that this very formulation casts doubt on the autonomy of categoreal knowledge, by suggesting that the dynamic explanatory impetus of theory is replaced by a merely descriptive stance. Classification can be a guideline, a useful tool of explanation;[37] when it tries to be self-sufficient, it is at best a bloodless copy of theory. It has proved attractive to some in our time, who would like to apply theoretical methods (reductive, imperialistic, manipulative) even to fields where there is little substantially to manipulate. The taxonomic urge, in its auto-manipulative splendor, can at small cost give us the uplifting feeling of being "scientific." Moreover, it can free us from the disquieting realm of experience with its dreadful need for interpretation, since it seems to propel us into a domain of sheer descriptiveness. Of course this is illusory, since interpretation is coextensive with understanding, a basic existential we are unable to shirk. But at least it is safely hidden in the taxonomy, so that we can receive it with averted eyes. How, then, can this activity give us such a profound subjective sense of understanding? But surely we know that there is such a thing as pseudo-understanding. It occurs each time we hear a word (a political slogan or an expression of modish jargon) and are content to accept it at face value. I am describing the *modus operandi* of the cliché—which is, precisely, a formula carrying collectively supplied, stereotypical implications vague enough to serve as an indefinite alloy of self-explanation and built-in interpretation. It can thus substitute itself for the full scope of understanding. And whenever we seek refuge in the mere application of a categoreal system, or for that matter of any autotelic construct abstracted from reality, we merely chichéify on a level of pseudo-sophistication. Self-rewarding taxonomy is not an autonomous, but a degenerated form of knowledge, and we should have no trouble identifying its exact artistic (pseudo-artistic) counterpart: it is known by the name of Kitsch.

There is, then, a *polarity* of understanding. Strictly speaking, the term "understanding" should be reserved for hermeneutic knowledge, but perhaps we should not speak too strictly here. Just as in art, the duality is a dialectic. We do and should use categorizations and methodical estrangements but should keep them at arm's length, flexible, instrumental to the aim of understanding. Alienation is then merely the preparation of a return to self—to a self whose barriers have been extended in the process. An expansion of consciousness: this is the deeper meaning of "objectified self-enjoyment." Admittedly, our *Lebenswelt,* in its very familiarity, is often sufficiently upsetting to tempt us into distantiation: Worringer's diagnosis of "spiritual agoraphobia" has, after all, much to commend it. And our flight from time and experience can all too easily be masked as a desirable triumph of strict "method." But it is our task as intellectuals to carry strictness one step further by seeing through such elaborate auto-masquerades. An ethics (and aesthetics) of temporality is needed. Let us not be minor Alexandrinians. Shunning experience, how could we grow? How could we help along the growth of others? Arrested time is arrested development.

Cornell University

NOTES

1 Wilhelm Worringer, *Abstraktion und Einfühlung: Ein Beitrag zur Stilpsychologie* (München: R. Piper, 1959), pp. 16 ff.

2 "Ars Una?" in Wilhelm Worringer, *Fragen und Gegenfragen: Schriften zum Kunstproblem* (München: R. Piper, 1958), pp. 155 ff.

3 See Wilhelm Worringer, *Abstraction and Empathy: A Contribution to the Psychology of Style,* trans. Michael Bullock (New York: International Univ. Press, 1953), p. 15 (hereafter cited as *AE*). Future quotations from Worringer's book will be taken from this translation, but will occasionally be altered to obtain a closer approximation to the original. In all cases, references will also be given to the German original as cited in footnote 1 above—hereafter cited as *G.* The present reference is found in *G,* p. 49.

4 Frank, incidentally, does point out the terminological difference in "Spatial Form in Modern Literature," in Mark Schorer, Josephine Miles & Gordon McKenzie, *Criticism* (New York: Harcourt Brace, 1958), p. 391. His exposition, uncharacteristically, is somewhat diffuse at this point. Could this be a symptom of the confusion to be referred to further down?

5 T. E. Hulme, *Speculations: Essays on Humanism and The Philosophy of Art* (New York: Harcourt, Brace 1924), p. 82. All Hulme essays referred to are to be found in this edition.

6 I have not been able to determine the date of this essay, but suspect that it was written earlier than the other two ("Modern Art" is dated early 1914, "Humanism" 1915). If so, then the classicism-romanticism duality may date from an earlier period and Hulme might eventually have discarded it. The attempts at a reconciliation of the two polarities (rather weak attempts, to be truthful) are chiefly found in the "Humanism" essay.

7 Hulme acknowledges this in passing on p. 54 (in "Humanism").

8 In José Ortega y Gasset, *The Dehumanization of Art and Other Writings on Art and Culture* (Garden City, N.Y.: Doubleday, 1956), pp. 1 ff.

9 Ortega, *The Dehumanization of Art,* p. 25.

10 Ortega's quotation on p. 27 of his book. Leverkühn, of course, goes still one step further at the end, finding his way back via the orchestra to expressivity and lament.

11 Ortega, *The Dehumanization of Art,* pp. 23, 25.

12 Ortega, *The Dehumanization of Art,* pp. 38, 40-41.

13 Ortega, *The Dehumanization of Art,* p. 21. Of course the emphasis lies very heavily on the dehumanizing pole.

14 Frank, "Spatial Form," p. 385.

15 Frank, "Spatial Form," p. 385. Italics mine.

16 Frank, "Spatial Form," p. 382: "For Eliot, the distinctive quality of a poetic sensibility is its capacity to form new wholes, to fuse seemingly disparate experiences *into an organic unity*" (italics mine).

17 Frank writes: "Proust forces the reader to juxtapose disparate images of his characters spatially," then goes on to compare this technique to that of the Impressionist painters who juxtaposed pure tones on the canvas "in order to leave the blending of colors to the eye of the spectator" (p. 387). The imprecision of the argument is patent. The painter does not at all force the spectator to do the juxtaposing, as Proust supposedly does, so there is no parallel at all if we accept Frank's account of Proust's procedure. In reality, of course, there *is* a parallel: Proust, just like the painters, does the juxtaposing and leaves the blending to the reader, and that blending is "temporal" and not "spatial."

18 At least if I understand correctly. Frank's vagueness is noticeable again: Proust erects a monument to his conquest of time by using "a method compelling the reader to experience its full emotional significance" (p. 386).

19 Frank, "Spatial Form," p. 392. "Space" now designates the timelessness of myth. In my opinion it means too many different things.

20 The following essays have been considered: "Modern Literary Criticism and the Spatialization of Time: An Existential Critique," *Journal of Aesthetics and*

Art Criticism, 29 (Fall 1970), 87-104; "Modern Drama and the Aristotelian Tradition: the Formal Imperatives of Absurd Time," *Contemporary Literature,* 12 (Summer 1971), 345-72; "Heidegger, Kierkegaard, and the Hermeneutic Circle: Towards a Postmodern Theory of Interpretation as Dis-closure," *boundary 2,* 4 (Winter 1976), 455-88; "Breaking the Circle: Hermeneutics as Dis-closure" *boundary 2,* 5 (Winter 1977), 421-57.

21 See Martin Heidegger, "Die Zeit des Weltbildes," in *Holzwege,* 4th ed. (Frankfurt/Main: Vittorio Klosterman, 1963), pp. 69 ff. I owe the reference to this essay to William V. Spanos (in "Breaking the Circle").

22 See Spanos, "Modern Drama," pp. 346, 349-350; "Breaking the Circle," p. 436. Goerg Lukács (*The Theory of the Novel,* tr. Anna Bostock, Cambridge, Mass., 1971) cites Gurnemanz as saying that the drama transforms time into space (p. 122).

23 Spanos, "Modern Drama," pp. 350-353.

24 Spanos, "Breaking the Circle," pp. 422, 437.

25 Also, the emphasis on the primacy of the medium threatens to relegate the visual arts to a basic inferiority or even inauthenticity.

26 See Spanos, "Modern Literary Criticism," pp. 94-95.

27 Actually, Spanos seems somewhat uncertain as to the identity of the interlocutor: does the dialogue take place with the author (as is asserted by romantic hermeneutics) or with the text (as Gadamer insists)? There seems to be a movement away from the author and towards the text. At one point, the dialogue is carried on with the absurd world itself.

28 Spanos, "Modern Drama," pp. 371-372.

29 Time is active temporalization. If it ceases to be that, we are in effect "lost in space." Worringer correctly speaks of *Platzangst.*

30 Spanos ("Heidegger, Kierkegaard," esp. pp. 472-76) writes at length about Kierkegaard's pseudonymous strategies, which are supposed to destroy the conclusive authority of his works. The reason he adopts these techniques of ironic indirection is, however, not that he is writing in a pre-Heideggerian age, still innocent about metaphysics, but that he is quite simply trying to convince us (without actually wanting to convince us) that he is destroying the indestructible specific character of the literary universe. He may be more subtle (rather than more innocent) than some contemporaries.

31 See Spanos, "Breaking the Circle," pp. 449-50. Spanos seems to be well aware of the trickiness of the problem of rereading, for he continually reverts to it, often dismissing it too quickly. The passage referred to is the one where he tries to come to terms with it. On that problem, see also my essay on "Mauriac and Sartre's Mauriac Criticism" (*Symposium,* Winter 1962).

32 Hayden White, *Metahistory: The Historical Imagination in Nineteenth-Century Europe* (Baltimore, Johns Hopkins Univ. Press, 1973).

33 The necessary distinction between art and the aesthetic was already made by J. Huizinga as early as 1905, in his inaugural lecture in Groningen, "Het aesthetische bestanddeel van geschiedkundige voorstellingen," in *Verzamelde Werken* VI, (Haarlem: H. D. Tjeenk Willink, 1950), esp. p. 25).

34 Ortega y Gasset speaks of Mallarmé's "extramundane" figures ("Dehumanization," p. 29) and of the "ultra-objects" of modern painting (p. 20). The precision of his terminology appears against the background of the preceding. Involved as some of us are in ultra-activities rolled into meta-enterprises, we should appreciate this!

35 These remarks are inspired by André Jolles's pages on the "Memorabile" in *Einfache Formen,* (Tübingen: M. Niemeyev, 1965), pp. 220 ff., esp. pp. 211-12). G. Lukács as well speaks of an intratemporal slowdown of duration: *Theory of the Novel,* p. 126—but the thought is clearer in the original: *Die Theorie des Romans* (Neuwied am Rhein: Luchterhand, 1963), p. 130.

36 Louis O. Mink, "History and Fiction as Modes of Comprehension," in Ralph Cohen, ed., *New Directions in Literary History* (Baltimore: Johns Hopkins Univ. Press, 1974), p. 116. Actually, Mink sees "configurational" knowledge far too much in extra-temporal terms (cf. esp. pp. 112, 115).

37 In Aristotle's statements on the various modes of cognition, classification is a characteristic of theoretical knowledge.

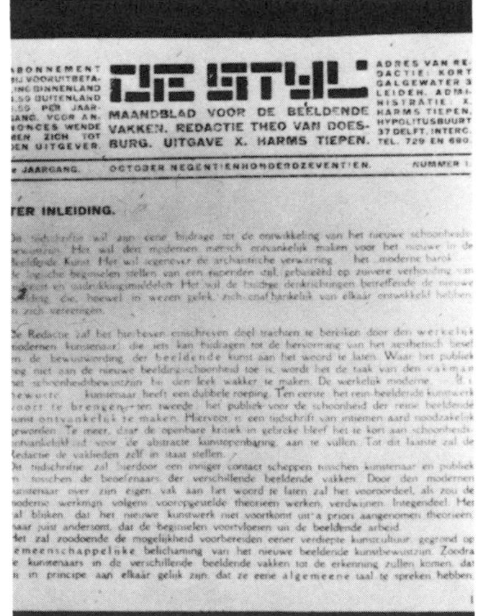
ABONNEMENT BIJ VOORUITBETALING BINNENLAND ... BUITENLAND ... PER JAARGANG. VOOR ANNONCES WENDE MEN ZICH TOT DEN UITGEVER.

DE STIJL

MAANDBLAD VOOR DE BEELDENDE VAKKEN. REDACTIE THEO VAN DOESBURG. UITGAVE X. HARMS TIEPEN.

ADRES VAN REDACTIE: KORT GALGEWATER 3 LEIDEN. ADMINISTRATIE: X. HARMS TIEPEN, HYPOLITUSBUURT 37 DELFT. INTERC. TEL. 729 EN 690.

JAARGANG. OCTOBER NEGENTIENHONDERDZEVENTIEN. NUMMER 1.

TER INLEIDING.

Worringer Among the Modernists

Joseph A. Buttigieg

It is Professor Holdheim's intent to demonstrate that Worringer's *Abstraction and Empathy* establishes a polarity which, properly understood and carefully developed, sheds important light on the complex problems torturing us today. In order to make his point Professor Holdheim has, first of all, to extricate or retrieve Worringer's classic from the clutches of those who have misread and misinterpreted it to such an extent that the importance of the polarity it posits has been lost, or at least forgotten. My intention in this brief response is to widen the scope of the discussion. Rather than voice my agreement or disagreement with Professor Holdheim's assessment of Worringer, I wish to regard his paper as the appropriate occasion to direct attention to those literary critics who used (or misused) Worringer's work. Why did the Modernist movement, or more specifically New Criticism, turn to Worringer's text to find the ideas it needed to buttress its own arguments? The corollary question is, of course, were these critics justified in co-opting Worringer the way they did? Professor Holdheim's exposition indicates that they were not. I will not offer an alternative reply; I will simply complicate the issue.

Like Professor Holdheim I find the mention of T. E. Hulme unavoidable, not simply because he discovered Worringer before anyone else in English and American literary circles, but more importantly because many adherents of the New Critical school regarded him as perhaps the earliest exponent of their most fundamental tenets. Cleanth Brooks, in an essay on "Metaphor and the Function of Criticism," refers to Hulme as "that remarkable figure of the twentieth century" and considers him "much more than an influence. He has been something of a prototype. . . ." He supports his claim by quoting from Robert W. Stallman's "The New Critics." "The affinity of several critics and Hulme lies in their common claim that our present disunity has been created by the confusion of two categories: the esthetic vision, which is concerned with quality, and the scientific vision, which is concerned with quantity."[1] We are reminded here that the Modernist and New Critical impulse was directed primarily against positivistic determinism and materialistic naturalism. More importantly, however, Stallman's allusion to the concern with quality as opposed to quantity echoes Bergson's discussion on the intensive and extensive manifolds. No treatment of the Modernist spatializing urge can be complete unless it takes into account the profound influence exercised by Bergsonian thought—an influence not only very evident in Hulme's scanty, unsystematic writings but also, indubitably, stronger than Worringer's. It is, after all, from Bergson that the phrase "spatialization of time" is borrowed, even though, as William Spanos has shown, this borrowing is confused and confusing.[2] Bergson used it to characterize the positivistic treatment of time; Joseph Frank applied it to the anti-positivistic works of the Modernists.

Cleanth Brooks finds Hulme exemplary in many ways. Among other things, Hulme insisted on the importance of original sin and foreshadowed the centrality of metaphor in modern poetry. (The enhanced position and understanding of metaphor brought with it, according to Brooks, a revival of interest in myth.) In both these respects Hulme is seen, quite rightly, as an antipositivist and Brooks believes it is not accidental "that so many of the modern critics who have been influenced by Hulme or who have taken a position sympathetic to Hulme in making metaphor the essence of poetry, have gone on, either to avow an orthodox religious position, or else to affirm the possibility and necessity for metaphysics as a science." Among these critics Brooks mentions T. S. Eliot, W. H. Auden, Allen Tate, J. C. Ransom, R. P. Blackmur, Ivor Winters and Austin Warren.[3] Clearly, Hulme's antihumanism was not the least of his virtues in the opinion of the New Critics; and it cannot have been for, after all, Hulme's sense of man's fallen nature and at the same time of man's ability to apprehend perfection stands at the very center of all his theorizing. He claims to have realized, even before reading Worringer, that Greek and Renaissance art emanates from rational humanism, and that the emergence of geometric art in his day implied a rejection or a collapse of humanism. His acquaintance with Worringer and his work helped Hulme clarify his ideas. It also helped him draw a sharper contrast between vital, organic art on the one hand and abstract, geometric art on the other. He did not fail to introduce his religious views into the scheme, either.

Hulme preferred geometric art for a number of related reasons. Among the most important are: (1) its "disgust with the trivial and accidental characteristics of living shapes"—an undisguised *contemptu mundi;* (2) its search "after an austerity, a *perfection* and rigidity which vital things can never have;" (3) its subordination of man "to certain absolute values"[4]—i.e., contrary to what one finds in Greek and Renaissance art, man is imperfect and sinful and not the measure of all things; (4) its rejection of the scientific dogma of progress. In brief, Hulme advocated an art that stemmed from a contempt of the world and aimed at reaching a perfection beyond it; an art, in other words, which dissociated itself from the phenomenal world of scientific and materialistic concerns. Worringer's description of "non-Classical, i.e., transcendental art,"[5] which he associates with "the ancient aristocracy of the Orient,"[6] is almost tailored for Hulme.

> Inextricably drawn into the vicissitudes of ephemeral appearances, the soul knows here only *one* possibility of happiness, that of creating a world beyond appearance, an absolute, in which it may rest from the agony of the relative. Only when the deceptions of appearance and the efflorescent caprice of the organic have been silenced, does redemption wait.[7]

The fragmentary world of appearances is the fallen world. The act of redemption consists in putting the pieces together again; the fragments must somehow be forged into a new whole. Worringer clearly suggests that this can only be done by transcending matter and reaching the purer level of the spirit—the level of angels. The religious vocabulary here is not accidental. The transcendental impulse is conceived as a religious drive, or else an impulse analogous to the religious. Redemption has inescapable religious connotations, and in transcendental art the redemptive act is the achievement of wholeness.

Further, according to Worringer:

> all transcendental art sets out with the aim of de-organicizing the organic, i.e. of translating the mutable and conditional into values of unconditional necessity. But such a necessity man is able to feel only in the great world beyond the living, in the world of the inorganic. This led him to rigid lines, to inert crystalline

> form. He translated everything into the language of these imperishable values. For these abstract forms, liberated from finiteness, are the only ones, and the highest, in which man can find rest from the confusion of the world picture.[8]

Here, again, Hulme finds in Worringer a support for his announcement that as a consequence of the rejection of Romantic organic art "a period of dry, hard, classical verse is coming."[9] Moreover, Worringer refers in this passage to the stasis which abstraction offers man caught up in the "great inner unrest inspired . . . by the phenomena of the outside world."[10] It is true that in this same passage Worringer refers to the dread of space, but it is obvious that the unrest he describes points to man's not-at-homeness in a decentered universe grounded in temporality. By contrast, the state of rest or stasis is found in a changeless, nonvital, hence imperishable realm—the realm wherein things stand still.

Professor Holdheim maintains that in Worringer's concept of abstraction this deorganicization constitutes the "means of distancing, deforming and stylizing reality, wrenching it out of human measure" and later in his paper states that "abstract art, born from disorientation, is defamiliarizing." One must not forget, however, that Worringer explained the urge to abstraction as a movement away from the restlessness experienced in a changing and ungraspable world towards a realm of rest and immutability. So, if abstraction defamiliarizes the world, it does so in a very specific way. This was well understood by the Modernists who, incidentally, also considered distancing a crucial feature of their aesthetics. The manner in which the Modernists accommodated defamiliarization is to be found in their "epiphanic" theories. The most influential articulation of the epiphanic mode comes from a fictional character, Stephen Dedalus, whose aesthetic theory, as William Spanos points out, served "with such scriptural authority as a primary source of New Critical doctrine."[11] According to Stephen's theory, the object singled out from its familiar surroundings is apprehended (i.e., *grasped* through *sight*) in three stages: *integritas, consonantia* and *claritas.* The epiphanic moment, although Stephen does not call it that in *A Portrait*—where, nevertheless, the religious vocabulary is pervasive—culminates in the luminous apprehension of the object "by the mind which has been arrested by its wholeness and fascinated by its harmony." This apprehension Stephen equates with "the luminous silent stasis of esthetic pleasure, a spiritual state. . . ."[12] Joyce did not write this under the influence of Hulme or Worringer. Yet, Hulme would certainly have concurred with Stephen's theory, as his successors did. I am not sure Worringer would have found Stephen's exposition unacceptable, except for the fact that Worringer would have accorded empathic art equal legitimacy.

Stephen's epiphanic apprehension of an object certainly entails a defamiliarization: the object is seen in a new way. But this remains the vision of the aesthete (in the full Kierkegaardian sense) and not the discovery of man-in-the-world. When Joseph Frank claims that the Modernist writer conquers time, he means, among other things, that the writer succeeds in freezing or crystallizing the moment of epiphanic vision—that is, he removes it from its temporal context and holds it still for eudaimonic contemplation. This can best be understood, perhaps, if Stephen's account of the epiphanic state were compared to Sartre's description of Roquentin's primordial experience in the public garden of Bouville. Not the least important feature that distinguishes the former's epiphany from the latter's antiepiphany, is the contrast between Stephen's insistent use of visual metaphor and Roquentin's real, physical feeling of nausea.

The superiority of sight and hearing over the other senses is affirmed overtly and indirectly by numerous Modernists and New Critics. Hulme, a prototype in this respect as well, repeatedly discusses literature in visual terms. This is another reason why he turned to Worringer and had no qualms about the propriety of applying the language of the visual arts and the theories of art criticism and art history to the study of literature. Not once did Hulme even doubt that the plastic arts and poetry belonged to the same sphere. In his fragmentary "Notes on Language and Style" he draws no distinction between the two. "Each *word* must be an image seen. . . . That dreadful feeling of cheapness when we contemplate the profusion of words in modern prose. The true ideal—the little statue in Paris."[13] Less than two decades after Hulme wrote this, Percy Lubbock in *The Craft of Fiction* tried to match prose to the same ideal—although Lubbock does not specify the size of the statue. Lubbock maintained that, seen from the vantage point of the end, the novel yields its "whole design," and "It may be absolutely satisfying to the eye." Furthermore, "with the book in this condition of a defined shape, firm of outline, its form shows for what it is indeed—not an attribute, one of many and possibly not the most important, but the book itself, as the form of a statue is the statue itself."[14] Hulme compares literature to yet another art form: "Poetry is neither more nor less than a mosaic of words, so great exactness required for each one."[15] In 1953, W. K. Wimsatt demonstrated the longevity of this view by publishing *The Verbal Icon.*

Percy Lubbock and W. K. Wimsatt approached literary works as if they could be perceived wholly and instantaneously like statues or paintings. They, and many others, frequently resorted to analogies drawn from the plastic arts to illustrate or elucidate points they wanted to make about literary works. Joseph Frank's discussion of Proust is in line with this school of criticism. He considers it his task to show how the various pieces of the mosaic fit together to form a complete and coherent picture. The picture, moreover, possesses all the characteristics Worringer attributed to abstract art. As Professor Holdheim has shown, Frank's enterprise fails and, indeed, Frank is blind to the fact that he is revealing something other than what he intended. Nevertheless, Frank's is not an exercise in hermeneutics, for he does not even engage the text in dialogue; rather, he seeks to master it. He goes through the process of reading, but he is not interested in it. He is more interested in *having read* the text so as to be able to look back at it or hover over it and obtain a bird's-eye view of its form—what Lubbock would call its "abstract beauty."[16] This is not hermeneutic understanding, this is cartography. And the urge to cartography is inspired by the desire to get out of the mess, the uncertainty of process—to get out of the dark woods, as it were, and soar above them to catch sight of the whole. Frank's misguided method may also be described by means of another favorite Modernist term: he is trying to demonstrate the *consonantia,* the relationship of part to part, the harmony of the object. I say *object* because Frank treats the text as if it were a thing. Indeed, he has to reify it before he can explicate it. The question is *why* does Frank do this? He is not merely applying an idea derived from Worringer (or from Proust himself) to Proust's text; he is coercing Proust into a form that supports and confirms an aprioristically formulated position. The aprioristic position and its consequences need to be questioned.

I should, before concluding, briefly mention the uneasiness I am caused by Professor Holdheim's phrase "the gradually clarified organism of artistic form." In what is probably a misreading, I see it as implying a movement towards grasping a whole, exhibiting a greater concern with the goal of completion than with the process itself of interpretation. There seems to be in the phrase a suggestion of an ultimate goal: the grasping of the whole, the apprehension of form. The hermeneutic of disclosure, about which William Spanos writes, is not concerned with the construction of wholes but with the process of deconstruction which does not have a final goal (*telos*), a *terminus ad quem.* If anything, the *telos* is for the deconstructor a *terminus a quo.* Professor Holdheim's description of rereading as bringing "deeper insight into the artificial organism's complex workings" carries a connotation of cumulativeness and recalls the Hegelian notion of *Bildung,* a propos of which Gadamer writes: "In accordance with the frequent carry-over from becoming to being, *Bildung* (as also the contemporary use of 'formation') describes more the result of the process of becoming than the process itself."[17] In the same context, it must be added, the empathic urge, described by Lipps as "objectified self-enjoyment," moves towards a contemplation of the unity of being. Empathy, according to Lipps—and Worringer follows him faithfully—involves self-participation. But Lipps also talks of contemplating the work of art. The participation of the viewer aims at totally objectifying the self; it strives for solidification, so that it can finally look at itself from a distance. There is a process involved, it is true, but what matters is the result of the process rather than the process itself. Romanticism, which Hulme associates with the empathic tradition, aims at perfection, i.e., completion, wholeness. In this respect it does not differ from abstract art. What Hulme objects to is that Romanticism introduces perfection in connection with the human and organic, whereas perfection "properly belongs to the nonhuman."[18] In other words, Hulme finds fault with Romanticism not because it accomodates temporality but, on the contrary, because it aims at the perfect and atemporal while dealing with the organic, unredeemed world. He insists that art should attain a perfection in order to emphasize man's inescapable fallenness—hence, abstract art which, by placing perfection in an ether world of geometric rigidity and immutability, avoids the error Romanticism is guilty of, the error of generating the illusion that perfection is attainable in the vital, living world.

I have not, in my necessarily sketchy remarks, touched upon William Spanos's treatment of Worringer. This is due partly to the constraints imposed by time and partly to the fact that Worringer matters to Spanos only in so far as he is important to and as he is seen by the New Critics. In this respect, perhaps, Spanos is not being sufficiently radical and is surrendering a text to the Modernists which may be worth retrieving. However, I will conclude by recalling the fact that Spanos's hermeneutic enterprise affirms the value of care (*Sorge*). Herein lies, in my opinion, the importance of his emphasis on the temporality of *Dasein.* Care stands in sharp contrast to the notions of distance, indifference, coercion. The New Critical approach, in its irritable reaching after fact or reason, coerces texts into predetermined molds. New Critics have never been care-ful detectives; rather, they embark on their investigations with the absolute certainty that there has to be a solution (a *telos* or *logos*) which can be reached if only the clues were juxtaposed in the proper fashion. So, when the clues do not fit, they are made to fit. This has led to distortions—and Worringer's text may have been, perhaps, one of the victims. These distortions are still with us, as are many other facets of New Criticism. What needs to be undertaken now is a reopening of the investigation. We need to rewrite literary history, but this time we have to be guided by care. In other words, we must let things be. We must also engage in this formidable task knowing that we will never reach *the* solution, we will always be on the way.

Notre Dame University

NOTES

1 Cleanth Brooks, "Metaphor and the Function of Criticism" in *Spiritual Problems in Contemporary Literature,* ed. Stanley Romaine Hopper (New York: Harper and Row, 1957), pp. 134, 136. Brooks quotes from Robert W. Stallman's "The New Critics," *Critiques and Essays in Criticism, 1920-1948,* ed. R. W. Stallman (New York: Ronald Press, 1949).

2 See, for example, "Modern Drama and the Aristotelian Tradition: The Formal Imperatives of Absurd Time," *Contemporary Literature,* 12 (1971), pp. 345-72.

3 "Metaphor and the Function of Criticism," p. 134.

4 T. E. Hulme, *Speculations,* ed. Herbert Read (New York: Harcourt Brace, 1927), pp. 53-54.

5 *Abstraction and Empathy,* trans. M. Bullock (New York: International Univ. Press, 1953), p. 133.

6 *Abstraction and Empathy,* p. 130.

7 *Abstraction and Empathy,* p. 133.

8 *Abstraction and Empathy,* p. 134.

9 *Speculations,* p. 133.

10 *Abstraction and Empathy,* p. 15.

11 "Modern Literary Criticism and the Spatialization of Time: An Existential Critique," *Journal of Aesthetics and Art Criticism,* 29 (1970), p. 97.

12 *A Portrait of the Artist as a Young Man* (New York: Viking, 1964), p. 213.

13 *Further Speculations,* ed. Sam Hynes (Minneapolis: Univ. of Minnesota Press, 1955), p. 79.

14 *The Craft of Fiction* (New York: Viking Press, 1957), p. 24.

15 *Further Speculations,* p. 84.

16 *The Craft of Fiction,* p. 20.

17 *Truth and Method* (New York: Seabury Press, 1975), p. 12.

18 *Speculations,* p. 11.

CONTRIBUTORS

David B. Allison is an associate professor of Philosophy at SUNY-Stony Brook. He is the editor of *The New Nietzsche* and of Derrida's *Introduction to Husserl's "Origin of Geometry,"* and the translator of Derrida's *Speech and Phenomena and Other Essays.* He has written on Derrida, Foucault, Levi-Strauss, Nietzsche, and Heidegger.

Jonathan Arac, associate professor of English at the University of Illinois at Chicago Circle, is the author of *Commissioned Spirits: The Shaping of Social Motion in Dickens, Carlyle, Melville, and Hawthorne,* and in 1978-79 held an ACLS Fellowship to work on *Rhetoric and Realism in Nineteenth-Century Fiction.* He is an assistant editor of *boundary 2.*

Alwin Baum teaches in the English Department at SUNY-Buffalo. He is the author of an essay, "The Metanovel: Robbe-Grillet's Phenomenal *Noveau Roman*" which appeared in the Winter 1978 issue of *boundary 2.*

Paul Bové is an associate editor of *boundary 2* and author of *Destructive Poetics*. He is currently writing a book on the cultural and theoretical implications of the academic study of English Literature.

Homer Obed Brown is a professor of English and Comparative Literature and a member of the Critical Theory Group at the University of California, Irvine. He has published a book on Joyce and articles on various other novelists, critical theory, and Romantic poetry. He is presently working on studies of the English novel and on modern critical theory and Romantic poetics.

Joseph A. Buttigieg is an assistant professor of English at Notre Dame. He is an assistant editor of *boundary 2* and the author of several essays in modern literature and criticism.

Stephen Crites, a philosopher of religion, is presently Chairman of the Department of Religion at Wesleyan University. His writings have been divided between speculative essays on aesthetics and religion and works of nineteenth-century scholarship, including a monograph, *In the Twilight of Christendom: Hegel vs. Kierkegaard on Faith and History.*

Jonathan Culler is professor of English and Comparative Literature at Cornell University and the author of *Flaubert: The Uses of Uncertainty, Structuralist Poetics,* and *Ferdinand de Saussure.*

Eugenio Donato is a professor of Comparative Literature and French at the University of California, Irvine, and the author of numerous articles on contemporary critical theory.

Edgar A. Dryden, the author of *Melville's Thematics of Form* and *Nathaniel Hawthorne: The Poetics of Enchantment,* is professor of English and Head of the Department at the University of Arizona.

Neville Dyson-Hudson is currently on leave from SUNY-Binghamton, where he is a professor of Anthropology. He is the author of a book, *Karimojong Politics,* and numerous articles on East African pastoralists.

Stanley E. Fish is a professor of English at Johns Hopkins University. His publications include *Surprised by Sin: The Reader in Paradise Lost, Self-Consuming Artifacts,* and *The Living Temple: George Herbert and Catechizing.* The present essay is taken from the forthcoming *Is There A Text in This Class? Interpretive Authority in the Classroom and Literary Criticism.*

Joseph Graham is an assistant professor in the Comparative Literature Department at SUNY-Binghamton and the author of several essays in linguistics and philosophy.

Michael Hays has published several essays on contemporary criticism and on semiology of literature and the drama. He teaches English and Comparative Literature at Columbia University.

W. Wolfgang Holdheim, the Frederic J. Whiton Professor of Liberal Studies at Cornell University, is widely published in the fields of literary criticism and theory. Among his books are *Theory and Practice of the Novel: A Study on André Gide.* His most recent work is *Die Suche nach dem Epos.*

David Couzens Hoy is an associate professor of Philosophy at Barnard College, Columbia University, and has recently published a book on literary hermeneutics entitled *The Critical Circle: Literature, History, and Philosophical Hermeneutics.*

Murray Krieger is University Professor of English at the University of California, Irvine and Los Angeles, and Director of The School of Criticism and Theory at Irvine. He has published several books including *The Classic Vision* and *Theory of Criticism.* The present essay will appear in the forthcoming *Poetic Presence and Illusion: Essays in Critical History and Theory.*

Marie-Rose Logan is assistant professor of French and Romance Philology at Columbia University where she is also a member of the Society of Fellows in the Humanities. She is editor of "Graphesis: Perspectives in Literature and Philosophy" and coeditor of "Rethinking History: Time, Myth and Writing." She is also Associate Editor of the *Columbia Dictionary of Modern European Literature.*

Daniel O'Hara, formerly an assistant professor of English at Princeton, now teaches at Temple University and has recently completed the study, *Tragic Knowledge: A Phenomenological Interpretation of Yeats's Autobiography*, to be published by Columbia University Press. He is an assistant editor of *boundary 2.*

Mark Poster is a professor of History at the University of California, Irvine. His books include *Sartre's Marxism, Critical Theory of the Family, Existential Marxism in Postwar France* and *The Utopian Thought of Restif de la Bretonne.* He is currently working on a study of the thought of Michel Foucault.

Joseph Riddel teaches modern poetry and literary theory at UCLA. He is currently at work on a study of "American" poetics to be titled, tentatively, *Purloined Letters.* His latest book is *The Inverted Bell, Modernism and the Counterpoetics of William Carlos Williams.*

Edward W. Said is Parr Professor of English and Comparative Literature at Columbia University. His most recent works are *Beginnings: Intention and Method, Orientalism, The Question of Palestine,* and *Criticism Between Culture and System.*

William V. Spanos, Editor of *boundary 2,* is the author of numerous articles on postmodern critical theory. He is currently working on three booklength projects: on hermeneutics, T.S. Eliot's major poetry, and a destruction of humanistic education theory, specifically the Harvard Core Curriculum Report.

George Stade teaches at Columbia University. He has edited numerous scholarly books and has published many reviews and articles in journals such as *Partisan Review, Hudson Review, Paris Review, Harper's* magazine, *Nation, New Republic* and *New York Times Book Review.* He is the author of the recently published novel *Confessions of a Lady-Killer.*

Dennis Tedlock is associate professor of Anthropology and Religion at Boston University and the editor of *Alcheringa,* a magazine of oral poetry. He is co-author, with Barbara Tedlock, of *Teachings from the Indian Earth: Indian Religion and Philosophy,* and translator of *Finding the Center: Narrative Poetry of the Zuni Indians.*

Evan Watkins is an associate professor of English at Michigan State University. He has published several essays on literary theory and a book, *The Critical Act: Criticism and Community,* on the relation between contemporary theory and recent poetry.

ILLUSTRATIONS

FINIS